William Hodgson

The lives, sentiments and sufferings of some of the reformers and martyrs before, since and independent of the Lutheran reformation

William Hodgson

The lives, sentiments and sufferings of some of the reformers and martyrs before, since and independent of the Lutheran reformation

ISBN/EAN: 9783337104443

Printed in Europe, USA, Canada, Australia, Japan

Cover: Foto ©Lupo / pixelio.de

More available books at **www.hansebooks.com**

Entered, according to Act of Congress, in the year 1867, by
WILLIAM HODGSON,
In the Clerk's Office of the District Court of the United States for the Eastern District of Pennsylvania.

PREFACE.

IN reading ecclesiastical history, it has often been a subject of disappointment that we cannot readily attain to a knowledge of the everyday course, and inner life and spirit, and so as it were enjoy the familiar intercourse of those pious men and women, who were, during the darkness of the middle ages, depositaries of a little of the true light of the gospel, and instrumental in preserving more or less of a testimony to the inward efficacy and simplicity of true religion, and transmitting it to succeeding times. The history indeed of the "inner court"—the true church of Christ, from the dark hour of its flight into the wilderness, until the dawn of day in the sixteenth century—has never yet been written, and probably never will or can be. The various ecclesiastical histories, though, many of them, deeply interesting and instructive, are, in their general scope, and with scarcely any exception, histories rather of the corruptions and confusions of the "outer court," which was "given unto the gentiles." They show that church history, as well as other history, teaches not only by examples, but by warnings. They display, in a remarkable manner, the stratagems of Antichrist, whereby that great deceiver of the nations established his throne in the professing Christian church, showed himself as it were God, was worshipped as a god, trampled on the bodies and souls of men, made merchandise of the gospel, enslaved the human intellect by superstition, intoxicated mankind with the cup of the wine of the wickedness of Babylon, and reigned even over the kings of the earth.

But the sweetness and humility and love of the true Christian life, which still lived, through all the darkness and death, in the hearts of a few, out of the sight of the world, but called and chosen and faithful, appears to have been scarcely an object of the research or commemoration of historians; and indeed was so much neglected by successive writers from century to century, that records of it, if any there were at all, are now scarcely to be found.

Thus the accumulation of matter connected with and arising from worldly motives, and transactions of men of a worldly spirit, though ostensibly acting for religion, seems almost to eclipse in such histories the light of truly Christian example and effort; and the reader is often discouraged in his attempts to commune as it were with the real disciples of Christ, by the necessity of wading through so much corruption and contention and intrigue, in order to obtain access to a little of that which is of a purer nature and more worthy of the name of Christianity.

Nor is he any less discouraged, in his endeavors to acquire a knowledge of the real sentiments and doctrines of many who have been considered as "disturbers of the peace," when they honestly testified against the corruptions introduced into the church. Historians have mostly given very imperfect, if not very partial and one-sided statements of opinions and doctrines so readily branded as heresy by interested parties; and in vain do we search, in the generality of church histories, for that which might be expected as a matter of justice, a clear and impartial statement of what such reformers really taught, couched in their own expressions. Perhaps the author who has approached the nearest to what is desired in this respect, may be said to be the late venerable and laborious Augustus Neander. Yet most readers are afraid to undertake the task of an intimate acquaintance with his ponderous pages.

And in like manner, many even of the modern biographical accounts of eminent worthies of the middle ages are encumbered with details of the results of minute research, valuable in themselves, and highly worthy of preservation, but rendering such works too bulky, whereby they lose much of the attractiveness of their subject, and are scarcely adapted for general perusal. That the public feeling evinces this want of a more intimate acquaintance with these reformers, is shown by the avidity with which even fictitious narratives, and diaries fallaciously purporting to portray their course, have of late years been received.

In a frequent realization of these circumstances, it has appeared to the author of the present volume, that it might not be unacceptable to many serious readers, to have spread before them in a simple and unpretending manner, and clear of extraneous matter, such a sketch, as the scanty materials now extant may permit, of the lives, examples, and sentiments of some of the sincere-hearted followers of the Lord Jesus, from the ninth century downward, who, having been taught more or less in the school of Christ, and faithful to the degree of light vouchsafed through the thick darkness, have been measurably enabled to discern the difference between genuine and fictitious religion, and made willing, at the hazard of their lives, to testify before the world against the falsities and corruptions which had crept in, so far as their eyes had been anointed and opened to perceive them.

In attempting these delineations, the writer has not felt called upon to dwell particularly on those points of doctrine in which these comparatively enlightened men and women, through the influence of education and an almost universal prevalency, were still in accordance with the tenets of the Roman church; but rather to endeavor to arrive at and give their own statements in regard to the points in which they diverged from Rome, and were constrained to protest against its apostasy from primitive Christianity. Neither has it been deemed needful here to include accounts of those eminent men, who were directly concerned in that mighty revolution which took place in the beginning of the sixteenth century; as their instrumentality therein, and the particular features of their character and lives, have been repeatedly and largely portrayed, and are already matter of open and general history, and freely accessible to the public at large.

Derived as the matter is, by compilation and condensation, from a considerable variety of detached works of ecclesiastical history and biography, and without much reference to intervening events, no attempt has been made to give to the volume the aspect of a connected history. Yet, as the accounts are generally arranged in chronological order, it is hoped that some glimpses at least may thence be gathered, of the condition of Christian truth in the respective periods, and of the successive efforts made to rescue it from the clouds of error.

The reader will perceive (however imperfectly accomplished) that one aim runs through the whole book—to show the superiority and sustaining efficacy of true spiritual religion—a religion, not of outward forms, and empty pomp and parade, nor yet of airy imaginations, but of inward and living virtue to cleanse and renew the heart—a religion deeper than all the precepts of human learning, and loftier and more expansive than the utmost soarings of the human intellect—a religion taught in the heart, by Him who taught as never man taught, and who is still the great teacher of his people; as near to them now in Spirit, as he was then in that prepared body, in which, though Lord of all, He condescended to walk lowly among men. Let the world call this religion by whatever name they may please to designate it, if it is the religion of our Lord and Saviour Jesus Christ, pure and undefiled before God the Father, it will be owned and accepted by Him whose name is above every name, and before whom every knee must bow.

TABLE OF CONTENTS.

	PAGE
PREFACE	5

CHAPTER I.
    CLAUDIUS OF TURIN 13

CHAPTER II.
    PETER DE BRUYS 26
    HENRI OF LAUSANNE 30
    ARNOLD OF BRESCIA 38

CHAPTER III.
    PETER DE WALDO 45

CHAPTER IV.
    NICOLAS OF BASLE 51

CHAPTER V.
    JOHN TAULER 62

CHAPTER VI.
    JOHN WYCLIFFE 80

CHAPTER VII.
    CONRAD WALDHAUSER 106
    JOHN MILICZ 108
    MATTHIAS OF JANOW 112
    MATTHEW OF CRACOW 118

CHAPTER VIII.
    JOHN HUSS 123

CHAPTER IX.
    GERHARD GROOT 170

		PAGE
CHAPTER X.		
	THOMAS À KEMPIS	179
CHAPTER XI.		
	JOHN RUCHRATH, OF WESEL	202
CHAPTER XII.		
	JOHN WESSEL	223
CHAPTER XIII.		
	JEROME SAVONAROLA	287
CHAPTER XIV.		
	JUAN VALDÉS	277
CHAPTER XV.		
	ANNE ASKEW	306
CHAPTER XVI.		
	MICHAEL DE MOLINOS	321
CHAPTER XVII.		
	JANE MARY GUION	342
CHAPTER XVIII.		
	WILLIAM DELL	428
CONCLUSION		461

REFORMERS AND MARTYRS

BEFORE AND SINCE

THE LUTHERAN REFORMATION.

CHAPTER I.

CLAUDIUS OF TURIN.

BEFORE entering on a brief delineation of the life of this pioneer of reform in the Roman church, it may be well to glance at the rise of certain corruptions of doctrine and practice, which had obtained more or less prevalence therein previous to the end of the ninth century.

Most of the corruptions had their origin after the profession of Christianity by the Emperor Constantine, which took place in the year 312, and the deliberations of the Nicene Council, which occurred about thirteen years thereafter.

The venerating of "saints' days" has been traced as far back as the martyrdom of Polycarp, who was cotemporary with the old age of the Apostle John, and suffered death at the stake about the year 166. After that, the honoring of the $\gamma\varepsilon\nu\epsilon\theta\lambda\iota a$ (literally *birthdays*), or anniversaries of the introduction of the saints by martyrdom into the heavenly life, became a frequent practice; and in the third century this form of superstition had extended so as to include an extreme veneration for their relics, if not an adoration of them; their blood being eagerly collected on sponges, cloths, etc., and their bones, and even garments, most sedulously preserved as holy. In the fourth and fifth centuries this veneration for saints had passed into actual worship.*

Although Ascetics and Hermits were known in the East at a very early date, and even, it has been said, before the introduction of Christianity, yet the monastic system, properly so called, embracing communities of monks and nuns living in seclusion under a lifelong vow, was not known, or at least no vestige of it has been discovered, before the end of the third century. But in the fourth it appeared with vigor, being introduced in Egypt by a friend of the celebrated Athanasius, called Saint Anthony, who established several communities called Cænobites in the Lower Thebaid, which were soon afterward extended into Upper Egypt. And about the year 341, Athanasius himself is said to have carried with him to Rome a number of Egyptian monks of that order; whose wild aspect, along with their devout demeanor, aroused the attention of the Romans, and induced the introduction of the system into Europe, and the foundation of several monasteries. In the fifth century the monastic system had become coextensive with the profession of Christianity.

The exposure of images and paintings of the Virgin Mary and of saints in places for public worship, is said to have originated in the fourth century.

In the early part of that century also, the celibacy of priests seems to have obtained a foothold, it being then established that no priest in the western church should marry after ordination. By the end of the fifth century, the rule of celibacy was commonly observed by the Romish clergy; but it was not strictly and universally enforced for several centuries afterward.

* Waddington's History of the Church, p. 213

The practice of private Confession to priests, called auricular confession, was established by Pope Leo I., surnamed the Great, about the middle of the fifth century, and gave so vast an addition to the influence of the priesthood that it has been considered as the laying of the cornerstone of the papal edifice.

The doctrine of Purgatory is not mentioned, nor does it appear to have been thought of (as afterward held), during the first four centuries. It began to obtain belief in the fifth and sixth ages, and was established in the church by Pope Gregory I., about the end of the latter century.

The same pope concentrated with the bishopric of Rome, the claim to "the power of the Keys of St. Peter," and (though with some appearance of caution) evidently aimed at establishing the supremacy of the Roman See; though both these arrogant assumptions were stoutly and permanently resisted by the Patriarchs of Constantinople on behalf of the Eastern or Greek church.

Gregory also introduced the pompous ceremonies of the "Communion," called "the Mass," regulated the prayers and chanting of the ceremonial, and established a school of chanters about the beginning of the seventh century.

The appropriation by the priesthood of the use of the Holy Scriptures, whereby the Bible was practically withdrawn from the knowledge of the people at large, may be dated about the seventh century.*

The doctrine of Transubstantiation, or the assertion that the bread and wine of the "Communion" became "the actual body and blood of Christ,—the same body which was born of the Virgin Mary, was crucified, and rose again,"— was broached by Radbert, abbot of Corbie, in 831; and this doctrine was at length, under the pontificate of Innocent III., confirmed in the Romish church about the begin-

* Waddington, p. 692.

ning of the thirteenth century. It was, therefore, only beginning to attract attention, in the age of Claudius of Turin.

Tithes do not appear to have been *claimed* by the priesthood, or paid at all, as such, by the ante-Nicene church; though Cyprian and Origen gave some hints in regard to the Levitical institution, and first fruits under the law. Ambrose and Augustine, in the fourth century, implied that in their time some such payments were voluntarily made; and the former seems to claim it as a divine requisition. Chrysostom and Jerome favored the same claim; but the system was very gradual in its extension during several centuries, and the first strictly legislative act conferring on the clergy the *right to claim* tithe, was passed by Charlemagne in the year 778.* But it was found very difficult to enforce the collection of tithes, and it was not until the end of the twelfth century that the claim could be considered as universally admitted.

Claudius, bishop of Turin, who has been styled "the Protestant of the ninth century," was a native of Spain, where he received his early education. As he grew up to manhood, he became attached to the clerical portion of the household of the Frank King Louis, surnamed the Pious, in Auvergne, and remained in this position about three years. While in the court of Louis,† he commenced a series of Commentaries on various books of Holy Scripture, by writing three books on Genesis, and one on Matthew, which he published in the year 815. In 816, he published a Commentary on the Epistle to the Galatians, soon followed by one on that to the Ephesians, and others on other books of the Old and New Testaments at intervals of a few years. Neander says that his object in writing these Com-

* Waddington, p. 231.
† Muston's "Israel of the Alps," vol. i. p. 9. English edition.

mentaries was the instruction and convenience of those ecclesiastics to whom the works of the older church authors were not readily accessible. As the Bible had now for more than a hundred years been secluded from the people at large, he had probably another object in view, to wit, the spreading of more correct views in regard to the contents of the Holy Scriptures than those which at that time prevailed. These Commentaries contained many original remarks, explanatory of his own religious sentiments, in addition to much compiled from the writings of Augustine and other ancient authors.

In the year 814, when Louis had succeeded to the imperial throne of Charlemagne, having imbibed a great regard for Claudius during his residence in his house, and hoping that his influence would be salutary in Northern Italy, he nominated him to the bishopric of Turin. On entering this new field of labor, his pious zeal, Neander tells us, found work enough to do in efforts to reform and improve a church so sunk in worldly views, ignorance, and superstition, as was that in Italy at that day.

The course taken by Gregory I., called "the Great," about the end of the sixth century, although a pontiff of uncommon energy and scope of mind, had greatly tended to fasten certain superstitious views and practices on the Roman church; especially the reverence for images and relics, and a belief in miracles performed by them, which extended to a degree most absurd and contrary to the common sense of mankind. The custom of exposing for public reverence in places of worship the images of saints, of the Virgin Mary, and even of Christ, which had arisen as early as the fourth century, had gradually advanced with the progress of bigotry, until the feeling toward these objects among the poor ignorant people became one of adoration. And though Gregory would not go so far as positively to sanction the actual worship of images, as such, yet he professed to believe that there was a benefit to be derived to the illiterate from the exhibition of them, and would not have them removed. Thus a sort of passive sanction was given by the pontiff to the superstitious veneration in which they were more and more held by the public; which was all that was needed, aided as it was by the cupidity of the priests·interested in the matter, to promote the prevalency of the practice; so that during the succeeding two hundred years the worship of images and of the relics of saints became very general in Italy, though not much prevalent among the Franks, and scarcely if at all allowed of among the simple inhabitants of the Alpine valleys of Piedmont.

The extension of the doctrine of Purgatory, as we have already seen, had also been greatly promoted by the same pontiff; and likewise the practice of pilgrimage to what were deemed holy places. But in nothing perhaps had the influence of Gregory more permanently fastened superstition on the succeeding ages, than in his extraordinary claims on the credulity of the people in regard to the most absurd stories of wonderful miracles performed by relics of the saints. His letter to the Empress Constantina,* who had solicited from him a donation for the enriching of a new temple of worship in Constantinople, exhibits a degree of bigotry which in our day would be considered unworthy of a reasonable intellect. The empress had requested the head, or at the least some portion of the body, of the Apostle Paul, for transportation to her new and splendid shrine, in order to give it importance with the people. But Gregory assured her that the bodies of the saints could not be approached within several feet for the purpose of abstracting any portion, without death to the daring invader; instancing several awful cases in point—one of which was

* For this letter, see Waddington's History of the Church, p. 152.

that a number of workmen engaged in some repairs near the tomb of the Saint Laurentius, had accidentally opened a portion of the grave and seen his remains, and that they all died within ten days. All that the pope would promise the empress was, that if it were possible to obtain any filings from the chains which the Apostle Paul had worn on his neck and hands, he would send them to her; but he added that this was very doubtful, for though a certain priest was stationed with a file, for the gratification of the solicitations of pilgrims, and could sometimes succeed in filing off a few grains from the chains, yet at other times all his efforts, though drawing his file over them for a long time, could scrape no filings whatever from the relics!

Under the powerful influence of pontifical encouragement, thus given by Gregory and his successors, such senseless superstitions had greatly increased in Italy, and taken the place of true religion; so that when Claudius assumed his episcopal functions in Turin, as Neander informs us, " He saw with extreme pain how the essence of Christianity was here placed, in making pilgrimages to Rome, in adoring images and relics, in various species of outward works; and how men were taught to trust in the intercession of saints, to the neglect of all earnest moral efforts of their own. He beheld a superstition which bordered closely on paganism, obtaining in the worship of saints, of images, of the cross, and of relics." With great zeal he both wrote and preached* against these superstitions, and even ejected the images and crosses from the places of worship, that they might no longer be objects of religious adoration. But, as might have been expected, his zeal provoked a bitter animosity on the part of some of the priests and people. In one of his works, written some years afterward, he says: "When I was induced to un-

* Milner's Church History, vol. iii. p. 209.

dertake the office of pastor, and came to Italy, I found, contrary to the true doctrine, all the churches full of the lumber of consecrated gifts; and because I alone began pulling down what all adored, I was calumniated by all, and unless the Lord had helped me, they would perhaps have swallowed me up alive." Among others who saw their craft placed in danger by Claudius's opposition to these superstitions, the Pope Paschalis I. was greatly displeased; but the favor of the Emperor Louis probably furnished a protection so powerful, that his enemies did not dare to put it to the test by commencing a persecution.

In the year 821, he published four books on Exodus, and in 823 a Commentary on Leviticus, which he dedicated to an old familiar friend, Theodemir, abbot of a monastery in the diocese of Nismes. These were followed by other similar works. In his various writings he took decided ground in favor of practical religion as opposed to mere outward forms; sanctification of spirit, and genuine love to God, were with him of the first importance as characteristics of true piety; and he displayed an earnest view of the nature of sin, and of the estrangement of the carnal nature from God; having no faith whatever in the monkish doctrine of the meritorious claims of what were called good works. His former friend, however, the Abbot Theodemir, was not prepared to undergo the odium of uniting with him in his sweeping measures of reform, and cleared himself of all connection with so dangerous a position by publicly denouncing several of his views (particularly some in his Commentary on the 1st Epistle to the Corinthians) as errors in doctrine. This he did before an assembly of bishops and nobles, at a time when Claudius supposed him to be still friendly to him. Theodemir did not, however, succeed at that time in procuring his condemnation; and when Claudius was afterward informed by his friends of what had taken place, he wrote to Theodemir: "May the Lord forgive thee—who is the witness of my life, and who gave me this work to do."

Claudius hereupon wrote a work in defense of his doctrines and conduct, wherein, says the translator of Neander, "he unfolded his principles with great boldness and the most violent zeal."* Whether this "most violent zeal" was anything more than the earnest asseverations of a man who felt convinced of the truth of the ground on which he stood, and of the necessity of maintaining it against all assailants, we are not informed; but Neander adds: "He declared that on no point had he set forth erroneous doctrines, or been a schismatic; but that he held firmly to the unity of the church, preached the truth, and defended the church; that he had always combated superstition and error, and would with God's help always continue to combat them. He attacked in this work every mode and form of image-worship; he exposed, as Agobard had done,* every false plea which could be employed in its palliation. 'If those, said he, 'who have forsaken idolatry, worship the images of the saints, then they have not forsaken idols, but changed their names. Whether thou paintest thy walls with figures of St. Peter and St. Paul, or of Jupiter and Saturn, neither the latter are gods, nor the former apostles. If men must be worshiped, it were much better to pay that worship to the living than to the dead; that is, to that wherein they bear the image of God, than to that wherein they are like to the brute, or rather to lifeless wood and stone. If the works of God's hands (the stars of heaven) ought not to

---

* Neander's own expression is, "heftigem Eifer"—simply, *sharp* or *vehement* zeal,—a comparatively mild term—not even "heftigstem;" so that the expression "*most violent*" is evidently an error of the translator. The contents of Claudius's document, as given in Flaccus Illyricus's *Catalogus Testium Veritatis*, from the work of Jonas of Orleans, his opponent, do not warrant any such epithet.

2*

be worshiped, much less ought the works of human hands to be worshiped; even the worship of saints will not bear to be excused, for these never arrogated divine honors to themselves. Whoever seeks from any creature in heaven or on earth the salvation which he should seek from God alone, is an idolater.'"

He objected also to the common custom of making the sign of the cross, with the idea of virtue attending it, believing that its tendency was to lead away the mind from spiritual communion with the Redeemer, and to fix it instead on outward symbols. In combating carnal views and superstitions of this nature, he frequently brought forward the Apostle's declaration: "Though we have known Christ after the flesh, yet now henceforth know we him (thus) no more." And he alleged that we have no more obligation to worship the cross, than to worship many other outward things with which our Saviour came in contact, or was connected, while in that body of flesh—such as mangers, from his being laid in one when an infant, lambs, from his being called "the Lamb of God," or ships, from the fact that he sometimes taught the multitude from on board of them.

Neander gives* this testimony to his spiritual views: "To point men away from the sensuous worship of the cross to the spiritual following after Christ in the fellowship of his sufferings, and in self-renunciation, was to him the principal thing; and hence the vehemence of his zeal against everything which tended to draw men away from this. Thus, he says, against the fleshly worshipers of the cross, 'What they do is quite a different thing from what God has commanded. God has commanded us to bear the cross, not to adore it. They are for adoring it, because they are unwilling to bear it either spiritually or bodily.

* Church History, 2d Amer. edit., vol. iii. p. 436.

To worship God after this manner means to turn away from him; for he has said, "Whoever will come after me, let him deny himself, and take up his cross and follow me;" for he who does not break away from himself cannot draw near to Him who is higher than himself,' etc. Again, 'By the shameful sacrilege of images you estrange them [men] from their Creator, and plunge them in everlasting ruin.' He invites men to seek after inward fellowship with Christ, when he says: 'Ye blind, return to the true light, which enlightens every man that cometh into the world; which light shineth into the darkness, and the darkness comprehendeth it not; ye who, not beholding that light, walk in darkness and know not whither you go, because the darkness hath blinded your eyes.'"*

On the word of the Lord, through the Prophet Ezekiel (chap. xiv. v. 14), "Though these three men—Noah, Daniel, and Job—were in it, they should deliver but their own souls by their righteousness," he observed : "This is said to warn us against trusting to the merits or to the intercession of saints; because no one who has not the same faith, the same righteousness and truth, whereby the saints obtained the divine approbation, can be saved." And in another place he reminds his readers that before the tribunal of Christ neither Job, nor Daniel, nor Noah can be of any use to us, but each one will have to bear his own burden.† In accordance herewith, he taught the utter emptiness of the idea of merit attaching to pilgrimages to Rome

---

* This primitive doctrine of the Christian religion, preached by Claudius in the ninth century, of the necessity of looking to and obeying the light of Christ, which enlighteneth every man that cometh into the world, and which the world so readily and willingly forgets, had to be proclaimed anew, in the demonstration and power of the gospel, eight hundred years afterward.

† Comm. on Galatians, p. 164. "Nec Job, nec Daniel, nec Noë rogare posse pro quoquam, sed unumquemque portare onus suum."

(except as the Almighty regards with *compassion* the *motives* of the honest-hearted), or that any one thereby made himself sure of the intercession of the Apostle Peter. On this subject, he says: "One gets no nearer to St. Peter by finding himself on the spot where his *body* was buried; for the *soul* is the real man." He denied that any power to bind or loose on earth what had been bound or loosed in heaven had been committed continuously to Peter, and those who came after him, in a sort of lineal succession. And he charged his opponent, the Abbot Theodemir, with culpable inconsistency or remissness, in retaining one hundred and forty monks in his own monastery, subservient to himself, instead of sending them to Rome, if his belief really was that pilgrimages to Rome were of so great a value in securing salvation; reminding him that there was no greater offense than that of preventing men from attaining to eternal blessedness.

Theodemir had reproached his former friend with incurring the displeasure of the "Dominus Apostolicus"—the apostolic lord—meaning the pope; to which Claudius replied: "The title 'apostolic' does not belong to him who administers a bishopric founded by an apostle, but to him who truly fulfills the apostolic vocation; to those who occupy the place, without fulfilling the vocation, should be applied the passage in Matthew, chap. xxiii. v. 12." He considered our Lord Jesus Christ as the true and only Head of the Church;* and that it was not allowable to obey the pope, further than as the pope himself stood in the apostolic doctrine. Thus boldly did Claudius defend the cause of practical Christianity, in accordance with the measure of light vouchsafed to him.

Theodemir now thought it necessary, in self-defense, to endeavor to sustain his charges; and before long Claudius

---

* Muston's "Israel of the Alps," vol. i. p. 9.

was cited to appear before an assembly of bishops, to answer certain allegations of heretical doctrine. This citation, however, he neglected to attend to, and it fell to the ground. But complaints were meanwhile made to the Emperor Louis, which came in so authoritative a shape, that the monarch at length deemed it advisable to institute an inquiry, especially as a certain Scotchman or Irishman, named Dungall, had undertaken to refute Claudius's opinions, calling on the princes of the empire to stop the spread of such errors. Lewis, apparently with some reluctance, laid it upon Jonas, Bishop of Orleans, to examine his writings, and prepare a refutation of what might be found to be heretical in them. But meantime Claudius was taken away by death, in the year 839 or 840, and thus probably escaped a continued and determined persecution. The seed, however, which he had sown was not lost. Many congenial minds had received his principles of reform in doctrine and life, and their influence was found to have extended so much in that part of the Frank empire, that it was deemed needful to endeavor to check it by the completion of the work of Jonas of Orleans, as ordered by the emperor. Whether this work produced the effect desired, we are not informed; but the northern parts of Piedmont continued for many years to be the seat of much comparative enlightenment and freedom from the bigotry so prevalent in more southern Italy; and by some writers Claudius of Turin has even been considered as the founder of the doctrines of the Waldenses.*

* See Milner's Church History, vol. iii. p. 369, note, and 415; and Morland's "Evangelical Churches of Piedmont," p. 11.

CHAPTER II.

PETER DE BRUYS.

About the year 1110, a preacher named Pierre de Bruys made his appearance in the south of France, and began to declaim against the corruptions of the church and the vices of its ministers. His opinions are now chiefly gathered from the representations of his adversaries, and may have contained or led him into some extravagancies. Neander avows, that "through the devotional study of the New Testament, he had embraced the pure worship of God, 'in spirit and in truth.'" Be that as it may, it appears that Peter was led to embrace and zealously to promulgate certain very extraordinary opinions for that age. Neander says that, "in the heat of an honest disgust, he attacked all outward ordinances, as inimical to the true worship of God; because he saw that the multitude confounded the means with the end, and placed religion in externals, to the prejudice of true devotion and morality. He was thus led to reject infant baptism, on account of the superstitious and indeed blasphemous representations which had for a long time been connected with it, as if those persons only could be saved who had received outward baptism. He brought forward in evidence the words of Christ, 'Whoso *believeth*, and is baptized, shall be saved.' Thus *no vicarious faith* could be availing. But he did not stop to examine whether, although the outward form of baptism were not of and by itself efficacious to the baptized person, it might not yet possess a sacred meaning, grounded on the intrinsic essence of Christian truth, and exhibited to man through this outward symbol; and whether the delusion might not have originated in the imperfect recognition of the relation between the sign, and the internal holiness which it symbolized."*

Neander adds : "In speaking against the conceits which his contemporaries had associated with consecrated places, he says justly, 'that God may be invoked in all places, from the shop as well as from the church and the altar, and will ever hear those who are deserving of it—that the church is formed, not by the piles of collected stones, but by the communion of the faithful.' From thence he drew the conclusion that churches [that is, church edifices] in general were unnecessary, and must therefore be pulled down."

"Disgusted," Neander adds, "with the pomp of public worship, and the multiplied ceremonies which had converted it into a lifeless mechanical service, and the artificial chanting, addressed rather to the senses than the heart, he truly says, 'that God taketh pleasure in the pious emotions of the heart alone, and that He is neither to be evoked by loud-sounding voices, nor conciliated by musical melodies;' but from hence he deduced [what Neander calls] the exaggerated inference, that 'God is only mocked by church chanting.'"

We also learn, from the same eminent author, that Peter spoke with great warmth against the worship of the cross, then so prevalent; going so far even as to say that "the cross, as the memorial of the sufferings and martyrdom of Christ, ought rather to be despised and banished, in revenge for his death, than to be honored among men." This doctrine, calculated to inflame the passions of men in that bigoted age, had more in it of personal danger to

* Neander's Life of Bernard of Clairvaux.

himself than any other of his testimonies against the corruptions which had crept in.

He totally rejected also, according to the same authority, the celebration of what is called "the Lord's Supper." "'Christ,' he said, 'had, once for all, before his suffering, produced his body in the bread, and distributed it among his disciples; therefore the celebration was not to be repeated.' 'Oh, trust not,' he exclaimed to the multitude, 'trust not to your misleading clergy; who, as in many other things, so also in the service of the altar, deceive you when they feign to produce for you the body of Christ, and to deliver it to you for the salvation of your souls!'"

"The honest man," adds Neander, "spoke sensibly enough against the efficacy of masses and almsgiving for the souls of the deceased; that delusion so prejudicial to the cause of practical Christianity. 'Every one,' he asserted, 'suffers after death, according to what may have been his deserts in life; there is no middle state.'" Herein he manifestly attacked the favorite dogma of Purgatory. He also opposed the observance of ecclesiastical fast days, and the abstaining from meats on those days.

For twenty years De Bruys promulgated such extraordinary sentiments with as extraordinary impunity and success, in the regions of the Pyrenees, in Provence, Languedoc, and Gascony. It would be difficult at this time, and with our imperfect sources of information, to determine how far his course was led and limited by the Lord's own requirings in his soul, or how far he may have participated in the heated enthusiasm which is said to have animated some of his disciples; who proceeded to destroy altars and crucifixes, making fires of their materials, and, it is added, even went so far as to personally attack the priests and compel the monks to marry. Neander seems to have thought that Peter de Bruys was in part accountable for these excesses; but he adds: "What other result could have been anticipated from the spirit of unbridled liberty pervading so rude an age,—when we see that at the kindred though more advanced era of the reformation, all the caution of the reformers was insufficient to prevent men from confounding earthly licentiousness with Christian freedom, and to restrain the wild bursts of human passion?"

But these deeds of his followers, particularly of destroying the adored crucifixes, though done by one mob, were more than another mob—composed of men attached to the old forms—could tolerate. The bigoted populace, whose feelings were thus outraged, and whose venerated priests had been thus insulted, at length rose in counter tumult, in the year 1130, seized Peter de Bruys, led him to the place of execution, and burned him at the stake, in a small town in the province of Languedoc.

It is evident that he took much the same ground in doctrinal opposition to the Romish Church, that was afterward taken by Luther and his companions; though he went further in some points, and may have advanced more rashly, and without a due consideration whether the age was ripe for measures of so sweeping a nature. His principles are, however, said to have taken deep root in the hearts of the people, and to have been cherished by many for a long time after his death.

HENRI OF LAUSANNE.

About the same time that Peter de Bruys came forth as a preacher of reform in the south of France, a youth of powerful talents and great mental activity, named Henri, incited by similar views, made his appearance in the district of Lausanne, in Switzerland. Neander's Life of Bernard of Clairvaux* thus delineates his extraordinary course, and the results of his teaching:

"He had been a monk in some monastery of the Cluniac order, probably devoted to the cloister by his parents, and brought up there. The diligent and devotional perusal of the Scriptures had opened his mind to the truth, which he ardently embraced in all its purity." [Rather too strong an expression of Neander's, considering all the circumstances.] "The picture of the apostles traveling in poverty through the world, for the purpose of publishing the truth; that of the affectionate fellowship of the primitive Christians, who, connected by no outward ties, lived together in the bond of a common faith and a mutual love, excited a holy enthusiasm in his soul, causing him to regard with still greater abhorrence the vices of his times and the corruption of the church, which had so widely departed from the apostolic model.

"Weary of the constraints of conventual life, and convinced in his own mind that he was in no wise bound by human ordinances, and the obligations grounded upon them, he abandoned his convent, in order to publish the pure doctrines of the gospel among the people, who were totally deficient in clear religious knowledge; to rebuke their vices from the Bible, and to exhort men to contrition and repentance. He himself always appeared in the garb

---

* English translation by M. Wrench. Lond., 1843.

of a penitent, meanly clad, and wearing a flowing beard. He went barefoot even in winter, carrying a staff before him, to which a cross was fastened, as a token that his object was to exhort men to follow the cross of Christ. On his arrival in any town, he took up his lodgings indifferently with any of the townspeople, and was satisfied with the meanest fare. He possessed all those qualities calculated to make a powerful impression on the people. His person was dignified and commanding, his voice loud and sonorous, and the effect of his discourses was heightened by the eloquent expression of a keen and flashing eye. His manner was like his character, impassioned; his words flowed with a natural eloquence, warm from the heart; and he was perfectly familiar with the texts of Scripture with which his representations were enforced. The fame of his sanctity and learning was soon spread abroad in that country; and young and old, men and women, came in throngs to confess their sins to him, and went away declaring that they had never before seen a man in whom authority and kindness were so admirably blended, at whose preaching even a heart of iron might readily be moved to repentance, and whose life might serve as a model to all monks, hermits, and priests.

"In the year 1116, Henri sent two of his disciples, arrayed in the garb of penitents, and bearing the standard of the cross, to the city of Maus, to announce his arrival to Bishop Hildebert, and to obtain his permission to preach there. The people, to whom Henri was well known by reputation, and who had for a long time been anxiously desiring an opportunity of seeing and hearing him, received his messengers as angels. At this era it was not unusual for monks to travel from country to country, preaching repentance. Hildebert therefore deemed Henri to be one of these, for he was not yet regarded as a heretic.

His discourses had been directed rather toward practical Christianity than to dogmatical subjects. He had attacked not the doctrines, but the vices of the church. Hildebert was one of those better bishops, who had the interest of religion at heart, and it was thus a personal gratification to him to welcome a man who, possessing such power of influencing the mind, made use of it to incline the heart to good. The bishop was also wise enough to perceive that, by refusing him admittance, he should only exasperate the people, and render himself obnoxious to them. He therefore gave a gracious and hospitable reception to Henri's messengers, and although he was himself on the eve of a journey to Rome, he left orders with his archdeacons, among other charges, to give free admission to Henri in his absence, and to allow him full liberty of preaching. His orders were obeyed, and Henri soon produced the same powerful impression at Maus that he had done elsewhere. Many of the inferior clergy, less influenced (than those of a more elevated position) by self-interest, were attracted by his discourses, and convinced of the truth of his allegations relative to the corruption of the church. They listened with the most eager attention, and were moved to tears by his words. Henri had hitherto acted wisely in bringing forward the truths of the gospel, and had attacked vice only through the medium of these truths, without personality. But the heat of youth now urged him to a series of passionate sallies against the clergy." [Or was it that his zeal was enkindled against their vicious course, and he could not refrain from exposing the falsity of their pretensions?] "And these, as is always the case, found the readiest reception from the people. The clergy became hateful and despicable in their eyes. They refused to have any intercourse with them. And it was only the protection of the nobles that sheltered the priesthood from their threatened vengeance. On one occasion, when some of the clergy came to remonstrate with Henri, they were so roughly handled by the people as to be too happy only to escape in safety. Not daring openly to proclaim the sentence of excommunication which had been pronounced against him, they sent it in writing by one of their members."

This remarkable document ends with the expression, that if he should presume to continue to scatter poison, he is excommunicated by the authority of Pope Paschal, the successor of Peter, the first of the apostles, and a desire that at the dreadful day of judgment Henri may be overtaken by the eternal curse of the Almighty!

Henri refused to receive the document, not recognizing the authority of the tribunal whence it issued, nor the truth of its assertions.

Neander continues: "That Henri, who believed it to be his duty far rather to obey the voice of God, by which he felt himself called, than the commandments of man, should utterly have disregarded this intimation, was but natural; and he went on laboring as before. His influence and authority continued to increase in the city. His word became law. Gold and silver he might have had at his pleasure. Had Henri been nothing more than a covetous and ambitious demagogue, he might easily have availed himself of his influence to enrich himself, and to usurp the government of the city, by arming the people against the nobility and priesthood. But he made use of his power only to realize his own ideas, and accepted only so much of the offered gold as he required for the execution of his plans. His first object was the establishment of Christian brotherly love and fellowship, in opposition to the prevalent corruption of morals and self-seeking worldliness. Women who had lived unchastely were to cut off their hair, and burn it, together with their garments, in public, in order to deter others from similar courses by this disgrace. Regarding celibacy, and the difficulties thrown in the way of marriage by the canonical impediments, as the most obvious sources of the prevailing dissoluteness of manners, he looked to early marriages as a means of improving the moral condition; and therefore he himself solemnized several marriages between the youths of the city, without respect to the canonical hinderances; which, in his opinion, were grounded on human tradition only. He believed marriage to be of perpetual obligation, and separations between those whom God had joined together inadmissible on any grounds. The woman took an oath before Henri, that she would preserve inviolable fidelity to her husband for life, and that she would renounce all pomp of dress—in this age the source of the most lavish expenditure. No considerations of property were in future to influence the matrimonial connection. Neither gold nor silver—neither dower nor possessions—ought to be the objects sought in each other by those whom God had brought together in a holy union. The distinctions occasioned by worldly possessions should be removed by Christian love. He therefore, in opposition to the existing custom, celebrated marriages between the free and those who had served as bondmen,—clothing the latter out of the fund he had formed with the money which had been given him.

"This was all beautiful and sublime, as flowing from a heart that had its home in a better world. It would have been well if such a community as Henri represented to himself could have existed in a world so beset with corruption and variety of hinderances; or if he could have looked into the hearts of those whom he thus united.

"The news of Hildebert's return from Rome induced

Henri to withdraw to some of the neighboring castles, from whence he continued his labors. The bishop made his entrance into the city, followed by a brilliant retinue. But he found that a great change had taken place, and when he would have given his blessing to the people, they contemptuously rejected it, exclaiming, 'We desire neither your learning nor your blessing. Let it fall to the ground. For we have a father and a priest who surpasses you in dignity, in sanctity of life, and in learning—him your clergy despise as a blasphemer. We feel that he lays bare their vices with a prophetic spirit, and rebukes their errors and excesses from the Holy Scriptures. But vengeance will swiftly overtake them, for having presumed to forbid the holy man to publish the word of the Lord.'

"It was a task of much difficulty to restore peace between the clergy and the highly exasperated people; but Hildebert's prudence and gentleness contributed greatly toward effecting it. A demagogue, who had been indebted for his reputation solely to those arts by which the hearts of the people are to be won, would have been quickly forgotten. The foundation of Henri's influence lay deeper. After the lapse of years, and the dissemination of the most scandalous reports concerning the life of the 'heretic,' his memory was still affectionately cherished in the minds of the people.

"Henri now turned to the south of France, and at Poitou, Bordeaux, and other cities, he produced a powerful impression. Coming farther south, he fell in with Pierre de Bruys, the man who was actuated by a like spirit; they united and labored in common. After the death of Pierre de Bruys, Henri became the leader of the sect, and made journeys throughout Provence, Languedoc, and Gascony. The bishops who presided over these provinces, and had been earnestly exhorted by Peter of Clugni to suppress the prevailing heresies, now strove, by every means in their power, to possess themselves of the person of the leader; and at length, in the year 1134, the Bishop of Arles succeeded in securing Henri, whom he took with him to the Council then held at Pisa. Here he was compelled [it is said] to retract all the errors of which he was accused.

"We must have a more accurate knowledge of the circumstances of the case, before we can venture to determine whether Henri really betrayed his convictions; for we learn from ecclesiastical history how little to be trusted are the statements of adverse partisans He was there given over to the custody of the Abbot of Clairvaux; but we soon find him again at liberty, probably owing to the negligence of Bernard, whose attention was at that time absorbed by greater matters, the restoration of peace to the Italian church.

"It was in the mountainous country about Toulouse and Albi, that Henri now made his appearance. The nature of the country rendered it a safe asylum to the sectaries; and the great feudatories who were seated there, instigated either by the preaching of Henri, or by their own hatred toward the ambitious clergy, found many adherents both among the inferior burghers and among the handicraftsmen, especially the weavers. His opponent Bernard has left the following picture of his influence: 'The churches are without congregations, the congregations without a priest. The priests are no longer treated with the reverence due to them. The churches are avoided as though they were synagogues. The sanctuary of the Lord is no longer held sacred; the sacraments are no longer reverenced; the festivals no longer observed. Men die in their sins, and souls are hurried before the awful judgment-seat of God without having been *reconciled to Him by penance*, or strengthened by the supper of the Lord. The way to Christ is closed against the children of Christians; the grace of baptism is denied; and those whom the Saviour called to Him with fatherly love, 'Suffer the little children to come unto me,' are no longer permitted to draw nigh unto heaven."

What should we now say of the professed minister of Christ who would substitute reconciliation *by penance* for reconciliation by Christ, and who would assert that the denial of baptism by water had closed the way to the Saviour and to heaven?

Neander proceeds to say that, "alarmed at the growing influence of Henri, whose doctrines were spreading more and more widely in the south of France, and who was now openly protected by several of the principal nobles, in particular by the Count of Toulouse; Pope Eugenius, who was at this time residing in France, dispatched the cardinal bishop Allerich of Ostia, accompanied by other bishops, into the south, with instructions to suppress the sect. The legate, knowing Bernard's power over the minds of men, persuaded him to join the expedition, and to him the cardinal was indebted for the final success of his efforts." "Bernard's arrival and preaching wrought a powerful effect in the city of Toulouse (and Albi), and Henri and his adherents were forced to make their escape."

"It was in the castles of the nobles that the Henricians now found their chief security; for Bernard had persuaded most of the people to unite in a league against the 'heretics'; by which they bound themselves to exclude them from the rights of burghership, and to renounce all commerce with them." "He urged them to pursue the 'heretics', till they had utterly driven them out of their borders; 'for,' said he, 'the sheep are not safe while there are serpents in their neighborhood.'" And while exhorting them to practise hospitality, he added the warning, "Receive not any strange or unknown preacher, unless he be sent by the pope or by your bishop; for there be preachers, who, assuming the appearance of piety, and renouncing its ways, introduce profane novelties in word and thought, mingling poison with honey."

"Henri himself was captured shortly after these transactions, through the exertions of the bishops, and led in chains before Pope Eugenius, at the Council of Rheims. But at the intercession of the Archbishop of Rheims his sentence was mitigated to perpetual imprisonment in some convent, where he soon afterward died," in the year 1148.

ARNOLD OF BRESCIA.

AMONG the pupils of the celebrated Peter Abelard, before the middle of the twelfth century, was a youth from the city of Brescia, in the Tyrol, named Arnold. Neander's Life of Bernard of Clairvaux contains a brief notice of this young man, the most interesting particulars of which are as follows, showing him to have a true place among the precursors of the reformation of the sixteenth century.

"He attended," says Neander, "on Abelard's teaching, and, like the rest of his disciples, led an ascetic life, seeking rather to satisfy the cravings of the spirit than to minister to their personal necessities. When Abelard represented the directing of the abstracted spirit to the contemplation of the Divine and Eternal One, as the necessary peculiarity of a monk; when in the lives of the apostles he drew the portrait of genuine Christian teachers; when he referred the church to her proper spiritual influence,* and, transported in these moments of pious zeal beyond the

* It must not, however, be forgotten that Abelard is said to have taught some sad and dangerous errors.

limits of the church system, forgot its restraints; then did his words imprint themselves deeply on Arnold's mind. He embraced with ardor the image presented in the apostolic writings, of the activity of the apostles, and the lives of the primitive Christians; and this served to augment his displeasure when he beheld the degeneracy of the clergy, and the corruptions of the church from its connection with the world. He went beyond his teacher in his controversy with the church; the ardor of his disposition rendering him bolder and more free. Possessed by the idea of a genuine Christian church, working only by spiritual means, and for spiritual ends, he sought its realization, and would fain have overthrown whatever of godless and earthly opposed this realization."

From France "Arnold returned to his native country a new man. He separated himself from the secular clergy, and appeared in the garb of a monk. The innocency and austerity of his life was never impeached, even by his adversaries; although they were wont to speak of it as a hypocritical mask, assumed by him in order the more readily to gain admittance for his heretical doctrines. With glowing eloquence he openly opposed to the worldly and vicious lives of the clergy and monks the doctrines and examples of the Bible, and ascribed the corruptions of the church to their having overstepped the boundaries of their real influence and peculiar jurisdiction, to appropriate to themselves the wealth, honors, and privileges of the courts. He declared that the monks and clergy ought to live together after the model of the apostles, in the communion of love, and to abandon all temporal possessions; that the abbots and bishops should resign all their temporalities and regalities, all worldly rank and jurisdiction, to their respective sovereigns, by whom the wealth which the clergy had abused to the purposes of luxury and sensuality should be administered for the benefit of their people. The first-fruits and tithes of the agricultural produce he would have assigned as most suitable for the support of the clergy in the bare necessaries of life; which, if they devoted themselves entirely to the duties of their calling, would be all they would desire.

"Arnold, who was chiefly anxious about *practical* Christianity, does not seem to have opposed further the dogmas of his church; but it is probable that his practical *mysticism* might have led him (when speaking against the ceremonial worship as prejudicial to the religion of the heart) into an actual or apparent deviation from the form of the church-teaching. Thus it might be, that in urging genuine conversion of the heart, he maintained that* *mere outward baptism was in and of itself* inefficacious to man unless connected with that *alone effectual baptism of the Holy Ghost,* through which the truly believing soul is purified and sanctified; that man was not reconciled to God by the outward participation of the Lord's Supper, but by that internal faith of the soul through which, by receiving Christ into it, man becomes united with Him in his heart, and manifests this union by a holy life.

"Arnold's animated discourses captivated the minds of those men who were as yet insensible of the vivifying power of religion (through the fault of the very ministers appointed to proclaim it), and their displeasure naturally fell upon those to whom the key of knowledge had been intrusted, and who entered not in themselves, and hindered those who would have entered. The clergy became the objects of general odium and derision. The magic pomp of the priests no longer made any impression on the people. There might, indeed, according to the usual course of hu-

* The expressions italicized are particularly placed as emphatic by Neander.

man events, be a mingling of impure motives with the purity of Arnold's purposes. The principle so loudly asserted by him, that all temporal possessions ought to be restored by the church to the state, to which they belonged, might indeed allure the desires of the covetous, and particularly of the great.

"The Bishop of Brescia, when he found the formidable consequences resulting to the church from Arnold's agency, accused him as a disturber of the public peace, at the Council held by Innocent II., at Rome, in the year 1139. The pope enjoined him silence, and banished him from Italy (branding his opinions with the name of 'heresy of the politicians');* and he was forced to bind himself by an oath not to return to that country during the life of this pope without his express permission. He returned to France just at the time when Abelard was hotly attacked by his enemies; and this circumstance did but cause him to adhere the more zealously to his old master, whose disinterested boldness he regarded as the origin of his persecutions. He thus drew upon himself the same odium that Abelard had incurred, and Bernard denounced him to the pope as Abelard's armor-bearer and herald. He incurred the same sentence as his teacher, being like him excommunicated, and condemned to imprisonment in a convent.

"In Abelard's case the sentence had been made void by the humane arrangement of the Abbot Peter of Clugni [receiving him as an inmate of his monastery with the sanction and indulgence of the pope upon his expressed submission]. But the youthful Arnold was little disposed thus to seek rest and peace by silence and retirement. Not one among the French bishops was found who would put the sentence against Arnold into execution; and being driven out of France, and repairing to the neighboring

* Sismondi's Hist. of the Italian Republics.

country of Switzerland, he found an asylum at Zurich, where his presence was tolerated by the Bishop of Constance." Sismondi says he influenced the citizens of Zurich to form a free constitution.

His "discourses were very influential in Zurich. We now lose sight of him for some years, but his principles had already produced an effect independent of his personal influence. These had become well known at Rome, through the papal condemnation, and had excited great attention."

Pope Innocent II. died in the year 1144, in the midst of great commotions in his capital, and strife between him and the Roman nobles. Soon afterward, either during the brief pontificate of his successor, Celestin II., who reigned only five months, or about the beginning of that of Lucius II., Arnold returned to Italy, and made his appearance at Rome. Here he seems to have taken part in the political struggles. "It appeared to him that it was through the usurpations of the church in temporal matters that the Roman Empire had lost its power and greatness, and the church its purity and its *spiritual* character. Arnold inflamed the Romans still more by reproving, from the Bible, the ambition of the popes and the vices of the Romish court. He pointed, as the source of all this corruption, to the temporal dominion which the popes had arrogated to themselves, and which he declared to be as little consistent with their position as with that of the clergy in general. They also ought to live on the offerings of the congregation. Stimulated by his harangues, the Romans established themselves in the possession of the Capitol, determined on reviving their ancient Roman constitution, the senate, and the equestrian order, and invited the Emperor Konrad to repair to Rome, and there set up the seat of his empire."

"Arnold placed too much confidence in the enthusiasm

of the fickle and light-minded Romans, which did not in general, like his, originate in the purest of motives. And he did not possess sufficient calmness to estimate the power of purposes, originating in temporary circumstances, on the minds of men. The Emperor Konrad regarded the language of the Romans as idle talk, and (on the other hand) received the embassy dispatched by the pope to solicit his protection, in the most respectful manner.

"Pope Lucius assembled a numerous body of armed men, and attacked the Capitol; but he was repulsed, and received a severe wound from a stone in the struggle, from the effects of which he died, in the spring of 1148."

A monk who had been employed in very humble duties in the monastery of Clairvaux, under Bernard, was now elected pope, and took the name of Eugenius III. But he was driven from Rome, and took up his residence at Viterbo, until at length the opposition was subdued and he was enabled to return to the city.

"Rome," says Neander, "was the last place where Arnold's pure spirit could have any influence. He had deceived himself when he had relied on finding, in that corrupt city, men capable of embracing his ideas, and of becoming animated by them in their purity. The spirit of wild rebellion, of passion, and of earthly covetousness ruled in Rome."

Neander here leaves him, and our information respecting Arnold from that period to the time of his death is very meagre. In the year 1154, the only Englishman who ever attained to that office, Nicholas Breakspeare, who had risen from a menial condition of life, was elected pope, and took the name of Adrian IV. He was a man of great energy and resolution, and in his contests with the Roman people, one of his cardinals being dangerously wounded in a popular tumult, he placed the city under an interdict, closing the places of worship and forbidding all religious services. This alarmed the fickle and superstitious populace, who, headed by the priests, supplicated the pope's recall of the formidable edict, so that they might once more be consoled by the formalities on which they were wont to place so great dependence. Adrian, however, would not relent until Arnold and his associates were expelled from Rome.

According to Waddington's History of the Church, Arnold soon afterward fell into the power of the Emperor Frederick Barbarossa, who was then in Italy, and who delivered him up to the pope. "He was conducted to Rome and subjected to the partial judgment of an ecclesiastical tribunal. His guilt was eagerly pronounced, the prefect of the city delivered his sentence, and he was burned alive, in the presence of a careless and ungrateful people. But lest this same multitude, with the same capriciousness, should presently turn to adore *the martyr*, and offer worship at his tomb, his ashes were contemptuously scattered over the bosom of the Tiber."

Sismondi says that he "was burned alive before the gate of the castle of St. Angelo, in the year 1155. But his precepts survived, and the love of liberty in Rome did not perish with him."* And Waddington adds to the account of his martyrdom, that "in respect to his disputes with the church, we may venture to rank Arnold of Brescia among those earnest but inconsiderate reformers, whose premature opposition to established abuses produced little immediate result except their own discomfiture and destruction; but whose memory has become dear, as their example has been useful, to a happier and a wiser posterity; whom we celebrate as martyrs to the best of human principles, and whose very indiscretions we account as zeal and virtue."

* "History of the Italian Republics."

CHAPTER III.

PETER DE WALDO.

PIERRE DE VAUX, or Peter Waldo, was a wealthy citizen of Lyons, born at the town of Waldum, or Vaux, in the vicinity of that city, and derived his surname from the place of his nativity. It has been supposed, from his having subsequently become eminent as a preacher among the Waldenses, that this people obtained their appellation from him; but this appears to be a mistake, inasmuch as the name of Waldenses, or Vaudois (valley-people), was given to those primitive children of the Alpine recesses long before his appearance among them. It is, however, very probable that his connection with them, and his agency in developing them as a distinct people in active, as they had been before in comparatively passive and silent opposition to Romish corruptions and encroachments, as well as the greater extension of their peculiar doctrines and practices from the time of Waldo's zealous and effective engagements among them, may have given him a claim to be considered in some sort as the founder of that denomination of Christians.

The time of his birth is supposed to have been about the beginning of the twelfth century. No account remains, so far as appears in history, of his education or early life; but he is stated to have possessed considerable learning, and seems to have been engaged for some years successfully in the pursuits of trade.

A remarkable circumstance was the means of awakening his mind to a conviction of the uncertainty of time, and the necessity of experiencing a preparation for eternity. But we are not informed at what period of his life this change in his character took place. He had supped one night with some opulent citizens of Lyons, and before separating, they engaged, as was common, in some amusement. In the midst of the sport, one of the company profanely used the name of the Almighty with an oath, and instantly fell dead on the floor. This sudden and awful event struck Waldo to the heart to such a degree that from that time he resolved to make the welfare of his soul his principal concern.* It is said that he formed a firm resolution thenceforward to detach his affections from earthly entanglements, to fix them on heaven and heavenly things, and to pass the remainder of his days as a "fellow-citizen with the saints, and of the household of God."

He now applied himself diligently to the perusal of the Holy Scriptures and the works of the ancient Christian writers, and thus became acquainted with the doctrines and practices of the early church. Some authors say that he occupied himself in translating some portions of the Bible into the Romance language, the vernacular tongue of that part of France; but it seems more probable that he employed others in this work; and Neander gives us the names of two individuals, Stephen de Ansa and Bernard Ydros, whom he hired to translate for him the four gospel narratives and some other portions of the Bible, as well as a collection of the sayings of the early authors on matters of faith and practice. The same historian informs us that copies of his version of the Holy Scriptures (being afterward extended to the whole Bible) were multiplied by him for circulation among the people at large.

He bestowed his wealth with great generosity in relieving and assisting the poor, and sending forth missionaries

* Blair's History of the Waldenses, vol. i. p. 249.

among the people of the country around Lyons. He proposed to form a society for the spread of evangelical truth among the more neglected inhabitants both of city and country, not particularly for an actual and open opposition to the doctrines of the papal system, but for the promotion of spiritual and practical religion, which was the great desideratum in his view.

His own house soon became a common resort for those who needed his aid in their outward necessities, and likewise for many who sought his advice and instruction on religious subjects. The number of his disciples increasing rapidly, he undertook to preach more openly in public places; and so many were attracted by his discourses that the usual houses for worship were comparatively deserted. In his preaching he took pains to prove his doctrines from the Holy Scriptures, and boldly asserted that the Church of Rome was in a state of apostasy from the true faith of the gospel, that she was the harlot of Babylon, and the barren fig-tree which our Lord cursed; that we are not bound to obey the pope, who is not the true head of the church; that monasticism is like corrupt carrion, and has the mark of the beast; and that masses, purgatory, the dedication of temples, and the worship of the saints, are inventions of the devil.*

After a time he began to preach, not only in Lyons, but likewise in the surrounding country, and sent forth numerous coadjutors to propagate the same doctrines, who met with a hearty welcome among congenial souls in the spurs and valleys of the Alps. His life, meanwhile, was consistent with his doctrines, and even his enemies have conceded to him a charity and Christian piety altogether rare in that corrupt age. Indeed, his character for virtue and integrity was beyond reproach. Blair says that "notwith-

* Blair's History of the Waldenses.

standing the opposition of the pope and clergy," his success as a preacher "was most singular. Some authors affirm that he and his followers denied swearing, and all *forms* of supplication, except 'the Lord's prayer.' Their other prayers would be extemporaneous. Be this as it may, Waldo and his fellow-laborers went on teaching all who chose to listen. They blamed the vice and luxury, the excesses and arrogance, of the pope and his dignitaries. In short, the new preachers removed almost all the sanctions of the Roman church as useless and superstitious." And it appears from the account given by Neander, that they not only disapproved of oaths, but also "held it unchristian to shed blood." For he tells us that a few years afterward, Pope Innocent III., being desirous to conciliate the Waldenses, granted permission (with certain reservations) to those of them who could be persuaded to remain in allegiance to Rome, not only to form a spiritual society among themselves, after the manner of other religious orders, but to be exempt from the liability "to be called upon for military service against Christians, or to take an oath in civil processes." How long they held these views on war and oaths, we are not informed, though it does not by any means appear that in their oft-repeated persecutions they always adhered to them.

At length the attention of the Council of Tours was directed to the heresies, so called, prevailing in the valleys of Piedmont and the district around Lyons; and the Archbishop of Lyons, alarmed at Waldo's progress, prohibited him and his companions from further spreading their sentiments, alleging that they, being only laymen, transcended the limits of their position in society, in taking upon them the function of preachers. He threatened that if the practice was persisted in, it should be met with excommunication and the punishment of heresy. But Waldo* replied,

* Milner's Church History, vol, iii. p. 419.

"that in a matter of such infinite importance as the salvation of men, he could not hold his peace, and that he must obey God rather than man." In accordance with the fulmination of the Council of Tours, the archbishop then endeavored to apprehend him; but Waldo continued in and about Lyons for three years afterward, notwithstanding the archbishop's efforts to have him arrested; being protected by his friends and relatives, some of whom were persons of much influence. At length, however, in the year 1166, the archbishop succeeded so far in his plans as to compel Peter Waldo and his followers to retire from the city to distant places. Neander says that they appealed to Pope Alexander III., transmitting to him a copy of their Romance Bible, and soliciting his approbation of their spiritual society; that the subject was discussed before the Lateran Council in 1170, but that the pope refused their petition and forbade them to continue to preach.

"They were dispersed," says Du Thou, "as strangers through the province of Narbonne, Lombardy, and especially among the Alps, where, having obtained a secure retreat, they lay hid for many years." And he adds that "Peter Waldo, being chased from Lyons, retired into the Low Countries, had a great number of followers in Picardy, passed into Germany, visited the towns of Saxony, and at last settled in Bohemia." He diligently propagated his sentiments in the various places where he travelled. By the accounts of other authors, it appears that on leaving Lyons he first proceeded into Dauphiny, making a great impression among the peasants of the mountains in that district, and founding congregations which withstood the assaults of persecution for many years. He next went into Provence, and thence into Languedoc, where he left zealous pastors over numerous flocks, in the field formerly occupied by Peter de Bruys and his companion Henri.

Thence he appears to have travelled northward into Picardy, where great multitudes adhered to his doctrines, who were afterward subjected to severe persecution. Here, in 1188, their enemies destroyed three hundred mansions of the more opulent among them, razed several of their walled towns, and consigned many of the inhabitants of the district to the flames.

Proceeding into the Netherlands and Flanders, he afterward visited Germany, and especially labored zealously in Saxony; after which he settled in Bohemia for the brief remainder of his life. Blair relates, on the authority of a Bohemian historian, that the disciples of Waldo, driven from France, arrived in Bohemia in the year 1176, and having selected for their residence Saaz and Laun on the Eger, they obtained an immense number of associates. But he does not state whether this was the district to which Waldo's own steps were directed. It would appear that they found in Bohemia congenial spirits, and were instrumental in leading many of these to a still purer doctrine, a more simple mode of worship than the Greek, to which they had been accustomed, and a stricter discipline.

The accounts, however, of the latter days of Peter Waldo are extremely defective, and contradictory in regard to dates. All that is certain appears to be the fact that in Bohemia he found not only an open door for his teachings, but also a secure asylum from ecclesiastical persecution, and a peaceful resting-place for his declining days. It is said by Milner that he died there in the year 1179; though even the date of his death is a matter of doubt, some authors alleging that 1184 was the year of his retirement to Bohemia.

Muston[*] assures us that 1179 was the year when Waldo presented to the pope a translation of the Bible into the

---

[*] Muston's "Israel of the Alps," vol. i. p. 15.

vulgar tongue; and was present at the Council of Lateran, where, according to the relation of Mapes, Archdeacon of Oxford, who was present at that Council, the pope showed Waldo some favor, and sanctioned his preaching, under certain restrictions. Muston adds that Waldo was condemned by Lucius III. in the Council of Verona, in 1184, when the emperor was exerting himself to extirpate "heretics;" and alleges that it was in consequence of this condemnation that, between 1185 and 1188, Waldo and his disciples were expelled from Lyons.

CHAPTER IV.

NICOLAS OF BASLE.

ONE of the most remarkable witnesses to the spirituality of true religion during the fourteenth century was Nicolas of Basle, a man who rather sought concealment or retirement than notoriety, and some of whose services in the cause of Christ were only identified with his name more than 450 years after he had sealed his testimony in the flames of the stake. He has, of later times, been ascertained to have been the long unknown instrument of a memorable change in the views and experience of the celebrated John Tauler, by which that eminent man was brought to a heartfelt acknowledgment of the necessity of the inward work of the Holy Spirit, and to a practical experience of its cleansing and sanctifying operations during the rest of his life. This occurred about the year 1340. Nicolas appears to have been born about or soon after the commencement of the fourteenth century, of a respectable family at Basle in Switzerland, and was a youth of good abilities and well esteemed; but being educated as a layman, pretended to no erudition, and had not for some years even the privilege of reading the Holy Scriptures. But it appears that he was in his youth visited with close convictions for sin, which resulted in great mental conflict for several years. Not being much acquainted with the way of the Lord, he sought to obtain religion by the efforts of his own reasoning powers; but found it in vain to endeavor in this way to fortify himself against temptation. S. Winkworth's Life of Tauler relates of this period of the life of Nicolas, that "one day, as he was meditating on the transitory nature of all earthly things, and the rapid flight of time, the thoughtlessness, sinfulness, and forgetfulness of God in all those around him were presented in such vivid colors to his mind, that it seemed inconceivable to him how man could take any delight in this vain world. And then, as the thought of his own wasted time rose to his remembrance, he was filled with such bitter remorse, that he resolved from that moment to renounce the world and dedicate his life to God."

He then began to peruse the lives of the saints (so esteemed by professors of that day), and to imitate the austerities with which some of them had sought to eradicate the carnal propensities of their nature. This kind of bodily exercise he continued for about five years, until it pleased the Most High, by the inshinings of the true Light in his soul, to show him a more perfect way than that of outward penances. After a time, it seems, he had opportunities of reading the Holy Scriptures, though it is uncertain in what language he perused them, as he was not learned in the Latin, in which tongue only, at that period, the Bible was generally accessible. He thought he had divine assistance in his application to the Holy Scriptures, and he says he was enabled, in about eight months, to understand them as well "as if he had studied all his days in the universities."

About that time, the most spiritual professors of religion in Germany and the neighboring countries were often designated as the "Friends of God," and this, sometimes, under circumstances which seem to indicate more or less of an association together into a community, though it does not appear that they ever separated organically or as a sect from the prevalent Roman church. It is clear that to some extent they had a common faith, and common views of the necessity of the spiritual life, and fellowship among each other as reformers of the practical corruptions of the times. Yet the most deeply spiritual men among them do not seem to have seen through many of the corruptions of doctrine which for ages had cast so deep a shade over the religion of Europe. They had glimpses thereof, and in their own life and conduct, as well as their expressed sentiments, often showed that they lived in an atmosphere raised far above these corruptions; and some of them, as we shall see, were willing to die for their testimony to the spirituality of true religion; yet they were not as a body led into open opposition to the Romish system. The times did not seem prepared to receive such a development at large. They may be said to have "worked out their own salvation with fear and trembling," in obedience to the degree of light vouchsafed, though still adhering to many errors of education, and tarnished with some superstitions. The writer of the Life and Times of Tauler, above quoted, and from whom we gather most of our information respecting Nicolas of Basle, expresses the opinion that "in the first instance, the sense of having entered into a living personal union with God, bringing with it a yearning pity for sinners, and a fervent desire to bring them to the same blessed state, was the sole distinction and bond of the 'Friends of God.'" To these people Nicolas soon attached himself, rather than enter the lists of the formal priesthood, which was so common a resort of those religiously inclined in those ages; and he acquired eventually great influence among them.

In the year 1340, he informed Tauler that for twelve years he had been the subject of the "wonderful dealings of God," though conscious of being but a poor sinner. It is probable there were at times, owing to his ardent imagination, and in accordance with the spirit of the age, some fantasies mixed more or less with true spiritual experience. We find him relating that on one occasion, during the night, an ardent longing came over his soul, so that he exclaimed: "Oh, eternal and merciful God, that it were Thy will to give me to discover something that should be above all our sensual reason!" Yet immediately a sense of presumption in this request alarmed him, and he prayed for forgiveness for its having entered into the heart of such a poor worm as himself to desire so great a gift of so rich a grace, when at the same time he was sensible that he had not always lived as he should have done, nor been thankful enough to the Lord, nor worthy of his favors. With this he resorted once more to scourging himself for his sin, until the blood ran down his shoulders. After a short time he believed himself favored of the Lord with a divine visitation of a wonderful nature, "insomuch," says he, "that I could have cried, with St. Peter, Lord, it is good for me to be here!" "In that hour," he adds, "I received more truth and more illumination in my understanding than all the teachers could ever teach me from now till the day of judgment, by word of mouth, with all their natural learning and science." However this may have been, whether this was all true experience, or somewhat amplified in his warm imagination, there can be no reason to doubt that it was a time of divine visitation to his soul, in which he received deep spiritual instruction. And going on in obedience to his convictions of duty, he learned more and more of the nature of true religion, and became a highly prized adviser of many in times of sore perplexity. That part of Europe was for some years the scene not only of political strife and war, but also of many afflictions, by pestilence, famine, and tempests; so that it might be said, "men's hearts failed them for fear, and for looking at the things which were coming on the earth." These tossings of the outward elements were doubtless a means whereby many were led to seek an anchorage for the soul more sure and steadfast than a dependence on the mere forms and ceremonies of the papal system, and the number of the spiritual seekers after God, or, as they were called, the " Friends of God," was probably thereby greatly increased.

It may be questioned whether Nicolas of Basle, in his zealous advocacy of immediate divine revelation, was always discriminating in his judgment between the real divine communications of the Holy Ghost to the soul, the "inspeaking Word," nigh in the hearts of all men and even dwelling with the faithful, and those emotions which sometimes assume that appearance in warm temperaments, especially in an age much given to legendary fancies. Yet it would appear that if he occasionally failed in this respect, the main bent of his life was a genuine testimony to the superiority of inward and immediate teaching by the Spirit of Truth, over all that can be learned by the mere powers of man's nature, or by outward preaching or forms of religion. And under such an experience in his own person, he could have well said with that spiritual man, King David, "I am wiser than all my teachers." He became highly valued among the "Friends of God" of that time, and perhaps by none of them more than by Tauler himself, though he continued a layman. Of his extraordinary influence upon the mind of the latter, we may have to speak in relating the life and sentiments of that eminent man. In the year 1356, he wrote a pamphlet on the decay of vital religion, a copy of which he sent to Tauler; in which, bemoaning the sinfulness which prevailed, he speaks of a warning vision which he had had, and foretells the approach of fresh calamities on the land. This is considered to have been, in part, at least, fulfilled in the almost total destruction of the city of Basle by a great earthquake* followed by a conflagration lasting eight days, which is said to have occurred during that same year. This year, also, one of his friends, Berthold von Rohrbach, was burned at the stake, at Spire, for preaching that a layman, enlightened by the Almighty, was as competent to teach others as the most learned priest.

In the little company or brotherhood around Basle, of which Nicolas was a sort of centre, both priest and layman united in regarding him as their most enlightened member; and all standing equally in a direct and individual relation to their Divine Master, they required no priestly mediation as such. Nicolas declared, "Not counsel from men ought we to seek after, but that which proceeds from the Holy Spirit; and so long as we have it from that source, it is indifferent whether it flow to us through priest or layman." And the author of the Life and Times of Tauler, already quoted, adds that "they regarded external observances as unimportant in themselves, and only excellent as a means of improvement, or a sign of obedience. Thus, while they admitted ascetic exercises and painful penances to be useful in the commencement of a religious life, in order to mortify the sensual inclinations, they declared them to be afterward a matter of indifference, nay, sometimes positively contrary to the Divine Will." How opposite were these views to the superstitious reliance of the Romish church on such austerities! Nicolas said, that to the advanced disciple such things might be self-sought penalties, and an evidence that God was not allowed to work in that soul himself alone; and he considered that it was their duty to endeavor to maintain the health and strength of the body, though in subjection to the spirit, that they might be adequate to the labors and fatigues which in the ordering of the Lord they might be called upon to undertake. Nevertheless, it is true that they often practised some of these austerities, as we have seen an instance of in the case cited of Nicolas himself.

For several years he did not, for some reason, allow the particular place of his abode to be generally known,—probably a measure of personal precaution in those disturbed and persecuting times,—yet he kept up a frequent correspondence from his seclusion, through the means of those few who had access to him, with brethren of the same faith on the Rhine, in Italy, Lorraine, and Hungary, and likewise with such as in their perplexities applied to him for spiritual consolation. In 1367 he and four chosen friends left Basle, and, in accordance with a dream, went into closer seclusion for a time in a place high up on a mountain in the dominions of the Duke of Austria, and far away from any human habitation. Here they remained some years. From this retreat, when he was above seventy years of age, Nicolas felt himself called upon to make a visit to Pope Gregory XI., who had recently gone to Rome from Avignon. He was under an impression that still heavier judgments were impending over sinful and distracted Christendom.

Accompanied by one of his intimate friends, and with the sanction of the community of his fellow-believers, Nicolas set out for Rome in the spring of 1377. The "Briefbuch" of Rulman Merswin, with whom he corresponded respecting his journey, gives the following particulars. When they came to Rome, the Layman (as Nicolas was always called except when styled "the dear Friend of God in the Oberland") inquired for a former acquaintance, now an inhabitant of that city; who received him and his companion with great hospitality, and insisted on entertaining them, with their servants and horses, during their stay in the city. Finding from Nicolas that they were very desirous of an opportunity of speaking to the pope, this man procured for them a private interview on the third day after their arrival. Coming into the presence of the pontiff, "the Jurist," as his companion was styled from having formerly been in the profession of the law, addressed him in Latin; but Nicolas, not being able to speak in that language, spoke to him in Italian; and among other things, to the following effect: "Holy father (following the common mode of addressing the pope), there are many grievous and heinous crimes wrought throughout Christendom by all degrees of men, whereby God's anger is greatly provoked. Thou oughtest to consider how to put an end to these evils." The pope answered, "I have no power to amend matters." They then told him of his own secret faults, which had been revealed to them of God by certain evident tokens; and added, "Holy father, know of a truth, that if you do not put away your evil doings, and utterly amend your ways, you will die within a year." The pope was greatly enraged at the boldness of these poor men in thus rebuking him; but they mildly assured him of their willingness to be imprisoned, or even put to death, if what they alleged were not found to be true. The mind of the pontiff seems to have been struck with conviction; for, rising from his throne, he embraced the two men and kissed them, requesting further conversation with Nicolas; and told them that they might do a great service to religion if they would deliver the same message to the Emperor of Germany. But this was not a part of their mission. Afterward the pope invited them to remain with him in Rome, offering to provide for their necessities, and to follow their counsel. But this they declined, wishing to return to their mountain home, and endeavor to obtain means for building a more commodious habitation. They informed the pope "that they sought no earthly gain, nor came thither for the sake of any such thing; but sought the glory of God and the welfare of Christendom above all perishable gifts of this present time." He then offered them a bishopric, and sundry revenues and grants; but they declined to receive them. He, however, wrote letters in their favor to the bishop and priests of their diocese. The simple and somewhat quaint account of their visit given in the "Briefbuch," thus winds up the story: "Now when these two dear Friends of God had settled their affair with the pope, and desired to depart from Rome, their host would not suffer them to pay for anything they had had in his house; and, moreover, gave the Layman a good ambling horse, instead of the heavy carriage in which he had come; saying that a soft-paced horse would be much easier for him to ride over the high mountains than the carriage, seeing that he was old and weakly. Now afterward the pope was unmindful of God's message, and obeyed it not, and died that same year, as they had prophesied." It is probable that the expression, "that same year," should be "within a year," in accordance with Nicolas's words; for the account adds that the pope died "about the fourth week in Lent, 1378."

After their arrival at home, through the kindness of the bishop and magistrates, and the liberality of "three foreign brethren," who had for some time wished to be received into their society, and now made over to them their property for the purpose of aiding the building, they were enabled to finish their house, and also a house for divine worship. How long they were permitted to rest in peace in their new habitation, does not clearly appear. Fresh troubles threatened that part of Europe, and Nicolas soon foresaw that events might come to pass which would compel the "Friends of God" to scatter themselves over the world. Meantime he advised that their part was to remain in privacy "until God shall do something, we know not what as yet." He entreated the prayers of his friends, in great trouble, and not knowing what might be the result. "It is evident," says S. Winkworth, "from such dark hints as these, that Nicolas and his friends now began to comtemplate the possibility of their duty calling them to use more public means of influence than the private, though by no means inactive or inefficient, line of conduct hitherto pursued. They must have foreseen the painful collision impending between their deep reverence for the outward authority of the church, and the inward authority of the indwelling light. Neither can they have been without forebodings of the martyr's doom, which actually befell all those of whose fate any traces are left."

The dissensions in the Romish church were now greatly increased by the election of two rival popes, producing a schism which lasted about forty years; and the "Friends of God" were greatly perplexed. Nicolas advised quietness and reliance on the Almighty, waiting His direction. The mysterious accounts of several meetings held by Nicolas and his associates in the mountains, with a few chosen friends from other parts, in which they sought for instruction in this time of deep trial to their faith, are so mixed up with what appears fanciful or symbolical, that we may pass them by. It is probable that too much scope was given to the imagination in their deep distress. "It is difficult," says the author already quoted, "to know in what light to regard the marvellous accounts that meet us in the writings of Rulman and Nicolas. Some of them seem to be simply symbolical; for it is clear that they were in the habit of presenting their views of human affairs under the form of an allegory, supposed to be seen in a vision or dream, as Bunyan does in his Pilgrim's Progress." "Whatever interpretation, however, we may be inclined to put upon the marvellous circumstances attending, it seems tolerably clear that the seclusion of the 'Friends of God.' was regarded by them as a time of preparation for their public work, when they should be 'scattered abroad over Christendom;' and that by their retirement they were breaking the ties that had bound them to those who had hitherto depended on them for guidance, and accustoming them to act for themselves against a time when they should no longer have their wonted counsellors at hand."

No clear accounts have come down to us respecting the dispersion of this little band, which, it is supposed, took place in the year 1383. "Most likely," says the author of the Life and Times of Tauler, "they went forth as preachers of repentance; for there occur in the letters of Nicolas frequent comparisons of the present state of the world to that of Nineveh, and hints that they may have to act the part of Jonah. But where, and how long they did so, is wrapt in utter darkness." "All we actually know respecting their subsequent history is, that in 1393 a certain Martin von Mayence, a Benedictine monk of Reichenau, in the diocese of Constance, who is called in the accounts of his trial a disciple of Nicolas of Basle and a 'Friend of God,' was burned at Cologne, after the same fate had befallen some other Friends of God a short time before at Heidelberg. Active researches were made after Nicolas, but as he had concealed himself from his friends, for a long time he was able to elude the efforts of his persecutors. At length, on a journey into France, in order to diffuse his doctrines, accompanied by two of his disciples, he fell into the hands of the inquisitors at Vienne. He was brought to trial, and persisted firmly and publicly" in his religious views, the most "audacious" of which seems to have been that he affirmed "that he knew that he was in Christ, and Christ in him" [in accordance with the apostle's testimony, 2 Cor. xiii. 5; Col. i. 27, etc.]. "He was therefore delivered over to the secular power, and perished in the flames, together with his two disciples, who refused to be parted from him." It is supposed that this venerable man was about ninety years old when he thus suffered martyrdom.

CHAPTER V.

JOHN TAULER.

JOHN TAULER, or Thauler, was born in the year 1290, most probably at Strasburg on the Rhine, though, according to some authors, at the city of Cologne. Being of a serious disposition, he determined in early life, in accordance with the practice of those times, to assume the clerical profession, and accordingly took up his abode in a monastery of the Dominican order in his native city. This is supposed to have been about the eighteenth year of his age; soon after which he went to Paris in order to study theology—a name given at that time to a laborious mixture of scholastic disquisitions with metaphysical speculations, almost to the exclusion of a true knowledge of God and of the nature of sin and redemption.

It does not appear what effect was produced on his mind by his studies and associations in the city of Paris. In its university might then be found almost every variety of speculation and belief. On his return to Strasburg he was probably thrown in contact with men more or less attached to mystical principles, including the famous Eckart, Nicolas of Strasburg, and others who were about that time there.

For several years after his return, his native city shared largely with others in the troubles consequent upon a long dispute between the pope and the emperor, during which the former had placed under interdict all who persisted in obedience to the latter. The ecclesiastics were thereby intimidated, and generally discouraged from pursuing their wonted functions, so that but a few remained in Strasburg, either to preach or to perform any of the usual services in their mode of worship. " The hireling fleeth because he is an hireling, and careth not for the sheep;" and thus these mercenaries left their flocks, mindful only of their own safety. This was in the year 1338. But John Tauler, when most of his fellow-priests had deserted their flocks, and left the city for two years to take care of itself, continued to preach as usual, and even with more diligence, not only there, but in several other places, ranging from Cologne to Basle. It was probably during his visits to the latter city about this time, that Nicolas of Basle first met with him, and was struck with the earnestness of his preaching. Here also he met with his old acquaintance, Henry of Nordlingen, a priest of Constance, who was then wandering about in great distress, in consequence of the pope's prohibition. He is described as a man of gentle pious spirit, "more fitted for a quiet contemplative life than for the energetic activity required by the troublous times in which his lot was cast. He, like Tauler, was filled with anguish at the sight of the distress of those around him; but while Tauler's grief stirred him up to vigorous efforts in their behalf, and his courage and energy rose with the emergency, the timid and hesitating Henry was unable to surmount the difficulties in which he found himself involved; and the greater the pressure of the times, the greater was his perplexity and longing for peace." Tauler endeavored to encourage him, and did actually prevail upon him at different times to venture to preach, notwithstanding the papal interdict; yet afterward he again gave way to his fears, and to the clamors raised against him among the priests. But Tauler was still undaunted and diligent, considering it to be his duty to preach without waiting for papal permission. He was evidently greatly esteemed as a fervent preacher, and was probably faithful to the best of his knowledge at that time; but he soon came to see, through the instrumentality of his friend, "the Layman," Nicolas of Basle, the "dear friend of God in the Oberland," that what he had hitherto attained to in conformity with the scholastic views of his education, was but as the outer shell of religious experience, and that, like Apollos of old, he needed to know for himself "the way of God more perfectly."

The following incident is said to have occurred to him during the time that he was earnestly concerned to find for himself a sure foundation for his faith and hope. He received an inward intimation that by going to a certain place of worship, he would find in the porch a man who would instruct him "in the spiritual life." On arriving at the place, he found a poor beggar, very meanly clad. He saluted him thus: "God give you a good day, my friend." The poor man replied: "Sir, I do not remember that I ever had an evil day." Tauler said to him: "God give you a good and happy life:" to which the beggar rejoined: "Why say you that? I never was unhappy." "Pray tell me what you mean," asked Tauler. The poor man replied: "That I shall willingly do. I told you first I never had an evil day; for when I have hunger, I praise God. If it rain, hail, snow, or freeze, be it fair or foul, or if I am despised or ill used, I return God thanks; so I never had an evil day. Nor have I ever been unhappy, since I have learned always to resign myself to His will; being very certain of this, that all His works are perfectly good; and therefore I never desire anything else but the good pleasure of God." Then said Tauler: "But what if the good pleasure of God should be to cast you hence into hell?" The poor man replied: "If he would do so, I have two arms to embrace him with: the one whereof is profound humility, by which I am united to his holy humanity; the other is love or charity, which joins me to his divinity. Embraced with these two arms, he would descend with me thither, if thither he ordered me; and there I had infinitely rather be, with him, than in paradise, without him." This was a deep lesson to Tauler, of the necessity of true resignation and humility, in order to attain to the love of God and acceptance with him. After this, he asked the poor man whence he came. He replied, that God had sent him. Tauler inquired of him, where he found the Almighty. He replied: "I found him when I had renounced all the creatures." "And where did you leave him?" asked Tauler. The beggar answered: "With the poor in spirit, the pure in heart, and men of charity." "But who are you?" again asked Tauler. "I am a king," said the beggar. "Where is your kingdom?" asked Tauler. "In my soul," replied he; "for I have learned to bring into subjection and govern my senses, as well outward as inward, with my affections and passions; which kingdom is undoubtedly superior to all the kingdoms of this world." Tauler then asked him by what means he had arrived at such an attainment; to which he replied, that it was "by silence, vigilance, meditation, and prayer, and the union I had with God. I could find no sure repose or comfort in any creature of the world; by which means I found out my God, who will comfort me world without end."

It was in the year 1340 that Nicolas of Basle believed himself warned of the Lord three times in his sleep to go to find out Tauler at Strasburg, more than ninety miles from his own residence. Accordingly he concluded to go, "and wait to see what God is purposed to do or to bring to pass there." The account given of his tarriance there, which was for several months, is somewhat prolix and quaint, after the manner of the times; but a brief abstract will not be without interest and instruction. It appears to have been chiefly drawn up by Tauler himself, and to have been given by him into the hands of Nicolas, about twenty years after the events, with the strict injunction that neither of their names should appear in it, and that it should not be printed during Tauler's lifetime. Accordingly, he is uniformly spoken of in the narrative as "the Master,"—a designation then given to priests—and Nicolas as "the Layman," or "the man." Neither of them appears to have been sufficiently enlightened to see through the popish superstitions of confession and the mass, though it is reasonable to believe that their esteem for these rites was at that time a subdued one, and their practice of them chiefly by way of obedience, or of acquiescence in the system of their education, at that period rarely questioned.

Nicolas, after hearing Tauler preach five times, became convinced that although he was of a very loving gentle spirit by nature, and had a good understanding of Holy Scripture, yet that he was "dark as to the light of grace;" and his heart so yearned over him, that after twelve weeks he ventured to go to him, with a request that he would preach a sermon, "showing how a man may attain to the highest point that is given to us to reach in this present time." He urged this request against Tauler's objections, and would not cease his entreaties till "the Master" promised him to do as he desired. His sermon, which "the Layman" took down in writing, was a remarkable one for those days of darkness; the following being the *qualifications* brought forward by Tauler as belonging to such an attainment, "so far as he could find from Scripture."

"The first is given us by our Lord Jesus Christ, when he says, 'Hereby [ye] shall know that ye are my disciples, if ye have love one to another,'—'even as I have loved you;' as much as to say, 'though ye should possess arts and wisdom, and high understanding, it is all in vain if ye have not withal fidelity and love.' We believe that Balaam was so replete with understanding that he perceived what things God purposed to do or reveal hundreds of years after his day; but it availed him nothing, forasmuch as he did not cleave with love and loyalty to the things which he understood.

"The second mark appertaining to a truly reasonable, enlightened man, is that he must become empty of self; and this must not make him proud, but he shall consider how he may ever more attain to this freedom, and sit loose by all creatures.

"Third, he shall resign himself utterly to God, that God may work His own works in him; and he shall not glory in the works as being his own, but always think himself too mean to have done them.

"He shall go out from himself in all the things in which he is wont to seek and find himself, whether belonging to time or to eternity, and by so doing he shall win a true increase.

"He shall not seek his own ends in any creature, whether temporal or eternal, and hereby he shall attain to perfect satisfaction and content.

"He shall always wait on that which God will have him to do, and shall try, with the help of God, to fulfil that to the uttermost, and shall take no glory to himself therefor.

"He shall daily, without ceasing, give up his will to the will of God, and endeavor to will nothing but what God willeth.

"He shall bend all his powers into submission to God, and exercise them so constantly and so strenuously in God, and with such power and love, that God may work nothing in him without his active concurrence, and he may do nothing without God.

"He shall have the sense of the presence of God in all his works, at all times, and in all places, whatever it please God to appoint, whether it be sweet or bitter.

"All his pleasure and pain he shall receive, not as from the creature, but from God; howbeit God ofttimes works through the creature, yet he shall receive all things as from God alone.

"He shall not be led captive by any lusting or desire after the creatures without due necessity.

"No contradiction or mishap shall have power to move or constrain him so that it separate him from the truth; therefore hold fast always and entirely by the same.

"He shall not be deceived by the glory of the creature, nor yet by any false light, but in a spirit of kindness and love he shall confess all things to be what they are, and from all things draw out what is best, and use it to his own improvement, and in no wise to his own detriment; for such a course is a certain sign of the presence of the Holy Spirit.

"He shall at all times be equipped and armed with all virtue, and ready to fight against all vice and sin; and with his good weapons he shall obtain the victory and the prize in all conflicts.

"He shall confess the truth in simplicity, and he shall mark what it is in itself, what God requireth of us, and what is possible to man, and then order his life accordingly, and act up to what he confesses.

"He shall be a man of few words, and much inward life.

"He shall be blameless and righteous, but in no wise be puffed up by reason of the same.

"His conversation shall be in all uprightness and sincerity; thus shall he let his light shine before men, and he shall preach more with his life than with his lips.

"He shall seek the glory of God before all things, and have no other aim in view.

"He shall be willing to take reproof; and when he striveth with any, he shall give way if the matter concern himself alone, and not God.

"He shall not desire or seek his own advantage, but think himself unworthy of the least thing that falls to his lot.

"He shall look upon himself as the least wise and worthy man upon earth, yet find in himself great faith; and above all, he shall take no account of his own wisdom and the works of his own reason, but humble himself beneath all men. For the Author of all truth will not work a supernatural work in the soul, unless he find a thorough humility in a man, and go before his doings with his perfect grace, as he did with St. Paul. But I fear, alas! that little heed is taken to this in these our days.

"He shall set the life and precepts of our Lord Jesus

Christ before him for a pattern to his life, words, and works, and without ceasing look at himself therein as in a mirror; that, in so far as he is able, he may put off everything unbecoming the honored image of our Lord.

"He shall comport himself as a man of small account— as nothing more than a beginner in a good life; and though he should therefore be despised by many, it shall be more welcome to him than all the favor of the world.

"Now these are the signs that the ground of a man's soul is truly reasonable [according to right reason], so that the image of all truth shineth and teacheth therein; and he who does not bear in himself these signs, may not and must not set any store by his own reason, either in his own eyes or those of others. That we all may become such a true image, in thorough sincerity and perfect humility, may He help us who is the Eternal Truth, the Father, Son, and Holy Ghost."

This discourse, on which many professing to be Christians nowadays might ponder with deep instruction, was heard with gratification by "the Layman," who took it down in writing, after he arrived at his lodgings, so accurately that on afterward reading it over to the preacher, the latter was struck with astonishment, and acknowledged that it seemed to be wonderfully word for word as he had spoken it. Still "the man" was impressed with a belief that "the Master" was trusting too much to his letter-learning, and needed more refinement of spirit under the immediate operations of the Holy Ghost, to fit and qualify him for so great a work. At length, after much hesitation, he ventured to inform Tauler of his uneasiness of mind in respect to him, and to open to him a little of his own experience. Among other things, he told him that neither his sermons, nor any outward words that man could speak, had power to work any good in him; for men's words had in many ways hindered him much more than they had helped him. "And this is the reason," said he: "it often happened that when I came away from the sermon I brought certain false notions away with me, which I hardly got rid of in a long while with great toil; but if the highest Teacher of all truth shall come to a man, he must be empty and quit of all the things of time. Know, that when this same Master cometh to me, He teaches me more in an hour than you or all the doctors from Adam to the judgment day will ever do." He afterward added: "Though you have taught us many good things in this sermon, the image came into my mind while you were preaching, that it was as if one should take good wine and mix it with lees, so that it should become muddy. I mean that your vessel is unclean, and much lees are cleaving to it; and the cause is, that you have suffered yourself to be killed by the letter, and are killing yourself still every day and hour, albeit you know full well that the Scripture saith, 'The letter killeth, but the Spirit giveth life.'—In the life you are now living, you have no light, but are in the night; in which you are indeed able to understand the letter, but have not yet tasted the sweetness of the Holy Ghost. And withal, you are yet a pharisee."

Tauler felt ready to recoil at being so closely pressed; but the layman re-affirmed the truth of what he had said, explaining to him that he was trusting too much to his "learning and parts," and did not purely seek the glory of God alone; but had an eye to self and a leaning to the creatures, and, therefore, not having a "single eye to God," his vessel was still unclean, and consequently his teaching was defective, "not bringing grace to pure loving hearts;" and thus it might be seen how it was that "so few received from his teaching the grace of the Holy Spirit."

As he spoke these words, Tauler fell on his neck and

kissed him, and compared himself with the woman at Jacob's well; "for he had had all his faults laid bare before his eyes," some of which he believed "no human being in the world knew of;" and he greatly marvelled, and doubted not that his friend had it indeed from God. He was greatly humbled, and made resolutions of beginning a better course, with the help of the Lord; and they had much sweet discourse to his edification. The layman told him of his own experience, according to what we have seen in the life of Nicolas; and in the course of the conversation related how he had, as he believed, been enabled by the Holy Spirit to write a letter "to a heathen far away in a heathen land," in such a manner as to answer the poor man's longings and prayer to be led to the knowledge of a "better faith than that in which he had been born;" and how this heathen had, through this instrumentality, been brought to the Christian faith. "Albeit I am unworthy of it," said he, "yet did the Holy Spirit work through me, a poor sinner."

Tauler expressing his astonishment at receiving so much instruction from so simple a man, the layman said to him: "Now tell me, dear master, how it was, or whose work it was, that the blessed Saint Katharine, who was but a young maid barely fourteen years old, overcame some fifty of the great masters, and, moreover, so prevailed over them that they willingly went to martyrdom?" The "master" replied, "The Holy Ghost did this." Then said "the man," "Do you not believe that the Holy Ghost has still the same power?"—which Tauler could not but acknowledge.

After much conversation, probably at various interviews, Tauler found himself so brought down from his former lofty position as to give himself up to the new life which he saw was required of him, and to resolve that, let the consequences be what they might to himself, he would, with the Lord's help, endeavor to cease from his earthly reasonings and course, and follow the counsels thus faithfully given him. His friend, at Tauler's request, consented to remain for some weeks longer with him, endeavoring to impart such counsel as should tend to his establishment in the spiritual pathway; and among other things, requested him to cease from both study and preaching for a time. "For know," said he, "that you must needs walk in that same path of which our Lord spoke to that young man; you must take up the cross, and follow our Lord Jesus Christ and his example, in utter sincerity, humility, and patience, and must let go all your proud, ingenious reason, which you have through your learning in the Scripture." "And then, when our Lord sees that the time is come, he will make of you a new man, so that you shall be born again of God. Nevertheless, know that before this can come to pass, you must sell all that you have, and humbly yield it up to God, that you may truly make him your end, and give up to him all that you possess in your carnal pride, whether through the Scriptures or without, or whatever it be, whereby you might reap honor in this world, or in which you may aforetime have taken pleasure or delight—you must let it all go, and with Mary Magdalene fall down at Christ's feet, and earnestly strive to enter on a new course. And so doing, without doubt, the eternal Heavenly Prince will look down on you with the eye of his good pleasure, and will not leave his work undone in you, but will urge you still further, that you may be tried and purified as gold in the fire. And it may even come to pass that he shall give you to drink of the bitter cup that he gave to his only begotten Son. For it is my belief that one bitter cup which God will pour out for you will be, that your good works and all your refraining from evil, yea, your whole life, will be despised and turned to naught in the eyes of the people; and all your spiritual children will forsake you and think you are gone out of your mind; and all your good friends and brothers in the convent will be offended at your life, and say that you have taken to strange ways.—Now if so be that you are minded to take these things in hand, there is nothing better or more profitable for you at this present than an entire, hearty, humble self-surrender in all things, whether sweet or bitter, painful or pleasant; so that you may be able to say with truth, 'Ah, my Lord and my God, if it were thy will that I should remain till the day of judgment in this suffering and tribulation, yet would I not fall away from thee, but would desire ever to be constant in thy service.' I see you are thinking in your heart, that I have said very hard things to you; and this is why I begged you beforehand to let me go, and told you that if you went back, like that young man, I would not have it laid to my charge." Then said the master, "Thou sayest truly: I confess it does seem to me a hard thing to follow thy counsel." The man answered, "Yet you begged me to show you the shortest way to the highest perfectness. Now I know no surer or shorter way than to follow in the footsteps of our Lord Jesus Christ."

Some time after this conversation, Tauler said to the man, "Ah, dear son, what agony and struggle and fighting have I not had within me, day and night, before I was able to overcome the devil and my own flesh!—but I am purposed to remain steadfast, come weal, come woe."

The layman soon after this took his leave. But within a year afterward, his prediction came to be fulfilled; for the strict spiritual life which Tauler now felt himself called upon to lead, in humility and renunciation of self, was so strange in the eyes of all his associates, that he came to be despised as much as he had before been looked up to.

During the distress into which he was hereby introduced, which at times seemed too much for him to bear without suffering in his bodily health, his friend came again to see him, and endeavored to encourage him to give up all to his Divine Master, and trust in Him through all. When he was about departing homeward, Tauler expressed the great loss his absence would be to him. But he referred him to the "Better Comforter, that is, the Holy Ghost, who," said he, "has called and invited and brought you to this point, by means of me, his poor creature; but it is *his* work which has been wrought in you, and *not mine;* I have been merely his instrument, and served him therein, and have done so willingly, for the glory of God and the salvation of your soul." Then said Tauler, "may God be thine eternal reward!" And he parted from him in tears.

After suffering for two years much humiliation and distress, both inward and outward, he again began to preach. His friend, the layman, had visited him in his trouble, and finding that the good work was going on in his soul, and judging therefore that as he had "now received the light of the Holy Spirit by the grace of God," his doctrine would "now come from the Holy Ghost, which before came from the flesh," he had encouraged him to resume his function as a preacher, "giving ear to the true Master, and obeying His commands." The first time that he tried again to speak in the congregation as a preacher, he was powerfully arrested in his feelings after he had gone into the pulpit, and could only exclaim, holding his hood before his eyes, "Oh, merciful eternal God, if it be thy will, give me so to speak that it may be to the praise and glory of thy name, and to the good of this people!" As he said these words, his eyes overflowed with tears, and though the people became impatient to hear him, he could say no more. He remained in silent supplication to the Almighty, casting himself on His wisdom and mercy, and at length apologized to the congregation and let them depart. After this, he became, it is said, a public laughing-stock of the town, so that they said, "Now we all see that he has become a downright fool;" and he was forbidden to attempt to preach any more. He was, however, after some time, permitted again to preach; and on this occasion many of his congregation appear to have been greatly affected by the fervency of what he delivered to them.

After this, continuing faithful according to the measure of the light vouchsafed through the clouds of those dark ages, he is said to have grown in spiritual understanding and in outward usefulness. He determined to preach altogether in the German tongue instead of the Latin. "In simple and earnest language he appealed to the consciences of his hearers, and showed them the way of escape from the wretchedness of their sinful lives to the peace of God, which passeth all understanding." It is said that it was a particular concern with him to promote a reformation in the lives of the ecclesiastics, many of whom were living in utter neglect of the duties of their vocation. The statutes of a synod called by Bishop Berthold, in 1335, even during the time of the interdict, described in sorrowful colors their indecorous conduct. It seems that they often alienated the church property in order to gratify their propensity to pleasure and ostentation. "The younger and more wealthy especially distinguished themselves by their extreme fondness for display, and the bishop complained, that instead of going about clad with due decorum, they allowed their hair to grow long in order to conceal the tonsure, wore boots of red, yellow, and green, and adorned their coats with gold lace and gay ribbons; that they strutted about in the streets equipped with rapiers and swords, attended tournaments, frequented the public taverns, and were the most jovial of boon companions at the drinking-bouts of the laymen. In some of the more wealthy nunneries too, things had come to such a pitch that the nuns dressed magnificently, took part in the amusements of the tournament, and even danced with laymen in their taverns!"

Tauler was zealous against such disorders, which provoked for him the hostility of many of the priests, who could not bear to be restricted or so exposed in their irregularities. His enemies ridiculed him for "making so much of the inward work," and called him and his friends innovators, Beghards, and belonging to the new spirits. But the magistrates befriended him; for though his preaching was in opposition to the papal interdict, and many of the priests in their anger against him forbade him to preach, yet he was sustained by the authorities of the city, who obliged them to rescind their prohibition. It is related, however, that under the influence of his admonitions "many of the priests became quite pious," and that by the people at large he was revered and greatly beloved, and often called upon to act as counsellor among them in weighty affairs. The "Friends of God" were closely attached to him, and it is believed that that eminent member of their community, Rulman Merswin, was convinced of their principles through his instrumentality.

Nor did he confine his piety to theory alone, but manifested his faith by his works in deeds of love and kindness to his fellow-creatures. In the year 1348 a plague visited southern Germany and France, called the Black Death; by which it was calculated that two-thirds of the population of southern France perished, and sixteen thousand in Strasburg alone. When it visited this his native city, he devoted himself to carrying consolation to the sick and dying; an employment rendered much more laborious by the fact that the other priests had generally deserted their flocks. Tauler and two of his friends, named Ludolph and Thomas, issued an address to the clerical body, showing them how wrong it was for them to desert the poor people under such circumstances of affliction, and declaring that "Christ had died for *all* men, and the pope had no power to close heaven against an innocent person who should die under the interdict." They afterward issued another address, in which they boldly proclaimed "that he who professes the true articles of the Christian faith, and only sins against the power of the pope, is by no means to be accounted a heretic."

As was to be supposed, the pope soon heard of such doctrine being promulgated, and took great offence at it. He commanded the bishop to burn the books of these three friends and forbid their perusal. The result was that they were expelled from the city which had been the grateful recipient of their benevolent exertions to its suffering people. After a while, the Emperor Charles IV. visited Strasburg, and, hearing much respecting Tauler and his two friends, sent for them to hear their defence. Tauler firmly advocated what he believed to be the truth, and plainly told the emperor why they were banished; and his discourse had so much weight with Charles, that he expressed his desire that no further proceedings should be taken against them, declaring himself (it is said) even favorable to their opinions. The bishops, however, who were present continued to condemn their writings, and enjoined upon them to recant, and write no more of the like nature on pain of excommunication. One writer declares, nevertheless, that they went on and wrote still better than before; but nothing can now be clearly known of this, for very little further has come down to us respecting Tauler until the occurrence of his last illness and death. It is known, however, that he left Strasburg and took up his residence in Cologne for a time, and afterward returned to his native city, where he died. He was visited with a long and painful illness, being confined to his bed for about twenty weeks with great suffering. Perceiving that he was about to depart, he sent for his old and valued friend Nicolas of Basle, informing him that he did not expect to be much longer in this world. On Nicolas coming to him and asking how it fared with him, he replied, "I believe that the time is very near when God purposes to take me from this world; for which cause, dear son, it is a great consolation to me that thou art present at my end. I pray thee, take these books, which are lying there. Thou wilt find written therein all thy discourse with me aforetime, and also my answers, and thou wilt find something concerning my life, and the dealings of God with me his poor unworthy servant. Dear son, if thou think fit, and if God give thee grace, make a little book of it." And when his friend assented, and spoke of writing an account of him and adding some of his sermons which he had written down, Tauler said to him, "Dear son, I lay upon thee my most solemn admonition, that thou write nothing about me, and that thou do not mention my name; for thou must know that of a truth the life, and words, and works, which God has wrought through me, a poor, unworthy, sinful man, are not mine, but belong to God Almighty, now and for evermore. Therefore, dear son, if thou wilt write it down for the profit of our fellow-Christians, write it so that neither my name nor thine be named, but thou mayest say, the 'master' and 'the man'. Moreover, thou shalt not suffer the book to be read or seen by any one in this town, lest he should mark that it was I; but take it home with thee to thy own country, and let it not come out during my life."

In this humble frame of mind he waited his summons for eleven days after this conversation, and died about the seventy-first year of his age, in the year of our Lord 1361.

CHAPTER VI.

JOHN WYCLIFFE.

JOHN DE WYCLIFFE, or Wickliffe, whose name has been spelled in nearly twenty different ways, is supposed to have been born about the year 1324, at or near Wycliffe, a village on the banks of the Tees, near Rokeby, and about eight miles from Richmond in Yorkshire, England; and to have derived his surname from the name of his birth-place. His parents are unknown to history, but are conjectured to have been the owners of the manor of Wycliffe.*

When about sixteen years of age, after obtaining the elements of learning nearer home, he went to the University of Oxford; at first entering Queen's College, but afterward removing to Merton College, which was of a more mature standing and offered greater advantages. It has been said, but on what authority we know not, that at that time this celebrated university contained the astonishing number of 30,000 students. Here he remained many years, and became a proficient in the literature and science taught at that day, and familiar with the intricate nonsense of scholastic philosophy which then occupied the disputations of the most polished minds of Europe.

In the year 1356, when about the thirty-second year of

* See Vaughan's Life and Opinions of Wycliffe, vol. i. p. 219.

his age, he wrote a small work entitled "The Last Age of the Church," in which he displays various speculative opinions of future events, but clearly manifests also the commencement of those sentiments which afterward distinguished him, of dissatisfaction with the corrupt condition of the church. Indeed, one author says that "even at this period of his history, the nefarious practices connected with the appointment of the clergy to the sphere of their duties had so far shocked his piety, as to dispose him to expect a speedy and signal manifestation of the displeasure of Heaven." Four years afterward, the mendicant monks took especial umbrage at his exposure of their many erroneous practices, and set on foot a controversy and opposition which continued to beset him during the rest of his life. These mendicants had originally appeared with the profession of correcting the abuses and vices attendant on the luxury and wealth to which the convents had attained, and which were the crying scandal of Christendom. But they soon showed themselves as disorderly as their predecessors, and indeed eventually became a public nuisance. About the year 1360, Wycliffe came forth with an exposure of their false pretensions, denouncing, as he did also some years afterward in a special treatise, their defective morals, their false claim to a monopoly of the privilege to preach the gospel, their wiles employed to seduce young children into their order, their hypocrisy in pretending to be poor while they were enjoying the luxuries accumulated by incessant itinerant begging, their encouragement of simony, their contempt of the civil authority, and their preference of the papal decrees to the obvious commands of Christ. From all these, he constantly charged them with being opponents of the gospel, and urged that nothing short of a removal of these intruders could restore the church to its long-lost order and prosperity. Of course such an attack upon these idle and privileged persons provoked them to great rage against its author.

In 1365, he was appointed warden of Canterbury Hall, a college recently founded by Islep, Archbishop of Canterbury. The next year, King Edward III. being required by Pope Urban V. to pay the annual claim of the papacy on the crown of England, which had not been paid now for thirty-three years, and which Edward considered an unjust and degrading acknowledgment of the tenure of the crown from the papal see, the question was, on the pope's urgently demanding the money, submitted by the king to his parliament. By this body the demand was indignantly refused, and plain intimations were given to the pontiff that the enforcement of such an insulting demand on England should be met by the strength of the nation. Soon after this decision, an anonymous writer appeared from among the monastic orders, supporting the claim of the pope, and calling upon John Wycliffe by name to prove the fallacy of his reasoning. Wycliffe was not backward to reply, though he knew he was entering on a dangerous theme; and knowing this, he was cautious in his own arguments, sheltering himself under the cover of the speeches which had been delivered in parliament; six or seven of which he quoted, showing great boldness, for that age, in resisting the claims of the papacy. One of the speakers went so far as to say, that "Christ is the supreme Lord, while the pope is a man, and liable to sin, and who, while in mortal sin, according to divines, is unfitted for dominion." Edward refused this badge of feudal homage demanded by the pope, and likewise the ancient tribute of " Peter's pence;" and appointed John Wycliffe to the office of royal chaplain.

In the parliament of 1371, an attempt was made to check the secular power of the ecclesiastics, by excluding them from various offices of state; a very large proportion of which they had for many years managed to obtain. Wycliffe came forth zealously against this practice, often using the words of the Apostle Paul, "He that warreth, entangleth not himself with the affairs of this life;" and as a consequence, he incurred the serious displeasure of the prelates and of the papal court; especially as the attempt of the parliament was partially successful, resulting at least in the resignation of the office of chancellor held by the Bishop of Winchester, and the removal of the Bishop of Exeter as treasurer of the realm. One of the first results of the papal displeasure was the loss by Wycliffe of his office of warden of Canterbury Hall; but receiving near the same time the chair of theology in the university, and the rectorship of Lutterworth, his efforts and opportunities for the spread of reforming sentiments were by no means diminished. He now published, among other small treatises, a Comment on the Ten Commandments, which contains some very remarkable sentiments in advance of the times, and the following expressions near the close: "Many think, if they give a penny to a pardoner, they shall be forgiven the breaking of all the commandments of God, and therefore they take no heed how they keep them. But I say thee for certain, though thou have priests and friars to sing for thee, and though thou each day hear many masses, and found chauntries and colleges, and go on pilgrimages all thy life, and give all thy goods to pardoners; all this shall not bring thy soul to heaven. While, if the commandments of God are revered to the end, though neither penny nor half-penny be possessed, there shall be everlasting pardon, and the bliss of heaven!" Such sentiments must have greatly tended to weaken the hold of the confessional on the minds of the thinking portion of the people.

During 1375, and six months of the next year, he was companion to Edward's second son, John of Gaunt, Duke of Lancaster, along with some prelates, in a mission to the city of Bruges, for the obtaining of certain concessions from the pope; and during these negotiations, although the pontiff did not personally appear, yet Wycliffe saw enough of the intriguing policy of the papal court, to return home with still clearer views of the corruptions which had overrun the church from the head of the hierarchy downward.

The parliament in 1376 issued an earnest remonstrance against the enormous extortions of the Romish See, and required that in future no papal collector or proctor "should remain in England, on pain of life and limb, and that no Englishman, on the like pain, should become such collector or proctor, or remain at the court of Rome." To read some of the parliamentary documents of this time, it would almost appear that but few additional steps were then needed to separate England from its allegiance to Rome altogether. The Duke of Lancaster, who was Wycliffe's avowed friend, now, in consequence of the death of his elder brother, "the Black Prince," presided in the councils of his aged and infirm parent. But at length Wycliffe's enemies broke ground, and prepared for open hostilities against him and the progress of reform. By the influence of Courtney, Bishop of London, he was cited to appear before his ecclesiastical superiors, "to answer on certain charges of holding and publishing many erroneous and heretical doctrines." The crowd in the cathedral was immense, attracted by anxiety or sympathy; so that, we are told, "the authority of Lord Percy, earl-marshal of the realm, and that of the Duke of Lancaster himself, were scarcely sufficient to procure for the accused an avenue of approach to the place of his judges. Some disturbance, arising from this difficulty, attracted the notice of Courtney, who was about to conduct the prosecution; and we may presume that his displeasure was not at all diminished, on perceiving the two most powerful subjects of the crown prepared to shield the Rector of Lutterworth (Wycliffe) from the meditated vengeance of his enemies. The prelate hastily accosted these noblemen with the language of reproof, proceeding so far as to express his regret that he had not adopted measures to prevent their admission to the court. The duke regarded this haughty intimation as an insult, and warmly replied, that in such matters the authority of the Bishop of London would be insufficient to regulate his conduct. Lord Perçy felt with his distinguished colleague under this attack, and resented it so far, as to call upon Wycliffe to be seated; observing, that such an indulgence might be necessary, as he would have much to answer. Courtney loudly opposed the advice of the earl-marshal, adding that such conduct in the person accused must be interpreted as a contempt of the court. The duke, however, applauded the suggestion of his friend. Some angry discussion arose, which becoming connected with the already excited feeling of the multitude, a tumult ensued, and the parties being compelled to separate in disorder, the prosecution was for the present suspended."*

This was early in the year 1377; and toward midsummer of that year Edward III. died, and was succeeded by Richard, son of the Black Prince, then in the twelfth year of his age. The parliament convened under his authority, however, pursued the same course as the previous ones, in declaiming against the arrogant pretensions and exactions of Rome; and, at the request ostensibly of the young king, Wycliffe again employed his pen in the cause. From various Scripture testimonies, and from the words of Ber-

* Vaughan's Wycliffe, vol. i. p. 338.

nard of Clairvaux, he undertook to prove "that the pope has no right to possess himself of the goods of the church, as though he were lord of them; but that he is to be, with respect to them, as a minister or servant, and a proctor for the poor." He concluded his treatise with the expression of an earnest desire, "that the same proud and eager desire of authority and lordship, which is now discovered by this seat of power, were aught else than a delusion, preparing the pathway of antichrist;" for the children of Christ's Kingdom are not produced by such means, and the same Bernard had said to Pope Eugenius, "I fear not any greater (evil) befalling thee, than this eager thirsting after dominion."

The pope was well informed of the state of things in England. Seventeen years had elapsed since Wycliffe first came out against the mendicant monks, and he had, since that time, repeatedly come forth with his pen in a manner calculated to excite the anger not only of the monastic orders, but of the papal chair. Letters were sent before long from the pontiff to the Archbishop of Canterbury, the Bishop of London, the King, and the University of Oxford, accusing Wycliffe of having "with a fearlessness, the offspring of a detestable insanity, ventured to dogmatize and preach in favor of opinions wholly subversive of the church;" and demanding that his person should be seized and committed to prison, that his tenets should be strictly inquired into, and that he should be retained in custody until further orders from Rome.

The result was, that Wycliffe, early in the next year, appeared before an ecclesiastical synod at Lambeth, near London. On this occasion his enemies were again frustrated in their endeavors to get him into their power. His opinions had gained much favor, not only in the court, but among the people at large; and many of these assembled around the place appointed for his examination, and, alarmed for his safety, forced their way into the building, and proclaimed their high esteem of his person and opinions. The tumult thus occasioned was increased by the entrance of Sir Lewis Clifford into the court, with a message from the queen mother, forbidding the bishops to proceed to any definite sentence respecting the doctrine or conduct of Wycliffe. Thus all proceedings were again suspended; but not before the reformer had presented to the court in writing a candid statement of his doctrines and sentiments, respecting the limits needful to be imposed on the pretensions of the papacy. He therein took the ground that in accordance with the law of Christ, the pope is as liable to be called to account as any other, when guilty of sin; and that even the laity may do this, if the cardinals omit it, and the welfare of the church demands it. He advocated the power of the civil government to take possession of the revenues and property of the clergy, when its possession by them is abused to improper purposes. He denied the sovereignty which the Roman bishops had so long claimed over the property of every religious establishment in Europe. He advocated the real equality, for the ministry, of priests with bishops, claiming that the difference between them was merely one of jurisdiction. He taught that Christian discipline should never be made an instrument of vindictiveness, that disposition itself being forbidden by Christ; and that the assumption of an unconditional authority of the keys, in the forms of binding and loosing, was usurpation of the divine power, and no less than blasphemy; saying, " we ought to believe, that then only does a Christian priest bind or loose, when he simply obeys the law of Christ." This was in direct opposition to the belief instilled into the people by the ecclesiastics, that their sentence of excommunication exposed the parties to the fires of purgatory, and often to eternal torments. This declaration was anonymously attacked soon afterward, and defended in a cogent reply by Wycliffe.

About the same time, the year 1378, he completed a work "On the Truth and Meaning of Scripture;" which is described as the most extended of any of his writings, and embodying nearly all his peculiar sentiments. It has only come down to us in a few copies preserved in manuscript. Vaughan gives the following account of a sickness which attended him at this period of his life. "The labor of producing such compositions, and the excitements inseparable from the restless hostilities of his enemies, so shook his frame at this period as to threaten his speedy dissolution, and in truth to lay the foundation of the malady, which, a few years later, was the occasion of his death. His old antagonists, the mendicants, conceived it next to impossible that an heresiarch so notorious should find himself near a future world, without the most serious apprehensions of approaching vengeance. But while thus conscious of their own rectitude, and certain that the dogmas of the reformer had arisen from the suggestions of the great enemy, some advantages to their cause were anticipated, could the dying man (as they supposed) be induced to make any recantation of his published opinions. Wycliffe was in Oxford when this sickness arrested his activity, and confined him to his chamber. From the four orders of friars, four doctors, who were also called regents, were gravely deputed to wait on him; and to these the same number of civil officers, called senators of the city, and aldermen of the wards, were added. When this embassy entered the apartment of the Rector of Lutterworth, he was seen stretched on his bed. Some kind wishes were first expressed, as to his better health, and the blessing of a speedy recovery. It was presently suggested, that he must be aware of the many wrongs which the whole mendicant brotherhood had sustained from his attacks, especially in his sermons, and in certain of his writings; and as death was now apparently about to remove him, it was sincerely hoped that he would not conceal his penitence, but distinctly revoke whatever he had preferred against them to their injury. The sick man remained silent and motionless until this address was concluded. He then beckoned his servants to raise him in his bed; and fixing his eyes on the persons assembled, summoned all his remaining strength, as he exclaimed aloud : ' I shall not die, but live, and shall again declare the evil deeds of the friars !' The doctors and their attendants now hurried from his presence, and they lived to feel the truth of the prediction."

His labors as a preacher were abundant, and he spared not to expose the manner in which the friars had abused their function of preaching, substituting for the truths of the gospel, "fables—chronicles of the world—stories from the battles of Troy"—and delusions intended to raise themselves into distinction, or gratify their avarice or sensuality. He denounced as the "foulest traitors" those priests who were found "in taverns, and hunting, and playing at their tables," instead of "learning God's law, and preaching;" since, among the duties of their office, "most of all is the preaching of the gospel, for this Christ enjoined on his disciples more than any other." It was no novelty, says Vaughan, to see him "in a village pulpit, surrounded by his rustic auditory; or in the lowest hovel of the poor, fulfilling his office at the bedside of the sick and the dying, whether freeman or bond. Over a sphere thus extended, his genius and influence were equally diffused." And he enjoined upon Christians a regular attention to the wants of the afflicted and the poor—" to visit those who are sick, or who are in trouble, especially those whom God hath made needy by age, or by other sickness, as the feeble, the blind, and the lame who are in poverty. These thou shalt relieve with thy goods, after thy power, and after their need, for thus biddeth the gospel." And he described it as a "cursed spirit of falsehood," which "moveth priests to close themselves within stone walls for all their life," instead of going into all the world to preach the gospel. Through the whole of his sermons, as they have been handed down to us, Vaughan says, "the multiplied corruptions of the hierarchy are vigorously assailed, as forming the great barrier to all religious improvement. The social obligations of men are also frequently discussed, and traced with a cautious firmness to the authority of the Scriptures; while the doctrines of the gospel are uniformly exhibited as declaring the guilt and the spiritual infirmities of men to be such, as to render the atonement of Christ their only way of pardon, and the grace of the Divine Spirit their only hope of purity." When attacking the hierarchy with a boldness worthy of Luther, he spared not its head, the pope: "As if ashamed to appear as the servants of Christ, the pope and his bishops show the life of emperors and of the lordly in the world, and not the living of Christ. But since Christ hated such things, they give us no room to guess them to be the ministers of Christ. What good doeth the idle talk of the pope, who must be called of men, *most blessed father*, and bishops *most reverend* men, while their life is discordant from that of Christ? In so taking of these names, they show that they are on the fiend's side, and children of the father of falsehood."

He vigorously opposed the idolatrous doctrine of transubstantiation, and in 1381, published a series of "Conclusions" in regard to it, denying that the bread and wine were to be considered as "Christ, or as any part of him," though he considered them "as an effectual sign of him." The great influence of the priests in the University of Oxford was now exerted to repel such an attack on a dogma in which their craft was so nearly concerned; and the result was, that in a privately convened assembly of twelve doctors, Wycliffe's views on this subject were denounced as erroneous and opposed to the decisions of the church, and suspension and excommunication were threatened against any member of the university who should inculcate such opinions, or even be convicted of listening to their defense. Wycliffe, who knew nothing of what was going on, was occupied in lecturing to his pupils on that very subject, when a messenger entered the room and announced, in the name of the chancellor and his coadjutors, the unlooked-for prohibition. Wycliffe paused a moment, in doubt what course to pursue in so formidable and unexpected an emergency; but presently recollecting the great importance of his position, he returned a message to the chancellor, that if the question must be one of force, and not of reason, he should appeal from this decision to the equity of the civil power.

He now published another piece, called "The Wicket," in which he continued to assail this favorite papal dogma, showing the idolatry of those who worshipped the bread supposed to be consecrated by the priests, and asking the plain question, "Where find you that ever Christ or any of his apostles worshipped it?" He shows the absurdity of the supposition that a thing which was made by man out of a natural product yesterday, should to-day be considered as God and worshipped, and affirms it to be reasonable to attach a figurative meaning to certain expressions of Christ in connection with the last supper.

His old enemy, Courtney, recently appointed Archbishop of Canterbury, and consequently primate of England, now took up the subject, and endeavored to extirpate the new views. An assembly of prelates, doctors, and monks was convened by him in the metropolis, which, after three days' deliberations, condemned as either heretical or erroneous, thirty articles alleged to be taught by the reformer and his disciples. Among these articles are the following propositions: that there is no change in the substance of the bread and wine—that deadly sin forfeited the power of priests and bishops—that auricular confession was unnecessary—that clerical endowments were unlawful—that tithes are merely alms, to be yielded to the clergy only as they are devout men, and according to the discretion of the contributors—and that the religious institutions (probably alluding to the monasteries) are in themselves sinful, and tend to the injury of piety. The Bishop of London and other prelates were then appealed to, to stop the progress of these innovations, and prohibit the preaching of such "heresies and errors." These prohibitions were accordingly transmitted without delay to the various rectors, vicars, and parish chaplains in the vicinity of Lutterworth, and doubtless also to Wycliffe himself. Yet various influential members of the University of Oxford were so convinced of the rectitude of the views advocated by the reformer, that they could by no means lend a hand to his condemnation, and for a time the denunciation seemed as if it might share the fate of previous attempts against him. But the youthful king and his court were soon assailed by the clerical party, with urgent appeals to interpose the power of the government in their behalf; and the result was the passage, by the parliament, of the first English statute law for the punishment of heresy. Under this statute several disciples of Wycliffe were prosecuted, and some of them induced by fear to renounce their convictions; but he himself does not appear to have been molested. Nearly sixty years old, his incessant labors with his mind and pen were producing their natural effect upon his bodily health; and his increasing infirmity, added to the dread of offending his friend the Duke of Lancaster, may have deterred his enemies from taking active measures against him.

He had been for some years engaged in preparing the greatest of all his works, a translation into English of the whole Bible from the Latin Vulgate version. In this arduous undertaking he was occupied at times during most of the remainder of his days, and finally succeeded in contributing to his fellow-countrymen the first copy of the Holy Scriptures in their vernacular tongue. It is worthy of remark that in this work he did not recognize the inspired authority of the books styled the Apocrypha, although included in the Vulgate version, and owned by the Romish church. As the art of printing was then unknown, the circulation of his English Bible was of course limited to manuscript copies; but there is no reason to doubt that it became eminently serviceable in England in promoting a knowledge of Scripture truth among the people. It would have been still more useful, if the reformer's acquaintance with the Hebrew and Greek languages had enabled him to make his version from the originals, instead of the incorrect version of the Latin Vulgate. But a knowledge of Greek and Hebrew was a rare accomplishment in England in those days.

In pursuance of his message to the chancellor of the university, toward the close of the year 1382, Wycliffe presented a memorial to the king and parliament, containing a summary of the most important of his tenets. He declares monastic vows to be a device of men, and of no obligation; and all human authorities assuming to be superior to Scripture, or really in opposition to it, he considers as mere usurpations; and advocates a return to the simplicity of the primitive church, when monachism was unknown. He combats the theory of certain friars, that the persons and property of ecclesiastics were beyond civil jurisdiction; showing its absurdity by exhibiting the natural results of such a notion fully carried out. Tithes he speaks of as rightfully limited to a voluntary offering of the needful food and clothing to those ministers who are devoted to their calling. The fourth and last subject of the memorial is in regard to the doctrine of the Eucharist; but in this portion of his declaration he chiefly declaims against "the worldly business of priests."

The impression made by the document was such, that the House of Commons petitioned the king to allow the repeal of the law lately passed against heretics, and levelled mainly against the disciples of the reformer. His converts had become numerous in various parts of the kingdom, and many zealous men, actuated by his precepts in regard to preaching without the motive of earthly profit or advancement, were engaged in travelling from place to place, publishing, either in the public places of worship, or when debarred from the use of these, in fields or markets or open streets, their views of the liberty of the gospel, without human ordination. They were, from their general poverty, their remarkable simplicity and apparent meanness of dress, and their obvious want of anything in the nature of benefices, generally styled "the poor priests;" and the effect of their preaching was such as to rouse the jealousy and determined hostility of the regular priesthood.

The parliament and the ecclesiastical convocation both met at Oxford. But by the craftiness of Courtney their attention was drawn away from the abuses in the church to the charges involved in the matter of the new doctrines, and to other matters entirely foreign from the repeal of the law against heretics. Wycliffe's attack on the received dogma of the Eucharist was paraded before them as requiring especial attention; and he was cited to appear before the archbishop, to answer the charges laid against him. He had not on this occasion the influence of the Duke of Lancaster to protect him from his enemies; for when it was found that he was attacking not only the abuses of the papal system, but some also of its most cherished doctrines, John of Gaunt was no longer willing to come forward to his assistance, but advised him to submit to the views of the church. But it is said by one of his adversaries (Walsingham), that on this occasion, "like an obstinate heretic, he refuted all the doctors of the second millenary." Though himself not entirely clear in his views in regard to the Eucharist, he clearly conceived the usual practice of the Romish church therein to be pure idolatry —the adoration of a piece of bread in the place of the Deity—and the presumption of priests in pretending to be endowed with a power to remake their own Maker, in professing to produce the body of the Lord Jesus in this bread, he vehemently denounced.

The assembly before which he appeared was a numerous one, consisting of the archbishop and six other bishops, the chancellor, and a great number of doctors and priests, besides a crowd of spectators. He laid before the convocation two confessions of faith, one in Latin and the other in English, chiefly relative to the doctrine of transubstantiation. In these documents, either through the confused mode of scholastic reasoning prevalent in those times, which was often calculated to obscure the clearest and most simple propositions, or from some other cause producing obscurity or apparent ambiguity, his enemies have taken occasion to assert that he abandoned some of his extreme views; and some have even gone so far as to allege that he recanted his main tenet on this question.

There appears indeed a want of clearness of statement in them, which we should not have expected from the author of so many powerful invectives against the papal superstition. There may have been an anxiety in his mind, on this threatening occasion, to go as far as his conscience would allow him towards the views of the church, to avert the impending danger; and this anxiety may possibly have produced an ambiguity of expression which he would not under other circumstances have given way to. Certain it is that the documents are not as clear as we should have hoped for, and that they were taken hold of to his disadvantage, after his death, by some of his hostile biographers. Yet at the time when they were presented, it does not appear but that they were looked upon even by his enemies as proofs of his guilt; and the result of the whole examination was, that his connection with the University of Oxford was dissolved by virtue of a letter obtained from the king. In a treatise published soon afterwards, he declared the "doctrine of the real presence" to be the "offspring of Satan," and expresses his sentiments thus: "Oh! that all who believe could see how antichrist and his instruments condemn the sons of the church, and persecute them even to death, because they maintain this truth as taught in the gospel. Truly aware I am, that the doctrine of the gospel may for a season be trampled under foot, that it may be overpowered in high places, and even suppressed by the threatenings of antichrist; but equally sure I am, that it shall never be extinguished, for it is the recording of truth itself, that 'Heaven and earth shall pass away, but so shall not my words.' Let the spirit of the faithful therefore awake itself, and diligently inquire as to the nature of this venerable sacrament, whether it be not indeed *bread*, as the gospel, the senses, and reason assure us. Certain verily I am, that the idolaters who make to themselves gods, are not ignorant of the real nature of these gods, though they pretend there is a something of deity within them, which is communicated as by the God of gods."* These do not seem to be the words of one who would recant before his judges. The ambiguity of his previous declarations seems to have arisen in part from a confused idea, broached also in the last mentioned treatise, that "this venerable sacrament is *naturally* bread, and *sacramentally* the body of Christ;" while in other places of his numerous works he would rather appear to substitute the word "figuratively," or "a sign," for *sacramentally*.

About this time also he was summoned by Pope Urban to appear at Rome, on account of charges preferred against him there. But independent of the great imprudence of trusting himself to the dangers which he would certainly have encountered there, he was now suffering from the effects of paralysis, which rendered such a journey impracticable. In his reply he expresses his entire willingness to tell his belief, "and always to the pope;" and hopes that if he be in error, the pope will wisely amend it. He declares his faith in the authority of Scripture, and his determination to follow the pontiff only as he shall be found to follow the Author of the gospel; warns him against worldly greatness by the example of Christ, who "had not where to rest his head;" advising him to "leave his worldly lordship to worldly lords, as Christ enjoins him," and "to move all his clerks to do so;" and tells him plainly, "I take as a part of faith, that no man should follow the pope, no, nor any saint that is now in heaven, only inasmuch as he followed Christ; for James and John erred, and Peter and Paul sinned." And he concludes this unwelcome expression of independence, after stating his willingness to retract his

* Vaughan's Life of Wycliffe, vol. ii. p. 132.

opinions if found erroneous, by the remark, "that as the providence of the Redeemer was plainly opposed to his visiting Rome, he trusts the pontiff will not show himself to be indeed antichrist, by insisting on a compliance with his pleasure on that point."*

It is probable that the difficulties in the popedom, occasioned by double papacy at this time, may have contributed to Wycliffe's safety from further molestation from Rome. But besides this, he had many influential friends in England, whose countenance of his opinions furnished more or less of a protection. Among these was Anne of Bohemia, the widow of the Black Prince, and mother to the young monarch, Richard II.—the same virtuous woman whom we have already seen to have prohibited proceedings against him in the convocation in London, some time previous. And though the Duke of Lancaster had lately withdrawn from any obvious patronage or protection of the reformer, yet it does not appear that he had openly opposed him, or given encouragement to his enemies; and his brother, the Duke of Gloucester, was believed to be favorable to him. But the king and court, influenced by the great body of the ecclesiastics, had turned against him. He retired to his rectory of Lutterworth; and perceiving that his disciples in various places, and especially those itinerant preachers of reform who were styled the "poor priests," were liable to suffer severely under the recent statute against heresy, the repeal of which had failed, he published a small defense of their position, under the title, "Why poor priests have no Benefices." We may condense the contents of this interesting treatise, furnished by Vaughan, partly in the words of Wycliffe himself, to show the condition of things in the priesthood of England at that period, as well as the character of these pious individuals

* Vaughan.

"Three reasons are assigned for their refusal of benefices—first, the dread of simony; second, the fear of misspending poor men's goods; and third, the hope of doing more good by itinerant labors than by limiting their exertions to a single parish. The customs connected with the system of patronage are said to be such, that whether an appointment to a benefice proceed from a prelate or from a secular lord, the demands usually made on the incumbent are of a description which must expose him to the guilt of simony. To prelates he must render the first fruits, and many other unlawful contributions; or he must descend to hold some worldly office, inconsistent with the life of a priest, and far from being taught by the example of Christ, or of his apostles. 'If there be any simple man who desireth to live well, and to teach truly the law of God, he shall be deemed a hypocrite, a new teacher, a heretic, and not suffered to come to any benefice. If, in any little poor place, he shall live a poor life, he shall be so persecuted and slandered that he shall be put out by wiles, extortions, frauds, and worldly violence, and imprisoned or burnt.' 'Some lords, to cover their simony, will not take for themselves, but kerchiefs for the lady, or a palfry, or a tun of wine. And when some lords would present a good man, then some ladies are the means of having a dancer presented, or a triper on tapits, or a hunter, or a hawker, or a wild player of summer gambols.' These practices are all denounced as treason against God—that prelates in selecting such men betray their trust and become vicars of Satan—and curates complying with such customs to begin with, are not likely to prove faithful afterwards. One reason, therefore, why poor priests have no benefices is, that it was scarcely possible to accept of them without the guilt of simony.

"The second reason was the fear of being compelled to misspend poor men's goods. Many rich entertainments must be made, sometimes for the gratification of lay patrons, and sometimes as a duty owing to the higher clergy when performing their feigned visitations. From such customs, it is said to follow, that beneficed clergymen 'shall not spend their tithes and offerings after a good conscience and God's law, but must waste them on the rich and the idle.' To avoid that expenditure which the ostentatious and luxurious manners of the clergy in that age required, was to become the object of almost every species of malevolence.—Yet, to be without a benefice, was not regarded as being thereby released from the obligation of preaching; and the voice of these conscientious men might often be heard in the precincts of the houses of public worship, or in the highway to the towns and villages.

"The last reason given is, that they should probably be thereby hindered from better occupation, and more profit to the church. The charge which they had received from above is declared to have respect to men in general, and to be binding 'wherever they may help their brethren to heavenward, whether by teaching, praying, or example giving.' 'And thus they may best, without any challenging of men, go and dwell among the people where they shall most profit, and for the time convenient, coming and going after the moving of the Holy Ghost, and not being hindered from doing what is best, by the jurisdiction of sinful men. Also they follow Christ and his apostles more, in taking voluntary alms of the people whom they teach, than in taking dymes and offerings by customs which sinful men have ordained, in the time of grace' (probably meaning, during the Christian dispensation).—'For these dreads, and for many thousand more, and for to be more like to the life of Christ and his apostles, and for to profit more their own souls and other men's, some poor priests think with God to travel about where they shall most profit, and by the evidence that God giveth them, while they have time, and a little bodily strength and youth. Nevertheless, they condemn not curates who do well in their office, and dwell where they shall most profit, and teach truly and stably the law of God against false prophets and the accursed deceptions of the fiend. Christ, for his endless mercy, help his priests and common people, to beware of antichrists' deceits, and to go even the right way to heaven!'"

After his exclusion from Oxford, he continued diligent with his pen. The most noted of his works published about this period was his "Trialogus," a conversation between three parties, Truth, Falsehood, and Wisdom, on various questions relating to religion and morality; including certain scholastic disputes of the time, with his own views on the far more important subjects of faith, sin, the love of God, the authority of Holy Scripture, the Eucharist, and baptism. It is not needful to follow his pen in all its activity at this period of his life. Many of the works then written are of no further interest at the present time than as coming from him, and tending to elucidate clearly what his sentiments really were. But it may be well to mention here, that in addition to the tenets alluded to in our previous pages, there were unmistakable indications in some of his works, of his disapproval of war, both offensive and defensive, as inconsistent with the law of Christ.* In his treatise "On the Seven Deadly Sins," he says that the doctrine of the clergy of that day was, "that it is lawful to annoy an enemy in whatever way you can;" but that "the charity of Christ biddeth the contrary."—"To keep men fighting, though humanity teaches that men should not fight, antichrist argues, that as an adder by his nature stings a man who treads on him, why should not we fight against our enemies, especially as

* See Vaughan's Life of Wycliffe, vol. ii. p. 243 to 248.

they would hence destroy us, and ruin their own souls? It is for love, therefore, that we chastise them! But what man that hath wit cannot see this fallacy?" As to the title of conquest, he says that unless it be clearly enjoined by the Almighty, as in the case of the Israelites in Canaan, it cannot be lawful; and in another place in the same work, in regard to defensive war, he holds the following emphatic and incontrovertible language, remarkable indeed as coming to us from the cloudy atmosphere of the fourteenth century. "Angels withstood fiends, and many men with right of law withstand their enemies, and yet they kill them not, neither fight with them. The wise men of the world hold this for wisdom, and have thus vanquished their enemies without striking them; and men of the gospel, by patience, and the prospect of rest and peace, have vanquished through the suffering of death, just as we may do now. But here men of the world come and say, that by this wise, kingdoms would be destroyed. But here our faith teaches, that since Christ is our God, kingdoms should be thus established, and their enemies overcome. But peradventure, some men would lose their worldly riches—and what harm were thereof? Well indeed I know, that men will scorn this doctrine; but men who would be martyrs for the law of God, will hold thereby. Lord, what honor falls to a knight, that he kills many men? The hangman killeth many more, and with a better title Better were it for men to be butchers of beasts, than butchers of their brethren!" After describing Wycliffe's earnest sentiments on this great subject, Vaughan adds: "The disastrous influence of war on civilization, and literature, and liberty, the reformer could deplore. But its demoralizing effects, and the desolation which it forebodes with respect to eternity, filled his mind with emotions of amazement and horror."

In various works he spoke of tithes, as a mode of contribution for which no divine authority could now be pleaded That sanction, he acknowledged, had been connected with this practice under the Mosaic economy; but he assumed, that both the ritual and the polity of that dispensation had passed away.* In a manuscript treatise entitled, "Sentence of the Curse Expounded," he uses the following language: "Men wonder greatly why curates are so unfeeling to the people in taking tithes; since Christ and his apostles took none as men now take them, neither paid them, nor spake of them, either in the gospel or in the epistles. But Christ lived on the alms of Mary Magdalene and other holy women, as the gospel telleth. And apostles lived sometimes by the labor of their hands, and sometimes accepted a poor livelihood and clothing, given by the people in free will and devotion, without asking or constraining. And to this end Christ said to his disciples, that they should eat and drink such things as were set before them, and take neither gold nor silver for their preaching, or their giving of sacraments. And Paul, giving a general rule for priests, saith thus, 'We having food and clothing, with these things be we content in Christ Jesus.' Paul also proved that priests who preach the gospel truly, should live by the gospel, and of tithes he said no more. True it is, that tithes were due to priests and deacons in the old law, and so bodily circumcision was then needful to all men; but it is not so now, under the law of grace. Christ however was circumcised, and yet we read not where he took tithes as we do; nor do we read in all the gospels that he paid them to the high-priest, or bade any other man do so. Lord, why should our worldly clergy claim tithes and offerings and customs from Christian people, more than did Christ and his apostles, and even more than men were burdened with under the law?"

* Vaughan's Life of Wycliffe, vol. ii. p. 284 to 291.

About this time also, many objections being set afloat against the publication of the Scriptures in the vernacular English, he wrote a treatise "On the labor of antichrist and his clerks to destroy Holy Writ," etc.; in which he answers these objections, and argues the far greater authority and value of the Holy Scriptures, than of the papal decrees and the teaching of antichrist and his clerks. "Christian men," he says, "are certain of the reality of their faith by the gracious gift of Jesus Christ, and that the truth in the gospel was taught by Christ and his apostles; though all the clerks of antichrist say the contrary never so fast, and on pain of their curse, and imprisonment, and burning. And this faith is not grounded on the pope and his cardinals, for then it must fail and be undone, as they fail and are sometimes destroyed. But it rests on Jesus Christ, God and man," etc.

Notwithstanding all the malice of his enemies, this eminent reformer was permitted to end his earthly career in peace. He had contended for many years with spiritual wickedness in high places; but the time approached for his rest. We may quote the language of Vaughan, in describing the close of his life.

"The temper of his chief opponents was sufficiently known, to satisfy him that the continuance of his personal liberty, and even of life, arose less from their inclination than from their weakness. But his anticipations of a season in which their power would be equal to their malice, were not to be realized. The fact admits of explanation. It was known that the Duke of Lancaster still entertained a favorable judgment of his character; the papal schism absorbed the attention of the pontiffs; and the domestic disquietudes of England had long rendered the factions who governed it, in a great degree fearful of each other. In addition to these causes, as serving to delay the introduction of more sanguinary persecutions, the declining health of the reformer should be noticed. It was probable that his career would soon terminate; and with him, his partisans may have been expected to disappear.

"Previous to his death, he needed the assistance of a curate in performing his parochial duties. In this infirm state, however, he continued at times to officiate; and he is said to have been employed in administering the bread of the Eucharist, when assailed by his last sickness. The paralysis which now seized his frame deprived him at once of consciousness; and after a short struggle, issued in the removal of his devout spirit to the abodes of natures more congenial with his own. This event happened on the last day of December, in the year 1384. Many good men have prayed to be called to their rest while thus occupied. We know not that it was so with Wycliffe; but we know that he was taken 'from the evil to come.'"

"Thirty winters had passed over his grave, when, in the Council of Constance, more than three hundred articles, said to be extracted from his manuscripts, were condemned, and with them the whole of his writings. And it was further decreed, that his memory should be pronounced infamous; and that his bones, if to be distinguished from those of the 'faithful,' should be removed from the ground in which they were deposited, and cast upon a dunghill. Tradition and history report, that in pursuance of this sentence, his remains were taken from their place, reduced to ashes, and thrown into the river which still passes the town of Lutterworth."

CHAPTER VII.

CONRAD WALDHAUSER.

Huss had his precursors, as well as Luther. One of these was Conrad Waldhauser, an Augustinian monk, and a preacher of great influence in Vienna from 1345 to 1360. When the pope, Clement VI., proclaimed the jubilee of 1350, Conrad was one of that immense multitude who undertook the pilgrimage to Rome to partake of the promised benefit, a plenary absolution of all sins. But instead of having his conscience more and more darkened, what he witnessed on that occasion seems to have opened his eyes to perceive the corruption of religion and the enormities of the priesthood, so that he returned to Austria a zealous preacher of repentance. He afterwards travelled as a preacher "through all Austria," and at length proceeded to Prague, in Bohemia.

Here, as is said by a recent American author,[*] "anxious to labor for the salvation of many, he went forth into the open market-place, and preached to immense audiences. The spirit of his sermons may be gathered from his own words: 'Not willing that the blood of souls should be required at my hands, I traced, as I was able, in the Holy Scriptures, the future dangers impending over the souls of men.'" He exposed the vices of the monks, and their hypocrisy, calling them wolves in sheep's clothing. He showed that their mode of life was not warranted by anything in the Scriptures, denounced their bodily mortifications and the mere machinery of religion which they had introduced, and protested against the perpetual vows to a

[*] Gillett, Life and Times of John Huss.

monastic life, which were imposed by parents on their children. "They only," said he, "are the sons of God, who are led by the Spirit of God." He did not inveigh against the original institution of monasticism, but against its degeneracy and the false pretensions by which the monks in that age were deluding the people. "The monks had become like the Pharisees of old. They had bound to men's shoulders burdens too heavy to be borne, which they would not themselves touch with one of their fingers. They had insolently set themselves up as teachers of the people; they had usurped the rights and privileges of pastors; they had refused men the Bible in their own language. They had encouraged superstition, and aggravated the prevalent corruption, by their vain questions and controversies, their useless school quarrels and nonsense. To carry out their designs, they made godliness a matter of traffic, introducing themselves into houses, and leading simple women astray."

The angry monks of course turned upon the zealous preacher who denounced their "craft," and endeavored to procure his overthrow. But they could not find any occasion of fault in the integrity of his life, nor successfully charge him with unsoundness of faith, especially as the emperor, Charles IV., was favorable to him. He is described, by a writer who outlived him,[*] as "a powerful preacher of repentance. He spoke forth to the people sharp warnings to flee from the wrath to come. No prevalent vice escaped his rebuke. Pride of dress, usury, lightness, and youthful vanities, were rebuked, and a powerful impression was made. The usurer gave up his ill-gotten gains. The thoughtless and giddy became serious. Quite a number of Jews were drawn to listen to his sermons. A radical change was effected in the hearts of a large num-

[*] Matthias of Janow, as quoted by Gillett.

ber of his hearers, while the purity of his own life exhibited an example of what he commended to them."

Some of the monks at length, in 1364, prepared a series of articles against him; but when the day of trial came, no one dared to present them. Conrad died five years afterwards, thus probably escaping a rancorous persecution.

JOHN MILICZ.

THIS cotemporary of Conrad Waldhauser was a native of Kremsier, in Moravia, who studied theology and law in the University of Prague, and in the course of his studies had been impressed with the superiority of the ancient Greek church in those countries.

He held in Prague several offices of public trust, besides that of preacher, being appointed archdeacon by the archbishop. But finding that his opinions as expressed in his sermons were displeasing to the latter functionary and the priests, he resigned his lucrative post, and took a very humble position, in which his maintenance depended on the voluntary offerings of pious citizens. He had preached against various corruptions, such as "the use of an unknown tongue in public worship, the celibacy and wealth of the ecclesiastics, the vows of religious orders, the false miracles and legends of the monks, and their self-invented sanctity;" and of course these were not palatable topics to those who felt themselves implicated.

But, says Gillett,* "the tide turned in favor of the man whose sincerity of purpose and simplicity of speech stood in striking contrast with the conduct and manner of his opponents. The people cherished toward him a strong

* Life and Times of John Huss.

affection. They would not suffer him to be silent, and sometimes he was constrained to preach three or four times the same day."

"His sermons were not unfrequently two or three hours long, and his only preparation—in many cases the only preparation possible—was prayer. His abstemiousness in eating and drinking was carried probably to an excess. He wore a rough hair shirt next to his skin; and in his voluntary poverty, as well as in his writings, administered a severe reproof to the mendicants, who violated vows which he never had assumed.

"Matthias of Janow said of him, 'Having been a simple priest, and secretary at the prince's court, before his experience of the visitation of the Spirit of Christ, he grew so rich in wisdom and all utterance of doctrine, that it was a light matter to him to preach five times a day—once in Latin, once in German, and then again in the Bohemian tongue—and this publicly, with a mighty force and a powerful voice; and he constantly brought forth from his treasure things new and old.'

"His preaching bore fruit in a striking reformation. Prague was noted for its depravity. It abounded in brothels. Milicz directed his energies, among other things, to the reform of licentious women. At first, twenty were converted, and a dwelling was procured for them. By enlisting the aid of devout women, the work was extended. Several hundreds were recovered from the paths of vice. A Magdalen hospital was founded. According to Janow the very face of the city was transformed. 'I confess,' he says, 'that I cannot enumerate even the tenth part of what my own eyes saw, my own ears heard, and my own hands handled, though I lived with him but a short time.'

"For six years Milicz continued to preach, unwearied in his efforts. But he was not satisfied with himself. His humility made him feel that he was unfit to preach. He felt a strong impulse to seclusion, and yielding to it for a time, he meditated on the corrupt condition of religion throughout the world. It seemed to him that he beheld antichrist, in the various errors and abuses which stalked abroad under a Christian name.

"Suddenly he felt called upon to visit the pope, narrate to him his visions, and utter his admonitions. He went, as he supposed, at the command of the Holy Spirit. He would have the pope originate a spiritual crusade for the overthrow of antichrist. A general Council should be called; the bishops should devise means for restoring discipline; and monks and secular priests should be exhorted to go forth as preachers."

Going to Rome during the absence of the pope, in 1367, he waited long for his expected arrival. After several weeks' detention, and employing his time in fasting, in prayer, and in reading the Holy Scriptures, he posted on the doors of the cathedral a notice that on a certain day he would address the people; adding, it is said, "antichrist is come; he has his seat in the church." This excited the monks, and he was arrested by the Inquisition, loaded with chains, and closely confined. "But," says Gillett, "he endured all with uncomplaining meekness. Not a bitter word escaped his lips, and his persecutors were confounded by his patient submission. After a prolonged imprisonment, he was asked what he had intended to preach. He replied by asking his examiners to give him back his Bible, pen, ink, and paper, and they should have his discourse in writing. The request was granted; and before a large assembly of prelates and learned men, he delivered his discourse, and it made a profound impression. Still he was kept in prison, and there composed his celebrated work on Antichrist."

On the pope's arrival at length at Rome, Milicz was set at liberty, to the disappointment of the monks, and returned to Prague, to the great joy of his friends.

He now recommenced his labors. Among other things, he instituted a school of two or three hundred young men, who received his instruction, and for whose use he copied books; engaging them also in the work of transcription, for the purpose of multiplying and extending the circulation of religious and instructive works. His school formed a brotherhood, without any external badge, or vow, or rule, such as characterized the monastic orders; but bound together by common sympathies and aims. Their exemplary conduct made them objects of vulgar reproach, and they were nicknamed, Miliczans, Beghards, etc.

"His extraordinary course of activity, and reproof of sin, drew down upon him envy and persecution. The priests, whose disgraceful connections he rebuked, united against him. The archbishop, with great reluctance, was forced to call him to account for his street preaching. Twelve heads of accusation were drawn up against him (in 1374) and sent to the pope."

Gregory XI., the pope at that time, enjoined the Archbishop of Prague, and several bishops, to arrest the progress of the innovation. But Milicz preferred to submit his case to the pope himself; and making his appeal to the pontifical chair, set out for Avignon, where the pope then was. We have no further information of his reception there, than that while his cause was still pending, he died in that city.

MATTHIAS OF JANOW.

MATTHIAS OF JANOW was a native of Prague, and for a short time a pupil of John Milicz. He studied and graduated at the University of Paris, travelled extensively, and afterward became a parish priest in the city of Prague, and confessor to the emperor Charles IV. By his own account it appears as if he had been powerfully visited by the immediate instructions of the Spirit of the Lord Jesus. He says, "Once my mind was encompassed by a thick wall. I thought of nothing but what delighted the eye and the ear, till it pleased the Lord Jesus to deliver me as a brand from the burning. And while I, worst slave to my passions, was resisting him in every way, he delivered me from the flames of Sodom, and brought me into the place of sorrow, of great adversities, and of much contempt. Then first I became poor and contrite, and searched with trembling the word of God [meaning here the Holy Scriptures]. Then did I begin to wonder at the exaltation of Satan, and the blindness with which he covered the eyes of men. And then did the most loving crucified Jesus open my ear, that is, my understanding, that I might understand the Scriptures appropriate to the present time; and he lifted my mind up to perceive how men were absorbed in vanity. And then reading, I clearly and distinctly perceived the abomination of desolation standing proudly in the holy place; and I was seized with horror and shuddering of heart. And I took up the lamentation of Jeremiah; and I went to them, and, between the porch and the altar, exhorted and admonished them to deplore the evils that had befallen Jerusalem, the daughter of my people."* He then speaks, says Gillett, of the fire in his

---
* Gillett's Life and Times of John Huss, vol. i. p. 27.

bones which would not let him rest; but he was forced to "dig through the wall" into "the chamber of imagery," and write what he had seen.

Who can say that this was not the genuine work of the Divine Spirit, enlightening his mind to perceive the truth as it is in Jesus, and to discern the corruptions which had overspread professing Christendom as with a thick cloud of abominations? "No one can peruse his writings," adds the author above referred to, "without feeling that he has come in contact with a mind penetrated with the love of truth, and possessed of a clear insight into the spirit of the gospel. In an age when the worldly spirit was triumphant; when, with thousands of the priesthood, gain was godliness and promotion was success, he withstood the bribes which were extended to his selfishness and ambition. It was not without a bitter inward struggle that he finally was brought to the point of self-renunciation and self-denial. The record which he has left us of his experience is exceedingly vivid. It portrays the spiritual conflicts through which he was called to pass, in words which reveal the process by which he was prepared for his work.

"'My feet,' he says, 'had almost gone; my steps had well-nigh slipped. Unless a crucified Jesus had come to my rescue, my soul had sunk to hell. But he, my most faithful and loving Saviour, in whom is no guile, showed me their counsels; and I knew the face of the harlot, by which she allures all that stand at the corners of the streets and the entrances of the paths. . . . . Nevertheless, I prayed to God and the Father of my Lord Jesus Christ. . . . . "O Lord and Father, who ordainest my life, leave me not to their thoughts and counsels, and let me not be taken in their net; lest I fall under that reproachful sin which shall sting my conscience and drive out wisdom from my soul!" . . . . . I confess, before God and his

Christ, that so alluring was this harlot antichrist, and she so well feigned herself the true spouse of Christ, or rather, Satan by his arts so tricked her out, that from my early years I was long in doubt what I should choose, or what I should keep; whether I should seek out and chase after benefices, and thirstily grasp after honors, which to some extent I did, or rather go forth without the camp, bearing the poverty and reproach of Christ; whether, with the many, I should live in quest of an easy and quiet life for the moment, or rather cling to the faithful and holy truth of the gospel; whether to commend what almost all commend, lay my plans as many do, dispense with and gloss over the Scriptures as many of the great and learned and famous of this day do, or rather manfully inculpate and accuse their unfruitful works of darkness, and so hold to the simple truth of the divine words, which plainly contravene the lives and morals of men of this age, and prove them false brethren; whether I should follow the Spirit of Wisdom with its suggestions, which I believe to be the Divine Spirit of Jesus, or follow the sentiment of the great multitude, which, in their self-indulgence, without show of mercy or charity, while lovers of this world and full of carnal vanities, they claim to be safe. I confess that between these two courses I hung wavering in doubt; and unless our Lord Jesus be our Keeper, none will escape the honeyed face and smile of this harlot—the tricks of Satan and the snares of Antichrist.'"

He was willing that all his opinions should be tested by their accordance with Holy Scripture. In his writings he rejects the authority of human traditions and popish decretals, and severely arraigns the conduct of the bishops and priests. He declares that antichrist is neither Jew, Pagan, Saracen, nor mere worldly tyrant, but the "man who opposes Christian truth and the Christian life by way of deception;—he is and will be the most wicked Christian, falsely styling himself by that name, assuming the highest station in the church, and possessing the highest consideration, arrogating dominion over all ecclesiastics and laymen;"—one who, by the working of Satan, assumes to himself power and wealth and honor, and makes the church, with its goods and sacraments, subservient to his own carnal ends.* He declares that the kingdom of antichrist is to be spiritually annihilated by the Almighty, —" by the breath of his mouth"—the utterance of his elect priests and preachers, who should go forth in the spirit of Elias and Enoch. This work was to go on like the operation of leaven, or like the growth of mustard seed. He laid open some of the causes of the great apostasy, in the neglect of the Holy Scriptures and reverence for popish decretals and human ordinances; the seeking of salvation in sensible and corporeal things, rather than in the crucified Lord; the censure and persecution of those who confessed Christ, while the stately ceremonies of the false prophet were extolled. But, said he, no multiplicity of human laws and ordinances can meet every contingency. The Spirit of God alone can do this. "So I have gathered from the Holy Scriptures; and I believe that all the above-named works of men, ordinances and ceremonies, will be utterly extirpated, cut up by the roots, and cease,—and God alone will be exalted, and his word will abide forever."

He called men back to the Scriptures; yet, as if aware that even here was not the original source itself of divine counsel or of salvation, he recurs to that wisdom and mercy which gave them forth; saying, according to Gillett: "But positive law has been ineffectual to recover fallen men, and Christ has left to them the Law of the Spirit: to its sound and simple beginnings the Christian church

* Gillett's Life of Huss.

should be brought back.—Monastic orders are not needed for the governing of the church. The unity of this is found in its union with Christ."

Matthias's principal writings are, his work on "Antichrist," that on "The Kingdom, People, Life and Manners of Antichrist," the "Abomination of Carnal Priests and Monks," and the books on the "Abolishing of Sects," and on "The Unity of the Church." In the first of these he comes forth with especial boldness against some of the false assumptions of the papacy. As quoted by Gillett, we find him describing three false principles "formed from the tail of antichrist. The first is, that as soon as any one is elected Pope of Rome, he becomes head of the whole militant church, and supreme vicar of Christ on earth. This is pronounced a bare lie! The second is, that what the pope determines in matters of faith, is to be received as of equal authority with the gospel. This is likewise pronounced false; for we must believe him who has so often erred in matters of faith, only when he is supported by the Scriptures. The third—that the laws of the pope are to be obeyed before the gospel—is declared blasphemous; for it is blasphemy to believe the pope or any one else, or accept his laws, in preference to Christ."

In his work on the "Abomination of Carnal Priests and Monks," he is unsparing in his reprehensions of the "lukewarmness of the prelates, their avarice, wealth, and simony, the negligence of the priesthood, the unseemly strifes between the monks and the regular clergy, the sacrilegious sale of sacred things, the barter of masses, indulgences, etc., the false worship offered to the bones of dead saints, while God's poor but devoted children are despised." The reign of hypocrisy, he thought, had become universal. "There were, indeed, not a few faithful still left, like the seven thousand in Israel that had never bowed the knee to

Baal. But by the iniquity of the times they were driven into solitude. Ambitious and worldly men, by disgraceful methods, attained power and influence in the church. Wickedness, if powerful and gilded with pomp, was flattered. — But, he says, antichrist is to be destroyed — 'Christ will destroy him by the breath of his mouth and by the brightness of his coming.' He will raise up those who shall proclaim his word, and thus consume the lies and errors of the great deceiver."

Matthias protests that he does not, in thus writing, direct his words against any individual, but at the general apostasy—that nothing is said in bitterness or pride—and that if his books are read as written, none will be injured. He declares that he would not have dared to write but for the irresistible impulse of truth.

It was wonderful that with all this boldness of invective against the prevalent system, he was not condemned as a heretic and burned at the stake. Gillett says, however, that he was considered as an innovator, and that, in 1389, he was arraigned before the synod of Prague, and his opinions condemned. He was afterward banished from the city, but, through the favor of the emperor, was soon enabled to return.

About five years afterward, in 1394, he died, and in 1410 his writings were committed to the flames. But the flames could not devour the effect they must have produced on the awakening minds of men of that age in Bohemia.

MATTHEW OF CRACOW.

MATTHIAS CRACOVIENSIS was descended from an ancient family of note in Pomerania. No account has come down to us respecting his parents, or the date or place of his birth; but it seems probable that he was born about the middle of the fourteenth century. He had a thorough education in the schools of philosophy and theology of that day. But he seems to have been a man of an active and energetic mind, preferring to think for himself on important subjects, rather than to be bound to keep in the beaten track of the schools of the middle ages. The corrupt condition of the Romish church, and especially of the ecclesiastical body, seems to have early engaged his serious attention. In 1384, he delivered a discourse on the improvement of morals, both in priests and people, before an archiepiscopal synod in Prague, in which city, as well as in the University of Paris, he was engaged for some time in lecturing, and in the latter city presided for a while over the faculty of theology.

Thence he was invited by the Emperor Rupert to a post in the University of Heidelberg, then in its infancy; he afterward became chancellor to Rupert, and in 1405, through the emperor's influence, he was made Bishop of Worms. Ullmann[*] says of him, that he "had in his travels and missions, and by his intercourse both with the great and the humble, collected a rich and extensive knowledge of mankind and experience of the world. In particular, his situation as bishop, and his repeated missions to Italy on affairs of high importance, could not but make him familiarly acquainted with the Roman court and the whole hierarchy."

He left behind him many writings in manuscript, some

[*] "Reformers before the Reformation," vol. i. p. 304.

of which were afterward published in print. We must remember that the art of printing by movable types was not known until several years after his death. Among the most noted of his works, is one which, from the indignant boldness of his invectives against the corruptions of the professing church in his day, justifies us in ranking Matthew of Cracow among the most decided of the forerunners of the Reformation. This work is a treatise " On the Pollutions of the Romish Court;" and appears to have been written a little previous to the year 1409, about the period when the schism in the papacy seemed to open a door for conscientious minds to cherish doubts, at least privately, yet sufficiently to afford a leaven for the future, respecting the boasted infallibility of the popes, and the degree of implicit faith and obedience due to their appointments and decisions. It may be that the weakness occasioned by this papal schism furnished a reason why the author of so bold an attack on the prevailing corruptions did not encounter the hostility and persecution of the ecclesiastical powers. His favor with the emperor was an additional source of impunity, and probably also his early death after the publication of the work.

At this period, the practice of simony, or buying and selling the ecclesiastical offices, had become almost universal, from the popes to the lowest priest. "No competition," says Matthew, "for any situation, however low, meets with any success at Rome, unless a ducat be first paid, and paid to the last penny." "This method of appointing to offices is a chief impediment to the promotion of able and honorable men; for these are restrained by good sense and shame from coming forward and stooping to the usual means. Whereas, on the other side, it is an easy way for light-minded persons and vagabonds, who are ready for everything, and demean themselves to the lowest services, to obtain high situations. Can anything be more lamentable?" "There is scarcely a person, however profligate and scandalous, who may not be admitted into the spiritual office. No attention is paid by those who have the power, to the correction of such offenders. To breathe a word on the subject would seem ridiculous—they have no time to spare for such a purpose—they are occupied day and night with vacancies, lawsuits, hunting after properties, and the ceremonies and forms of the papal court."—"Even the bishops are seldom possessed of a Bible—they are blind leaders of the blind, and in place of guiding the people in the paths of righteousness, rather mislead them." This was the language of a German bishop, more than one hundred years before Luther's appearance at the same city.

In the same treatise he combats boldly the right of the Romish chair (whether paid for it or not) to fill the offices of bishops and other high dignitaries of the church; calls it an encroachment on the long established privilege of election; designates some of the practices often connected with it as nothing short of fraud; and says, "What has resulted from the practice which has hitherto obtained? Nothing but a mass of simony. Simony however is heresy, and no venial but a very heinous sin. It robs all who commit it of grace, and places them in the state of eternal perdition; so that the pope, and all who take part in the sale of offices, are living in a state of condemnation. For the practice and encouragement of simony, as now carried on in the court of Rome, is neither accidental, nor proceeds from want of thought; but on the contrary is deliberate and intentional, has grown into a habit, and is therefore unpardonable. This assertion will appear harsh to many, and I myself at first shrank not merely from the words, but even from the thought."—"And how ruinous are other consequences of such practices! The churches are cheated with unworthy priests; the spiritual office is abused; able and godly men are excluded from it; the universities and schools fall into decline, etc."

Some of the Romish courtiers, he says, excuse this buying and selling of offices by the allegation, that the money is not received for *the place,* but for the *trouble of bestowing* it; to which he replies that it is none the less to be considered a low-minded transaction, unworthy of so great a prince; and suggests that for the *trouble* of the business "a florin would be quite a sufficient fee!" To the excuse, that "the pope is the lord of all," and that consequently all the property of the church belongs to him of right, Matthew replies: "God alone is the absolute Lord of all. All other lordship is limited. No man, not even the pope, has any more power than what God has given him;" and he goes on to show that the pope, like other men, is liable to error, and, as a man, insufficient for such a lordship. "How," asks he, "could it ever have been the will of the Lord, who bought the church with his blood, that any one man, who may possibly be ignorant and ill-disposed, but who, at any rate, is subject to mistake and error, should govern it merely according to his own fancy?"—"In Scripture not a word is said of the right of the pope to keep benefices in his own hand, or to put them into his purse. Nor does this tend to edify the church, for it drives away from it the poor, however fit they may be for the duties, and it fosters avarice and cupidity."

Matthew allows that the pope ought to have sufficient means to live respectably; but insists that these means must be legitimately obtained. "If," says he, "the necessities of the pope be really urgent, and if his object be not the mere accumulation of treasure, all he has to do, in order to raise money in a pious way, is just to assemble the bishops and advise with them. Were they indeed to refuse to assemble, it would be no more than the Church of Rome deserved, because by her neglect of the Councils she has dishabituated the prelates from attending them.— From the neglect of the Councils, numerous evils have arisen both in past and present times, etc."

In reply to the allegation, that although the pope does wrong, yet it is right to obey him, Matthew says that even the pope cannot escape from the inward and mental judgment which is every one's right respecting his public acts, and that he is, moreover, liable to be condemned by a judgment of the church as a whole, or by its representatives. "No doubt," he adds, "the apostle justly says that 'whosoever resisteth the power, resisteth the ordinance of God;' but the pope *has no power to govern badly*, or to destroy; and he who resists him in any such attempt, resists not the power, but the abuse of it, and so does not resist God, from whom the abuse does not come."

To the objection, that subjects ought not to judge their rulers, he thus boldly answers, "that the principle is true in all matters that are either good or indifferent; but where there is a manifest mischief, the case is altered. The head ought to govern the members, but not to mislead or destroy them. When he does that, he does not govern them, and then neither are they bound to obey him, because he thereby ceases to fulfill the duties of the head."

It is evident that Matthew of Cracow desired a reformation, but not a revolution, in the Romish church. He did not apparently see the errors of doctrine which were in some sort at the root of the gross errors in practice which he so boldly denounced. He looked to a correction of the abuses, but not to a subversion of the whole system. Yet this treatise, published even before the dawn after a long dark night, was calculated to arouse the dormant minds of men, and bring them to question whether the basis was not corrupt, on which so much corruption had accumulated; and he opened the way for such thoughts to find favorable entrance, by denying the infallibility of the pope, and showing that he was, like other men, liable to human frailty, and amenable to trial and even to the forfeiture of his position, by a judgment of the church.

We have no information of the effect immediately produced by this treatise; but it shows that the harvest of the sixteenth century was even then in its germ, and it seems like some of the seed toward that harvest, sown for a hundred years, to produce fruit in the times of Luther and Melancthon.

Of the closing days of Matthew's life, we know little more than that, in 1409, he attended the Council of Pisa, and that he died the next year in his episcopal city of Worms. He was buried in the cathedral there, where an epitaph still marks the place of his sepulture.

CHAPTER VIII.

JOHN HUSS.

THE life of this eminent man was so mingled with the political disturbances of Europe and the ecclesiastical intrigues and hierarchical changes of the day, that to develop it fully in its relations thereto, would require a volume of itself. It is moreover already so much a matter of history that our present purpose will be answered by a brief delineation of the main features of his course as a reformer and a martyr, leading the way in men's minds for the more successful upheaving of the mighty revolution in the profession of religion, which took place in the following century.

John Huss was born at the village of Hussinitz, in the southern part of Bohemia, in the year 1373, or according to some writers, four years earlier. His parents were poor, but honest, and worthy peasants,* who spared no pains to give their son a good education. At first he was sent to a school in his native village, kept in a monastery not far from his parents' residence. Here he devoted himself zealously to his studies, and his quiet habits and lively intelligence won for him the favor of the monks who taught the school. They were however too ignorant to instruct him in Latin, and as he became ambitious to acquire a knowledge of many books which he found written in that language only, he was, after a time, transferred to a higher school at the neighboring village of Prachatitz. Here he made rapid progress in rhetoric, and in the Latin and Greek languages, and after completing the course of study in that institution, his widowed mother took him to the city of Prague, and placed him in the university. He obtained a position in the house of one of the teachers, receiving his food and clothing in return for his services in the family, and having the advantage of access to a good library. He was then about sixteen years of age. He pursued his studies with such assiduity and success, and was so highly esteemed by the faculty and by the students, that in little more than twelve years he received all the degrees which that celebrated school could bestow (except that of Doctor in Theology, which it does not appear that he ever took) and was made rector of the university.

There were during those years quite a number of religious persons in Prague, whose minds were burdened with the

* "Von schlechten und gerechten Ælten." Zitte: Leb. des Joh. Hus, p. 20.

prevailing corruption, and who longed for a reform. The writings of Wycliffe also had found their way into Bohemia, and had attracted much attention in kindred minds. Huss however at first looked coldly on these, suspecting that the Englishman had gone too far with his innovating views. But his mind was gradually led to understand the sad degeneracy of the church, and to take a deep interest in the question of a thorough practical reform; and after a time he was able more truly to appreciate and more fully to approve of many of the sentiments presented to him in the writings of Wycliffe.

He became greatly afflicted with what he now saw of the profligacy and vice of those who had assumed the place of pastors and teachers to the flock, and with the general neglect of the Holy Scriptures, and the substitution of popish decretals.

In the year 1401, he was appointed confessor to Queen Sophia, wife of the King of Bohemia; and soon afterward he was selected by the founder of Bethlehem Chapel in Prague, to occupy the important position of preacher there. This chapel had peculiar endowments, and privileges, leaving the possessor of its pulpit free from ecclesiastical control or restraint, except such as might be exercised by the direct intervention of the pope. Here John Huss therefore occupied a comparatively independent position, and here he continued to preach for twelve years to crowded audiences.

His sentiments meantime were gradually maturing and developing, respecting the great question of a reform from the corrupt state into which the mass of the professors of Christianity had lapsed. The writings of Wycliffe, though they had been condemned in England in 1403, attracted more and more of his approval, and of the attention of multitudes both in and out of the university. The Bohemian students were mainly favorable to the reforming sentiments; but those of other nations attending the school, chiefly Germans, to the number of many thousands,* stoutly opposed what they looked upon as heretical innovations; and thus the university became greatly divided in feeling. To some of his fellows in the school, who had come upon him while reading one of Wycliffe's books, and reproached him with it, Huss replied: "I only wish that my soul, when it leaves this body, may reach the place where that of this excellent Briton now dwells." And this desire he frequently afterward repeated, it is said, in his sermons in the chapel.

He fearlessly exposed the base artifices of the priests, by which they attempted to palm off upon the ignorant and superstitious people their false pretensions to miraculous intervention. After some years he lost the position of rector of the university, through the dissatisfaction of the German students with the advancing sentiments of reform. But at length, probably instigated by Queen Sophia, the king interposed his authority, by which the Bohemian students were put on an equality of influence with the foreigners. The latter consequently lost their preponder-

* Gillett supposes about 5000; but many authors greatly exceed this number. Gillett had probably misconstrued what Æneas Sylvius says on the subject, who states that upwards of 5000 departed for Leipsic alone within a few days. Palacky, however, who quotes this, adds that a Bohemian Annalist, of that period, affirms that more than 20,000 in all left Prague. Zitte (Leb. des Joh. Hus, vol. i. p. 95) quotes Balbinus the Jesuit, as saying that Hagek computed them at 40,000, Lupacz at 44,000, and even Lauda, a cotemporary, at 36,000, who left Prague for various other universities. Zitte indorses the latter number, incredible as it may appear to us; for he says (p. 92): "Their trains amounted to three or four thousand persons; and in a period of eight days, there had departed 36,000 students, with their professors and teachers." Hœfler, a modern writer against Huss, says that at any rate they exceeded 20,000; and quotes a cotemporary Bohemian chronicler, as asserting that 34,000 attended the university, besides those who took lessons outside (p. 249).

ancy in the affairs of the institution, and in their anger and disappointment left the city. Upon this, Huss was again elected; but this circumstance called forth much hostile feeling against him in Prague, among those who favored the German element in the school, and who were opposed to the party who had adopted or approved the writings of Wycliffe. The monks also found themselves set aside, and the many tradesmen who had gained by the custom of the students were greatly exasperated.

At length the books of the English reformer were condemned by the Archbishop of Prague, and all possessing them were required to give them up to that functionary. Huss remonstrated with him, but in vain. More than two hundred manuscript volumes, many of them very expensively executed, were collected for the flames. The pope sustained the archbishop, ordered the books to be burned, and prohibited Huss from continuing to preach in the chapel. But the pope died, the king interfered, Huss refused to be silenced, and for a time it appeared as if the burning of the books might be averted. The archbishop however resolved to perform his part, and in the summer of 1410, protected by bands of soldiers, and accompanied by several bishops and a large number of ecclesiastics, with the tolling of the tower bells and much pomp, he proceeded to burn the books in the court of his palace. But a cry of indignation went through Bohemia. Even some of the priests, and several of the nobility, protested against the deed; the queen wept, and the king cursed aloud. The populace became excited, and some tumults occurring, the archbishop began to tremble in his palace. He had barbarously destroyed more than two hundred costly volumes; but he had by no means obtained them all, and those which escaped his vigilance became increasingly valued.

Meantime Huss appealed to the papal chair against the prohibition to preach, and went on with his functions as before. The evils which he rebuked, says his American biographer Gillett, "were too glaring to be denied. He held up to view the purity and holiness required by Christ, and in this mirror exposed the avarice, ambition, luxury, sensuality, and violence of the profligate ecclesiastics. He could not compromise with his convictions; and with a high consciousness of his responsibility to God rather than men, he aimed to discharge his whole duty."

Huss having appealed to the pope, that functionary placed the matter, first in the hands of a commission, and afterward in charge of Cardinal Otho de Colonna; who gave a ready ear to the charges against the reformer, and required him to appear personally before the pope at Rome. This, at a distance of 1200 miles, and through a country filled with his reckless foes, Huss could not with a reasonable regard for his own safety attempt. The king and queen of Bohemia, the University of Prague, and many lords and barons, united in sending an embassy to request the pope to dispense with his presence in Rome, and to suffer him to continue to preach in the chapel; and Huss himself sent three agents to plead his cause. But the cardinal refused to listen to them, and the request to the pope was treated with contempt. Colonna issued a decree of excommunication against Huss, for disobedience in refusing to appear at Rome. This was in the spring of 1411; but Huss still continued to preach as before, and the archbishop in anger closed the places of worship and placed the whole city under an interdict.

This prohibition of their accustomed religious ceremonies the populace could not endure. They appealed to the king, and the archbishop becoming weary of the contention, and perhaps fearful of the people's hostility, agreed to a compromise, by which all proceedings against Huss, as well as the interdict upon the city, were suspended until further orders should arrive from Rome. Archbishop Sbynco soon afterward died at Presburg, on his way to solicit assistance in his difficulties from the Emperor Sigismund, who was also King of Hungary.

Huss now became fully aroused to the necessity of clearly exposing the false pretensions of the papacy. He maintained before the university that antichrist was already come, and had obtained the highest dignity in Christendom, exercising authority over all Christian people; but that being a chief enemy and adversary of Christ, obedience was no longer a duty, but rather resistance of his usurpation. The papal court was occupied by a contest with Ladislaus, King of Naples, and issued a bull, calling on all to engage in a crusade against him, and offering indulgences* to such as should enlist in the papal army or pay a sum adequate to purchase a substitute. This bull and offer of indulgence Huss stoutly opposed, as totally at variance with the spirit of Christianity. "One ought rather," said he, "to endure wrong patiently, after the example of Christ and his apostles, than spur on Christians to exterminate one another. Does any one say that these commands (of Christ) belong only to those that are perfect? Then the pope should be the most perfect among the clergy."†

In the summer of 1412 that notoriously wicked man, Belthazar Cossa, who had been elected to the papacy through corrupt means in 1410, after the death of Alexander V., and had assumed the name of John the Twenty-third, put the case of this reformer into the hands of one of

* "Die Nachlassung aller der Sünden die sie dem Herzen bereuen und mit dem munde beichten." See the bull at length in Zitte, vol. i. p. 252.
† Gillett's Life and Times of John Huss, vol. i. p. 210.

the cardinals, who issued another bull of excommunication against Huss. In this terrible instrument not only was Huss nominally cut off from the church militant, but all men were forbidden to give him food or drink. "None might buy of him or sell to him; none were to converse or hold intercourse with him; none might give him lodging, or allow him fire or water. Every city, village, or castle where he might reside was put under interdict." "If he died excommunicate, he was to be denied church burial; or, if buried in consecrated ground, his body was to be dug up again from its grave!"* The pope himself followed this up by still another fulmination, ordering the person of John Huss to be seized, and his chapel to be levelled to the ground. On this being reported at Prague, a mob of Germans, bitterly opposed to Huss, marched in arms to the chapel, for the purpose of tearing it down. But finding Huss then in the pulpit, encompassed by a large assembly, their zeal failed them, and they went away without accomplishing their nefarious project.

Huss continued to preach in Bethlehem Chapel till near the close of the year 1412. The king had issued a decree to relieve the city, in some measure, from the effects of the interdict; but Huss found his position there not only increasingly difficult for himself, through the continual efforts of his enemies for his destruction, but constantly affecting also the great body of the citizens themselves with what they looked upon as a great disaster; the papal interdict being only partially and irregularly counteracted by the intervention of the king. The pope's power was considered paramount to the authority of the king, even in his own dominions. Huss therefore concluded, for a time at least, to leave Prague, and toward the end of that year he returned to his native village. In doing so, he drew up a

* Gillett's Life and Times of John Huss, vol. i. p. 226.

solemn appeal to his Divine Master against the injustice of "this pretended and frivolous excommunication."

In his absence from Prague he did not give himself up to inaction, but preached in various places around his residence much as he had done in his chapel. We are told that "throngs crowded to hear, and were curious to see, a man who had been excommunicated, yet who spoke with" such earnestness and fervor; "who had been driven out of Prague by the interdict, yet whose blameless life shamed his persecutors. His eloquence was as effective in the open fields as in Bethlehem Chapel. Poor peasants and proud nobles gathered around him, in the forests and highways, to hear his forcible expositions and applications" of the Holy Scriptures. "From city to city, and from village to village, Huss pursued his mission. His hearers came in crowds from their homes, fields, and workshops. The impression made was in many cases deep and abiding; years did not efface it."

During this time also, he composed several of his most important works, and wrote many letters of counsel and encouragement to his friends. He made his home for a time at the castle of Kozi-Hrádek, and afterward found a hospitable refuge in the castle of Cracowec, both belonging to his firm friends. In the former place he wrote his most elaborate and systematic work, "On the Church." It is not necessary to enter at large into the contents of the writings which now proceeded from his pen. Many of his views were undoubtedly characterized by the errors of his education and of the times; so that he saw as it were the truth by glimpses, mixed with much that we cannot now unite with; but where he saw through the bigotry and corruption of the papal system, which he did in some important particulars, he was deeply concerned to be faithful to his convictions. He is said to have been quite as strong an advocate as Calvin for the doctrine of predestination; and he evidently believed in that of purgatory, though in a modified way, calling that condition "the sleeping church." Some of his views are thus compiled by Gillett from the above-named work.

"Christ is the sole supreme head of the church, the true pontifex, high-priest, and bishop of souls. The apostles did not call themselves heads of the church, but servants of Christ and of the church. Even Gregory would not allow himself to be called universal bishop. . . . . . But in truth the pope is no more a successor of Peter than the cardinals are successors of the apostles. He is only to be considered as Christ's and Peter's successor and vicar, when he resembles Peter in faith, humanity, and love; and cardinals are successors of the apostles only when they emulate their virtues and devotion. But this same might be said of others who have never been popes or cardinals. . . . . . . If, instead of fulfilling their calling, and having Christ's example before them, they rather strive for worldly things, splendor, and pomp, and excite avarice and envy in believers, then are they successors, not of Christ, of Peter, or of the apostles, but of Satan, Antichrist, Judas Iscariot.

"It cannot therefore be said that the pope, as such, is the head of the church. The pope can know no more than any other man, in regard to himself with absolute certainty, whether he can be saved. . . . . . . The popedom is not essential to the well-being and edification of the church."
. . . . . . "In the early church there were but two grades of office, deacon and presbyter; all beside are of later and human invention. But God can bring back his church to the old pattern, just as the apostles and true priests took oversight of the church in all matters essential to its well-being, before the office of pope was introduced. So it may be again." . . . . . . "As of the pope and car-

dinals, so of the prelates and clergy. There is a clergy of Christ, and a clergy of antichrist. The former is built on Christ and his laws, labors constantly for the glory of God, and seeks simply to follow Christ. The latter, though wearing the robes of Christ's clergy, rests upon privileges savoring of pride and avarice, finds itself obliged to defend human ordinances, strives after a proud splendid equipage."

...... "Faithful Christians keeping the commandments are the magnates of the church; but prelates who break them are least, and if reprobates, have no part in the kingdom of God." ......

"Every true Christian, when a command issues to him from the pope, must deliberate whence it originates — whether it is an apostolic ordinance and a law of Christ, or mediately such; and he is then to regard and honor it. But if the opposite is the case, he must not honor, but rather firmly oppose it, and not by subjection incur guilt. Opposition in such a case, is true obedience." ......

"The power of the keys, that is, the power to receive the worthy, and reject the unworthy, belongs to God alone, who ordains salvation, or foreknows perdition. The priest has no power to release from guilt and eternal punishment. The pope even has not this power—it belongs to God only. The priest has only the churchly office of declaring, not of binding or loosing, unless this is already done by God. The absolution must *follow* the grace of God and the sinner's repentance. Intellectual knowledge is not essential to the soul's salvation, but true contrition and confession of the heart."

During the year 1414 Huss occasionally reappeared in Prague, and the active opposition to him seemed somewhat suspended. The cause of reform, and views more and more evangelical, seemed to be steadily advancing. "Huss no longer," says Gillett, "approved of the worship of the wooden cross. He condemned the adoration paid to the pictures of the saints."

The "evangelical party" seemed to be gaining the ascendancy. Bohemia appeared in danger of being lost to the Romish church. Something must be done. The university was already lost. "Help, if any was to be found, must come from abroad. There was a conviction becoming deeper and more general on every side among the papal party, that Huss could only be managed, and his heresy restrained, by a General Council. This was a question not only agitated in Bohemia, but all over Europe. There were many reasons which conspired to urge its convocation. The scandalous condition of Christendom, divided in allegiance to three rival pontiffs, was a problem which, by general consent, demanded the assembled wisdom of the church for its solution. There was, moreover, on all sides, a loud demand for ecclesiastical reform. How could measures which had this for their object be initiated, except by the action of a General Council?"*

The Emperor Sigismund had other and strong reasons for desiring a Council; and the pope, John XXIII., reluctantly agreed to it, and the city of Constance was fixed upon as the location. John Huss was cited to appear before the Council, and answer such charges as might be brought against him; and so confident was he in the justice of his cause, that he only asked the privilege of a free audience before the assembly.

"Nor was he without encouragement in the affection of his fellow-citizens From the time when, on the withdrawal of the Germans, he had been elevated to the rectorship of the university, the sympathy of the nation had rallied to his side. A large number of the educated men of the country had been brought under his influence,—while

* Gillett's Life of Huss.

the patriotic feeling, both of the nobility and of the common people, was strongly enlisted in his support."

He believed he was required by the Almighty to maintain the position which he had taken. In one of his letters written during his absence from Prague, he holds the following language: "What to me are riches, honors, or disgrace? My sins alone grieve me. What if the just man lose his life? It is only to find the true life. God will yet destroy antichrist. Be prepared for the conflict. Woe is me, if I do not expose the abomination of desolation by preaching, teaching, and writing." And in another letter, he says: "I count it all joy that I am called a heretic, and excommunicated as disobedient. With Peter and John, it is better to obey God than man."

Before quitting Prague for Constance, Huss took occasion to make a full declaration of his doctrinal views; a safe conduct was granted him by the emperor; and two knights, John de Chlum and Wenceslaus Duba, were appointed by the King of Bohemia to accompany and protect him on the journey. Gillett says: "In the month of October, 1414, Huss bade adieu to his chapel, where his voice was never more to be heard, and to his faithful friends and disciples, some of whom were to follow him in his path of suffering, self-denial, and martyrdom. He left behind him his faithful companion and bosom friend, Jerome, and the scene of parting was one of deep emotion. 'Dear master,' said Jerome, 'be firm; maintain intrepidly what thou hast written and preached against the pride, avarice, and other vices of the churchmen, with arguments drawn from the Holy Scriptures. Should this task become too severe for thee,—should I learn that thou hast fallen into any peril,—I shall fly at once to thy assistance.'"

He went with a full hope that he would have free liberty to state and explain his views before the Council, and to show their accordance with the Scriptures. In this he was to be sorely disappointed. He had not properly realized the determination of his enemies to compass his destruction, nor the tricks and management that unprincipled ecclesiastics were capable of bringing to bear, in order to accomplish their purposes.

Before setting out (or, as Zitte says, from Krakowicz, a short distance from Prague), he addressed a letter to the priest Martin, one of his disciples, in which he spoke of himself with great humility, accusing himself of faults which many would deem trifling—of having felt pleasure in wearing rich apparel, and wasted precious hours in frivolous occupations—and adding the following exhortation: "May the glory of God and the salvation of souls occupy thy mind, and not the possession of benefices and estates. Beware of adorning thy house more than thy soul; and above all, give thy care to the spiritual edifice. Be pious and humble with the poor; and consume not thy substance with feasting. Shouldst thou not amend thy life, and refrain from superfluities, I fear thou wilt be severely chastised, as I am myself—I, who also made use of such things, led away by custom, and troubled by a spirit of pride.—I conjure thee by the mercy of our Lord, not to imitate me in any of the vanities into which thou hast seen me fall."

He experienced great kindness from the people in various places where he rested during his journey. On his arrival at Constance he found the city completely thronged with strangers. "From every direction," says Gillett, "crowds were thronging to the famous Council. Multitudes had already arrived, and more were on their way. The buildings were insufficient to accommodate the immense concourse. Booths and wooden buildings were erected outside the walls, and thousands of pilgrims were encamped in the adjoining country. The whole neighborhood presented a curious and novel scene. All classes of society, laity as well as clergy,—representatives of every nation, with their peculiarities of costume and manner— the soldier in his armor, the prince followed by his escort, the prelate in his robes, the magistrate with his symbols of authority, servants hastening on errands, thousands providing for the food and entertainment of those who had gathered for the Council,—all contributed to make Constance a miniature Christendom! To consult the various tastes of the immense crowd of strangers, there were shows and amusements of all kinds, dramatic entertainments and representations of every description, varied with the solemn or gaudy pomp of religious proceedings.*

...... Who that walked these crowded streets, or gazed upon the princely robes, the rich and costly attire sparkling with jewels and shining with gold, the waving plumes, the burnished armor, the embroidered standards, the splendid equipage, the lengthened cavalcade, would have imagined that amid such scenes of worldly pomp and pageantry were to be sought, decisions and counsels inspired by the Holy Ghost, sentiments accordant with the Galilean fishermen, or sympathy for the evangelical simplicity of the Bohemian reformer?"

The pope had arrived before them, and the next morning Huss's companions visited the pontiff, to announce his arrival under a safe conduct from the emperor, and to request to be informed by the pope whether he might remain

* Zitte gives a copy of a manuscript in the library at Vienna, by which it would appear that among the vast throng collected on this occasion professing to consult the welfare of Christendom, there were "1500 herumvagirende Nachtnimpfen!" (Lebensb. des J. Hus, vol. ii. p. 51.)— A sad commentary on the morals of this "miniature Christendom," where, it has been said, 23,000 prelates, priests, and monks were assembled.

in Constance free from the risk of violence. The pope replied: "Had he killed my own brother, not a hair of his head should be touched while he remained in the city." The sequel will show how far this fair promise was to be fulfilled. For a few weeks Huss enjoyed tolerable liberty and quiet, being left unmolested at his lodgings in the humble dwelling of a poor widow. The excommunication was suspended, but he was cautioned to avoid any appearance at the public mass, or any occasion of scandal to the ecclesiastics. But his enemies soon followed him to Switzerland, and exposed placards in the public places, denouncing him as a heretic and an excommunicate. They set spies to watch him, and presently persuaded the cardinals in the city to summon him before them. Articles of accusation, some of them utterly false, were drawn up with malicious diligence, and the substance of them repeated wherever it was possible to excite prejudice. We are told* that two bishops, the Mayor of Constance, and a certain knight, carried the citation to Huss to appear before the pope and cardinals, in accordance, as they said, with his expressed desire to give an account of his doctrines. Huss replied with calmness, yet with firmness, "I did not come hither with the intention of pleading my cause before the pope and cardinals; and I never desired any such thing; but I wished to appear before the General Council, in the presence of all, and there, openly and plainly reply, on every point proposed to me, according as God shall inspire me for my defense. Yet I do not refuse to appear previously before the cardinals; and if they act unfairly toward me, I shall put my trust in the Saviour Jesus Christ, and shall be more happy to die for his glory than live to deny the truth as taught in the Holy Scriptures."

The bearers of the citation had taken the precaution to

* Gillett, vol. i. p. 343.

place soldiers near the house, to obviate any resistance on the part of Huss or his friends; yet they conducted themselves gently and respectfully toward him. Huss obeying the summons prepared to leave the house, and struck with a prospect of what awaited him, took a solemn and tender leave of his widowed hostess. Arriving at the bishop's palace, he was told by the cardinals that many very grave errors were imputed to him; to which he replied that he would rather die than be convicted of any heresy, especially of any of a very grave character as was expressed; that to this end he had cheerfully come to attend on the General Council, and if any could convince him of any error, he would unhesitatingly abjure it. The cardinals withdrew soon after, leaving him and his companion, John de Chlum, in custody!

Meantime his enemies appear to have sent a man in disguise, to converse with him apparently in a friendly manner, and endeavor to entrap him, or induce him to say something which might be reported to his disadvantage. But Huss and his friend suspected the snare, and avoided it. He afterward learned that the pretended ignorant monk was one of the most learned theologians in Lombardy. As night approached, the provost of the palace announced that Huss must remain in custody, though his friend, John de Chlum, was at liberty to depart. The latter, indignant at the base and perfidious detention of his friend, bitterly complained that a worthy and upright man had thus been lured into an infamous snare, and hastened to the pope to remonstrate with him on the violation of his promise. The pope coolly protested that he had to act according to the wishes of the cardinals and bishops.

After remaining for eight days in charge of the Bishop of Constance, Huss was conveyed to the prison of the Dominican monastery on the banks of the Rhine. "His enemies," says Gillett, "could scarcely have selected a place of confinement more nauseous and unhealthy. The monastery was situated near the spot where the Rhine issues from the Lake of Constance. Here he was thrown into an underground apartment, through which every sort of impurity was discharged into the lake. . . . The noxious stench and effluvia of the place were not long in producing their effect on the health of the prisoner. In a few hours Huss was thrown into a violent fever, which threatened his life."

When Chlum went to remonstrate with some of the cardinals on the gross injustice of thus confining a man who had the emperor's safe-conduct, one of them alleged that the council could act as it pleased with such documents; another, that no faith need be kept with heretics; and two others, learning the nature of his errand beforehand, closed their doors against him. The emperor had not yet arrived in Constance, but Chlum determined to write to him, requesting redress of the gross outrage. At first the emperor was indignant at this violation of his authority and promise, and dispatched an embassy at once to Constance to insist on the immediate release of Huss. Meantime the prisoner's physicians having insisted on his removal from his noisome underground cell, as essential to his life, he was removed to a more healthy apartment above ground. Here he was presented with a list of charges against him; and on his asking, on account of his inability from imprisonment and sickness to defend himself, that he might have an advocate to assist him in his defense, his request was denied, and he was cruelly told that, according to canon law, no one could be allowed to plead the cause of a man suspected of heresy!

Every day some new accusation seemed to be devised, and the vexations and insults to which he was subjected, and the artifices and intrigues employed to prevent his having a hearing before the Council, we are told, "were enough to drive him to despondency. But, in spite of all, his trust in God and in the justice of his cause, remained unshaken; and the writings which issued from his prison-cell attest his incessant activity." The order from the emperor for his release was not obeyed, but the strictness of his confinement was increased. The pope had a secret purpose to engage the attention of men's minds on the supposed heresy of Huss, in order to screen himself from the measures which he was well aware his own wickedness might bring down upon himself, should the attention of the Council be turned toward the correction of hierarchical abuses or corruption.

About the end of the year 1414, the Emperor Sigismund at length arrived in Constance, but from motives of policy he connived at the confinement of John Huss. During the spring of 1415, Huss was removed to the Franciscan monastery, with the intent, it is supposed, of having him more an object of attention to the members of the Council. But the intrigues set on foot in that body for a time struck at the man who occupied the papal chair, instead of his prisoner; and to such a pitch did the dissatisfaction with John XXIII. increase, that it culminated in a demand for his abdication, and he fled secretly from the city of Constance. The Council, however, continued its sittings as before; and, at its eighth session, the writings of Wycliffe, which had previously been submitted to a commission of examination, were condemned as heretical, the decree adding, that the body and bones of the English reformer, if they could be found and distinguished, should be disinterred, and cast out from sepulture!

The flight of the pope, with several of his adherents, threw the custody of Huss into the hands of the Emperor

Sigismund. In a few days a scene occurred which may be best related in the words of his biographer Gillett: "The reformer's faithful friend, De Chlum, accompanied by other Bohemian nobles, waited on Sigismund in the hope of procuring his release. They pointed out to him the favorable occasion now afforded of delivering an innocent man from indescribable sufferings, while he would vindicate his own honor and that of the empire from the contempt to which they had been subjected. Sigismund listened in embarrassed silence. He protested, not without confusion excited by a sense of his own injustice, that the future destiny of the professor lay not in his hands, but in those of the four presidents of the several nations of the Council. All that he himself would consent to was, that the nobles might pay the invalid a short visit in the presence of witnesses.

"Conducted by the emperor's attendants, the Bohemians proceeded to the Franciscan convent. There they found Huss, to outward view a pitiable object. He lay stretched on a miserable couch, emaciated, and wasted almost to a skeleton. On the ground before him lay a small strip of paper. They picked it up, and though the writing upon it was scarce legible, it told the story of neglect which would soon have saved the stake a victim: 'If you still love me, entreat the emperor to allow his people to provide for me, or else enable me to find sustenance for myself!' Such were the words they read.

"Huss had formerly been scantily supplied from the pope's kitchen; but since his flight, had been entirely overlooked. For three days the weak, enfeebled prisoner had been without food. Meekly and uncomplainingly did he endure what God had seen fit to suffer wicked men to inflict upon him. At the melancholy sight, the bearded warriors were melted into tears, but their resentment was roused. With uplifted hands and eloquent eyes, they besought Heaven to give them, at some future period, an opportunity of avenging with their swords such inhuman cruelty and injustice. . . . . . The meeting of Huss and his friends, says the chronicle, was very melancholy, and the parting was still more sad. For they loved Huss as their father, and their hearts were full of gloomy forebodings. When the sufferer had received the last embrace of his countrymen, he sank back fainting on his chains.

"The next day he was given over by the emperor and the Council to the rigid custody of the Bishop of Constance. By order of the latter, he was conveyed by water to the castle of Gottlieben. Armed men accompanied the prisoner till they reached the spot, on the banks of the Rhine, three miles distant from Constance. He was thrown into the tower, and treated with a severity which would have been harshness even to the greatest criminal. Irons were fastened to his feet, and during the day he might move the length of his chain; but at night he was chained by his arms to the wall. With such inhuman cruelty—enough to crush the boldest. spirit—Huss was to be prepared to stand up alone against a host of enemies that thirsted for his blood. Undoubtedly there were men among them who would deliberately prefer to browbeat an invalid, or argue with one too weak to defend his own cause, than contend with the living vigorous energy of thought and action that had electrified a whole kingdom."

During the spring an attack was made in the Council on Huss's ardent and faithful friend, Jerome of Prague, then in that city. This generous and impulsive man, possessed of much less coolness and prudence than John Huss, hearing of the imprisonment and danger of his venerated teacher, had determined to proceed to Constance and exert his endeavors for his relief or defense. He was probably at that time unaware that two citations had already issued from the Council, at the instigation of that notoriously bad man, Michael de Causis, for his own appearance to defend himself before that body. The Bohemians in Constance, on his arrival in that city, urged the risk of his staying there, and the impossibility of his being of any service to his suffering friend. Jerome, however, seems by some means to have found admittance to Huss's prison; but when he saw his dismal condition, and the chains about his limbs, and found the harsh treatment to which he was subjected, and the still more cruel prospect which, in all probability, awaited him, he was seized with a sort of panic, and took to flight with great precipitancy. It was soon found that he had been in the city, and had left it; but he contrived, by the help of some of his countrymen, to reach the free city of Uberlingen, where he deemed himself more secure. Here he was, on reflection, struck with shame at the thought of fleeing without having really attempted anything for the safety of his friend. He wrote therefore both to the emperor and the Council, requesting a safe-conduct for himself, in order that he might appear at Constance and justify himself and Huss from all calumnious charges. The emperor coldly refused the request. The Council replied that they would grant him a safe-conduct, but that "they had nothing more at heart than to catch the foxes which were ravaging the vineyard of the Lord;" and warned him also that the safe-conduct should be "excepting always the claims of the law, and that the orthodox faith does not in any way prevent it"—a pretty clear intimation of what it was worth, and what were their real intentions. Seeing no hope of doing anything effective, or of even safety for himself, he commenced his journey back to Prague, bearing with him a testimony from seventy Bohemian nobles, then in Constance, of his having done all in his power to render reasons for his faith, and of his having departed only because he could not safely remain.

Jerome reached the village of Hirschau, in the Black Forest; but here his natural rashness was the means of his being taken into custody. Being in a company of priests, and the conversation turning on the transactions of the Council, his indignation got the better of his discretion, and he launched forth invectives which soon excited the suspicions of his hearers that he was a heretic. Hearing him style that grand assembly "a synagogue of iniquity," they went and informed the officer in command of the place, and Jerome was at once arrested, cast into prison, and bound with chains. He was soon afterward conveyed to Constance, chained to a cart, his heavy irons clanking upon his limbs; and on his arrival, the Duke of Bavaria, surrounded by a mob as brutal as himself, undertook to pull and drag him about by his chains, and led him through the city as if he had been some wild beast. He was taken to the convent of the Minorites, and examined by the priests assembled for the purpose, in the midst of much agitation and noise. Gillett says that "a multitude of persons volunteered to give evidence against him. He had visited all the universities of Europe, and the fame of his eloquence, if not the vanquishing force of his arguments, had excited the jealousy and envy of many who were here present." As might be expected, there was a great clamor against him, and many frivolous and empty charges were brought. He replied that if he had taught erroneously, he desired to be instructed in what respect it was erroneous, and he would be corrected with all humility; and requested them to specify any error distinctly. A murmur soon arose among them, "Let him be burned, let him be burned!" To which he said: "If it be your pleasure that I should die, in the name of God be it so." The Bishop of Saltzburg was the only one to show the least feeling of compassion, reminding the assembly that it was written, that the Lord "willeth not the death of the sinner, but that he should turn and live." But the clamor was such that his appeal was of no avail. Jerome was remanded to prison, bound, and placed in charge of the Archbishop of Riga. This professed minister of Him who is boundless in goodness and mercy had Jerome removed to the dungeon of a tower in a certain cemetery, ordering him to be heavily ironed. "His chains were riveted to a lofty beam in such a way as to prevent his sitting down, while his arms were forced by fetters to cross on his neck behind, compelling him to incline his head forward and downward. For two days he was kept in this posture, his only food being bread and water.* At length a friend of his found out his distressed circumstances, through one of his keepers, and obtained for him the indulgence of better food. His health giving way under his grievous restraint, some of his irons were, after a time, taken off; but he was kept in prison for a whole year before he was subjected to the penalty of the flames.

Soon after Jerome's arrest, the Bohemians in Constance appealed to the Council in behalf of Huss and of his threatened disciples at Prague. They spoke of him as an innocent man, insisting that he should be liberated, or, at least, that his restraint should be alleviated, and that he should be allowed a public audience, especially as he had been confined in violation of his safe-conduct. His enemies in the Council parried all arguments in his favor either by further false charges or by evasions and clamor, and nothing was effected for his relief. The Council was busy deposing Pope John XXIII., whose iniquities were too scandalous to allow him to be screened from public reprobation. This was at length, after many intrigues on his part,

* Gillett's Life of John Huss.

accomplished, and the ex-pontiff was actually imprisoned in the same building which contained his own former prisoner, the Bohemian reformer. This, however, did nothing for Huss's safety; for the Emperor Sigismund, for political purposes, had turned against him, and his enemies therefore had entire control in the Council.

But after the pope was disposed of, and some measures taken toward ordering the election of another, the Council had to listen to another remonstrance from the Bohemian nobles, demanding an alleviation of Huss's cruel constraint in irons, and a public audience for his defense. They reluctantly consented to the latter, and fixed a day for his appearance before them. A commission was appointed to draw up the charges against him, who visited him in his prison a few days before the time appointed, endeavoring to ensnare him by insidious questions, or to shake his constancy by insults and threats. But he was cautious and firm, and gave them no advantage, while he distinctly let them know that he did not wish to maintain anything obstinately, but was willing to receive instruction from any one.

They had drawn up thirty articles against him, and urged him then and there to answer in regard to them. But he preferred to defer his answers till he should come before the Council. In one of his letters to his friends, describing the occasion, Huss says: "Michael de Causis stood by, with a paper in his hand, urging the patriarch to use force to make me reply to his questions. The bishops then came in and interrogated in their turn.—God has permitted Causis and Paletz to rise up against me for my sins. The one examined and remarked on all my letters, and the other brought up conversations that had taken place between us many years back.—The patriarch would insist on it that I was exceedingly rich, and an archbishop even named the very sum, namely, 70,000 florins.—Oh, certainly my sufferings to day were great! One of the bishops said to me, 'You have established a new law;' and another, 'You have preached up all these articles.' My answer simply was, 'Why do you overwhelm me with outrage?' "

We are told by Gillett, "It was on the fifth of June, 1415, that Huss was removed from the prison at Gottlieben, where he had remained for more than two months, and brought to Constance. But even here he was not permitted to meet his friend, Jerome. The latter was confined in the tower of St. Paul's Cemetery, while the former was placed in the monastery of the Franciscans, where he was to remain, for the greater part of the time loaded with irons, till the hour [day] of his martyrdom."

Several hours previous to his arrival before the Council, they were occupied in forwarding measures looking to his condemnation. The emperor on being informed of this became indignant at such flagrant injustice, and sent to the Council to enjoin it upon them not to determine the case, until they had heard Huss with calmness and impartiality. Huss was accordingly at length produced before them, and on some of his books being presented to his notice, he acknowledged that they were his, and promised "that he would rectify, with the most hearty good-will, any error or mistaken proposition which any man among them would point out." The reading of the articles then commenced; but as soon as Huss undertook to reply, such a clamor and disturbance arose through the whole assembly, that he could by no means be heard. This disturbance went on as they proceeded from article to article; so that one who was present has testified that the proceedings were characterized rather by the ferocity of wild beasts, than by the serious deportment of Christian teachers assembled to decide one of the gravest questions. At length, during a lull,

Huss was heard appealing to the Holy Scriptures. This produced another outbreak of invective and derision. They laughed him to scorn, and any attempt to make himself heard and listened to, was perfectly futile. Some there seemed to be struck with a degree of sympathy for the prisoner, so beset by determined enemies, but their voices were smothered in the general uproar. It was like a mob. No order was preserved. The members were crying out against Huss, and interrupting each other at the top of their voices. The prisoner at one brief interval remarked: "I supposed that there had been more fairness, kindness, and order in the Council." Even for this he was rebuked. When he asked to be instructed in what respect he had erred, the presiding cardinal replied, "As you ask to be informed, you must first recant your doctrine!"

As the disturbance continued, Huss gazed over the disgraceful scene, and was impelled to express his surprise: "I anticipated a different reception, and had imagined that I should obtain a hearing. I am unable to make myself audible over so great a noise, and I am silent because I am forced to it. I would willingly speak were I listened to." The more moderate members were disgusted with the disorder, and urged an adjournment for two days, which was acceded to. Meantime, on the day adjourned to, there was an almost total eclipse of the sun; and so awe-struck were these guilty ecclesiastics, that they did not assemble till about one o'clock, when the eclipse had passed away. Sigismund attended the adjourned sitting, having been requested by the Bohemian nobles to be present, in the hope that by that means some decent order might be maintained. Huss was led in, loaded with chains, and attended by a body of soldiers. He was placed directly in front of that monarch who had given him a safe-conduct, but whose word had been thus trampled on by others, and the outrage connived at by himself. He may now have encouraged a hope of saving the prisoner's life, by restraining the violence of his enemies; yet he was giving way, little by little, to those who were presently to prove too strong a current for him to resist.

The views of Huss were sought to be identified with those of Wycliffe, the more readily to bring about his condemnation; though he had never sanctioned all the doctrines of the English reformer, and indeed in several respects did not go so far. The Cardinal of Cámbray dishonorably strove to entangle him in a scholastic dispute on a question of the idle and fantastical philosophy to which he was accustomed in the University of Paris; but Huss warily gave him such a reply as left his adversaries no advantage. Several false charges were brought against him, some of which he plainly asserted were groundless, and others he showed from his books to be falsified quotations, or perversions of his meaning. Some of the articles which were brought forward as heretical, he maintained to be sound doctrine according to Holy Scripture. One priest charged him with having said "that St. Gregory was a jester, or a wag;" which he firmly denied, complaining of the injustice done him, as he had ever very highly esteemed Gregory. But the Cardinal of Florence alleged that they had twenty men to testify to the truth of it; though it does not appear that his witnesses were brought forward. This man spoke to Huss in such a manner as to show that he meant to intimidate him to a recantation. But Huss replied, "I call God and my own conscience to witness, that I never have taught, or even thought of teaching, as these men have dared to testify in regard to what they never heard. And even though there were many more arrayed against me, I make more account of the witness of the Lord my God, and of my own conscience, than I do of the judgments of all my adversaries, which I regard as nothing."

At one time, Huss having spoken of appealing "to Christ, the sovereign judge," he was asked whether it was lawful for him, not having received absolution from the Roman pontiff, to appeal to Christ. And, on his seriously and earnestly maintaining that no appeal could be more just than to implore the aid of Christ, the judge over all, and the ready helper of the afflicted and oppressed, he was met by a shower of jeers and mockery from the whole Council.* And again, on his stating the falsity of a certain charge in regard to Wycliffe, but adding that "he would that his soul might be where John Wycliffe was," this was a signal for another outburst of jeers and derision against their helpless prisoner.

When several charges were disproved, his enemy Paletz seized an opportunity to say, "Yes, most reverend fathers, not only men of other nations, but of Bohemia itself, have been driven out by John Huss and his counsels, some of whom are yet in exile in Moravia." "How," asked Huss —astonished at such a falsehood—"how can this be true, since I was not once at Prague at the time when those men you speak of were sent away?" Their banishment had in fact occurred after his withdrawal from the city. He was repeatedly charged with obstinacy, and the emperor, after a while, advised him to submit to the judgment of the Council, rather than run the extreme hazard which otherwise awaited him. Huss respectfully replied, calling the Almighty to witness, that he had never cherished anything like obstinacy or stubbornness, and that he came among them with this intent, that if any one could give him better instruction, he would unhesitatingly change his

* "Die heiligen Väter brachen darüber blos in ein lautes Hohngelächter aus," says Zitte (vol. ii. p. 113).

views. The soldiers then took him back to his quarters, and the Council adjourned.

The next day, at his third audience, much the same conduct was pursued toward him. Thirty-nine articles, professedly taken from his writings, were read. Those which had been fairly taken, he acknowledged; but others had been drawn up by Paletz in such a manner, that he would not acknowledge any responsibility for them. He was, besides, reproached with several things which he showed clearly to be falsehoods, and he replied to all the articles in a firm but calm and dignified manner. To those articles which had been shown to him beforehand, and of which he had a transcript, he replied in writing; but many things were charged against him verbally, any member of the Council thinking himself at liberty to interrupt and browbeat the prisoner, by allegations of what he professed to know, without adducing any proof; and the Cardinal of Cambray repeatedly declared that Huss's writings contained many things that were "still more detestable and atrocious" than what the articles contained. A great deal of sophistry, and still more of puerile reasoning, if reasoning it could be called, was thrown out against him. Some of the charges, if faults in Huss, were equally against the late transactions of the Council in deposing the pope; and Huss took occasion to let them see that if they condemned what he had said, they condemned their own position. But such things were generally passed over as slightly as possible, to save their own authority. When they could not reply to what he said, as for instance, when he reminded them that at one time the Romish church, having elected a woman, Agnes, to be pope, was in fact without a real earthly head for nearly two years and a half, and that it was quite as well governed during that time by its heavenly head, Christ Jesus, and added that in the times of the apostles the church was infinitely better ruled than it was now; and that at present they had no earthly head at all, but yet Christ did not fail to rule his church; the Council could not undertake to refute what he said, but treated it with sneers and derision.

When all the charges had been gone through, a discussion arose in regard to the steps to be taken with the prisoner. At length they concluded that, "in the first place, Huss was to confess that he had erred; secondly, he was to promise that he would never teach again the same doctrines; and thirdly, he should recant the articles charged against him." The Cardinal of Cambray then addressed him. "You have heard," said he, "of how many atrocious crimes you are accused. It is your duty now to consider what course you will take." And he went on to exhort him to submit to the judgment of the Council. Others also urged him to submission. Huss reminded them of what he had already told them, that he came not in stubbornness, but with an entire willingness to submit to be instructed, if his views were in any point incorrect; and he therefore asked that he might have a further opportunity of defending the correctness of his views and course; and then if he did not bring plain and sufficient proof, he would readily submit to their direction. On this, some one shouted at the top of his voice, "Notice the sophistry of his words. He says 'direction,' not *correction* or *decision*." "Yes," replied Huss, "as you wish it—direction, correction, or decision; I protest before God that I spoke in all sincerity of mind."

Cambray and several others now again urged him to recant. But he replied, "Again I say that I am ready to be instructed and set right by the Council. But in the name of Him who is the God of us all, I ask and beseech of you this one thing, that I may not be forced to that which, my conscience being repugnant to it, I cannot do under peril of the loss of my soul—recant, by oath, all the articles against me." He went on to say that to recant or abjure was to renounce an error previously held, and that many of these things charged against him he had never held; but in regard to such as were indeed his own, if he could be instructed that he was in error, he would readily yield. The emperor attempted to persuade him that he might properly *renounce* all errors whatever, without its necessarily following that he had held errors. Huss meekly answered him, "Most merciful emperor, the word has a very different signification from that in which your majesty has used it." Sigismund then plainly intimated to the prisoner the danger he incurred by persisting in his refusal to recant. But Huss continued to request to be heard further. After much altercation, and many attempts again to ensnare and intimidate their almost exhausted victim, the day drawing to a close, further proceedings were deferred till the day following, and Huss was again led to his prison. After the adjournment, the emperor expressed to some of the prominent members his view that the charges against Huss were such, that "each of them was deserving of death by fire:" yet if he would consent to banishment and silence, and this could be effectually accomplished so as to insure the destruction of the heresy now afloat by his means, he thought it ought to be done.

About a month was now passed by Huss in prison at Constance, awaiting the conclusion of his judges. During that time he was preparing his mind for the result which he deemed almost inevitable, though the delay at times seemed calculated to inspire some hope that his life might yet be spared. He was during this month constantly urged by various people, and even by a deputation from the Council at one time, and from the emperor at another, to submit to the judgment of the assembly, and abjure the errors imputed to him. He still felt that he could not with a clear conscience renounce or recant doctrines which he had never held, nor disavow those, of the error of which he was not convinced. The Cardinal of Florence, Zabarella, who was inclined to moderation, was really anxious to save his life, and is said to have prepared a form of recantation which it was thought by some of his friends he might safely subscribe, as it was as little as could be expected by any who desired the infallibility of the Council's judgment to be maintained by the submission of the prisoner. But Huss looked at it with the feelings of one to whom clearness of conscience was of far more value than personal safety. He saw that to adopt it would be a compromise of principle. He expressed his gratitude for the kind feeling which had prompted the suggestion, but calmly informed them that he dared not submit in the way proposed, for he must needs thereby condemn many truths, and perjure himself by confessing that he had held errors, thus occasioning scandal to the people of God who had heard his preaching.

He was perfectly beset by the repeated importunities of many who respected his character and talents, and desired that his life might be spared. But in his mind there appears to have been no wavering. "I would sooner," he said in one of his letters to his friends, "have a millstone bound about my neck, and be cast into the sea, than give occasion of scandal to my neighbor; and having preached to others constancy and endurance, I will set them an example, looking for help to the grace of God." One of the doctors urged him to submission by this argument: "Even though the Council should tell you that you have but one eye, when you have two, you would be bound to assent to their statement." But Huss replied, "While

God spares my reason, I would never allow such a thing, though the whole world were agreed upon it, because I could not say it without wounding my conscience."

In another letter, in speaking of his conviction that he should thereby "commit perjury and give offense to many of God's children," he says: "Far be it, far be it from me! For my Master, Christ, shall be hereafter my reward, while even now he gives me the aid of his presence." He wrote many letters during this brief month of respite, encouraging his friends at home to faithfulness, and giving them parting admonitions. In these letters his humility is often conspicuous, as well as his Christian firmness. In several he warns them not to be misled by anything in him that may have been wrong. He confesses that he had in time past done wrong in playing at chess, and in indulging in dress. And in one letter he says, among many affectionate and earnest exhortations: "I beseech, moreover, if any one has observed any levity in my speech or conduct, that he copy not my example, but intercede with God in my behalf that such levity may be forgiven me." It is an epistle of some length, toward the conclusion of which he thus alludes to the approaching event: "This letter have I written to you in prison and in chains; and this morning I have heard of the decision of the Council, that I must be burned. But I have full confidence in God that he will not forsake me, nor permit me to deny his truth, or with perjury confess as mine the errors falsely imputed to me by lying witnesses. But how gently God my Master deals with me, and supports me through surprising conflicts, ye shall learn, when, amid the joys of the life to come, we shall, through the grace of Christ, behold one another again."

In still another letter to his friends at home, he thus expresses the grounds of his comfort and confidence: "That word of our Saviour much consoles me, 'Blessed be ye when men shall hate you. Rejoice ye in that day, and leap for joy, for behold, great is your reward in heaven.' A good consolation—nay, the best consolation; difficult, however, if not to understand, yet perfectly to fulfill, to rejoice amid those sufferings. This rule James observes, who says, 'My beloved brethren, count it all joy when ye fall into divers temptations, knowing this, that the trial of your faith worketh patience.' Assuredly it is a hard thing to rejoice without perturbation, and in all these manifold temptations to find nothing but pure joy. Easy it is to say this, and to expound it, but hard to fulfill it in very deed. For even the most steadfast and patient warrior, who knew that he should rise on the third day—who by his death conquered his enemies and redeemed his chosen from perdition, was, after the last supper, troubled in spirit, and said, 'My soul is exceeding sorrowful, even unto death'—and he sweat, as it were, great drops of blood falling down to the ground. But he who was in such trouble said to his disciples, 'Let not your heart be troubled,' etc. Hence his soldiers, looking to him as their king and leader, endured great conflicts, went through fire and water, and were delivered. And they received from the Lord that crown of which James speaks, i. 12. That crown will God bestow on me and you, as I confidently hope, ye zealous combatants for the truth, with all who truly and perseveringly love our Lord Jesus Christ, who suffered for us, leaving behind an example that we should follow his steps. It was necessary that he should suffer, as he tells us himself; and we must suffer, that so the members may suffer with the Head; for so he says, 'Whoever would follow me, let him take up his cross and follow me.' O, most faithful Christ, draw us weak ones after thee; for we cannot follow thee if thou dost not draw us.

Give us a strong mind, that it may be prepared and ready. And if the flesh is weak, succor us beforehand by thy grace, and accompany us, for without thee we can do nothing; and least of all, can we face a cruel death. Give us a ready and willing spirit, an undaunted heart, the right faith, a firm hope, and perfect love, that patiently and with joy we may for thy sake give up our life."

Such were some of his last expressions to those who had shared his friendship and his conflicts at home. Here was no self-confidence, no boasting of his own attainments, but an evidence of humble trust and faith in divine help.

His confinement continued very strict, and his treatment by the authorities is said to have even increased in harshness. None of his friends were allowed to visit him, and the wives of his jailers, who had evinced a disposition to show him kindness, were prohibited from any such attentions.

We are told by Gillett, that "an assembly was held on the first of July (1415) in the Franciscan monastery, and Huss was brought before it, and publicly urged to abjure. He now presented a paper, drawn up by his own hand, in which he once more stated the grounds of his refusal: 'I, John Huss, in hope, a priest of Jesus Christ, fearing to sin against God, and fearing to commit perjury, am not willing to abjure all and each of the articles which have been produced against me on false testimony. For, God being my witness, I have not preached, asserted, nor defended them as they have said that I have preached, defended, or asserted. Moreover, in regard to the extracted articles, if any of them implies anything false, I disavow and detest it. But through fear of sinning against the truth, and speaking against the views of holy men, I am unwilling to abjure any of them. And if it were possible for my voice now to reach the whole world,—as every falsehood and every sin which I have committed will be brought to light in the day of judgment,—I would most cheerfully recall everything false or erroneous which I ever spoke or thought of speaking, and I would do it before the world. These things I say and write freely, and of my own accord.'—Such a position as Huss had taken did not pay that homage to the infallibility of the Council which was considered essential. He was led back to prison."

Four days afterward, the emperor, who appears to have had fears of the consequences of Huss's execution, particularly in Bohemia, and was anxious to avert any danger of public disturbance in the heart of Europe, once more sent to inquire if he would not recant. The deputation consisted of the cardinals of Cambray and Florence, the patriarch of Antioch, six bishops, and a doctor of laws; accompanied by Huss's friends, Chlum and Duba; who probably eagerly seized this opportunity of once more seeing and conversing with a man whom they so truly esteemed, and whose case they so deeply commiserated. To the solicitations of the deputation Huss made the same answer he had done to all others, declaring with tears at the same time, in the presence of the Almighty, his readiness to be instructed if in anything he had taught error. Chlum encouraged him, if convinced of error, to yield without hesitation; but if in his conscience he felt himself innocent, to beware of leaving the path of duty and committing perjury, through any apprehension of death. At last, "See," said the bishops, "how obstinately he perseveres in his errors!"

The day at length arrived when his faithfulness was to be put to the last test. "It was on the following day," says Gillett, "that Huss appeared for the last time before the Council, now in its fifteenth session. There was a full attendance. ..... The emperor himself was present," crowned and seated on a magnificent throne, surrounded by the princes and ecclesiastical dignitaries of his empire, in all their splendor. "An immense crowd had assembled from all quarters. ..... The celebration of mass had already commenced when Huss arrived; but he was kept outside the door till the religious services were over, under the pretence that the holy mysteries would be profaned by the presence of so great a heretic. At length Huss was brought in. ..... He was required to take his stand in front of the platform, on a stool, so as to be visible to the whole Council. Here he fell upon his knees, and remained for some time engaged in prayer in a low tone."

The Bishop of Lodi then ascended the pulpit, and addressed the assembly with a long discourse calculated to prepare them for the scene which was to follow; concluding by almost idolatrous adulation of the emperor, as elected by God, deputed in heaven before chosen on earth, endued by the Almighty with the wisdom of divine truth for the performance of so holy a work as destroying heresies, "and especially *this* obstinate heretic, by whose malign influence many regions have been infected with the pest of heresy;" blasphemously adding, "From the mouths of babes and sucklings shall thy praises be long celebrated, as the avenger of the Catholic faith, and the destroyer of its enemies." After this, silence was proclaimed in "the holy Council of Constance, lawfully assembled by the influence of the Holy Spirit;" and all language, murmuring, and noise "which may disturb this assembly convoked with the inspiration of God," was forbidden under penalty of excommunication and imprisonment. Such was the high assumption which this wicked assembly dared to arrogate!

After pronouncing condemnation on the doctrines of Wycliffe, the Council proceeded with reading thirty articles against Huss, some of which had not before been publicly read. Huss attempted to reply to some of them as they were read; but was stopped by the Bishop of Cambray, who ordered him to be silent, and, when he answered, to reply to all at once. Huss reminded him, but in vain, that it would be out of his power to remember the whole list of accusations. When he again attempted to defend himself, the officers were ordered to seize him, and force him to be silent. Being unwilling that the assembled multitude should be induced to believe that he acquiesced in the truth of these charges, with a loud voice, and his hands lifted toward heaven, he exclaimed, "In the name of Almighty God, I beseech you, deign to afford me an equitable hearing, that I may clear myself at least before those who surround me, and remove from their minds the suspicion of errors. Grant me this favor, and then do with me what you will." "Here he was again interrupted, and ordered to be silent; at which he kneeled down, and commended his cause in prayer to God, the most righteous judge." A great variety of charges were brought, in order to prove his heresy. One of them was, that he had given out that he was a "fourth person in the holy trinity!" "Give me the name," said he, "of the lying doctor who testifies thus against me." But he was told by the bishop who read the accusation, "There is no need of it." Huss solemnly asserted its falsehood, denying that such a thing had ever been thought of by him.

When they charged him with a contempt of the papal excommunication, he had to go into a relation of the circumstances that had attended him for some time, and reminded the Council that he had come thither freely, "relying upon the public faith of the emperor, who is here present, assuring me that I should be safe from all violence, so that I might attest my innocence and give a reason of my faith." As he spoke thus of the safe-conduct, he fixed his eyes steadily upon the emperor, and a deep blush at once mounted to the imperial brow. Sigismnnd felt the shame and meanness of which he had been guilty.

After all the accusations had been gone through, one of the judges of the court made a statement, that Huss had repeatedly given out that he would submit to the judgment of the Council, but that he still persisted in his position, notwithstanding all the means of *persuasion* (not convincement) that could be made use of. A long document was then read, referring to the already condemned writings of John Wycliffe, whom they style a man "of damnable memory," confirming the decree of the Council of Rome respecting them, and then charging John Huss with being a disciple of that "heresiarch," and condemning his books to the flames wherever they could be found. After this paper was read, Huss said to his judges, "Who are ye, that ye can justly condemn my writings? For I always desired that they should be corrected by a better application and understanding of Christian truth; and this is still my wish. And yet, hitherto ye have not presented any solid arguments against them, nor have ye convicted of error a single word of my writings. Why, then, have ye been impelled to destroy my books, whether rendered in the Bohemian or other language—those, moreover, which doubtless ye have never seen? And, if ye were to see them, your ignorance of the Bohemian language would prevent your understanding them." After complaining of other injustice in the accusation, he knelt down in supplication, with his eyes upturned toward heaven.

They then read the sentence condemning Huss himself. After asserting that the charges have been "made most clearly manifest," that he "has taught many things evil, scandalous, seditious, and dangerously heretical, and preached the same through a long course of years," it declares that "this most holy Council of Constance—the name of Christ being invoked—having only God before their eyes"—pronounces that the said Huss is a manifest heretic, has taught errors and heresies, etc., and treated with contempt the keys of the church, and has interposed his appeal to the Lord Jesus Christ, laying down many positions false and scandalous in regard to the apostolic see, and that he is pertinacious and incorrigible; wherefore they condemn him as a heretic, and decree that he be deposed and degraded from the priesthood "in the presence of this most holy synod."

When the charge of obstinacy was read, Huss promptly denied it, saying: "This I do utterly deny. I have ever desired, and I still desire to be better instructed from Scripture; and I solemnly declare that such is my zeal for the truth, that if, by a single word, I might confound the errors of all heretics, there is no danger that I would not face in order to do it." After the sentence was all read, he once more fell on his knees, and, in earnest and distinct tones, prayed for his enemies; while "scorn and derision were traced in the features of the members of the Council, and were uttered in their sneers."*

The persons appointed now approached him to perform the ceremony of degradation. He was clothed in the usual priestly robes instead of his prison garments, and the mass cup placed in his hand. When thus clad, he was made to stand up on the platform to be seen by the people, to whom he now expressed a few solemn and clear words of exculpation, in order that they might not be misled. He was then made to descend from the platform, and was stripped of his priestly robes by the bishops. First they took from him the cup, saying, "O, thou accursed Judas!

* Gillett, vol. ii. p. 62. See also Zitte, vol. ii. p. 242.

—behold we take from thee this chalice, in which the blood of Jesus Christ for the redemption of the world is offered." Huss exclaimed: "But I have all hope and confidence fixed in my God and Saviour, that he will never take from me the cup of salvation; and I abide firm in my belief that, aided by his grace, I shall this day drink thereof in his kingdom!" What a heavenly foretaste he evidently experienced! Well worth all the sufferings of the body that wicked men were about to inflict upon him.

As they proceeded to strip him of the remaining symbols of the priestly office, accompanying the removal of each with an awful curse upon him, Huss said: "All these insults I can endure, undisturbed and calm, for the name and truth of Jesus Christ."

The Council then, by declaration, delivered him over "to the secular arm," for execution under the civil authority. As they prepared to place upon his head the paper crown—a sort of tall pointed cap, conical at the bottom and three-sided upward, with frightful figures of demons painted on its sides, and the word *heresiarch* distinctly written in large characters—they said, "We devote thy soul to the devils of hell!"—"But I," replied the martyr, lifting his eyes to heaven, and reverently folding his hands, "I commend it to my most merciful Master, Jesus Christ." He looked at the hideous crown as they placed it on his head, and calmly said: "My Lord Jesus Christ, though innocent, deigned to bear to an ignominious death, for wretched me, a far rougher and weightier crown of thorns."

He was then placed in the hands of the executioners, who were commanded to burn him, with his clothes, and all that belonged to him, "even to his knife and his purse, from which they were not to take so much as a single penny." He was led to the place of execution without his chains, accompanied by several officers, and escorted by the princes, a body of eight hundred soldiers, and an immense multitude of people attracted by curiosity or pity. The procession went by the episcopal palace, apparently that their victim might have an opportunity of seeing his books consuming in the flames in front of that building.

There was a pause as they approached the meadow outside of the city, where the execution was to take place; and Huss kneeled down and prayed to the Almighty, using some of the psalmist's words in the thirtieth and fiftieth Psalms of the Vulgate, or thirty-first and fifty-first of the English version—the latter being the same psalm on which Savonarola, nearly a century afterward, wrote meditations in his prison a few days previous to his own martyrdom. After this he fervently exclaimed, "Into thy hands I commit my spirit—thou hast been the salvation thereof, O God of Truth!"* Some among the crowd were struck with the evidence of his piety and devotion, and exclaimed, "What this man may have done before, we know not; but now, certainly, we hear him speak and pray in a godly and devout manner!"

A man was now appointed to act as confessor, who desired him to renounce his errors; but Huss once more declined, and requested the privilege of addressing the people in the German language. Instead of granting this last and reasonable request, the Elector Palatine, who had charge of the execution, gave orders that he should be immediately committed to the flames. Huss then lifted up his voice again in prayer: "O Lord Jesus, I would endure with humility, for thy gospel, this cruel death; and I beseech thee, pardon all my enemies," etc. Obtaining permission to speak to his keepers, who had felt commiseration for him, and been affected by his pious example, he thanked

---

* Zitte, vol. ii. p. 250.

them in German for their kind treatment while they had him in charge, adding, "Ye have shown yourselves not merely my keepers, but brethren most beloved. And be assured that I rest with firm faith upon my Saviour, in whose name I am content calmly to endure this sort of death, that I this day may go to reign with him."

He was now fastened to the stake by seven wet cords, and an iron chain around his neck, with his hands bound behind his back. Two piles of fagots were placed about his bare feet, and bundles of straw were put round the stake, reaching upward as high as his neck. When everything was thus made ready, the emperor sent once more to make a final effort to induce his prisoner to evade death by recantation. The marshal of the empire brought the message to him; but Huss replied to it as he had done to all others, with a loud, clear voice, calling the Almighty to witness his innocency of the falsehoods charged against him, and his willingness to seal by his death the truth of what he had taught. The flames were then kindled; and, amid the smoke and blaze, Huss was once more heard engaged in prayer. Twice the words were heard, "O Christ, thou Son of the living God, have mercy upon me!" And again he was heard indistinctly, and at length bowed his head in the flames, and all was silent. The spirit had fled. The executioners barbarously struck and pushed the charred remains of the martyr, crushing his skull with a club, and utterly consuming everything to ashes. These were then carefully collected and carted away, to be thrown into the Rhine. Huss had that very day completed the forty-second year of his age.*

The biographer whom we have so often quoted in the delineation of his life, says of him: "The character of John Huss is one that the most virulent calumny has scarce

* Zitte, vol. ii. p. 258.

dared to touch. The purity of his life, the simplicity of his manners, his love of truth, his deep conscientiousness, his aversion to all assumption or display, his strong sympathy for the poor and ignorant, his readiness to obey each prompting of duty though it might carry him to the prison or the stake, are plainly legible in the whole story of his life. He has no false pride that forbids him to retract an error, or reject a truth. He only asks to be convinced, and he is willing to confess his mistake. We can see at times the impetuousness of his nature breaking out under the indignant sense of wrong or injustice. He utters his feelings in sharp and even burning words. Fearing not the face of man, he dares avow his doctrines before the world; and if the occasion demands, can lash the vices of men in power, with unsparing invective and reproof. And yet, so thoroughly is he master of himself, so perfectly has he schooled his passions to self-control, that rarely a word escapes his lips, or a step is taken, which he needs to recall. In all the prominent men of his age we look in vain for that combination of qualities by which he was eminently fitted for the task committed to his hands. He showed throughout his trial a presence of mind, and a power and quickness of apprehension, which are perfectly surprising, when we consider the hardships of his protracted imprisonment, for the most part deprived of books, and the tumultuous scenes in the Council, which at times made it more like a mob than a body of men assembled to deliberate and judge. In other reformers we can in almost every instance detect some weakness or excess that led them into blunders, and which we sadly regret. . . . But Huss pursued a course in which his decision and moderation, his conscientiousness and docility, his loyalty to truth and his respect for the rights and judgment of others, are happily blended. . . . Frank, genial, and confiding, he scorned all disguise of his views or feelings. His motives are transparent and avowed, and he is never ashamed to confess them. . . . . That he valued and desired the love of all good men, is obvious. But he seems never to have been carried away by the mere love of applause. In his controversies he never descends to personal abuse. He expresses, in strong language, his disapproval of the course of some of his party in the use of reproachful epithets. . . . . His social affections were warm and tender. . . . . We have indeed in Huss a man whose faculties were admirably balanced—true and devoted as a friend, powerful yet courteous as an antagonist, eloquent in the pulpit, faithful as a witness to the truth before the Council, a hero in the prison, and a martyr at the stake." And we may add, that although it was not given him to see through all the mysteries of iniquity attendant on the Romish system, nor all the corruptions of doctrine introduced by centuries of blind submission to its priesthood, yet he had the rare virtue of unwavering faithfulness, through all provocations and threats of the powers of this world (so far as appears even by the accounts of his enemies), to those principles of divine truth which had been made manifest to his understanding, and was willing to attest them at the stake by the sacrifice of his life, rather than purchase his personal safety by a base denial of his conscientious convictions.

The Bohemian historian Palacky gives the following estimate of the character of Huss:[*] predicated, he says, especially upon manuscripts of Huss in the Bohemian language which still exist, but which for the most part remain unpublished. After expressing his opinion that "the

---

[*] Kindly furnished to the author by Wm. G. Malin, of Philadelphia, who has made the history of the times of Huss, and of the Council of Constance, a special study, and has materially assisted in certain items of this account.

course of sermons preached by John Huss in the Bethlehem Chapel at Prague were among the most weighty and important events of his time," Palacky continues thus: "Less harsh in his language than Konrad Walthauser, less fanatical or visionary in his views than Milic, he wrought no such stormy emotion in his hearers as they had done; but the impression he made was much more enduring. Huss addressed himself especially to the understanding of his hearers, awakened reflection, first informed and convinced, and then failed not in impression and eloquent exhortation. The acuteness and clearness of his mind, the tact with which he at once penetrated to the core of any question, and the ease with which he unfolded and exhibited it to the eyes of all men; his great reading, especially of the Holy Scriptures, and the solidity and consistency with which he established and enforced his propositions, gave him pre-eminent influence among his colleagues and cotemporaries. To these great qualities were added powerful earnestness of purpose, a truly pious spirit, a daily life in which his bitterest enemy could find no subject of blame, a burning zeal for the moral elevation of his countrymen and the reformation of their church;—but also uncalculating boldness, regardlessness of consequences, inflexible determination, a strong thirst for popularity, and an ambition which regarded the martyr's crown as the highest object to which a mortal might aspire."

About ten months after his death, his friend Jerome, who had through weakness and fear given way so far as to disavow his true sentiments in hope of saving his life, found that such a compliance afforded him neither safety of body nor peace to his soul, and candidly came forward before the Council, condemning his recantation, and nobly advocating the principles which had really actuated him in the course in which John Huss and himself had been so closely united. The Council, as was to be expected, condemned him to the stake; and he perished in the same place that had witnessed the martyrdom of Huss.

CHAPTER IX.

GERHARD GROOT.

Much of what we know of this pious and benevolent man is from the warm and loving pen of Thomas à Kempis, with the addition of some other information collected recently from various sources by C. Ullmann.*

Gerhard Groot was born in the year 1340, at Deventer, in the Netherlands. His father, Werner Groot, was sheriff and burgomaster of that town. Of a feeble constitution of body, but endowed with superior mental powers, after receiving the rudiments of his education at school, he was induced by an ambition for knowledge to place himself, when about fifteen years of age, at the University of Paris, where he remained three years. He graduated as Master in his eighteenth year, and, at the desire of his father, returned home, furnished, it is said, with a good knowledge of the studies in which he had been engaged, but "with his youthful mind somewhat unhappily engaged with the curious and illicit arts" of magic—a strange sort of knowledge for a student at that far-famed academy. He afterward further pursued his studies at Cologne, became a professor there, and obtained several preferments.

Though he had thus entered the clerical ranks, yet, hav-

* " Reformers before the Reformation," vol. i.

ing ample pecuniary means, and his mind unrestrained as yet by subjection to the cross of Christ, but, on the contrary, enamored with the delights of the world, he seemed likely to pursue the usual path of self-indulgence. "He took part in public amusements, treated himself to the richest food and most costly wine, dressed his hair, wore gay clothes, a girdle with silver ornaments, and a cloak of the finest fur.* With prominent intellectual acquisitions, he was then a man according to the prevailing spirit of the times. But soon deeper and more serious sentiments awoke within him." While present one day as a spectator at some public game, an unknown person said to him, "Why dost thou stand here intent on vanities? Thou must become another man." But he was still more shaken by some expressions of an old Parisian acquaintance, Henry Aeger, who, meeting with him at Utrecht, took the opportunity to "admonish him with deep earnestness on the vanity of earthly things, and on death, eternity, and the chief good." This, it is added, struck the right chords in Gerhard's heart—no doubt reached the witness for truth in his own conscience—and, overcome with emotion, he promised that, with the help of the Almighty, he would renounce the world and change his course of life.

From that time he became indeed "another man." He "renounced the use of the emoluments of his prebends," and even of his patrimonial inheritance, "burned his costly books of magic, shunned all diversions, put on plain gray clothing, and calmly braved the derision which this conduct brought upon him." He gave up his lectures and orations, retired into the seclusion of a monastery, and there spent three years in serious reflection, reading the Holy Scriptures, and practising rigorous penitential exercises. He passed a considerable portion even of his nights in watch-

* Thomas à Kempis, *Vita Gerhardi Magni.*

ing and prayer, abstained from many things usually considered lawful, and thus endeavored to bring his body into subjection to the spirit. "His object," says Thomas à Kempis, "was first to learn for himself, what he was afterward to teach others."

It seems that he now refused to become a priest. He said, "I would not, for all the gold of Arabia, undertake the care of souls even for a single night." He would only consent to be ordained a deacon, in which office he would be at liberty publicly to instruct the people, without the pastoral care and responsibility. He then came forward as a Christian teacher of the people; and Ullmann says of him at this time, that "after obtaining from the Bishop of Utrecht a license to preach over the whole of his diocese, Gerhard was seen, as of old Peter de Bruys and Henry of Lausanne, and as in more recent times George Fox, William Penn, and others, in mean attire, travelling through towns and villages, and everywhere exhorting the people to repentance and amendment, with overpowering eloquence. As depicted by Thomas à Kempis, he labored in the spirit of John the Baptist, laying the axe to the root of the tree, and by preaching the law and repentance to his cotemporaries, now more and more generally sinking into wickedness, he again prepared them for the reviving gospel. His discourses, listened to by the great and the humble, by clergy and laity, went to the heart. It was not merely the copiousness and easy flow of his eloquence that struck the hearers, but a very different thing. Here was a preacher who spoke, not because it was his professional duty, nor for the sake of the pay (it is expressly mentioned that he received no pay from them to whom he preached, nor sought any temporal or ecclesiastical benefit), but freely and gratuitously, and because impelled by the zeal of love—a preacher in whom it was impossible not to mark deep concern and intense seriousness, and who sealed, by the actions of his life, the sentiments taught him by his own experience." He did not address the people, as many did, in the Latin language, which was foreign to them, but in the dialect of the country. Hence, in many places in Holland, where he first preached in low Dutch, the whole population, it is related, neglecting their meals and most urgent business, thronged in such multitudes to hear him, that the houses of worship were not able to contain them, and he was compelled to bring his audience into the open air. He frequently preached twice a day, often for three hours at a time, and the result was not mere wonder and transitory excitement, but actual conversion and permanent amendment. Many were induced, says a cotemporary, to renounce a worldly life, to devote themselves to God, to restore stolen property, give up usury, and live in chastity and temperance.

But he was by no means ignorant that the suspicions and hatred of the monks and common clergy followed him wherever he went. He had attacked unsparingly the corruption of this class, especially the manners of such as led impure lives; and this aroused many bitter enemies to him and his doctrine. The Bishop of Utrecht was at last prevailed upon to withdraw his license to preach; and though Gerhard modestly protested against this prohibition, yet on its being insisted upon, he avoided appealing to the indignant feelings of the people, and submitted to the mandate.

His exertions for the good of his fellow-creatures were now turned into a somewhat different though a congenial channel. Being thus prohibited from continuing to preach publicly to the people, his mind was directed to the education of youth, and, the art of printing not being yet known, to the copying of books of piety. In the year 1378, when about thirty-eight years of age, he paid a visit to the monastery of Grünthal, of which the aged John Ruysbroek was then prior. He was particularly struck with admiration in witnessing the social life—the family spirit—which prevailed among the canons of that religious house. They seemed to him, in their simplicity, to realize the idea of a brotherhood rather than of a monastic institution; and Thomas à Kempis says that, impressed by the edifying and simple life of Ruysbroek and his brethren, Gerhard thenceforth felt himself determined to form an institution of a similar kind. But this particular prospect was frustrated by his early death. He extended his journey to Paris, where he expended a considerable sum in the purchase of books for the instruction of youth. He then returned to his native town of Deventer.

He had always been fond of the society of young men. In Deventer there was a considerable school; and many of the youth who frequented it attached themselves to Gerhard Groot; who advised them about their studies, maintained with them scientific intercourse, read with them good books, entertained many of them at his table, and procured for them the opportunity of bettering their pecuniary condition, by earning a little money in useful employment.

Gerhard himself had quite a solicitude for the multiplying of copies of good books, especially of well-written copies of the Holy Scriptures. "Hence," says Ullmann, "he had long before employed young men under his oversight, as copyists, thereby accomplishing the threefold end of multiplying these good works, giving profitable employment to the youths, and obtaining an opportunity of influencing their minds. The circle of his youthful friends, scholars, and transcribers, became from day to day larger, and grew at length into a regular society. Having thus in part owed its origin to the copying of the Scriptures and devotional books, the society from the outset and through its whole continuance, made the Holy Scripture and its propagation, the copying, collecting, preserving, and utilizing of good books, one of its main objects."

Young Florentius Radewins, then Vicar of Deventer, one day said to Gerhard: "Dear master, what harm would it do, were I and these clerks, who are here copying, to put our weekly earnings into a common fund and live together?"—"Live together!" replied Gerhard; "the mendicant monks would never permit it; they would do their worst to prevent us."—"But what," said Florentius, "is to prevent us making the trial? Perhaps God would give us success."—"Well then," said Gerhard, "commence; I will be your advocate, and faithfully defend you against all who rise up against you." In this manner they formed themselves into a private society; and, as their manner of living in community was imitated, they grew at length into an extensive confederation, under the designation of "The Brethren of the Common Lot."

Thus was Gerhard Groot instrumental in founding an association which afterward, ramified through many parts of Germany and the Netherlands, exercised a powerful influence for good in the promotion of a pious education of youth, and in preparing the minds of the succeeding generation for the Reformation of the sixteenth century. These societies had in them something akin to those of Monachism, but without the vow, and without much of the superstition and mere legal performances, especially without the idleness and awful corruption of morals which had then fastened upon a very large proportion of them; on the contrary, they formed a union of brethren endeavoring after the apostolic pattern according to their apprehension of the primitive church, and combining for the cultivation, not of absolute recluseness, but of practical piety and usefulness to their fellow-men. Ullmann says they procured for themselves the means of a simple livelihood, partly like the Apostle Paul, by manual labor, and partly by receiving voluntary donations; which, however, none of the brethren were permitted to solicit, except in a case of urgent necessity. In this, too, they were clearly distinguished from the mendicant monks. To insure their common subsistence, and in token of their fraternal affection, they had introduced the principle of a community of goods. In most cases, each member surrendered what property he possessed, for the use of the society. But there seems to have been no strict or general law on the subject; all was to proceed from individual freedom and love. The object of the societies was the exemplification and spread of practical Christianity. This they endeavored to accomplish by the moral rigor and simplicity of their manner of living, by religious conversations, *mutual* confessions, admonitions, lectures, and social exercises of a devotional nature. For the promotion of the same object outwardly, they labored by transcribing and propagating Holy Scripture and other religious treatises, but most of all by the instruction of the people and the revival and improvement of the education of youth. In the schools of most of the large towns such wages were exacted from the scholars as only the more wealthy could pay; while the style of instruction was nevertheless very defective. The schools of the monks were equally unsatisfactory, very superficial, and often coarse and superstitious. "The Brethren of the Common Lot," says Ullmann, "on the contrary, not merely gave instruction gratuitously, and thereby rendered the arts of reading and writing attainable by all, both rich and poor; but, what was of most consequence, they imbued education with quite a new life and a purer and nobler spirit." Gerhard's views of school learning for the masses, were that it should be simple, practically useful, carefully guarded, all consistent with the doctrines of Holy Scripture, and all with a view to self-acquaintance, improvement, and progress in true piety; and these institutions thus arranged, constituted a turning point in the general system of juvenile and popular education; the beneficial results of which soon displayed themselves so convincingly, that Brother Houses were erected in a short time in different places in Holland, Westphalia, Saxony, etc.

Their practice of mutual confession to one another gave an indirect yet a very decided blow to the prevalent superstition of priestly confession and absolution. They also carefully avoided the use of oaths in their speech, preferring a simple affirmation or negation. Their efforts were directed to the great object of promoting prudence, rectitude, and the utmost conscientiousness, not merely in regard to actions, but even to the most minute word or expression. They introduced a much more substantial and correct method of teaching Latin and Greek than was then common in the schools, and were so successful in this, as to train and send forth some of the most eminent of the revivers of ancient literature at the close of the fifteenth and commencement of the sixteenth century. The use of the *mother-tongue* in religious matters, as practised by them, was a very important step in advance, greatly promoting the circulation of the Bible in the language of the people.

Gerhard was still a member of the Romish church, and probably attached from education to many or most of its doctrines. Yet was he a reformer in very deed, and helped essentially to pave the way for entire emancipation from its corruptions. He insisted earnestly upon the diligent use of the Holy Scriptures, and aided, as we have seen, in the multiplication of manuscript copies of them, which was no small labor. In the Scriptures, he sought chiefly that doctrine which is vital and efficacious, considering Christ as the root of life, and the sole foundation of the church. The primitive church was in his eyes a model of perfection; and in it he found a piety and zealous fervor, which, in his own days, he no longer beheld. While upholding the system of priesthood, he desired its reorganization on a genuine spiritual standard, and labored to correct its corruptions as then existing.

But he lived not long to carry all his purposes into practice. Toward the close of his life, but whether after he was attacked with his last sickness we are not informed, he often expressed a desire for death. Once, when longing after eternal life, he said to one of the brethren: "What have I any longer to do here on earth? Oh that I were with my Master in heaven!" In the year 1384 the plague visited the town of Deventer, and attacked one of Gerhard's friends. He hastened to his help, having some skill in medicine; but was himself smitten with the disease. And now, when he felt death obviously approaching, he met it with exemplary resignation, saying, "Lo, I am now summoned by the Lord. The hour of my departure is come." To the brethren who stood weeping around his bed, and lamenting the anticipated loss of so valued a preceptor, he said: "Set your confidence in God, my dear friends, and fear not what the men of this world may say. Be steadfast; for man cannot prevent what God has determined to accomplish." And commending his beloved pupil and friend Florentius to their confidence, he calmly breathed his last, in his native city, in the forty-fifth year of his age.

He bequeathed his library to the Brother House at Deventer. Besides this he left no property, except some old furniture and clothing; having long disentangled himself from all the encumbrances of worldly affairs.

CHAPTER X.

THOMAS À KEMPIS.

AMONG the numerous pupils of the schools of the "Brethren of the Common Lot," none became more justly eminent for genuine piety, or was more truly and widely beloved by cotemporary and succeeding Christians for the loving and lamb-like spirit pervading his writings, than the humble but celebrated author of the "Imitation of Christ."

Thomas Hamerken, or Hamerlein, was born in the year 1380, at the little town of Kempen, in the great plain of the Rhine, near the city of Cologne. From the name of his native place, according to the custom of those times, he was generally called Thomas à Kempis. His parents, John and Gertrude, were in humble life, his father earning their subsistence by his daily labor as a mechanic; his mother was a woman of exemplary piety, exerting a favorable influence on the tender mind of her son, in cherishing a love for heavenly things.

When about thirteen years of age, he went to Deventer, where the school of the Brethren of the Common Lot offered an opportunity for his obtaining a good education without much expense to his family. He was, however, not at first a resident in the Brother House, but being introduced to Florentius Radewins, the superintendent, he obtained through him a lodging in the house of a pious matron, and pursued his studies in the grammar school. Florentius soon won his respect by his venerable manners, and his affection by acts of kindness and attention to the poor boy. He furnished him with books, which his limited means did not enable him to purchase, and supplied him with money to pay the school expenses. The rector of the grammar school at that time was John Boehme, who, according to Thomas's account, was an intimate friend of Florentius, and exercised rigid discipline. Thomas having one day gone to him to pay the school fees, and to redeem a book which he had temporarily pawned, the rector asked him, "who gave you the money?" On hearing that it was Florentius, Boehme dismissed the boy, with the words, "Go, take it back to him; for his sake I shall charge you nothing." He thus obtained his schooling for the future on the funds of the Institution.

Thomas was evidently a youth of very conscientious, tender, and susceptible feelings; and being deeply imbued with sentiments of piety, was struck with love and admiration whenever he witnessed evidences of it in others. In his memoir of his friend Florentius, Thomas mentions many traits of that simplicity, dignity, gentleness, and self-sacrificing activity for the good of others, which had won his ardent admiration. Before he became a boarder in the Brother House, he was directed by the teacher to attend with some other boys in the choir of the chapel. Here Florentius attended also. Thomas says, "Now whenever I saw my good master Florentius standing in the choir, even though he did not look about, I was so awed in his presence by his venerable aspect, that I never dared to speak a word. On one occasion I stood close beside him, and he turned to me, and sang from the same book. He even put his hand upon my shoulder, and then I stood as if rooted to the spot, afraid even to stir, so amazed was I at the honor done me."

Thomas, in course of time, came to dwell in Florentius's house, and closer acquaintance strengthened his love for him. When he happened to be troubled in his mind, he applied, like the other youths on similar occasions, to his respected master; and such was the effect of even a sight of his placid and cheerful countenance, or of a few words of conversation, that he seldom failed to leave his presence comforted and encouraged. This attachment showed itself in small matters. In consequence of weak health, Florentius sometimes could not partake of the common meals, but ate at a small table in the kitchen. Thomas then considered it an honor to wait upon him. "Unworthy though I was," he says, "I often at his invitation prepared the table, brought from the dining-room what little he required, and served him with cheerfulness and joy." If Florentius was at any time more sick than usual, it was customary with the Brethren to inform the neighboring Brother Houses and request their remembrance of him in prayer. On such occasions Thomas often undertook to carry the message, delighting to be so employed. Doubtless Florentius's pious example had great effect in moulding the after-life and character of his affectionate pupil.

Another inmate whose example made a deep impression upon him was Henry Brune, a memoir of whose life also is among the productions of his pen. He says, "One day in winter, Henry was sitting by the fireside, warming his hands, but with his face turned towards the wall, for he was at the time engaged in secret prayer. When I saw this, I was greatly edified, and from that day loved him all the more." Little incidents of this nature, told in Thomas's simple familiar style, let us into the inward character of his mind perhaps more readily than events of apparently greater importance. He was deeply interested in the religious exercises of the Brethren at Deventer, and attached himself entirely to their mode of life, entering into full outward communion with the society. He obtained from Florentius a place in the Brother House, in which at that time twenty-three members dwelt together and received maintenance. His chief companion, and soon his most intimate friend, was Arnold of Schoenhofen, a youth of fervent piety, with whom he shared a little chamber and bed. Here Thomas occupied himself in copying and reading the Holy Scriptures, taking part also unremittingly in the religious exercises of the family. What he earned by writing, he put into the common fund; and when it fell below what was needful for his support, the lack was supplied by the generosity of Florentius. The pious example of his young friend Arnold deeply impressed him. Arnold would rise every morning exactly at four o'clock, and after a short prayer at his bedside, quickly dressed himself and hastened to the place of worship, where, at all the exercises, he was the first to come and the last to depart. Besides, he frequently withdrew to some solitary place, in order to devote himself unobserved to prayer and meditation. Thomas sometimes accidentally became a witness of these outpourings of his friend's heart. He says, in his biography of Arnold, "I found myself on such occasions kindled by his zeal to prayer, and wished to experience, were it only sometimes, a devotion like that which he seemed almost daily to possess. Nor was his fervor in prayer at all wonderful, considering that wheresoever he went or staid, he was most diligent in keeping his heart and mouth." Arnold expressing once to him his earnest wish to learn quickly and well the art of neat writing, so usefully applied by the Brethren, Thomas thought within himself, "Ah, willingly would I also learn to write, did I but first know how to make myself better. But," adds he respecting his friend, "he obtained special grace from God, which made him skilful in every good work." Thomas evidently looked upon him as far more advanced in the spiritual life than himself.

He thus spent seven happy years, industriously engaged in prosecuting his studies and transcribing religious books, in the school and Brother House at Deventer. He was probably about completing the twenty-first year of his age, when one day Florentius called him to him at the close of the religious exercises, and addressed him seriously on the importance of the choice which he must now look towards making, of an avocation for life. It seems that having often observed Thomas's pious disposition, he was inclined to promote his entering into some monastic order; and Thomas, who had unbounded confidence in his master's judgment, finding it to accord with his own inclination towards a quiet contemplative religious life, at once acceded to his advice. The Brethren of the Common Lot had been instrumental in founding a monastery which they called the Monastery of St. Agnes, by the Dutch since known as Berg Clooster, situated on a pleasant and healthy elevation near the town of Zwoll. Recently erected, and with but slender means, it was as yet but little known. This institution, as being in Florentius's estimation the most eligible, he recommended to Thomas's choice, and gave him a letter of introduction to the prior. Thomas was kindly received, duly installed there at first for five years as a novitiate, and afterward as a priest, and spent the rest of his long and quiet life within its cloisters.

We must now contemplate Thomas Hamerken as a monk, for that he truly was during about seventy years of his life. Yet his monastic habit appears as if it had ever been covered by the genial warmth of a truly Christian spirit. How far it was wise in him to make the choice of this mode of life, we may certainly have doubts. But we must take into consideration the tendencies of the age, and the almost universal practice at that time for religious persons to seek refuge, in such institutions, though often a fallacious one, from the pollutions, temptations, and dangers of the world around them.

Thomas, however, led no idle life in his monastic condition. He still diligently occupied himself with the copying of books, and writing original works, as well as in the daily routine of the monastery. He is said to have been quite a fine penman, taking delight in having books well written and even in an ornamental manner. He made many copies of his own works, and the monastery preserved for many years a beautiful copy of the Bible in four volumes, executed by him, and several other large books. He was a great economist of time, and, to the neglect of his health, busied himself from the earliest hour in the morning. His maxim was: "In the morning, resolve; and in the evening, examine thy behavior; what thou hast that day been, in thought, word, and deed; for in all these, perhaps, thou hast often offended God and thy brother. Gird thy loins like a valiant man, and be continually watchful against the malicious stratagems of the devil. Bridle the appetite of gluttony, and thou wilt with less difficulty restrain all other inordinate desires of animal nature. Never suffer the invaluable moments of thy life to steal by unimproved, and leave thee in idleness and vacancy; but be always either reading, or writing, or praying, or meditating, or employed in some useful labor for the common good."

During many years of his life, and until his decease, he held the office of sub-prior of the monastery. His life flowed on like a placid stream, with quiet industry, lonely contemplation, and secret drawings to the Source of all good in prayer. Ullmann says of him, partly on the authority of Franciscus Tolensis, that all who were acquainted with him have borne witness how, during the whole course of his life, he evinced love to God and love to man, cheerfully bearing all afflictions, and kindly excusing the faults and foibles of his brethren. In his whole nature and habits, he was cleanly, moderate, chaste, inwardly happy, and outwardly cheerful. His great endeavor was for the attainment of uniform tranquillity and peace of mind, and the calm happiness of communion with the Most High. With this in view, he did not willingly or needlessly entangle himself with the affairs of the world, avoided intercourse with its great and honorable, observed a marked silence when the conversation turned on temporal things, and was ever fond of solitude and meditation. Yet he was by no means void of sensibility, and had from early youth a warm and lively sense of friendship, chiefly founding it on a mutual love of heavenly things. His Biographies of eleven of his fellow-inmates at the Brother House of Deventer evince this in a lively manner. He was full of zeal for the welfare of the community in which he lived, and an eloquent advocate of their views of divine truth. Multitudes are said to have flocked to hear him, even from remote places. It is said that during the exercise of singing the psalms, he stood erect, never studying his ease by leaning against anything to support his body; his look was reverentially upward; and his countenance and whole frame showed the heavenly direction of his soul. We must not omit to add, that on certain occasions, in conformity with the practices then prevalent, he resorted to the use of the scourge as a part of his private personal discipline.

Thomas's outward appearance corresponded to the gentleness of his inward nature. He is described as below the middle size, but well proportioned. The color of his face was fresh, with a slight tinge of brown. His eyes were piercingly bright, and notwithstanding almost constant use, retained their acuteness of vision to extreme old age; so that he never used spectacles, though he lived to be over ninety years of age.

Besides his eleven Biographies already mentioned, which were probably the product of his somewhat early years, he wrote a series of Sermons, for the especial use of the "Novices" in religious institutions: and his more important works, the "Soliloquy of the Soul," the "Garden of Roses," the "Valley of Lilies," and especially his great work on "The Imitation of Christ," with some minor pieces, are supposed to have been written during the later and more mature period of his life. He wrote also some Discourses addressed to Monks, a few religious poems, and other small works of but little interest at the present time.

From what we have already seen of his life and character, it is hardly needful to say that in all his writings his great object is to uphold and maintain the spiritual nature of all true religion, and to bring it home to the heart of man as a renovating power; yet that his views, excellent and edifying as they are in this respect, are by no means free from the cherished bias of his mind towards the system prevalent in his day. He was a great reformer, yet still holding to the forms and ceremonies of the Romish church, notwithstanding the real incompatibility of many of his principles with the outwardness and legal formalities of that system. His eye seems to have pierced as it were into the dawn of a brighter day, and his heart to have seized it in the love of it; but without being conscious that he was in measure preparing the way for it; for shut up as he was from the world in the seclusion of his cloister, the scope of his vision was limited, and he could not freely range over the field of gospel truth in the liberty and clear light of the gospel, as might have been the case had he not been bound by the ties of his order, and had he felt himself free to contrast his own inward convictions with the falsities which had been forced upon mankind in the name of Christianity. He might thus have seen that the system then in vogue, and to which he clung, was, in its tenor and in its spirit, no more like his own spirit and the secret tendencies of his heart, than a dead and dry nutshell is like the rich and living fruit. But he felt himself a pilgrim and a sojourner in the world, his mind was ardently bent heavenward, his childlike spirit was satisfied with nothing short of the incomes of heavenly consolation, and he seemed to shrink from looking outward at the inconsistent dogmas which were afloat, or from endeavoring to meddle with things which, without direct guidance and help from on high, he might have found too hard for his gentle nature. In short, he was not made for that warfare; and it would not be right to judge him unfaithful, for not seeing what had never been clearly unfolded to his view, when we have abundant evidence of his constant concern to be found walking acceptably with God, according to the measure of light and grace vouchsafed.

It is true, as Ullmann remarks, that he adhered strictly to the creed of the Romish faith as it had been handed down, and did not assail any of its doctrines. He practised with zeal the exercises of worship which then obtained currency, and believed them to be right, not feeling disposed to enter into what he might have considered as a rash spirit of criticism, in doubting their correctness or efficacy. In some of his writings his views seem more or less tinged with the legalism of the schools of the middle ages; but in other parts he displays remarkably clear and sound views of the nature of regeneration and redemption through Christ our Saviour. His mind was not fond of the intricacies of doctrine. He made war, not with heretics, but with the world, sin being the great heresy in his eyes, and the object of perpetual hostility. To the hierarchical system he seems to have paid no attention. He just let it stand where he found it, and looked to something more inward. In his numerous writings, Ullmann says, he only mentions the pope once [he should have said twice], and that only for the purpose of saying that he and all other men are nothing in the sight of eternity, and that his bulls are powerless to obviate the certainty of death. This he has expressed in two odd lines of *Latin rhyme:*

"Omnia sunt nulla, Rex, Papa, et plumbea bulla.
Cunctorum finis: mors, vermis, fovea, cinis."

Ullmann further says, "The secularization of the church, so far as he was acquainted with it, must have been, to one who had so little of a worldly spirit, an abomination. All he did and thought was [in accordance with] the saying of Christ, 'My kingdom is not of this world.' Hence he speaks against striving after honors either academical or ecclesiastical, against the wealth of churches and monasteries, simony, plurality of ecclesiastical offices, and the secularities of monachism.... He ever insists upon the Christian principles of spirituality and freedom which formed the basis of the reformation.... To him the inward life, the disposition of mind, is the great matter. No work or external thing is of any value except through love. Where there is genuine love, it sanctifies all. In the spirit of the fraternity of which he was a member, he did many things to pave the way for reform. These consisted chiefly in zealously inculcating the reading of the Bible and the transcription of copies of it,—in laying the chief weight, not upon Moses or any sort of law, but upon Christ and his gospel, upon grace, repentance, faith, love, and the appropriation of the spirit of Scripture by the Spirit of God in the soul— in laboring much for the religious revival and instruction of the people—and in practically evincing a lively concern for the literary education of the rising generations. All this included the germs of future evolutions, although the harvest which they bore was such as Thomas never anticipated, and, if foreshown to him, he would scarcely have recognized as the growth of his own seed."

Scarcely anything is known of the latter days of this eminently humble and heavenly-minded Christian. He appears to have been permitted to attain to a somewhat unusually prolonged life. No particular incidents of his last illness have come down to us, but he died in the summer of 1471, about the ninety-second year of his age.

But few of his works have been translated from their original Latin into the English language. His "Imitation of Christ," written about the sixty-first year of his age, is so well known and so highly appreciated, that it is scarcely needful here to enter into any analysis of its contents. It consists of three books, to which some editors have attached a fourth, being "the Book of the Sacrament;" which, however, evidently by no means belongs to it, and has probably been in the first place appended by some who desired thereby to impart a more Romish character to the whole work.

There are in this truly valuable treatise, as might be expected, here and there, slight allusions to some of the views peculiar to the church of Rome, such as those on monastic obedience and duties, purgatory, and the merit of good works; yet these are very slightly touched upon. And his advocacy of good works is by no means such as to counterbalance the evidence, contained in various portions of the work, of his sound acceptance and true appreciation of the great and fundamental doctrines of the Sonship and atonement of Christ;* though it is true that he has not

* In his "Book of the Sacrament" (chap. ii.) he says: "The love of Christ is as incapable of change or diminution as his own being; and the treasures of his propitiation are not to be exhausted." This is evidently the expression of one to whom that doctrine was a settled conviction.

9*

given the latter any particular prominence in the treatise. This may have arisen from the pre-eminently practical nature of the work, to the exclusion of almost all that might, in a sense, be termed abstract doctrine. As he fully believed in the apostolic declaration that "faith without works is dead," so he desired also that all men should be induced, and enabled by the grace of God, to show their faith by their works. A few detached extracts may give an idea of the value of the book, to such readers as are unacquainted with this instructive collection of aphorisms on the practical doctrines and duties of the Christian life. He seems to speak from his own experience.

"'He that followeth me shall not walk in darkness, but shall have the light of life.' These are the words of Christ, by which we are taught, that it is only by a conformity to His life and Spirit that we can be truly enlightened, and delivered from all blindness of heart.... The doctrine of Christ infinitely transcends the doctrine of the holiest men; and he that had the Spirit of Christ would find in it 'hidden manna, the bread that came down from heaven.' But not having his Spirit, many, though they frequently hear his doctrine, yet feel no pleasure in it, no ardent desire after it."

"He whom the Eternal Word condescendeth to teach is disengaged at once from the labyrinth of human opinions. For of One Word are all things; and all things, without voice or language, speak Him alone. . He is that Divine Principle, which speaketh in our hearts, and without which there can be neither just apprehension nor rectitude of judgment. Now he to whom all things are but this One, who comprehendeth all things in His will, and beholdeth all things in His Light, hath his 'heart fixed,' and abideth in the peace of God. O! God, who art the Truth, make me one with thee in everlasting love! I am often weary of reading, and weary of hearing; in thee alone is the sum of my desires. Let all teachers be silent; let the whole creation be dumb before thee; and do thou only speak unto my soul."

"A holy life makes a man wise according to the Divine Wisdom, and wonderfully enlargeth his experience. And the more humble his spirit is, and the more subject and resigned to God, the more wise will he become in the conduct of outward life, and the more undisturbed in the possession of himself."

"Not eloquence, but truth, is to be sought after in the Holy Scriptures; every part of which must be read with the same Spirit by which it was written. And as in these, and all other books, it is improvement in holiness, not pleasure in the subtlety of the thought or the accuracy of the expression, that must be principally regarded, we ought to read those parts that are simple and devout, with the same affection and delight (at least) as those of high speculation or profound erudition."

"As much as lies in thy power, shun the resorts of worldly men; for much conversation on secular business, however innocently managed, greatly retards the progress of the spiritual life. We are soon captivated by vain objects and employments, and soon defiled; and I have wished a thousand times, that I had either not been in company, or had been silent."

"The hope of consolation from outward life, utterly destroys that inward and divine consolation which the Holy Spirit gives us, and which is the only support of the soul under all its troubles. Let us therefore watch and pray without ceasing, that no part of our invaluable time may be thus sacrificed to vanity and sin; and whenever it is proper and expedient to speak, let us speak those things that are holy, by which Christians edify one another."

"If the progress to perfection is placed only in external

observances, our religion, having no divine life, will quickly perish with the things on which it subsists. But the axe must be laid to the root of the tree, that, being separated and freed from the restless desires of nature and self, we may possess our souls in the peace of God."

"It is hard, indeed, to relinquish that to which we have been accustomed; and harder still, to resist and deny our own will. But how can we hope to succeed in the greatest conflict, if we will not contend for victory in the least? Resist then thy inordinate desires in their birth; and continually lessen the power of thy evil habits; lest, as they increase in strength in proportion as they are indulged, they grow at length too mighty to be subdued. Oh, if thou didst but consider, what peace thou wilt bring to thyself, and what joy thou wilt produce in heaven, by a life conformed to the life of Christ, I think thou wouldst be more watchful and zealous for thy continual advancement toward spiritual perfection."

"The life of a religious man ought not only so to abound with holiness, as that the frame of his spirit may be at least equal to his outward behavior; but there ought to be much more holiness within, than is discernible without; because God, who searcheth the heart, is our inspector and judge, whom it is our duty infinitely to reverence, wherever we are, and as angels to walk pure in his sight. We ought every day to renew our holy resolutions, and incite ourselves to more animated fervor, as if this was the first day of our conversion; and to say, 'Assist me, O Lord God, in my resolution to devote myself to thy holy service; and grant, that this day I may begin to walk perfectly, because all that I have done hitherto is nothing.'"

"The good resolutions of the righteous depend not upon their own wisdom and ability, but upon the grace of God, in which they perpetually confide, whatever be their attempts; for they know that though 'the heart of man deviseth his way,' yet the Lord ordereth the event; and that 'it is not in man that walketh, to direct his steps.'"

"Appropriate a convenient part of time to retirement and self-converse; and frequently meditate on the wonderful love of God in the redemption of man. Reject all studies that are merely curious, and read only what will rather penetrate the heart with holy compunction, than exercise the brain with useless speculations."

"No man can safely go abroad, that does not love to stay at home; no man can safely speak, that does not willingly hold his tongue; no man can safely govern, that would not cheerfully become subject; no man can safely command, that has not truly learned to obey; and no man can safely rejoice, but he that has the testimony of a good conscience."

"Lift up thy eyes to God in the heavens, and pray for the forgiveness of thy innumerable sins and negligences. Leave vain pleasures to the enjoyment of vain men, and mind only that which God hath required of thee for thy own eternal good. Make thy door fast behind thee; and invite Jesus, thy beloved, to come unto thee, and enlighten thy darkness with his light. Abide faithfully with him in this retirement; for thou canst not find so much peace in any other place."

"The end of thy present life will speedily come. Consider therefore in what degree of preparation thou standest for that which will succeed. To-day man is; to-morrow he is not seen; and when he is once removed from the sight of others, he soon passeth from their remembrance. Oh, the hardness and insensibility of the human heart, that thinks only on present enjoyments, and wholly disregards the prospects of futurity! In every thought, in every action, thou shouldst govern and possess thy spirit so absolately, as if thou wast to die to-day; and was thy conscience pure, thou wouldst not fear thy dissolution, however near. It is better to avoid sin, than to shun death. If thou art not prepared for that awful event to-day, how wilt thou be prepared to-morrow? To-morrow is an uncertain day, and how knowest thou that to-morrow will be thine?"

"It is better to provide oil for thy lamp now, before it is wanted, than to depend upon receiving it from others, 'when the bridegroom cometh;' for if thou art not careful of thyself now, who can be careful of thee hereafter, when time and opportunity are forever lost? This instant, NOW, is exceedingly precious. 'Now is the accepted time, now is the day of salvation.' How deplorable therefore is it, not to improve this invaluable moment, in which we may 'lay hold on eternal life!' A time may come when thou shalt wish for one day, nay one hour, to repent in; and who can tell whether thou wilt be able to obtain it?

"Awake then, dearest brother, and behold what inconceivable danger thou mayst now avoid, from what horrible fear thou mayst now be rescued, only by 'passing the time of thy sojourning here in fear,' and in continual expectation of thy removal by death. Endeavor now to live in such a manner, that in that awful moment, thou mayst rejoice rather than fear. Learn now to die to the world, that thou mayst then begin to live with Christ. Learn now to despise all created things, that being delivered from every incumbrance, thou mayst then freely rise to Him."

"Now, therefore, dearest brother, now turn to God, and do whatever his Holy Spirit enables thee to perform; for thou knowest not the hour in which death will seize thee, nor canst thou conceive the consequences of his seizing thee unprepared. Now, while the time of gathering riches is in much mercy continued, lay up for thyself the substantial and unperishing treasures of heaven. Think of nothing but the business of thy redemption; be careful for nothing but the improvement of thy state in God."

"Live in the world as a stranger and pilgrim, who hath no concern with business or pleasures; and knowing that thou hast 'here no continuing city,' keep thy heart disengaged from earthly passions and pursuits, and lifted up to heaven in the patient hope of 'a city that is to come, whose builder and maker is God.'"

"'The kingdom of God is within you,' saith our blessed Redeemer. Abandon therefore the cares and pleasures of this world, and turn to the Lord with all thy heart, and thy soul shall find rest. If thou withdrawest thy attention from outward things, and keepest it fixed upon what passeth within thee, thou wilt soon perceive the coming of the kingdom of God; for 'the kingdom of God' is that 'peace and joy in the Holy Ghost,' which cannot be received by sensual and worldly men. Christ will come to thee, and bless thee with the splendor of his presence, if thou preparest within thee an abode fit to receive him. All his glory and beauty are manifested within, and there he delights to dwell. His visits there are frequent, his condescension amazing, his conversation sweet, his comforts refreshing, and the peace that he brings passeth all understanding."

"That man only is poor in this world, who liveth without Jesus; and that man only is rich, with whom Jesus delights to dwell."

"The vicissitude of day and night in the spiritual life, is neither new nor unexpected to those who are acquainted with the ways of God; for the ancient prophets and most eminent saints have all experienced an alternative of visitation and desertion. As an instance of this, the royal prophet thus describes his own case: 'When I was in prosperity,' says he, and my heart was filled with the treasures of grace, 'I said, I shall never be moved.' But these treasures being soon taken away, and feeling in himself the poverty of fallen nature, he adds, 'Thou didst turn thy face from me, and I was troubled.' Yet in this disconsolate state he does not despair, but with more ardor raises his desire and prayer to God: 'Unto thee, O Lord, will I cry, and I will make my supplication unto my God.' And to show how mercy and help were manifested, he adds, 'Thou hast turned my mourning into joy, and hast compassed me about with gladness.' The Holy Spirit cometh and goeth, 'according to the good pleasure of his will;' and upon this principle the blessed Job saith, 'Thou visitest man in the morning, and of a sudden thou provest him.'"*

"The ground of this vicissitude of comfort and distress, is in general this: the consolations of the Spirit are given to man, to enable him to bear the adversity of his fallen state; and they are taken away, lest he be so much elevated with the gift, as to forget the giver.

"After all, remember, that the devil slumbereth not, nor is the flesh yet dead. Be therefore continually prepared for contest; for on the right hand and on the left, thou art beset with enemies that are never at rest."

"Though a man give all his substance to feed the poor, it is nothing; though he mortify the desires of flesh and blood by severe penance, still it is of little importance; though he comprehend the vast extent of science, yet he is far behind; and though he hath the splendor of illustrious virtue, and the ardor of exalted devotion, still he will want much, if he still wants this 'one thing needful,' this poverty of spirit, which, after abandoning the creatures about him, requires him to abandon himself; to go wholly out of himself; to retain not the least leaven of self-love and self-esteem; but, when he hath finished his course of duty, to

* Job, vii. 18—Vulgate version.

know and feel, with the same certainty as he feels the motion of his heart, that he himself hath done nothing. Such a man will set no value upon those attainments, which, if under the power of self-love, he would highly esteem; but, in concurrence with the voice of Truth, 'when he has done all that is commanded him,' he will always freely pronounce himself 'an unprofitable servant.'"

"There is no redemption, no foundation for the hope of the divine life, but in the cross. Take up thy cross therefore, and follow Jesus, in the path that leads to everlasting peace. He hath gone before, bearing that cross upon which he died for thee; that thou mightest follow, patiently bearing thy own cross, and upon that die to thyself for him. And if we die with him, we shall also live with him; 'if we are partakers of his sufferings, we shall be partakers also of his glory.'"

"Blessed is the soul that listeneth to the voice of the Lord, and from his own lips heareth the word of consolation! Blessed are the ears that receive the soft whispers of the divine breath, and exclude the noise and tumult of the world. Yea, truly blessed are they, when, deaf to the voice that soundeth without, they are attentive only to the Truth teaching within! Blessed are the eyes that are shut to material objects, and open and fixed upon those that are spiritual. Blessed are they that examine the state of the inward man; and by continual exercises of repentance and faith, prepare the mind for a more comprehensive knowledge of the truths of redemption. Blessed are all, who delight in the service of God; and who, that they may live purely to him, disengage their hearts from the cares and pleasures of the world."

"The children of Israel once said to Moses,.' Speak thou with us, and we will hear; let not God speak with us, lest we die.' I pray not in this manner. No, Lord, I pray not so; but, with the prophet Samuel, humbly and ardently entreat, 'Speak, Lord, for thy servant heareth.' Let not Moses speak to me, nor any of the prophets; but speak thou, O Lord God, the inspirer and enlightener of all the prophets; for thou alone, without their intervention, canst perfectly instruct me; but without thee, they can profit me nothing. They indeed can pronounce the words, but cannot impart the Spirit. . . . If thou art absent, they do not influence the heart. They administer the letter, but thou openest the sense. They utter the mystery, but thou revealest its meaning. They publish thy laws, but thou conferrest the power of obedience. They point the way to life, but thou bestowest strength to walk in it. Their influence is only external, but thou instructest and enlightenest the mind. They water, but thou givest the increase. Their voice soundeth in the ear, but it is thou that givest understanding to the heart."

"Some place their religion in books, some in images, and some in the pomp and splendor of external worship. These 'honor me' (as said Christ) 'with their lips, but their heart is far from me.' But there are some, who with illuminated understandings discern the glory which man has lost, and with pure affection pant for its recovery. . . . These hear and understand what the Holy Spirit speaketh in their heart, exhorting them to withdraw their affection from things on earth, and set it 'on things above;' to abandon this fallen world, and day and night aspire after reunion with God."

"I bless thee, O heavenly Father, the Father of our Lord Jesus Christ, that thou hast vouchsafed to remember so poor and helpless a creature! O Father of mercies, and God of all consolation, I give thee most humble and ardent thanks, that, unworthy as I am of all comfort, thou hast been pleased to visit my benighted soul with the enlivening beams of heavenly light! Blessing, and praise, and glory, be unto thee, and thy only begotten Son, and thy Holy Spirit, the Comforter, forever and ever!"

"I stand astonished, when I consider that 'the heavens are not clean in thy sight.' If thou hast found folly and impurity in angels, and hast not spared even them, what will become of me? If the stars have 'fallen from heaven,' if 'Lucifer, son of the morning,' hath not kept his place; shall I, who am but dust, dare to presume upon my own stability? Many whose holiness had raised them to exalted honor, have been degraded most deeply by sin; and those who have fed on the bread of angels, I have seen delighted with the husks of swine. There is, therefore, no holiness, if thou, Lord, withdraw thy presence; no wisdom profiteth, if thy Spirit cease to direct; no strength availeth without thy support; no chastity is safe without thy protection; no watchfulness effectual, when thy holy vigilance is not our guard. For no sooner are we left to ourselves, than the waves of corruption rush upon us, and we sink and perish; but if thou reach forth thy omnipotent hand, we walk upon the sea and live."

"Bring my will, O Lord, into true and unalterable subjection to thine, and do with me what thou pleasest; for whatever is done by thee, cannot but be good. If thou pourest thy light upon me, and turnest my night into day, blessed be thy name! And if thou leavest me in darkness, blessed also be thy name! If thou exaltest me with the consolations of thy Spirit, or humblest me under the afflictions of fallen nature, still may thy holy name be forever blessed!

"I am he (might Christ say) that exalteth the humble and simple mind, and suddenly imparteth to it such a perception of eternal truth, as it could not acquire by a life of laborious study in the schools of men. I teach not, like men, with the clamor of uncertain words, or the confusion of opposite opinions; with vain learning, or the ostentation of learning yet more vain; or with the strife of formal disputation, in which victory is more contended for than truth. I teach, in still and soft whispers, to relinquish earth and seek after heaven; to loath carnal and temporal enjoyments, and sigh for spiritual and eternal; to shun honor, and to bear contempt; to place all hope and dependence upon me, to desire nothing besides me, and above all in heaven and on earth most ardently to love me. . . . Though my written word speaks the same language to all, yet, without me, it does not impart the same instruction. I, as the internal principle of light to angels and men, am the only teacher of divine truth. I search the heart, and comprehend the most secret thoughts. I am the author and finisher of every good work; and, for the ornament and perfection of my mystical body, I bestow upon the members of it 'a diversity of gifts, dividing to every man severally as I will.'"

"I give thee thanks, O Father of mercies, that thou hast not spared the evil that is in me; but hast humbled sinful nature by severe chastisements, inflicting pains, and accumulating sorrows, both from within and from without. And of all in heaven and on earth, there is none that can bring me comfort, but thou, O Lord my God, the sovereign physician of diseased souls; 'who woundest and healest, who bringest down to the grave and raisest up again.' Thy chastisement is upon me, and thy rod shall teach me wisdom!"

"From self-love, as the corrupt stock, are derived the numerous branches of that evil, which forms the trials of man in his struggles for redemption; and when this stock is plucked up by the roots, holiness and peace will be implanted in its room, and flourish forever with unfading verdure. But how few labor at this extirpation! How few seek to obtain that divine life which can only rise from the death of self! And thus men lie bound in the complicated chains of animal passions, unwilling, and therefore unable to rise above the selfish enjoyments of flesh and blood. But he that desireth to follow Christ in the regeneration with an enlarged heart, must endeavor to suppress and kill the evil appetites and passions of his fallen nature; and not by a partial fondness, which hath its birth from self-love, adhere to any creature "

" Come then, O Meekness of the Lamb of God! thou who makest the poor in spirit rich in goodness, and the rich in goodness poor in spirit; oh come, descend into my soul, and fill it with the light and comfort of thy blessed presence, lest it faint and perish in the darkness and barrenness of its fallen state!"

" Come, my beloved brethren, let us take courage, and hand in hand pursue our journey in the path of life. Jesus will be with us! For Jesus' sake we have taken up the cross; and for Jesus' sake we will persist in bearing it. He, who is our captain and our guide, will be our strength and our support. Behold, our King, who will fight our battles, leads the way! Let us resolutely follow, undismayed by any terrors; and let us choose death, rather than stain the glory of which we are made partakers, by deserting the cross."

Finally, "'unto thee,' therefore, 'do I lift up mine eyes, O thou that dwellest in the heavens!' In thee, my God, the Father of mercies, I place all my confidence! Oh, illuminate and sanctify my soul with the influence of thy Holy Spirit; that being delivered from all the darkness and impurity of its alienated life, which thine eyes cannot look upon, it may become the living temple of thy holy presence, the seat of thy eternal glory! In the immensity of thy goodness, O Lord! and 'in the multitude of thy tender mercies,' turn unto me, and hear the prayer of thy poor servant, who has wandered far from thee into the region of the shadow of death! Oh, protect and keep my soul, amidst the innumerable evils which this corruptible life is always bringing forth; and by the perpetual guidance of thy grace, lead me in the narrow path of holiness, to the realms of everlasting light and peace! Amen!"

CHAPTER XI.

JOHN RUCHRATH, OF WESEL.

PERHAPS no one in the fifteenth century more clearly saw and more indignantly protested against the corruptions of practice and morals which had crept in during the middle ages, than John Ruchrath. He is generally styled John of Wesel, from the town of Ober Wesel on the banks of the Rhine, which was his birth-place; but as this was not his true name, and has the disadvantage of confounding him with a subsequent reformer, John Wessel, it seems preferable to designate him by the name of his birth and parentage, Ruchrath, or Richrath.

He was born probably about the year 1410, but the precise period has not come down to us, neither have we any information of his early education. Ullmann, from whom we derive the particulars now presented respecting him, and who has industriously collected together all that could be found in regard to him, says that he first appears in history at the University of Erfurt, in Thuringia. It is supposed that he commenced his studies there about the year 1440, as he graduated in 1445 as Master of Arts. He entered the clerical profession, but without taking the monastic vow; and in process of time became one of the professors in that university, and took the degree of Doctor of Divinity about the year 1456. He is said to have been greatly distinguished as a preacher; and Martin Luther, who many years afterwards studied at the same school, gives this testimony respecting him: "John Wesalia *ruled* the university *by his books;* and it was out of these that I studied for my Master's degree."

The year 1450 was distinguished throughout western Europe as a great Jubilee, by order of Pope Nicolaus V. Very great multitudes made pilgrimage to Rome, under the superstitious belief, that, according to a bull issued by a previous pope on a similar occasion, "every one who should, during that year, visit with reverence the churches of the apostles Peter and Paul in Rome, and there do penance and confess his sin, should obtain the *very fullest forgiveness of all his sins;* the citizens to visit them once a day for thirty days, and foreigners for fifteen days." This scheme of the priests had brought, it is said, no less than 200,000 poor deluded pilgrims to the city during the first year of its appointment (viz. A.D. 1300), and continued to attract great crowds, and brought incalculable gain to the citizens of Rome and to the papal treasury. But the pope in the Jubilee of 1450 was not satisfied with confining the profits of its celebration within the city of Rome. Knowing that vast multitudes were not able to leave their homes in distant parts of Europe for so great a journey, he adopted a substitute for the pilgrimage, by the sale of Indulgences to such as were under the necessity of remaining at their homes; and sent forth the Cardinal Nicolaus of Cusa into Germany, to "collect the gifts made by the penitent," and to preach the great efficacy of the spiritual favors now offered to the poor people for their money.

This man, as he travelled from place to place, attended by a meagre retinue to simulate poverty or humility, and mounted on a mule, was everywhere received by the princes, the clergy, and the common people, with the utmost reverence, and escorted with songs of praise into the places where he preached or celebrated mass. Among other places he visited Erfurt, where he preached several times with the usual solemnities, and doubtless with the usual success to his simoniacal trade. John Ruchrath probably was one of his hearers; but if so, the effect of what he then witnessed appears to have confirmed him in his sentiments of the entire inconsistency of such a practice with the gospel of Christ; for he soon afterwards completed a work on which he had been some months engaged, viz. his Disputation against Indulgences.

It would be incompatible with our limits, to go at length into an explanation of the manner in which this abominable abuse gradually crept into the Romish system of operations. The doctrine of Indulgences ran its course for centuries before it reached its acme. We may briefly condense its successive stages, from the somewhat elaborate description of Ullmann.

Indulgence was originally a remission of penance, or ecclesiastical pains and penalties. The early church exercised so strict a watch over the purity of its members, as to exclude from communion all who were openly guilty of sin. In order to readmission, a series of penitential discipline was imposed, often wearisome and severe. If evidences of true amendment were distinctly visible, the severity of the discipline might be mitigated, or its duration abridged; and this was the commencement of remission or indulgence. This penitential discipline, at first imposed on excommunicated persons for their readmission, was eventually extended to all delinquents. It seems to have greatly promoted, in its course, the doctrine of satisfaction by good works, so prevalent in the western church during the middle ages; and in its turn to have derived great strength from that doctrine; for its supposed efficacy was gradually extended from a matter of church discipline to the remission of sin in the view of the Almighty himself. In order to favor this extended view of the doctrine, the idea was promulgated that the authorities of the church, possessing the power of the keys from Christ, possessed also a treasury to be opened by those keys; containing the supererogatory or superabundant merits of Christ and the saints, for distribution among the penitent. It was alleged that as " even one drop of the blood of Christ would have sufficed to expiate the guilt of all mankind, and as he shed infinitely more than one drop,"* the rest had, along with a similar superabundance of meritorious works on the part of the saints, beyond what was necessary for their own salvation, been mercifully treasured up and granted by the Almighty to the keeping of the church, and especially to the Pope, as Christ's vicar, for the salvation of souls that have no merit of their own. It was after a while alleged that such was the plenitude of the grace thus kept in store, that it might even be made available for the souls which were undergoing purification in Purgatory, and might thus shorten the period of their purgation!

Albert, surnamed The Great, who died about the year 1280, thus advocated the doctrine of Indulgence, as "the remission of some imposed punishment or penance, proceeding from the power of the keys and the treasure of the superfluous merits of the perfect. A penalty," he thought, "can only be remitted to a party by whom it is due, on condition that some other party, who has done *more* than was obligatory upon him, furnishes an equivalent for it;

---

* Alexander of Hales, as quoted by Ullmann.

and this *more* is kept in store in the treasure belonging to the church, and containing the fullness of the merits of Christ and the saints. Some," he says, "imagine that Indulgence has no efficacy at all, and is merely a pious fraud [and no wonder they did!], by which men are enticed to the performance of good works, such as pilgrimages and alms-giving. These, however, reduce the action of the church to child's play, and fall into heresy. Others, carrying the contrary opinion farther than is necessary, assert that Indulgence at once and unconditionally accomplishes all that is expressed in it, and thus make the divine mercy diminish the fear of judgment. The true medium is," says he, "that Indulgence has that precise amount of efficacy which the church assigns to it." [Comfortable doctrine to those who wished implicitly and blindly to rely upon it.]

Thomas Aquinas, about the same period, was one of the strongest advocates of the efficacy of Indulgences; and in attempting to prove it, alleges "that the church in general is infallible, and as it sanctions and practises Indulgence, Indulgence must be valid. This, Thomas is persuaded, all admit, because there would be impiety in representing any act of the church as nugatory!"—"The reason of its efficacy," he says, "lies in the *oneness of the mystical body*, within which there are many who, as respects works of penitence, have done more than they were under obligation to do; for instance, many who have patiently endured undeserved sufferings sufficient to expiate a great amount of penalties. In fact, so vast is the sum of these merits, that it greatly exceeds the measure of the guilt of all the living, especially when augmented by the merit of Christ." It may be safe to say that no more monstrous perversion of the doctrine of salvation through the mercy of God in Christ Jesus was ever invented by the agents of antichrist, to delude the hearts of the simple, and make merchandise of the gospel. Ullmann says that "during the fourteenth century, Indulgences were multiplied from the most multifarious causes, and more and more came to be granted for money. At last, indeed, a regular list of prices was drawn out, so that what had been already treated in theory as a sort of traffic with ecclesiastical blessings, now also assumed in practice the shape of a mercantile transaction; and the business was carried on with a punctuality and attention which would have done honor to the first commercial house in the world." — "Many of the preachers of Indulgence, in order to promote its sale, extolled its efficacy upon both the living and the dead, by arguments which either absolutely omitted, or at least cast into the shade, all religious and moral requirements."

John Ruchrath, in the introduction to his Treatise against this abuse, takes the ground that neither in Holy Scripture, nor in the writings of the early and most celebrated teachers for several hundred years, is a word to be found respecting Indulgence. He afterward through the work stands upon this ground, and affirms it as his persuasion, that if in the writings of subsequent authorities anything is found contrary to the testimony of Scripture, it is not to be received as true merely because it has high human authority. He declares himself entirely opposed to the belief in any treasure of merits from the saints, quoting the Scripture testimony that "their works do follow them." He endeavors to instill more correct ideas than at that time prevailed, respecting the nature of sin and repentance, and forgiveness through the grace of God. He takes a position in advance of the doctrine of the Romish writers, yet still not clear of entanglement with the notion of the power of priests to grant absolution. He says that in offenses against the church, there is also an offense against God; and that "He can forgive the offender his sin, even when the offended party refuses to do it. If from this point of view, then, we contemplate the plenary power of pardon committed to priests, it is evident that no priest can dispense pardon originally and effectively, but only by the divine assistance, which lies in the communication of grace." He lays, says Ullmann, a marked stress upon the principle, that there is no virtue in "the sacrament of penitence," to produce any effect, *prior* to the communication of grace. Aware that in this opinion he differs from many masters and teachers, he yet says that he cannot help it, because the honor of God constrains him; requiring as that seems to do, that *God alone*, of his pure goodness, should be the author and giver of grace.

It seems scarcely needful to follow him through the course of his reasoning on the subject of sin and forgiveness, inasmuch as his views are evidently mixed up with those of the age respecting penance and purgatory. They seem somewhat like the efforts of a man who sees in degree the grossness of the popular errors, but is depending too much on his own attainments and powers to comprehend with entire clearness the mysteries of redeeming love and mercy through Christ. In his 51st chapter, he calls Indulgences "a pious fraud practised upon believers," in inducing them to make pilgrimages, give money for pious purposes, etc., under the notion that they will be thereby absolved from the penalties due to them for their sins; yet he does not deny that a degree of merit may attach to those who comply with the requisitions or terms stated in the Indulgences, if done in the love of God and a spirit of piety.

After proving that Indulgences are not warranted by anything in Scripture, he turns to the allegation of the advocates of the doctrine, that the church has sanctioned it, and the church being infallible, Indulgence must be valid. To this he replies, "that the Catholic church is infallible, is a mere assertion, in support of which no proof is advanced either from reason or Scripture." And he endeavors to draw the distinction between the Catholic or Universal church, as it exists as a gathered and visible body, and that portion of it which is truly the church of Christ, being founded on a rock, and against which the gates of hell shall never prevail. "Inasmuch," he says, "as this church (the Christian church in a narrower sense) is holy and undefiled, there exists no error in it, none at least self-induced, because that would be a spot or wrinkle :" but that the Universal church, as it is found mixed with the world and in part composed of wicked men, does err, and that therefore the argument of the infallibility of the Catholic church (applying as it does to only a part of it) is inconclusive. He concludes that the proposition, that the church grants Indulgence, comes from that part of the church which does err, and that the church ought not to dispense it, because it is founded upon error.

On the whole, though his reasoning appears in many respects much entangled with some of the errors which he still adhered to, yet the treatise was a bold and great advance beyond the superstition of the age, and doubtless had considerable effect in moulding the opinions of thinking men toward those convictions which ripened into the reformation of the sixteenth century.

About ten years after completing this work, John Ruchrath was called from Erfurt to occupy the position of a preacher at Mayence, at the confluence of the Rhine and Mayn. But it is said that he left his post there, not long afterwards, from fear of a pestilence then raging. If this were the case, it seems to indicate, either that he was convinced that his call thither had been defective, or that he had not that living faith which would have sustained him in an honest endeavor to discharge what might be really required of him, as a pastor of the flock, through a trying dispensation.

He then obtained a similar position in the city of Worms, which he occupied for seventeen years. Here he was considered an effective and fervent preacher, though perhaps not always a discreet one. He saw more and more clearly into the corruptions which prevailed among the monks and in the clerical body at large; and while here he published his most celebrated work, "Concerning the Authority, Duty, and Power of Pastors;" a work which gave great offense to those whose easy nests were stirred up and exposed by it. He attacked the corrupt priests with great boldness. "The church," said he, "has lapsed so far from true piety into a certain kind of Jewish superstition, that wherever we turn our eyes, we see nothing but an empty and ostentatious display of works, void of the least spark of faith; the Pharisaic pride of Rabbis, cold ceremonies, and vain superstition, not to call it idolatry. All seem intent on reaping a golden harvest, pursue only their own interest, and totally neglect the duties of Christian piety."*
Again, "It is certainly a hard task to be one of the princes and rulers of the people; for they have to answer not merely for their own sins, but also for the errors of others; and if men would reflect on this, they would never canvass for the office of a ruler or pastor, nor pursue or purchase it with gold, but would *wait the call of the Lord;* for they who obtain this dignity without vocation are, according to the language of our Saviour, thieves and robbers, having entered in by another way and not by the door of Christ. The preachers of eternal wisdom ought to be the salt of the earth. 'But if the salt have lost its savour, wherewith shall it be salted? It is thenceforth good for nothing, but to be cast out and trodden under foot of men.' If the doctrine of

* Ullmann, from whom this account is chiefly compiled.

priests and prelates be not the doctrine of Christ, it ought to be rejected and trampled in the dust; so little is it our duty to listen to pastors, who would fain besprinkle and season us with salt that has lost its virtue. Rare as a black swan, is the priest who discharges the apostolical office with apostolical fidelity. And the reason is, because the Word of the Lord is fettered by human devices, and cannot be freely preached. Tyranny and oppression on every side cry out against it, and the ordinances of many bishops oppose it; not to speak of the legends of the saints, the imposture of indulgences, the labors of fraternities, which one must in every way extol to the skies, in order to enjoy favor, and escape the chance of losing one's stipulated pay. 'Speak to us what we like to hear,' say the people in their folly, 'or we will call down the wrath of God upon your head.' The consequence is, that, as good pastors either hide in a corner, or are proscribed and shamefully banished, the great majority discharge their office with no other view but to feed themselves and not the sheep, and seek to promote their own interests instead of nourishing them. Nay, sometimes, not satisfied with their wool and milk, they flay and wholly devour them. How extreme the misery of the Christian flock! The little ones call for bread, and there is no one to give it them. They seek for water, and there is none, and their tongue faileth for thirst."

"It is the duty of a Christian man," he says in another place, "to exercise not power, but love, over those whom he governs; measuring all with one line, viz.: the communion of faith and the confession of Christian charity. In this religion there is no difference, the righteousness of God which is by faith in Jesus Christ being in all and upon all them that believe. They have made thee a prince, saith the Scripture, therefore exalt not thyself, but be as one of them. Yea, the Lord commands, 'Whoever will be chief among you, let him be your servant.'—'The ruler,' says Jerome, 'ought, by his humility, to be the companion of them that do well, and by his zeal for justice, to stand boldly up against the sins of the wicked, yet so as never to prefer himself to the good.'"

He places before every other requirement this, that the preacher should deliver, unalloyed and uncurtailed, the pure gospel according to Holy Scripture. "It is clear," he says, "that he only who teaches the word of the Lord is a true apostle and pastor. Whoever delivers a contrary doctrine is not to be believed."—"Whoever teaches that Christ has been made unto us for righteousness, the same is a teacher whom the Lord has given."—"As the law is not given for the righteous, but for the unrighteous and unbelieving, every one has, in the Holy Spirit, a leader who is above the law. For there is no other fulfilling of the law, but the shedding abroad of the love of God in the heart. He who has obtained this has become one spirit with God, and can say with the apostle, 'I live, yet not I, but Christ liveth in me.'"—"Whoever does the work of the law, even as respects its moral requirements, only in consequence of the law's constraint, keeps it in a more carnal way, and does not really satisfy its demands; but whoever, from the spirit of faith, and with a willing mind, executes the law's work, even as respects outward things, for him alone is the law truly spiritual. This genuine fulfillment of the law is the gift of that Spirit by whom every pious man is certainly actuated."

We must be indulged in a few more extracts, to show the bold character of his invectives against the carnal clergy.

"I despise," he says, "as a vain mask, the name and title, the honor and quality of whomsoever they may be, were it even an angel, not to speak of the pope, or a human being, *provided* they do not utter the words of life, but merely vaunt their office and dignity, and pretend that by these they have received authority to ordain what they please. Christ himself despised all this in the apostleship of the traitor Judas; and Paul would have all honor withheld even from angels, unless they minister as messengers of Christ.—So far am I from believing that outward show, and vain splendor, and pompous words, and the heathen salutation of Master, have any weight."

"The Apostle Paul himself claimed the belief of men solely for the sake of the gospel entrusted to him by God, not on account of his person, and not for the weight of his name. Even he aspires to be no more than a minister, apostle, and herald, and glories so little in what he suffers for the gospel, that he declares it to be folly to speak of his labors. Before such a pattern, let the flatterers, whom the Bishop of Rome permits to honor him with the titles of 'Holy' and 'Most Holy,' be silent and not breathe a word."

"The man from whom I hear nothing of Christ's righteousness, and in whom I perceive no insight and knowledge, I refuse to confess as a master; I own not in him the authority of a bishop, nor reverence him as a pastor.—I care not for the two-horned mitre—the shining *infula* affects not me—I abominate the priestly slippers decorated with precious stones and gold. High-sounding names are mere semblances, and anything rather than the badges of a true pastor, bishop, or teacher, when that is lacking which alone gives them worth, and renders them tolerable."

In reply to the plea of *antiquity*, for the papal traditions and devices, he says: 'It is an argument easily parried by any one who reflects that the Babylonian Empire is not commended for having stood for several centuries.—Be-

10*

sides, the Lord curses those who, for the sake of human traditions, transgress the divine commands. They who burden the people with new precepts show themselves not ambassadors of God and stewards of his word, but assume the airs of masters and usurp dominion. Wherefore, dear brethren, let us follow the exhortation of the apostle, and be no longer children, tossed to and fro by every wind of doctrine. We have a right to require from the pope and the priests, as successors of Christ and the apostles, the word of God [the pure doctrine of the gospel]. If they feed us with that, let us listen to them—but if not, then will we not admit them to dwell in our hearts, that so we may not seem to have fellowship with their wicked works and lying words."

"Let every one to whom a pastoral charge is entrusted, hear the words of the apostle, 'Feed the flock of Christ, not by constraint, but willingly, not for filthy lucre, but of a ready mind; neither as being lords over God's heritage, but being ensamples to the flock.' Nowadays however (alas for the mischief!) there are in the church more who feast and hunt than who labor, and who in this respect are very different from the apostle, who sought not gifts but fruit.—Not only is the salvation of souls little attended to; it is not attended to at all. The prelates ought not to be lords over God's heritage—but servants and stewards of the mysteries, even as Christ, the true Lord and Shepherd, took upon him the form of a servant, and bequeathed to us an example of humble ministering."

"The zeal with which the Saviour sought to extinguish ambition may be inferred from the fact, that he does not leave his followers at liberty to take a name designative of pre-eminence, but expressly forbids them to assume the proud titles of Master and Lord. For this reason I am often surprised that these names have found their way to the spiritual heads of the church, and that theologians and philosophers assume them as their peculiar privilege; although there is but One who is our Lord and Master, and in whom are hidden all the treasures of wisdom and knowledge; not to speak of the blasphemous and fulsome titles of most wise, most venerable, most blessed, vicar of Christ, hero, demigod, and even most godly, with which his flatterers fawn upon the pope, and which, considering the self-love of man, can scarcely fail to make him vain of his ornaments, and lead him to exult and fancy himself beautiful."

With respect to divine worship, he remarks: "Behold, Christian brother, how the whole face of the primitive church of Christ has been changed! It is considered priestly merely to move the lips, and coldly and unintelligently to mumble the prayers. It is thought a glorious thing when the deacons in churches *bray forth* the gospels and epistles. They only are considered to have done their part well, and gain the public applause, who, in chanting, lift their voice to the loudest pitch. None cares whether the psalm is likewise sung with the spirit and the heart; so that one is disposed to believe that theirs is no mistake who look upon human life as a comedy, and imagine that this is nowhere more manifest than in the church, and among the clergy."

Respecting the duty of obedience to superiors, he says: "I acknowledge the authority of rulers, in things which may be required of us without prejudice to piety. In such cases we have the example of Christ; for although bound by no law, he yet paid tribute to Cæsar; and in such cases no less do the apostles recommend obedience." But when rulers "inculcate things which are diametrically opposed to the law of charity and good will," he says, "we must obey God rather than man, and with body and soul resile from that which the princes enjoin, that we may not appear to have fellowship with their wicked works. It will even be lawful to protest, to resist them in season and out of season, and openly to rebuke them.—We have examples of such conduct in the prophets, apostles, and martyrs, nay in Christ himself."

These were certainly very remarkable sentiments to be put forth in that age. "He had," says Ullmann, "penetrated to the centre of Christianity, to the very essence of the gospel, to the righteousness, spirit, and life of Christ, in short, to that Saviour who, to all who embrace him by living faith, becomes a source of peace, love, and true morality. He recognized the love which is the offspring of faith, as the sole true fulfilling of the law; and this knowledge, embraced with his whole soul, gave him confidence and alacrity, both to labor undauntedly amid the difficulties of the present, and hopefully and joyfully to anticipate the future. He knew that the word of God was not held in great esteem, and that it could scarcely be preached except at the risk of life. Against this, however, he sought to steel his mind. He says, 'The language of our Rabbis is like that of the Jews in the days of the Saviour: Thou wast altogether born in sin, and dost thou teach us? How odious and intolerable to these proud and inflated Moabites is a preacher of Christ! Their cry is—

'Dii nostris istas terris avertite pestes!'

If, however, thou art enjoined to teach evangelical piety, than which nothing is so greatly disrelished, then suffer not thyself to be frightened and discouraged by the papal fulminations, curses, and interdicts. From bulls (made of paper and of lead), they dart but a harmless flash. The excommunicator was himself under excommunication by the Divine Judge, before he uttered his sentence; and with a curse upon his own head, he has no power to excommunicate others. There is therefore much greater cause to fear the curse which says, 'Woe unto you who call evil good, and good evil,' than that which human tyranny presumes to utter."

He seems to have looked forward to a time of deliverance for the afflicted church. "Come it will;" he says: "Our souls will perish with hunger, unless from on high some star of mercy rise, and dispel the darkness, and clear our eyes from the delusions with which they are bewitched by the falsehood of our rulers, and restore the light, and at last, after so many years, break the yoke of our Babylonish captivity.—Deliver, O God! thy people from all their tribulations!"

These few extracts will show the spirit and tenor of this extraordinary work. In his sermons he was no less bold in declaiming against many human ordinances and customs by which religion had been burdened. "The style of his preaching," says Ullmann, "was, in many respects, of distinguished excellence. He possessed intellect, fervor, and vivacity.—The effects which he produced, and the celebrity which he attained, give us ground to conclude that his gifts were considerable. But pure and irreproachable as a preacher he certainly was not. His boldness sometimes degenerated into arrogance, his popularity into pungent and provoking jests, such as, making all allowance for the rude spirit of the age, we cannot consider but as too strong for a man of otherwise so earnest a character. When (for instance) combatting the exaggerated estimate which was formed of priestly rites, such as unction with consecrated oil, he would venture to say, 'The consecrated oil is no better than that which is in daily use in your kitchens,' etc."—Yet it may be that some eccentricities of this character have been more or less exaggerated by those who put them forth, in that day, as specimens of the "Paradoxes" of the preacher, who so greatly roused the minds of the people, and kindled the animosity of the monks.

For about seventeen years he continued to promulgate, in the city of Worms, his views of the corrupted condition of the Romish church, and the great need of a reformation. Would that he had been endued with that fortitude and living faith, in a time of trial, which would have enabled him to seal his testimony with the offering up of his natural life for Christ and his gospel. But now comes the dark side of the picture. The monks and clerical body were enraged at his continued attacks and exposures; and the bishop, Reinhard of Sickingen, a man of very different character from his predecessor, Matthew of Cracow, became determined to put a stop to invectives which he doubtless felt were partly aimed at himself. John Ruchrath was accused of heresy, and charged with cherishing familiarity with Jews (then greatly hated and persecuted), and with the followers of John Huss. It is supposed that the charge of his favoring the Jews, was occasioned either by his pity for them under their cruel treatment by the populace, or by his seeking from some of them instruction in the Hebrew language, which at that time could not be obtained elsewhere. As regards the Hussites, there is no reason to doubt that he was convinced of the truth of some at least of their opinions; and he had probably manifested it by correspondence with certain of their number.

On these charges, in the beginning of 1479, he was arrested, and arraigned before a Court of Inquisition held in the city of Mayence, the seat of the archbishopric. The Court of Inquisition, with the archbishop, met at the Convent of the Minorites, where Ruchrath was in prison, and summoned him to renounce his errors and plead for mercy. John was now old and infirm, and rendered weak also by sickness. He came before them between two Minorite friars, pale, looking like a corpse, and supported by a staff. Instead of offering the old man a comfortable seat in his weakness and distress, a place in the centre, exactly opposite the archbishop and chief Inquisitor, was pointed out to him, where he might sit down *on the floor*. The Inquisitor Gerard Elten then addressed to him in person the offer of mercy. He was about to reply in his own defense, when he was interrupted by Elten, who told him to be *brief* in what he said, and to declare at once whether he meant still to adhere to his opinions, or was willing to subject himself to the decision of the church. He replied, that he had never taught anything contrary to the decisions of the church; and that if in his writings he had erred or said what was wrong, he was willing to recant, and to do whatever was right. On this he was asked: "Do you then ask mercy?" to which he answered, "Why should I ask mercy, having as yet been convicted of no crime, fault, or error?" "Well," said Elten, "we shall recall it to your remembrance, and commence the examination." Other members of the Court then joined in exhorting John to sue for mercy, probably suggesting to his mind the terror of the flames, to which he would otherwise undoubtedly be committed. At last he uttered the words, "I ask for mercy." This, however, weakened himself, and did not satisfy his judges, who concluded to proceed with the examination. They put to him, during two days, a great number of entangling interrogations, many of them of so trifling or irrelevant a nature that it is not worth while here to dwell upon them. To some of them he appears to have answered weakly or somewhat ambiguously; to others with candor and firmness.

Being asked whether he believed that infants, before birth, are yet without original sin, he replied that he certainly believed so. This was considered very heretical.

To the question, whether he believed or had written, that there are *no kinds of mortal sin*, except those which are designated as such in the Bible?—he replied that he did believe this, and will believe it till better taught.

Being asked whether he had written a book on Indulgence, and what he believes on the subject, he answered, that he had written such a treatise, and believes what is therein contained. He had replied to a query, that he did believe that the Bishop of Rome was Christ's Vicar; but being afterward queried of, respecting the vice-gerency of Christ upon earth, he answered, that he did not believe that Christ had left any vice-gerent, and appealed for proof to what Christ himself said when about (as to his bodily presence) to leave the world: "Lo, I am with you always;" inasmuch as these words distinctly intimated that he did not intend to appoint any one as his substitute, because it was his will to be present, and do everything himself; and added, that "if a vicar signifies one who in the Master's absence is to perform his work, then Christ has no vicar upon earth."

Being interrogated, what were his sentiments respecting the consecration and benediction of altars and cups, ornaments, lights, palms, herbs, " holy water," and other things, he replied that he believed there was no virtue in them to drive away evil spirits, or to effect the forgiveness of venal sins; and that "holy water" had no more efficacy than other or common water.

On the second day of the examination, he declared, " Though all forsake Christ, I, though I should do it alone, will adore Him as the Son of God, and continue a Christian." To which the Inquisitor answered, "All heretics say the same, even when already fastened to the stake." Being urged to ask for mercy in regard to his errors, after considerable colloquy he at length told them that they were compelling him to confess and sue for pardon, and added, "Well then, I do ask for mercy." Upon which he was told that this was not satisfactory, but that he must come voluntarily and ask for it; and he was again conducted to prison.

The next day he was visited in his prison by a deputation of three doctors from the Court, who came to exhort him to recant. He replied, "Ought I to act contrary to my conscience?" The deputies said, "No, for the articles are false, as you see yourself." John replied, "You say so, indeed, but you do not prove it." The deputies assured him they were sentiments which were condemned by the church, and questioned him respecting some other points of his belief. After much conversation, John finally declared that he would recant, if they would take the responsibility upon their own consciences; to which, of course, they readily assented. Here it is sorrowfully evident that he gave away what little strength he had left, to save himself from the punishment which he saw impending.

The day after, a form of recantation was presented to him, and he expressed his willingness to comply. Accordingly, about seven in the morning of the following day, the archbishop and chief Inquisitor, the doctors, prelates, and many of the clergy and laity, assembled in the refectory of the Minorites; and, after an harangue from Gerard Elten the Inquisitor, Ruchrath, with fear and trembling, but in a distinct voice, uttered the following words: "Most honorable Father in Christ, Archbishop of this renowned diocese, reverend father Inquisitor, and you, doctors, masters, and other reverend gentlemen, I voluntarily confess that errors have been found in my writings and sermons. These errors I now recant, and am also ready to recant them publicly. I submit myself to the commandments of the holy mother church, and to the tuition of the doctors.

I will endure the penance which has been imposed upon me, and I supplicate forgiveness and mercy."

Thus, through unwatchfulness, did Satan get the advantage, and thus weakly fell John of Wesel, after many years of advocacy of the truth, according to the measure to which he had attained.

After being somewhat further questioned, he declared himself ready to recant and abjure publicly in the Cathedral; but entreated that he might be allowed some decent place of habitation, instead of being sent again to the dark and filthy prison. The Inquisitor, however, would not permit this change until after his public recantation. This was accomplished on the following day before the people; after which he had doubtless expected to be set at liberty. But his enemies, who had him now completely in their own hands, were far from being satisfied with a mere recantation. His writings were condemned to be committed to the flames from which he had barely escaped; and he was sentenced to be confined for the rest of his life in the Augustinian Monastery at Mayence.

It does not really appear that his judgment was convinced or convicted of error in his teachings; for when he beheld his writings carried to the fire, remembering the good sentiments contained in them, and how much labor they had cost him, he wept bitterly, and exclaimed, "Oh, thou God of mercy, must all the many good things I have written bear the punishment due to the little that was evil? Such is not *thy* sentence, O thou God! who wast ready at Abraham's prayer to have spared an innumerable multitude for the sake of ten righteous. It is the sentence of men, inflamed against me with I know not what zeal!"

What must have been the feelings which forced themselves upon the mind of such a man, as during the ensuing two years he looked back upon his former faithfulness to his convictions! May we not hope that through the mercy of the Most High, he was brought to see the nature of his dereliction, and led to ask for a renewal of that divine favor and acceptance, which he had slighted in cringing to the power of the false church? He died in his place of confinement in the year 1481.

CHAPTER XII.

JOHN WESSEL.

JOHN WESSEL was born about the year 1419 or 1420, at Gröningen in Friesland. His parents were respectable citizens, his father, Herman Wessel, being by occupation a baker, and his mother descended from a family of good repute in the town. But losing both of them in early youth, he was kindly cared for by a benevolent matron of good estate, who educated him along with her own son. John was lame in one foot, having the ankle distorted; which circumstance may have promoted an inclination, as he grew up, to sedentary and scientific or literary pursuits. He was placed for some time in a school at Gröningen, and afterward in the institution of the "Brethren of the Common Lot" at Zwoll, where he had the advantage of forming an acquaintance with Thomas à Kempis, whose residence was within about half a league from the town. This acquaintance ripened into an intimate friendship, although Thomas was about forty years his senior; and this friendship appears to have had an important influence in moulding his opinions and forming the character of his subsequent life. It was about that time that Hamerken had just written his admirable work on the Imitation of Christ; and John Wessel has acknowledged that the perusal of that book was mainly instrumental in first leading him to a decidedly religious course of life. The instruction which he received at Zwoll, and the pious example of his teachers there, doubtless contributed to promote this inclination. But his active and inquiring mind was not fully satisfied with the amount of learning to be obtained in the schools of the "Brethren of the Common Lot," which was in some sort elementary, though practically useful and substantial. Indeed, it appears that he had an almost insatiable thirst for knowledge, in the departments both of science and literature, as well as in what was then called theology. His desire, says Ullmann, was to master everything the age offered as worthy of being known. And another of his biographers, Hardenburg, tells us that from his boyhood he had always something peculiar, and entirely repugnant to all superstition. Thomas à Kempis had a great veneration for the Virgin Mary, and on one occasion exhorted his young friend to evince the same reverence for her. Wessel replied, "Father, why do you not rather lead me to Christ, who so graciously invites those who labor and are heavy-laden to come unto him?" Thomas was also zealous in fasting, as in other parts of the usual discipline, and was once inculcating it upon Wessel, when he received from him this answer, "God grant that I may *always* live in purity and temperance, and fast from sin and vice!" The narrator of this incident adds that Thomas à Kempis was so much struck with his youthful friend's reply, that "he took occasion to alter some passages in his writings, which now show fewer traces of human superstition."

John Wessel had complied with all the usages and discipline of the school at Zwoll, and was appointed submonitor or lector to the third class of scholars; but the freedom of certain of his opinions, indicating the opposition which he afterward maintained to various superstitions, gave some umbrage to the inmates and authorities, which is supposed to have induced him to leave the school sooner than he might otherwise have done. From the comparatively sheltered and domestic roof of the "Brethren of the Common Lot," Wessel departed for the renowned University of Cologne, where he found a very different state of feeling among both students and professors. "Theology," says Ullmann, "reigned supreme at Cologne;" but it was characterized by "the stiff, gloomy, intolerant spirit of scholastic dogmatism;" very different from the warmth of practical piety with which young Wessel had before been associated. Cologne was the chief seat of the Inquisition in Germany. Laurentius, the founder of that part of the establishment in which Wessel now resided, had boasted that he had himself pushed that great reformer John Huss into the fire at Constance! Wessel was disgusted with the condition of things in the university, yet he went through his studies regularly, and in due time received his degree of Master of Arts. But he has complained that he there heard scarcely anything but the doctrines of Thomas Aquinas and Albert Magnus, calculated either to rivet his youthful mind to superstition, or else to satiate and disgust him with the scholasticism so much in vogue. The latter seems to have been the result with him, and he placed himself in opposition to many of the dogmas and traditions taught in the university. At the same time he highly prized the opportunities of consulting the valuable libraries with which Cologne abounded, and he made himself well acquainted with the Latin, Greek, and Hebrew languages.

After remaining several years at Cologne, he visited the seats of learning in several other countries; a learned education in those days requiring many years of assiduity, and the inspection of various libraries, as the art of printing was then in its infancy, and books were comparatively rare and enormously costly. A copy of the Bible is still to be seen in Utrecht, written by Jacob Enkhuysen about the year 1458, for which he charged 500 gold guilders; although money was then many times more valuable in comparison with the commodities of common life than it is at the present period; when, nevertheless, the poor can purchase a good copy of the Holy Scriptures for half a dollar.

It appears that Wessel spent many years of his middle life in Paris, arriving there about the thirty-second year of his age, and residing there chiefly until 1470, when he went into Italy for about two years, and then returned to Paris. Here in 1473, he met with the celebrated John Reuchlin, who has been called "the restorer of Hebrew literature among Christians,"* with whom he afterward at least renewed his acquaintance at Basle in 1475, if he did not even become his tutor.

The University of Paris, at the time of his residence there, was the scene of endless disputes among the learned on subjects which now appear worthy only of ridicule. Abstruse questions, of no practical importance whatever, assumed vast proportions in the interest of the opposing factions of Nominalists and Realists, though really too childish to be worth dwelling upon, and at length became the subject of a royal *ex parte* interference and interdiction. For an example of the entangled nonsense which, in the middle ages, was called philosophy, we may refer the curious to what Ullmann has said of these disputes in his elaborate memoir of the life of Wessel.† It is indeed sorrow-

* McCrie's History of the Reformation in Italy, p. 29.
† Translation into English by Menzies, p. 300. "The antithesis between *Realism* and *Nominalism*, which runs through the whole theology and philosophy of the middle ages, has its extreme roots in the philosophical sys-

ful to consider that such empty disputations constituted a large portion of what was then deemed the study of theology. Wessel became involved in these discussions, along with almost every one else in the University of Paris, probably to his own injury in so far as they drew his mind away from the comparatively simple views of religion which he had imbibed among the Brethren at Zwoll. Yet he did not blindly follow the popular religious current. Whatever he found openly contrary to the Holy Scriptures, he felt bound to call in question. Thus he was led to oppose

tems of antiquity, especially in the antagonistic modes of thinking of Plato and Aristotle. . . . . Taken in the most general point of view, the dispute related to the question, *whether* so-called *universals possess objective reality*, or have merely *ideal existence* in our thinking? . . . . By universals two things could be meant, either the five general ideas of the Aristotelian logic, which were likewise called predicables—or generic ideas. . . . . In the sequel, universals were usually understood to mean generic ideas; and respecting these, Realism taught that they had an objective existence even apart from our thought; whereas Nominalism asserted that they were merely abstractions of human thinking, verbal signs, names, nay, as Roscellinus is said to have expressed it, a breath of the mouth. For example, the Nominalist required to say : That which we call mankind does not exist as such, but only in this or that person. It is merely an idea abstracted from the generality of the individuals—a form of thought in which these are all comprehended. The Realist, on the other hand, maintained that mankind is also something actual, either the prototype of humanity . . . . or their proper and formative substance. . . . . At first the contest possessed merely a metaphysical interest. But in course of time, by the application of the philosophical conclusions to particular doctrines . . . . . it also acquired great ecclesiastical importance . . . . (p. 301). When Wessel lived, there were four different systems upon the subject . . . . viz., a twofold form of Realism and a twofold form of Nominalism."

The above brief statement is important as affording a sample of the utterly empty scholastic disputes with which the universities wasted the time and intellects of their students. Applied as this jargon was to theology, it seems like an awfully daring and impious attempt to scan, by the powers of the human intellect, the incomprehensible mystery of the Divine Being, as Father, Son, and Holy Spirit.

some of the cherished articles of the Romish creed, and even to doubt the absolute authority of the Romish church, and of its head, the pope. He was willing to go along with the pope, only when the pope went along with the Scriptures. He trusted in Christ as his Redeemer, rejecting all personal worthiness as forming a claim on the favor of the Most High, and of course all desert or merit accruing from ecclesiastical penances or what were deemed good works. In this respect he seems to have advanced further than the pious friend of his youth, Thomas à Kempis. He was decidedly opposed to Indulgences, and attacked at the same time the Romish doctrine of Purgatory. He desired a return to the primitive condition of Christianity, so far as he understood it, in the constitution of the church. The traditions and the hierarchy of Rome he considered as something interposed between Christ and his church. The sale of Indulgences was to his candid mind an abomination, and he openly expressed his sentiments respecting it, says Ullmann, before all descriptions of men. The degradation of morals among the students of the Universities of Cologne and Paris greatly disgusted him. He looked there in vain for Christian piety, or even good morals. He thus expresses his feelings in regard to it. "In fact, what I saw when living at Cologne and Paris was doubtless odious to God; I mean not the study itself of the sacred sciences, but the moral depravity with which it was mixed up."

During a portion of the time of his residence in Paris he appears to have been engaged in imparting instruction, partly in the form of lectures, both there and in cities within a convenient distance. At Angers, in particular, he delivered public lectures, in which he took occasion to advocate freely his opinions concerning Indulgences.

In the year 1470 he went into Italy, and visited Rome; where he cultivated an intimate friendship with Francis de

Rovere, who, the next year, while Wessel was still there, was elected pope, and took the name of Sixtus IV. With this pope's particular friend the Cardinal Bessarion, Wessel had previously made acquaintance in Paris; and (what seems remarkable) he now sheltered himself under their friendship to promulgate in Rome itself, with greater security, his liberal and reformatory opinions. He had considerable medical knowledge and skill, and it has been said that he attended Sixtus in the capacity of a physician. Whether it was through his influence that this pope gave his sanction to the institutions of the Brethren of the Common Lot, is a matter of doubt, but it seems not by any means improbable. On one occasion soon after the elevation of Rovere to the papal chair, Wessel waiting on him was invited to ask for some favor from the new pope. To this he modestly and frankly replied: "Holy father, you are well aware that I have never aspired after great things; but now that you occupy the place of supreme priest and shepherd on earth, my desire is that your reputation may correspond with your character; and that you may so administer your exalted office, that when the Chief Shepherd shall appear, he may say to you, 'Good and faithful servant, enter into the joy of thy Lord;' while you on your part may be able confidently to aver, 'Lord, thou deliveredst unto me five talents; behold, I have gained beside them five talents more.'" On the pope remarking that this was a matter which belonged to him, and that Wessel should now ask some boon for himself, he said, "Well then, I ask you to give me from the library of the Vatican a Greek and Hebrew Bible."— "It shall be done," replied Sixtus, astonished; "but, foolish man, why did you not ask a bishopric, or something of that sort?"— "Because," rejoined Wessel, "of that I have no need." Ullmann adds that the Bible was accordingly given to him; and this remarkable manuscript, which was more precious to Wessel than the possession of a bishopric, is said to have been long preserved in a convent near Gröningen, where he spent part of his declining years.

He very undisguisedly expressed his sentiments respecting the subject of Indulgences, among all classes at Rome, not excepting those belonging to the papal court. But many of these persons had long ago divested themselves in reality of all religious sensibility, so that they could treat the prevailing prejudices, or even opposing views, with indifference if not with ridicule. Thus Wessel could for a time express his opinions with the more impunity; but he learned by personal observation the hollowness and corruption of the Romish priesthood, and returned to France with his reformatory sentiments practically confirmed. This was probably about the year 1472, and he does not appear to have ever afterward felt any inclination to revisit Rome.

Resuming his residence in Paris, he was soon afterward invited by Philip, Elector Palatine of the Rhine, to a position in the University of Heidelberg; which invitation he accepted about the fifty-eighth year of his age. In this same city Jerome of Prague had, about seventy years before, on publicly posting up reformatory theses, been peremptorily forbidden to call in question the prevalent dogmas. Here also Melancthon afterward studied, and Luther at a still later day kindled much ardor for the doctrines of the reformation. The elector, it seems, was desirous that he should lecture on theology; but here an obstacle soon presented itself. Wessel had never taken a degree as Doctor of Theology, and had always refused on any account to submit to the tonsure as a priest; and the faculty would by no means consent to such an innovation as to place one who was not holding such an ecclesiastical position, in that professorship. He therefore took the chair of

Philosophy, in his capacity of Master of Arts. His lectures included some reference to the Greek and Hebrew languages, and afforded him frequent opportunities of freely speaking his sentiments on the defects and corruptions of the Romish system, and of what was called theological science. He continued his labors at Heidelberg for but a few years. "It was he," says Ullmann, "who sowed the first seeds of that purer Christian doctrine, which we find springing up here, with so rich a growth, about the commencement of the sixteenth century."

But his free teachings, so opposite to the scholastic dogmatism of those times, were not likely to make his abode in Heidelberg a couch of ease. A jealousy also ensued among the other teachers, who saw and felt his preponderating influence. The monks hated him for his determined opposition to their bigotry and superstition; and their inclination to bring him into trouble showed itself at various times in a way which convinced him that they only wanted opportunity for the commencement of persecution. About the year 1479, his friend John Ruchrath of Wesel was imprisoned, and his writings condemned by the Inquisitors, and a report reached Wessel that he was even condemned to be burned. This he looked upon as a clear indication of what might perhaps soon befall himself. He had already retired from Heidelberg into his native country of the Netherlands, being weary of the animosity which pursued him. He now appears to have taken the resolution to spend the approaching evening of his life in comparative privacy. The dreaded prosecution, however, was averted, probably owing in part at least to the known protection and hospitality extended to him by David of Burgundy, Bishop of Utrecht and half-brother of Charles the Bold; a man who delighted in the society of men of great talent and celebrity, and endeavored to promote some reform in the ecclesiastical body.

This prelate once wrote to Wessel: "I know there are many who seek your destruction; but while I am alive to protect you, this shall never be."

The biographer of Wessel to whom we have so often referred, says in regard to this period of his life: "Wessel believed that the time was now come for him to direct the current of his life more into the channel of peaceful contemplation. In doing so, however, he did not cease to employ his pen and tongue as industriously as ever, but only gave to his industry a more calm and exclusive character. He frequently visited his friends, and received visits in return. It was his custom annually to repair to the scene of his early education, Zwoll and the contiguous Mount St. Agnes. Here he was surrounded with the memories of former years, especially of his paternal friend Thomas à Kempis, and in no spot of his native land did he love so much to dwell. From the abode thus endeared to him by the remembrances of youth, Wessel was wont to resort to the monastery Adwerd [about two leagues from Gröningen], where he had many friends and scholars, to whose number he was continually adding." Belonging to this monastery "there was a sort of academy, frequented by the youth from all Friesland, who, in a lower school, were taught the elementary branches of knowledge, and then promoted to a higher, where, under professors of greater learning, they prosecuted their studies in philosophy and theology. These schools had formerly been in a very flourishing condition . . . . . but they were now somewhat upon the decline. Wessel made great efforts to revive them, in which, at the outset, he was supported by the abbot, Henry Rees. At his death, however, hindrances were cast in his way. During his visits to Adwerd, he endeavored to operate on the minds of the monks and the susceptible youths. He encouraged them to the study of Hebrew, explained to them the Psalms, pointed out the mistakes in the Vulgate, answered the questions and solved the difficulties they proposed; and occasionally read aloud a passage from the original Hebrew text, at which all that the monks could do was to wonder at the outlandish sounds. These exertions were not unsuccessful. Adwerd, for a time, united together all the men of learning in Friesland and the surrounding countries."

"In like manner Wessel everywhere endeavored to operate upon the young, and sow the seeds of improvement in their souls. He directed their attention to what was defective and pernicious in the prevailing method of education.... and prepared their youthful minds for the rise of a brighter day, which he never doubted would come at last, but of which he only caught a distant view." "Wessel used to foretell, with the most perfect certitude, the speedy and total overthrow of scholasticism. To one of his favorite pupils, who applied to him for advice about the prosecution of his studies, he said, 'Young friend, you will live to see the day when the doctrine of Thomas Aquinas and Bonaventura, and such other modern dialectical theologians, will be rejected by all truly Christian divines.'" This was literally fulfilled, Oestendorp, the student alluded to, being still living about the year 1528, at which time scholasticism had received its fatal blow from the reformation.

"Upon another occasion he declared, 'It will come to pass ere long, that these irrefutable teachers, with their hoods and cowls, both black and white, will be forced to retreat within due bounds.' In this manner Wessel guided the current into a new and better channel ... and as they had once done to Gerhard Groot and Florentius Radewins, persons of all ages from the surrounding district resorted to the old and experienced man for advice and instruction." "In the list of Wessel's scholars, the two who, both as the oldest and the most distinguished, undoubtedly claim the highest place, are Rudolph Agricola, and John Reuchlin." In this manner, as well as in his published works, did Wessel's labors serve to prepare the minds of his countrymen for the great change which took place in the next century.

"The piety of Wessel," says Ullmann, "evinced itself most of all as a vital consciousness of dependence upon God, and complete devotedness to his will. . . . 'All that I have,' he says, addressing the Divine Being, 'is from thee. Not by my own wisdom, or my own device, or my own labor, am I what I am; but I am this and all else because such has been thy will. Thou hast commanded, and I am here. And for this reason, I do not merely commit myself to thee with confidence, or devote myself to thee in faith, but, as is my duty, I give myself wholly up to thy will. Use me according to thy free pleasure. Created for thy sake and by thyself, out of nothing, I ought to seek and expect nothing but thy glory. Then, whatever befalls me, provided it comes from thee, will be right. . . . Let this one thing suffice for my comfort, to know that such is the will of Him, without whose will not even a leaf drops from a tree; and in all situations let it be the firm anchor of my tossing bark, to have no other will but thine.'"

"And no less does his piety manifest itself as sincere and profound humility. Thoroughly as his mind was imbued with love to the Divine Being, he yet possessed that childlike modesty which considers its affection as far beneath the dignity of its object, and a consciousness that all he had to offer to God bore no proportion to what he had received from him. 'What shall I render to him for his gifts,' he asks, 'to whom I can render nothing which is not already his own, nothing which I have not obtained from him, and obtained as a boon? Woe is me! I must not be ungrateful, and yet to give him gift for gift in the least degree, is impossible. My very self and all that is mine is thine, O Lord, whether I choose or not. I received it without desert, and I possess it without the power of making any return for it..... With immeasurable obligations on the one hand, and total penury on the other, all that is left for me is to acknowledge and confess, and refer all to Him, and to admire, love, glorify him, and sweetly enjoy his bounties.' And in another place : ' What can I give to Him who gives all to me ? The violet of spring exhales its fragrance to the fostering sun. The winged gnat sports in its beams. But to Him who is my spiritual sun, what can I give in return ? In truth, to render to him anything of my own is impossible, and, toward such a lover, would be dreadful ingratitude and neglect of duty. . . . The only thing which I can give is a grateful heart.'"

In another passage of the same work (*Exempla Scalæ Meditationis*), he thus fervently expresses his feelings on the love of God to be perfected in heaven : " Oh, that will be a happy day, when I shall love, and not merely love, but love with all my heart, and soul, and spirit ! Nor will it even suffice that I truly, and sincerely, and purely love, but the nerve and force of my affection will be unspeakably heightened by Him who was born and gave himself for me. So that my love will then be exalted as far above that which we now feel, as heaven is above the earth, the sun above a spark, and the universe greater than a grain of mustard seed. And with a love thus elevated and inflamed will I keenly and fervently long and hunger and thirst after my God, and when at last my desires shall be crowned, and I shall possess and embrace their object, who will then paint my bliss ? Who can comprehend it, that has not burned with the same ardor ? Blessed, therefore, yea truly blessed that day ! Its blessedness is such as no eye hath seen, nor ear heard, neither hath it entered into the heart of man to conceive."

Yet it appears that toward the clôse of his life his mind was permitted to be brought into some painful conflicts. To a friend who visited him in his last illness, he is reported to have said, that according to his time of life and condition he was well, but had great trouble one way; for that he was tossed to and fro by conflicting thoughts, and even began to doubt of the truth of the Christian religion. Ullmann says that " even at former periods he had not been exempt from inward conflicts and scruples. But that which was the inmost and highest power of his life soon obtained the victory in the breast of Wessel. Many a time before, in a lively faith in the Redeemer, he had obtained inspiring glimpses into the eternal world, and long had he anticipated and extolled the happy day on which he would pass to an infinitely perfect life of love. And now, when the hour of his departure approached, he met it with steadfastness and joy. To the friend, when he repeated his visit, he said, 'Thank God, all the vain thoughts of which I spoke have vanished, and now I know nothing but Jesus Christ and him crucified!' . . . . A peaceful death at length emancipated his spirit, on the 4th day of October, 1489, and, supposing him to have been born in 1419 or 1420, at the age of sixty-nine or seventy." He left quite a number of works on various religious subjects, many of which, probably published only in manuscript, have been lost.

CHAPTER XIII.

JEROME SAVONAROLA.

JEROME, or in his native Italian, Girolamo Savonarola was the third son of Nicolo Savonarola, and was born in the city of Ferrara in the year 1452. During his childhood, his grandfather, Michele Savonarola, a physician of great eminence, distinguished as a professor of the physical sciences and as the author of several medical works, undertook the charge of his education, but died when the youth was only ten years of age. Under his care, however, he had already made good progress in elementary studies and in the Latin language; and when afterward he was sent to the public schools of his native city, he is said to have evinced indications of the finest talents and the most acute intellect. He applied with such assiduity to the study of the liberal sciences as then taught, that in a short time he became famous for his acquirements, and far surpassed all his fellow-students. The scholastic theology and metaphysics of that age were much in vogue in these schools, and a great deal of valuable time was lost in endeavoring to imbue the minds of the young with what was scarcely any better than pagan philosophy. Young Savonarola at length became disgusted with "the jargon of Aristotle," and, being seriously inclined, betook himself principally to the works of Thomas Aquinas and the Holy Scriptures. He had at one time taken pleasure in the philosophy of Plato, but later in life he said, "I was then in the error of the schools, and studied with assiduity the Dialogues of Plato; but when God brought me to see the true light, I destroyed and cast away from me those futilities which they had incited in me the idea of writing. What does all this wisdom of philosophy serve for, if a poor old woman, established in the faith, knows more of the true wisdom than Plato?"

As he grew up toward manhood, his mind became more and more absorbed in meditation on religious subjects, and in those studies which have reference to the improvement and elevation of society. "All historians who treat of Savonarola," says his recent biographer, Madden, "are agreed that his youth was full of promise, and of evidence of great virtues as well as extraordinary intellectual endowments..... Though of a sanguineous temperament, and his nervous system most delicately organized, rendering him remarkably susceptible of external impressions, and sensitive even to atmospheric influences, he possessed bodily strength and robustness that made him capable of enduring great fatigues, of going through extraordinary labors. He possessed, moreover, a penetrating spirit, an ardent love of truth and justice, natural feelings affectionate, kind, and pitiful. He had strong sympathies with poverty and suffering, and equally strong antipathies for pride, oppression, and meanness of every kind."

Again he says, "We are told that Girolamo was a silent, joyless child, given to seclusion; that he shared neither in the amusements nor occupations of young people of his age; that he arrived to the age of twenty without ever having been seen in the fashionable resort for the citizens of Ferrara, the public promenade..... One opinion of his mind, from a very early period of his career, from his first entrance into college life, was a profound conviction of the vanity of all earthly honors and enjoyments."

These sentiments seem to have increased with his years. To use his own words, he saw and felt "the great wretchedness of the world, the iniquity of men, the debauchery, the theft, the pride, the idolatry, the dreadful profaneness into which this age has fallen, so that one can no longer find a righteous man.... I could not endure the great wickedness of certain parts of Italy; the more also seeing virtue exhausted, and trodden down, and vice triumphant." He longed to retire altogether from such scenes, and at length, in 1475, before he had attained to his twenty-third year, he took a resolution, so often taken in those disturbed times by those who were oppressed with a sense of the wickedness which surrounded them, and saw not clearly that the evil one can penetrate into the secret recesses of the cloister, as easily as into the busy streets of cities. He determined to leave his father's house, and devote himself to a religious life in a Dominican convent at Bologna. His first purpose was, not to become a priest or monk, but merely as a lay brother, to reside there permanently as a safe refuge from the vices and dangers of the world; but the monks of the convent soon appreciated the importance of indissolubly attaching to their community a youth of such promise; and by the time that his year of residence there had been accomplished, which was requisite for a noviciate, they induced him to assume the full habit and obligations of their order. Here he applied himself with great assiduity to the perusal of the Holy Scriptures, so that it is said he almost had them word for word in his memory. He was also diligent in studying the writings of those who were esteemed as fathers in the church.

The Dominican monks were distinguished for their great diligence in preaching, and after a time it fell to Savonarola's lot to engage in this public function of the order. But his first attempts in the pulpit gave no indication whatever of his subsequent eminence and success. "In the commencement, he had neither voice, nor gesture, nor any manner that was suitable and fit," says an Italian author; "so that there was nothing whatever agreeable in his delivery, nor was any person pleased with it. But by a special gift of God, he afterward became a wonderful and admirable preacher." The same author adds, as an instance of his effective appeals in this way in after-life, that "On one occasion, when he was going by water from Ferrara to Mantua, he found himself in a boat with eighteen soldiers, who were indulging in ribaldry and filthy conversation. He begged to be allowed to say a few words to them, and having obtained their permission, he addressed some observations to them, exhorting them to change their mode of life and habits. But he had not spoken long, before they gathered round him, threw themselves at his feet, and confessed their sins, accusing themselves of many grievous crimes—and with many supplications and tears they humbly asked his pardon." Whether he then directed them to Him who only can forgive sins, this author does not say.

When he entered the monastic order, he abandoned all worldly property, except some clothing and a few religious books. Though somewhat delicately brought up, he now took pleasure in using the coarsest materials for his clothing, and food of the most simple quality and most sparing quantity that would suffice for his nourishment. No luxury or delicacy did he allow himself. His bed consisted of a few boards, on simple supports, with a sack of straw for a mattress. He had a very kind regard for the poor, and often spoke of them as his children. He feared, it is said, nothing in this world so much for the church and its ministers, as wealth.

When about thirty years of age, he had been appointed to preach in Florence; but his signal failure on his first attempts so discouraged him, that he resolved to leave the city, to appear no more in the pulpit, and to devote himself to more private instruction. This was in 1482, and the next seven years he passed in teaching noviciates in several convents in Tuscany and Lombardy, and in the convent at Brescia.

It seems probable that this discouragement in regard to his first attempts at preaching, was the means of leading him to more attention to the inward operations of the Great Teacher within his own soul. The Italian author* quoted above says that about a year after his leaving Florence, he "began to be made a partaker of the divine illumination;" and mentions the occurrence of what Savonarola believed to be a special revelation to himself respecting "the renewal" of the church, and likewise respecting a great and most distressing calamity, which was to attend the city of Brescia within the lifetime of some then living. In that year he spoke of it in private to some individuals, and also gave some cautious hints of it in public discourse; and on one occasion he was so greatly confirmed, that "all doubts were dissipated respecting the events foreseen; as he afterward related to the Count of Mirandola, and often declared in public, that of the things revealed to him, he had more certainty than philosophers had of the first principles they so much depend on." Sensible of the judgments impending on that city, it seems that again in 1484, in a public discourse, he felt himself called upon to exhort the inhabitants to repentance; and afterward, in the year 1494, in speaking during one of his sermons of his sense of the need of a renovation of the church, he mentioned the same circumstance, and declared that his mind was confirmed in it, "not only on account of the divine light," but also " on account of the enormity and infinite number of sins arising from the scandalous lives of prelates of every grade, and the great lukewarmness and relaxed discipline" of those professing highly

* Burlamacchi, Vita de Savonarola.

in religion The calamity thus foretold, came to pass six years after his thus reannouncing it, and two years after his own death, when, in the year 1500, the people of Brescia were so cruelly spoiled by the French, against whom they had risen in revolt.

In 1490, Savonarola was sent by the superiors of his order, to preach in Genoa, and he afterward returned to Florence. Here he was fearless in his denunciations against the corruptions of the times, and especially among the ecclesiastical dignitaries. His boldness of invective began to irritate those against whom his shafts were aimed, and soon the Franciscan monks were incited by the powerful family of the Medici to raise a popular outcry against Savonarola and the Dominicans. But he stood his ground, and from the time of the election of Alexander VI. to the papal chair, he ceased not to testify against the flagrant wickedness of that pontiff.

On his return to Florence, Madden informs us that the citizens "received him with joy and satisfaction ; and we are told their surprise was wonderful, at observing how great a change had taken place in his deportment, demeanor, voice, and gesture. A gracious sweetness that seemed to them ineffable, had spread over his features, and extended to his mode of speaking, and to his mien and manners. His instructions to the community were usually given in the garden of the convent, from a small chapel in the centre, and were attended by a vast concourse of people of distinction in the city, of the court, and of the schools. The intellect and piety of Florence were taken as if by storm by the irresistible eloquence of Fra Girolamo; his fame extended even to Rome itself." He was at length prevailed upon to deliver his discourses in one of the public places of worship ; and on the occasion of his first thus occupying the pulpit, a remarkable circumstance is said to have occurred. "He seemed for some minutes to be absorbed in deep and solemn thought—he then proceeded with his discourse—and after another solemn pause, and apparent meditation on things of high importance, he said, calmly and distinctly, 'I shall preach in the church tomorrow, and shall continue to do so for the space of eight years.' This was in the middle of 1490; in the spring of 1498 he was put to death."*

The account given by his Italian biographer, Burlamacchi, of what followed for some days after this remarkable prediction, is very curious. He says, "At this time [Savonarola was engaged in several discourses on the Apocalypse] there arose great diversity of opinions in the city; some saying that he was simple and well-intentioned; some, that he was learned, but very designing; many, that he gave credence to false and absurd visions.... There were three propositions that he especially enforced, and endeavored to impress on the minds of the people. The first was, That the church of God had to be renewed, and that in our own times—the second, That all Italy would be chastised by God's wrath—the third, That all the things predicted would speedily come to pass. Which things he satisfactorily showed were to be expected, by argument and resting on the authority of the Holy Scriptures, abstaining then from further reference to visions, the people not appearing much disposed to give credence to them.... Then the exceedingly disturbed and divided state of public opinion becoming daily more manifest, reflection made him apprehensive and timid, and he resolved to preach no more in the same style. But nevertheless, every other subject that he studied or read, dissatisfied him, and when he preached on other matters, he became still more discontented with his labors, and finally he felt his being, as it were, a burden

* Madden's Life of Savonarola, vol. i. p. 112.

to himself. Wherefore, commencing a series of sermons the first day of the Septuagint, 1490, in the church of the D'Uomo, in the first week having preached sufficiently on future events, he proposed on the following week to abandon that subject, and to preach on it no more. But, throughout the succeeding Saturday and the night of that day, he could not by any possible efforts apply his mind to other subjects, finding the way to every other consideration closed, and this one alone (of the Revelations) open to him. The morning came, and found him, after the long mental conflict during a sleepless night, wearied in mind and body; and in this state he heard a voice saying to him, 'Foolish man that thou art! Dost thou not see that it is the will of God that thou shouldst preach in the appointed manner?' Thus aroused, he immediately felt restored to himself; and shortly after ascended the pulpit, and preached a most admirable and wonderfully effective sermon."

He was appointed Prior to the convent "San Marco," the same year; and it is said that on this occasion he irritated the feelings of Lorenzo de Medici, by declining to call upon him as had been customary, to offer him thanks and request his protection for the convent. Savonarola took the ground, that his thanks were only due to the Almighty, and that to Him alone could he pray for protection. Lorenzo, however, covered up his anger, and endeavored for some time to gain him over to friendship and familiarity. But Savonarola steadily pursued his course of avoiding to court a familiar acquaintance with the great of this world. He continued, says Madden, "preaching and reprehending vice in severe terms, and menacing Italy with tribulations, declaring that there would shortly be seen a tempest which would shake all things, and put an end to the sunshine and fine weather which were now enjoyed." Many of the citizens became greatly offended at his preaching so continually in this manner, which sadly disturbed their couches of ease; especially the wealthy, with "the magnificent," the luxurious, and the haughty Lorenzo de Medici at their head. The latter at one time sent five principal citizens to endeavor to induce him to change his style of preaching to a more palatable one, charging them however not to let it be known that they came from him. But Savonarola, after hearing their persuasions, told them distinctly, that though they said they came of their own accord, yet he knew it was not so, but that Lorenzo had sent them; and he bade them charge Lorenzo "to repent of his sins, for God had ordained the punishment of him and his." Many at this time told him that he would be exiled, if he continued to preach thus; but he did not regard their threatenings. A famous preacher in Florence, one Mariano Genezanno, for whose convent Lorenzo de Medici had erected a most beautiful building, shortly afterward went to Rome, and in a sermon denounced Savonarola to the pope and cardinals, mentioning him by name, and using these words, " Oh, holy father, burn this agent of Satan; burn him; burn, I say, this scandal of the whole church!"

In the year 1492, the same year that Rodrigo Borgia commenced his pontificate under the name of Alexander VI., Lorenzo de Medici died. On his death-bed, being struck with fear and remorse, he sent for Savonarola. There are contradictory accounts of what passed on this solemn occasion; and Roscoe, in his Life of Lorenzo, seems to have desired to suppress all that was not favorable to the idea that this "magnificent" man died with the firmness and calmness of a *philosopher*. But the most reliable account seems to be,* that Lorenzo de Medici, conscious of many crimes, and especially weighed down by the remembrance of three great acts of enormity; first, the sacking of

---

* See Madden's Life of Savonarola, vol. i. p. 153, etc.

the city of Volterra, with the shocking cruelties ensuing; second, the taking of certain endowments from a charitable institution, by which many poor people suffered wrong; and third, the butchery of more than one hundred of his fellow-citizens, many of them under the very walls of his palace, and many of them, as he confessed, entirely innocent, after the defeat of a certain conspiracy; sent twice for Savonarola to consult with him in his distress, and to receive if it were possible some spiritual comfort. On the second entreaty, Savonarola went to him; and on his opening to him the state, "almost of despair," to which he had been brought by the consciousness of the near approach of death, Girolamo reminded him that God is merciful, but that he believed there were three things which it was needful for Lorenzo to be willing to do. On the latter asking what they were, Savonarola replied, that the first was, that he should strive after a great and lively faith in the pardoning mercy of the Almighty—to which the dying man assented. The second was, the necessity that everything wrongfully acquired should be restored as far as possible, leaving to his children as much as might be a decent maintenance for them as private citizens. At these words, Lorenzo roused somewhat, but after a little while said, "And even this will I do." The third requisite was, that he should restore to Florence her liberty, and to the people their former state of a republic. At these words, Lorenzo turned round in his bed with his back to his adviser, and gave him no answer. Savonarola then left him, and after some time Lorenzo departed this life. Some writers say that before Savonarola entirely left the room, being called back and solicited for a blessing, he did in some manner comply with the dying man's entreaty. What it amounted to, does not clearly appear.

Savonarola having been appointed Prior of the convent

in which he lived, and afterward to some official supervision of other convents of the same order, was diligent in promoting the practical reforms which he had so deeply at heart. Yet it is said that "there was always in his manner and in his looks a remarkable sweetness, which gave a peculiar but indescribable feeling of satisfaction and comfort to all that approached him." He slept only five hours during the night, and "his great recreation was to converse familiarly, though on subjects of solemn interest, with the novices," whom he called his children; and when he was with them "he always spoke to them of divine things, and of the sacred Scriptures."

The plague at one time committed great ravages in the city, and made its appearance in his convent; but he "kept his ground, undaunted by the closest contact with the sick, when nearly all the other members of the community had fled."

Early in the year 1492, he "relates that he had a vision, and in that vision he thought he saw a hand projecting from the heavens, holding a sword, with this inscription: 'The sword of the Lord upon the earth, soon and sudden!'" A few months later, this vision is thought to have been fulfilled, in the seating of that scourge of the earth, Alexander VI., upon the papal chair, bringing down untold evils upon Italy, and great scandal to the name of religion.

It appears also that he predicted the invasion of Italy by the army of Charles VIII. of France, in one of his sermons preached about the middle of the year 1494 in Florence. Guicciardini says, that "having publicly preached in Florence during many years, and combining a singular reputation for sanctity with much sound doctrine, Savonarola had acquired the character of a prophet, and obtained an immense influence in the estimation of a great number of people; because, when there appeared no sign (of danger) in Italy, but all were rejoicing in a profound tranquillity, he had predicted several times in his sermons the arrival in Italy of foreign armies, formidable on account of their strength and numbers, which would cast down their walls, destroy their troops, and burn their cities; declaring that these predictions, and many others which he introduced continually into his sermons, he did not make by means of human science, nor the interpretation of the Scriptures, but by a special divine revelation." And these predictions, says Madden,* "were accomplished sooner or later." Whether there were indeed any mixture of the workings of a vivid imagination in these remarkable predictions, it would be difficult now to decide; but it seems impossible fairly to doubt that he was sincere in his belief of a divine communication of the warnings through him, and equally impossible to deny that the events in a very few years evinced the truth at least of what had been predicted. In one of his numerous works he has expressed himself as follows on the subject of prophecy, adding that he had himself "attained to the knowledge thereof, and had always been certified of the truth, by the aforesaid light."—"Far removed from the scope of natural knowledge of every creature are future contingent events; chiefly those which are dependent on free will, which in themselves cannot be known by men, nor by any other created beings, because they are only present to the Eternal, whose knowledge embraces all times. . . . . . . Their future contingency cannot be known by any natural light, but solely by God, who knows them in the eternity of His light; and by him only are the things communicated to those to whom He deigns to reveal them. In such revelations there are two things done. One is, that God infuses a supernatural light into the mind

* Life of Savonarola, vol. i. p. 106.

of the prophet, which light is a certain degree of participation of His eternity [of light]. By such participation, the prophet judges of that which is revealed to him, that the revelation is true, and that it comes from God. And of such efficacy is this light, that the prophet is made certain of those things above mentioned, as the natural light makes philosophers certain of the first principles of science, and as people are made certain that two and two make four. The other thing that God does in those revelations is, that he propounds distinctly to the prophet that which he wishes him to know and to declare; and that he does in various ways, as it is written in Hosea, chap. xii. 10." He then mentions his views in regard to the revelation by visions, the manifestation of types and signs, and angelic mediation; adding, "And by the divine light, the prophets clearly know those apparitions to be angelic, and that which is spoken to them to be true."*

Savonarola's predictions at various times were quite numerous, and many of them were known to be fulfilled, some even during his own life-time. Yet there does not appear to have prevailed in his mind any spirit of exaltation on that account. He constantly gave the glory and praise to the Almighty, and spoke of himself as "an unprofitable servant," and unworthy of such favors from the Most High; but that the Lord, who had a right to choose whom he would for his instruments, had deigned to make use of him as "an arrow in His quiver."

Toward the close of that year, 1494, Italy was invaded by the French, the Medici family was expelled or forced to fly from Florence, their splendid palace was sacked, and a republican government was regained by the citizens. When

---

* "Compendio di Revelatione dello *Inutile Servo* di J. C., Hiero. da Ferrara."

the French king arrived in Florence, and demanded of it 120,000 crowns of gold, to enable him to continue his march on Naples, and, in default of payment of this great sum within twenty-four hours, had determined on the spoliation and utter ruin of the city, Savonarola went to him only an hour or two before the time of the night appointed for the wholesale massacre, and in a solemn manner warned him to abandon his design and leave the city harmless, or the cries of the innocent would ascend to the throne of God, and confusion and destruction would fall on him and his army. So powerfully did Savonarola plead for the safety of the city, that Charles was turned from his fixed purpose, and made a treaty with the inhabitants, accepting an honorable capitulation, ratifying the republican form of their government, and withdrawing his army from them. On Charles's return from the South, Savonarola again warned him of divine judgments.

After so remarkable and beneficial an interposition on his part on behalf of the doomed city, it was a natural result that his influence with the people became greater than ever. And here was a trying time for Savonarola's humility and integrity. "The gravest charge laid to his account in history," says Madden, "is that of his interference in temporal affairs." Yet he held no post or place in the government. His counsel was for several years freely requested and as freely given, in the attempts made by the citizens to settle the republican form of government for Florence. Like the great Pennsylvania legislator about two hundred years afterward, he earnestly desired that the laws should be conformable to, and based upon, the divine will; though, walking as he did in the mist of those dark times, surrounded by superstition, and entangled in the trammels of popery by his education, he saw not with equal clearness what that will was. The state of society, too, throughout Europe, was not then such as to warrant a reasonable expectation of the permanency of pure and liberal institutions in one isolated city. Yet during the few short years that his personal influence prevailed, and indeed for several years after his death, to some extent, a great reform was manifested in the morals of the people, which had previously been at a very low ebb.

He proposed four things to the people as conducive to their security: first, the fear of God, and a reform in their manners and customs, so as to do all things in a Christian manner and for Christian ends; second, a love of the commonwealth, sacrificing to it every private consideration; third, a universal peace, and amnesty for political offenses; and fourth, such a constitution of government as should secure to every class of citizens, by representation, a participation in the control of its affairs. The aristocratic class were dissatisfied with his suggestions; but the bulk of the industrial part of the population approved them, and prevailed.

A late author has thus described Savonarola's style of preaching: "Proverbs, questions with replies interrupted by pathetic enthusiasm, scriptural passages, practical applications of a surprising kind, but ever open to the plainest understanding—these stood in plentiful abundance at his disposal. . . . . . His stores seemed inexhaustible. He spoke in short sentences; without ornamental epithets; quick and practical as we speak in the streets; but uniting his ideas together in a current that carried away his hearers."*

Besides his diligence as a preacher, his pen was indefatigably employed, so that he left behind him many works on subjects of importance to the welfare of his fellow-men of that age. Madden says his writings and published sermons

* Hermann Grim's Life of Michael Angelo, vol. i. p. 153.

are characterized by "an all-pervading spirit of piety toward God, of compassion toward mankind, united with a profound conviction of the depth of the misery into which human nature has fallen, and the height of the excellence to which it is capable of being elevated by the grace of God. In every work of Savonarola these great sentiments are found embodied, and are always remarkable for the piety which pervades them." The same author says that by his preaching "a complete revolution was effected in the manners and morals of the people. High and low, rich and poor, young and old, gave edifying proofs of the wonderful power of the reforming friar of San Marco." . . . . . "People came three or four hours before the time appointed for the sermons, in order to procure a place, so great was the difficulty of getting even room to stand, when Fra Girolamo preached. But the most remarkable change that was apparent in the manners of the people, in their recreations and amusements, was the abandonment of demoralizing practices, of debauchery of all kinds, of profane songs of a licentious character, to which the lower orders of the people especially were greatly addicted. The amount of the restitution of money wrongfully acquired was enormous. Vast sums were advanced by opulent people to send to foreign countries for grain, of which there was a dearth at this period; and the supply thus obtained was disposed of at a moderate price to the poor. Money was also lent to a large extent to the industrious poor by the rich, free of interest, which had not been done previously, except on a very small scale, by some charitable persons." The effects of his labors were especially manifested in the behavior of the children and youth of both sexes. "They sedulously avoided theatrical spectacles and balls, masquerades, and public sports; they were simple in their clothing, and vanities and superfluities they were taught to look on with contempt." A juvenile confraternity* was formed under the sanction of Savonarola and the Signorial Council, the members of which were "not to be found at public worldly spectacles, such as theatres and masquerades." They were to be diligent in their religious duties. "Their clothing was to be simple, according to the condition of each, without *slashings* or other vanities. They should cut their hair close about their ears, avoid games and bad company like serpents, never hear or read impure books, either in their own language or in Latin, should shrink from lascivious poets as from deadly poison, and occupy themselves on festivals with divine things, not going to schools for fencing, dancing, singing, or playing." Another author says, that "It was an extraordinary sight for the Florentines, to see that youth formerly so boisterous, so undisciplined, so insubordinate, submit to a rule of life so contrary to its customs and to its natural impetuosity, and to have a great desire for pious exercises—during seven consecutive years."

Savonarola desired for the youth a solid school education, but one guarded from baneful influences. He once thus counselled the Florentines: "Ye fathers, let your children learn grammar, and keep able men as teachers

* M. Young, in his Life and Times of Palcario (vol. i. p. 574), does great injustice to Savonarola, in displaying in a ridiculous point of view certain public celebrations of these youthful confraternities, as if Savonarola was accountable for every extravagance or folly of an excitable people like those of Florence. He also very unjustly charges him with "cruelty and intolerance," "fanatical enthusiasm," and a "stern harsh spirit," that "knew nothing of the love of Christ," adding that he "was totally ignorant of the benign influence of the gospel," and "so little was he spiritually enlightened, that he thought of no other reform but substituting one kind of excitement for another." Such vituperations, unsupported by the smallest shadow of an attempt at proof, against a man of acknowledged piety and great public and private virtues, are unworthy of so judicious a biographer.

who are accomplished, and not players. Pay them well, and see that the schools are no holes and corners. All should practise grammar in some degree, for it wakens the mind and helps much. But the poets should thereby not destroy everything else. There should be a law made that no bad poet should be read in the schools; such as Ovid, *de Arte Amandi*, Tibullus, and Catullus, and of the same sort, Terence in many places. Virgil and Cicero I would suffer. Homer in the Greek, and also some passages from Augustine *De Civitate Dei*, or from Jerome, or something out of the Holy Scripture. And where your teachers find in those books Jupiter, Pluto, or the like named, say then —children, these are fables—and show them that God alone rules the world. So would the children be brought up in wisdom and in truth, and God would be with them."

A certain writer* says of him: "Drunkenness, sensuality, and profanity were overcome by Savonarola, and the triumph endured for some years during his life—nay, for upwards of thirty years after his death, the traces of it were to be witnessed in Florence. Is it exaggeration in sentiment or language to say that humanity owes more to the memory of the poor friar of Ferrara, of the fifteenth century, than to the merits of all the military heroes of Europe put together, who have flourished during the last 400 years?"

He earnestly deprecated all works of art that pandered to the depraved inclinations of fallen man, of which works, both statuary and pictures, there were abundance in Italy; and in consequence, a vast number of immodest paintings were given up to be destroyed. We are told by Rio that "His success so far exceeded his expectations, that he himself thought he could not attribute it to any cause but the miraculous intervention of the Divine mercy; and he was

* Quoted by Madden, vol. i. p. 404.

never more moved than in the effusion of his acknowledgment of the Author of that benefit."

But in 1495, it became evident that a reaction had been set on foot against his influence. His interposition in secular affairs, and above all, his invectives and active measures against the rapacity of the money-dealers, had exasperated these avaricious men; and they, in their turn, had incited the monks of the Franciscan order to endeavor to break down his popularity. He had constantly testified against the simony and corruption of Pope Alexander VI.; and in 1484, under the previous pontificate, in one of his sermons in the city of Brescia, he had publicly used the following bold language, after reproving the vices of the people and of the clergy. "Popes have attained, through the most shameful simony and subtlety, the highest priestly dignities, and even then surrender themselves to a shamefully voluptuous life and an insatiable avarice. The cardinals and bishops follow their example. No discipline, no fear of God is in them. Many believe in no God. The chastity of the cloister is slain, and they who should serve God with holy zeal, have become cold or lukewarm..... After the corrupted human race has abused for so many centuries the long-suffering of God, then at last the justice of God appears, demanding that the rulers of the people, who, with base examples, corrupt all the rest, should be brought to heavy punishment."

Still his enemies had not been able entirely and successfully to undermine him, or bring him into trouble with the authorities; and the people generally highly venerating him, the pope was for a time reluctant to proceed to extremities. From 1495, however, the opposition to him gradually augmented, particularly among the bigoted and immoral portion of the community. Many insults and annoyances were attempted, apparently with a view to intimidate him and drive him from his post. They set up a dead ass in his pulpit. They fixed sharp nails in the cushions along the edge in front of his pulpit, with the points upward, so that when he should strike his hands on the cushions he might inflict a severe wound. More than once his life was attempted to be taken, and mobs were raised for the purpose of exciting the passions of the worst of the populace.

About midsummer of that year, the pope issued a citation, requiring him, in moderate language, to "come as soon as might be to Rome, where he would receive him with paternal love!" Doubtless if he had trusted himself to this smooth invitation, he never would have lived to return to Florence. But he was sick at the time of its reception, confined to his convent, and attended by a physician, so that the citation fell to the ground. He replied by stating his inability for the journey, and protesting his fidelity to the church. After this a brief was sent from Rome, prohibiting him from public preaching in Florence. But on the remonstrance of the city government this prohibition was withdrawn. "He resumed his labors," it is said, "with an amount of vigor in his denunciations against ecclesiastical abuses, such as he never before displayed."

In one of his sermons, after alluding to the troubles coming upon him, he addressed the Almighty with these emphatic expressions: "I am come to a deep sea, and now long for the haven once more; and I look all around me for it, and I see no possibility of returning. I will say to thee, as the Prophet Jeremiah said (Jer. xx. 7, Vulgate version), 'Lord, thou hast persuaded me, and I have let myself be persuaded. Thou hast been too strong for me, and thou hast conquered. But I, on the contrary, have become a mockery—I am scoffed by every one.' Now,

Lord, that thou knowest I am at the mercy of this deep sea—thy will be done! But I pray God for this one boon, that the thought of death may always with me be associated with a firm hope, and a constant thinking of the Lord. If thou givest me the living knowledge of the glory prepared for thy elect, I will fear no danger on the waves of this world, but in the midst of all the troubles that beset me, I will be firm and joyful. Now, Lord, I am content with the path thou hast persuaded me to go, for it is full of sweetness and holiness. I thank thee that thou hast thought me worthy to be made an arrow in thy quiver, and to make me, in sufferings and troubles, like unto thee!"

In 1496, he received a second citation to Rome, accompanied by threats of excommunication against himself if disobedient, and against the city government, unless they compelled him to obey it. For several months he refrained from preaching; but at length, "at the instance of the authorities" of the city, and "the solicitation of vast numbers of respectable citizens," who represented to him the disorders that began to prevail again in Florence, he resumed his function, preaching, with even more earnest appeals than before, against the scandals given to religion, and the conduct of the dignitaries of the church. He said, "We must obey God, rather than man."

He soon received another citation, peremptorily charging him to abstain from all preaching, until he should appear in Rome; and a brief was sent to his convent, accusing him of blasphemy, rebellious language, craftiness, destructive doctrines, and of giving forth that he was sent from God. Yet the crafty pontiff, who was not yet sure but that he might bribe him to obedience, if he could not prevail by intimidations and the thunders of the Vatican, sent a confidential messenger to Savonarola, a "Master of the Sacred Palace;" who, after many long discussions lasting three days, finding he could prevail nothing by mere persuasion, at length said to him, "It has pleased his holiness, having been informed of your virtue and wisdom, to desire to elevate you to the dignity of the office of a cardinal, provided you proceed no further with revelations of future events!" To this Savonarola replied, in the true spirit of the martyrs, "The Lord save me from it! The Lord save me from it!—that I should resign the legation and embassy of my Lord!" The next day, from the pulpit, he alluded in a moving manner to his frequent warnings of the people, and, in allusion to the proffered dignity, made use of these solemn words, "I wish no other red hat, than that of the martyr's blood-stained crown!"

On one occasion during this year, after a suspension of preaching for some time, he again addressed the people, and in allusion to the circumstance of his appearing to act in opposition to authority, he made use of the following expressions:—"I act, in coming here, in obedience to authority! To whom?—Know then, that I have ascended the pulpit to obey Him who is the Prelate of all prelates, the Supreme Pontiff of all popes, and who makes known to me what is contrary to His will, and in nature opposed to it. It would be much more willingly that I would repose; but I cannot do otherwise than I do, because I must obey; and it is not as formerly, when I derived honor and glory from so doing; for now, things and times are turning to tribulation. . . . . My obedience, as you see, brings hatred on me, reproaches, mortal perils, and invectives from all quarters. . . . . He who confides in his own strength, and not in God, is a proud man, and the pride of man is a great weakness."

In the latter part of 1496, various conspiracies were concocted in Milan to assassinate Savonarola, and were defeated only by the vigilance of the government. An attempt was also made in the convent itself, to take his life by poison.

At length the pope became exasperated by the discovery that Savonarola had been writing to several sovereigns of Europe, calling on them to convoke a General Council to consider the sad condition of the church, and if possible to apply a remedy. Lodovico Sforza, Duke of Milan, whose fall from prosperity, and death in a prison, Savonarola had predicted (and which afterward came to pass), had intercepted two letters from Girolamo, one of which, to the Emperor of Germany, held the following language:—" Under heaven. there cannot be a greater sin, than to prevent the true worship of God, and turn it to the dishonor of the Divine Majesty; which crying sin to leave unpunished, and affect not to see it, and what is urgently required (for a remedy), is no other than to give sin a sanction, and a support to the enormous vices of men. For at present, in the church of God, we see a state of things in which, from head to foot, there is no soundness, but an abominable aggravation of all vices; you standing by quietly, and even bowing down to the great iniquity that usurps the seat of Peter, and which without shame runs into all disorders; and it is now long that the church is without a true pastor. I testify, *in verbo Domini*, this Alexander the Sixth is not a Pontiff, and cannot be recognized as such. For, putting aside his wicked crime of simony, by means of which he bought the papal throne, and every day makes larger sale of ecclesiastical benefices, and by other manifest vices, I affirm, among other things, that he is not a Christian, and does not believe in the existence of God, which surpasses every species of infidelity. And before all the world, in opportune time and place, I will discover his other occult vices, as my God has commanded me to do." And finally he solemnly calls upon the emperor " to have at heart the desire and the design to purify the church, and to liberate it from such astounding and contaminating pollution."

The other intercepted letter was to the Queen of Spain, much to the same purport. These two letters it is supposed the Duke of Milan transmitted to his brother, the Cardinal Ascanio, at Rome. It is at least known that he sent to Ascanio another letter of Savonarola's of the same import, addressed to the King of France, urging him to call a General Council for remedying the calamities occasioned by the scandalous life of Alexander. From the time of his obtaining a knowledge of these letters the pope conceived "a deadly hatred" of the faithful friar, "which nothing could appease to the last hour of Savonarola's life."

A brief of excommunication was issued from Rome, late in the spring of 1497, both against Savonarola and against "all who abetted him, spoke with him, or attended his sermons." The Signoria of the city remonstrated against it in two appeals to the pontiff, but in vain. "Savonarola remained," says Madden, "a silenced and anathematized friar, scorned by his brethren of *other* orders, scowled on by the secular clergy, and, in the sight of the Borgias, a son of perdition, a sower of sedition, and a heretic. The father bore the ignominy with becoming meekness and resignation. He was advised to solicit the pope to remove the excommunication, and acknowledge the errors imputed to him— but this he refused to do."

Yet another, and an almost incredibly absurd attempt was made to corrupt him who had renounced all worldly property for conscience' sake, who had for years held as an abomination all bargaining in sacred things, and who had so recently refused to purchase the dignity of cardinal at the price of his faithfulness to apprehended duty. Cardinal Piccolomini of Sienna, subsequently Pope Pius III., wrote to Savonarola from Rome, "making a tender of his good offices with the pope on certain conditions, more or less important, for the removal of the excommunication, and undertaking to have that object effected, if he would pay the sum of 5000 scudi to his (the cardinal's) creditors in Rome!"* It is almost needless to add, that Savonarola declined to purchase such services. He replied, that he had preached the truth, and he would stand by it, though the earth should open beneath his feet, and the sky should fall on his devoted head.

Things were now fast drawing to a crisis in Florence. The excommunication let loose upon Savonarola a state of open warfare, instead of covert and insidious attempts to undermine him. The agents of the Medicis and of Sforza were also secretly at work among the aristocratic party in the city, and among the Franciscan friars; and soon a conspiracy was discovered and frustrated, the object of which was to bring back the son of Lorenzo de Medici to tyrannize as before over the liberties of the city. On this occasion Savonarola did not escape censure among those who desired an occasion against him, on account of his not having interposed to prevent the execution of five of the citizens implicated in this conspiracy. It was said that he ought to have prevented the shedding of blood. But there is no evidence to prove that any intervention on his part would have been availing, in the highly excited state of the public mind at that time, when their recently-established republican government was threatened with destruction; nor had Savonarola any other than advisory influence, and certainly no other authority whatever to meddle with the administration of justice, than attached to any one of the citizens having the welfare of the city at heart.

But notwithstanding the discovery of this plot, the party opposed to Savonarola, before the middle of 1497, had in

* Burlamacchi, as quoted by Madden, vol. i. p. 436.

various ways insinuated themselves into power, and they gradually absorbed the authority of the state. The wealthy families, together with the corrupt portion of the citizens, the Franciscans, and the agents of Rome, proved too strong for the continued maintenance of power in the hands of the people who were on the side of morality and improvement. The government went into the hands of those who with scarcely an exception were hostile to Savonarola. The Signoria issued their command that he should preach no more. In his last sermon he said to the people, "Let the Lord do his work. He is the master of the forge who handles the hammer; and when he has made use of it, he lays it not on what he has wrought, but casts it from him. Thus he did with Jeremiah, whom he permitted to be stoned to death when his preaching mission was accomplished; and thus also will he do with *this* hammer, when he has used it after his own manner."

The Franciscans now became more furious in their attacks upon him from the pulpit. Savonarola had more than once in his discourses expressed his willingness to seal the truth of his testimony, if needed, with his natural life. His enemies now took up this matter to make the most of it for his ruin They put forth a Franciscan monk to offer to undergo with Savonarola the ordeal of fire—a barbarous relic of the dark ages—to test the truth of his doctrines or their own by the escape or destruction of either party. One of Savonarola's brethren, Domenico da Pescia, volunteered to accept the challenge on the part of Girolamo. It is to be feared that Savonarola was not sufficiently firm on this occasion in discountenancing this antichristian and barbarous mode of settling the question; though we have no evidence from history to show that he really approved of it. He seems to have taken up the persuasion that the infuriated populace demanded it, and that there was no escape from it. The Signorial Council, anxious for his destruction, urged it forward, and without waiting to hear from Rome, made preparations in the spring of 1498 for its accomplishment. In the middle of the public square a platform was erected, and on it two long piles of wood and other combustible matter were placed, leaving a space between them for the passage of the two contestants. An immense crowd of people assembled at the appointed time. The Franciscans, however, when the matter came to the point, began to cavil against certain arrangements. They pretended a suspicion that Domenico da Pescia might have enchanted clothing upon him, and insisted on his removing them. This was complied with. They then quarreled with his intention of carrying the crucifix, or "the symbols of the sacrament," into the fire with him. This was a matter which da Pescia could not dispense with, and Savonarola also insisted on it. After a length of time consumed in this manner, the commissaries returned to the Signoria, and reported what had passed. " It now became manifest," says Madden, "that there was no serious intention on the part of the Franciscans to venture on the trial, but solely a purpose to protract discussions about arrangements, and to tire the patience of the people. The commissioners returned, and one of them said to Fra Girolamo, 'The Franciscans are raising so many objections that it is impossible to satisfy them. It may be truly said, that on your part there is nothing wanting. The failure has been on theirs.'" Savonarola said he feared it would not be possible to restrain the people. This pagan experiment having been thus frustrated, "the Signoria then sent a strong guard to protect them, and thus the Dominicans were conducted to their convent through an enraged populace, disappointed at not enjoying a great spectacle."

It is much to be regretted that Savonarola ever gave

any countenance to such a proposal. But we must bear in mind the customs of those dark ages, from which society had not yet emerged; we must remember that Girolamo, with all his piety and all his comparative enlightenment, was yet a monk, and subject, by his education and associations, to the influence of much of the bigotry and superstition which hung over him like dark clouds, obscuring the brightness of that light which at times beamed with glowing effulgence upon his mind; and we must also take into account the fact that this spectacle was not a new one in Florence, and was demanded by the voice of a mob, thirsting for such a sight.

Madden says: "On the evening of Friday, the 7th of April, 1498, Savonarola retired from the Piazza, the scene of the proposed ordeal, to his convent, a doomed man. His enemies had effectually worked upon the evil passions of a giddy multitude, ignorant and superstitious, fickle, and prone to fanaticism, passionately fond of spectacles and pageants, and fierce and brutal in their anger when their gratifications were interfered with. The Franciscans and their adherents circulated a statement among the populace, calculated to excite them to some desperate act of outrage on the Dominicans, that Fra Girolamo and his associates wished to burn the blessed Eucharist, and were only prevented doing so by the Franciscans. This rumor, extensively circulated, produced feelings of great exasperation against the Dominicans. On the following Sunday evening, the 9th of April, a number of the faction hostile to Fra Girolamo congregated about the Duomo, and began to cry 'to San Marco!—to San Marco!' The crowd was augmented by a great many of the idle, dissolute youths of the city, who commenced arming themselves with stones. There were evidences of a preconcerted plan of attack on the convent and on the friars. . . . . . Some armed villains met a young man of noble family going to the church of the Annunziata, and repeating to himself some devotional verses. They attacked him with their lances, exclaiming, 'Villain! still we have psalm-singing,' and slew him on the steps of the church of the Innocents.

"Arrived at San Marco, they immediately commenced an attack on the chapel with a shower of stones, while the monks were singing vespers. They waited for night before they made any attempt to break into the convent..... The doors of the convent were made as secure as possible by the monks, and the friends of the father, who had been able to gain admission, for his protection..... The father observing some of the monks with weapons in their hands, said to them, 'The arms of monks should be spiritual, and not carnal.' He desired those monks to throw down their weapons immediately...... Notwithstanding Fra Girolamo dissuaded his brethren from using arms in their defense, Fra Domenico da Pescia and some others assisted the citizens who had come to their assistance." But "the majority of the community remained with Fra Girolamo in prayer .... momentarily expecting death. Amid the horrid tumult, whenever there was a pause, they were heard singing all in unison, as if with one voice and mind, 'Salvum fac populum tuum, Domine, et benedic hereditati tuæ.'" Ps. xxviii. 9.

Fire was, after a time, applied to the doors, and an entrance thus effected by the furious rabble, who rushed in, with bloodshed, plundering, shouting, and shrieking, and a portion of them reached the choir, where Savonarola and some of the monks were still at prayer. On seeing them he calmly asked them what they wanted, and reproached them for the tumult. Meantime many attempts were made by the other monks and some citizens to defend the place. The chapel became filled with smoke from the fires which had been kindled; but Burlamacchi says, "It appeared miraculous, that though there were about two hundred of the community congregated around the great altar in the choir, none were wounded there, though stones were almost incessantly flying in from the windows, and shots fired at them." Several were killed and wounded in other parts of the building. At length Savonarola was informed that artillery had been brought and planted in various places round the walls, to demolish the building. The commissaries of the Signoria made their way into the convent, and exhorted him to present himself before the Council along with Domenico and another friar, or otherwise the building would be totally destroyed. On receiving the order for their appearance in writing, along with a distinct promise that they should be safely restored to their convent, Savonarola and the two other friars declared they would obey the command of the Signoria. But before leaving his brethren, he called the community together for the last time, in the Greek library attached to the convent. There, says Madden, quoting Burlamacchi, "he delivered an admirable exhortation to them in the Latin tongue, entreating them to stand fast in the faith, keeping their souls in patience, and acquiring fortitude by prayer. The road to heaven, he told them, was by tribulations, and they were not to allow themselves on any account to be cast down. He was ready to suffer all things with alacrity and contentment, for the love of his Lord Jesus Christ, knowing that a Christian life consisted in doing good and enduring evil."

It was now about five o'clock in the morning of the 10th. After taking a little food, and speaking with his usual sweetness and serenity to those about him, he took his leave of his brethren, tenderly embracing them, and bidding them to persevere in the faith. "He then proceeded to the door of the library, where the commissaries, with arms in their hands, were waiting for him and his two companions." They bound his hands behind his back, and led him forth as a criminal. "No sooner did the prisoner issue forth from the convent, than a savage shout of exultation was raised, and the brutal populace rushed on the fettered prisoner, with the design of killing him on the spot; and were only prevented with the greatest difficulty by the guard. But as he was led along the streets, the populace showered maledictions, filthy names, and ribald abuse on him, beat him with their fists, kicked him, and flung stones at him."

The convent was plundered, and Savonarola was taken before the Signoria, with his two companions, Silvestro Maruffi and Domenico da Pescia. They were immediately examined, and to the inquiries put to Girolamo, he asserted that "those things which had been predicted by him were from God." Madden says, "This answer enraged the lords of Florence. They seemed to require no further proof of guilt; and forgetting the solemn pledge they had given of restoring the three friars to liberty, they gave directions on the spot to have them shut up in three separate places of confinement. And for the especial charge of the prisoners, and the conduct of the proceedings against them, they appointed a magistracy of sixteen persons, all notoriously hostile to Fra Girolamo and his ministry." One of these sixteen, however, though opposed to Savonarola, very soon perceiving the great malignity of the measures against him, declared "he would not stain his hands with the blood of the innocent," and entirely left them.

Savonarola and his fellow-sufferers were kept in prison forty-three days, and it is said that during that time Savonarola was put to the torture seven times. On one of these occasions he cried out, in the agony of his sufferings, "Tolle, Domine, tolle animam meam!" But as soon as the torture was suspended, he dropped on his knees and prayed for those at whose hands he had endured those sufferings.

During some of these occasions of torture, it is said by authorities hostile to him, that his enemies succeeded in extorting from the sufferer, in the extremity of his anguish, some ambiguous words, which they made the most of to spread the idea that Savonarola had confessed his error in assuming to predict future events. It is well known that the notary Ceccone, an abandoned character, whose life had been saved on a former occasion by Savonarola's kind intervention, was bribed by the offer of 400 scudi if successful, to endeavor to procure his benefactor's condemnation, and that this man, by the connivance of one of the judges, had a perverted and falsified account of the examinations by torture entered on the records of the court. It is, however, entirely possible, and perhaps probable, that Savonarola, during his sufferings, may have remembered that in some instances he had, through temptation and the frailty of human nature, gone beyond what the Inspeaking Word of the Lord had revealed to his soul as the message to be delivered to the people, and that he had added something from his own imagination, for which he felt now condemned; and he may have confessed this in his agony, in tones more or less distinct, to his tormentors. But it is on the other hand certain, that during the intervals of suspension of the torture, he warned them not to trust in words that might be spoken by him during the agony of suffering, when he might scarcely know what he was saying, and that he renewedly asserted his divine commission for his ministry. It is greatly to be regretted, if the weakness of nature induced him to say anything not true, either in exculpation or inculpation of his previous course; yet, were it even so, it would only furnish another evidence of the liability of the servants of Christ, through unwatchfulness, to fall, under great temptation, similar to the sorrowful case of the ardent and impulsive Peter, who denied his Divine Master even with cursing and swearing! If even all that Savonarola's enemies allege respecting his confessing his error in predicting future events were correct, it was acknowledged that this was only during the tortures, and that afterward he recalled all such expressions. And where is the man that is sure he would not himself have given way under such excruciating sufferings? Truly, it may be said, let him who has already made proof of his fidelity under such a trial, be the one to cast the first stone at Savonarola on this account. His enemies now determined to make themselves sure of his condemnation, by "packing" the Great Council of the city. Shortly before the day of election "about two hundred citizens were expelled from the Council," and when the elections took place "none but men of *the right sort*,'" says Madden, "were returned."

Meantime, in his prison, during the intervals allowed him, Savonarola endeavored to prepare for the event which he knew well was approaching. Among other engagements he occupied himself with writing meditations on Psalm li. (l. in the Vulgate version), beginning, "Have mercy on me, O God! according to thy loving-kindness." He had some years before written commentaries on the other Psalms, omitting this one, and giving as a reason, that he would reserve this Psalm to the day of his own calamity. His remarks upon it, written within a few days of his death, touchingly evince a deep sense of his own sinfulness and unworthiness, but also a reliance on the unbounded mercy of the Most High through Christ our crucified and risen Lord. This effusion of the dying martyr fills about thirty octavo pages, in the English version of it given by Madden.

At length, the public being admitted to the concluding scenes of the mock trial, " in an assembly of some thousands of persons," says Madden, " by order of the magistrates, the notary Ceccone [the bribed man before mentioned] publicly read the false process. At the end, he said he had omitted all the unimportant matter, and read only that which was indispensably requisite, being 'unwilling to divulge secrets of state'!"

" When, finally, it came to the question of condemning the prisoners to death, or sending them to Rome to be dealt with by the pope, the majority of votes appeared in favor of condemnation. Of the members of the Council, Agnolo Niccolini, a person of great experience in public affairs, spoke in the following terms to the assembly:—' Magnificent Signori, honorable magistrates, and most noble citizens—if we consider the history of the present time, and of past ages, we shall find that it would be difficult to meet, in any part of the world, a man of such excellent qualities, and of so high and noble an order of intellect, as this friar, of whose death we are now debating. Then, to lay to our doors the blood of so great and rarely gifted a man, whose like may not be born for many centuries, would seem to me to be an act too impious and execrable to be thought of by grave and prudent men. It appears to me then, that it is not for us to quench a light like that, which is capable of giving lustre to the faith, even when it had grown dim in every other part of the world; and not of shedding lustre on the faith alone, but on all the sciences, with the knowledge of which he is so fully endowed. I say, it appears to me, that if it were necessary, for the punishment of some fault, to imprison him, it should be in some safe place of custody, within some fortress if you choose, affording him commodious apartments, with pens, ink, and paper, and such abundance of books as he might desire to have. For in this manner, I have no doubt that he would write most valuable books, in honor of God, leading to the exaltation of our holy faith, and of a great utility to posterity. While consigning him to death, without utility of any kind, would bring on our republic, so honored and illustrious, perpetual dishonor and discredit in the minds of all men throughout the world.'"

But this was all of no avail. They condemned this "man of such excellent qualities," and his two brethren to death; and this condemnation was afterward ratified and sanctioned by two commissaries sent by the pope, who had heard of Savonarola's arrest, and was delighted at the anticipation of his destruction. The words of the sentence of condemnation "show plainly and indisputably that Savonarola was condemned on the charge of heresy, and on that alone."

Savonarola and his companions were now taken from the great hall of the Council to the common prison, through a dense crowd of people, "who heaped on them all sorts of abuse and scandalous indecencies of language as they passed by. The officers of this new place of confinement were far more rigorous and cruel than their former jailors. They obliged the prisoners to sleep on the bare flags, without bedding or covering of any kind. They allowed them no lights at night, and prohibited any communication between them. These officials were men degraded by debauchery and licentiousness to the lowest rank in the scale of human beings. . . . . . In their detestable jocularity, indignities of the grossest kind were offered to their prisoners. Sometimes they were struck on the face to rouse them, and desired to perform some miracles to amuse their tormentors."*

The prisoners received the intelligence of their condem-

* Madden, vol. ii. p. 88.

nation with calmness. Savonarola spent most of the ensuing night in prayer. During a part of it, at his request, the three prisoners were allowed a brief interview, after which they were again separated. Wearied at length with hardships, tortures, and mental conflicts, and with the want of all outward comforts, the fettered Savonarola requested of a friendly priest, Jacopo Nicolini, who attended him during the night, to be allowed to lay his head on his knees, in the absence of any other pillow, that he might take a little repose; and thus he took a short but very sweet sleep. On awaking, he expressed his obligation to his kind attendant, and added: "You know what tribulations I have predicted for this city. To you will I communicate the time of those terrible calamities. Know then, and bear it in your mind, that they will come when there will be in the chair of Peter a pope named Clement." Nicolini made a note in his pocket-book of this prediction, sealed it, and placed it in a convent for safe keeping. It was, after many years, delivered into the hands of Pietro Soderini, Duke of Florence, who had heard of it and sent for it. Strange as it may appear, this prediction of the dying Savonarola was fulfilled in the year 1530, during the pontificate of Clement VII.; when Florence was besieged and taken, after enduring great calamities, "having lost 8000 citizens, and 14,000 men, foreigners enlisted in her service. The city was utterly impoverished; for the citizens had expended all they possessed for the maintenance of the troops. It was full of lamentation and misery, of suspicions, strife, and suffering; it was scourged by the plague, which manifested itself still more violently after the capitulation, the imperial troops having been long previously infected by it."*

In the morning, the prisoners were again allowed to

* Madden, Life of Savonarola, vol. ii. p. 97.

communicate with each other, and after some religious exercises, in which Girolamo supplicated for the forgiveness of his sins through the precious blood of Christ, who was now his Comforter, the officers of justice came to announce to them that the hour was come for their execution. Several platforms were erected in the principal square of the city, for the accommodation respectively of the bishop, the pope's commissaries, the civil authorities, and the executioners with their scaffold of twenty feet high surrounded with a pile of fagots. The prisoners were led to the first tribunal in the Square, half naked and barefoot, where with a mock solemnity they were again clothed, only to have their sacerdotal garments taken from them by the hands of the bishop; who impiously said to Savonarola, "I deprive you of the church triumphant and militant!" Girolamo immediately replied, "Of the church militant, yes; but of the church triumphant, no; that does not belong to you." A person approaching him and inquiring whether his mind was calm and resigned to death, he replied, "My Lord died innocent of all crime, for my sins; and shall not I willingly give my soul for the love of Him?" Some persons offered him refreshments on his way; but he said, "What need have I of those things, who am about to depart from this world?" Many vile indignities were offered them while they ascended and stood on the scaffold. Savonarola requested for decency's sake, that a tunic might be wrapt around his bare limbs when he was about to be suspended; but this was barbarously refused. His two companions were then hung by the neck, and lastly the great Savonarola himself, the executioner pushing them off the platform after the rope had been adjusted round their necks, and then mocking them with antics, while life was departing from the bodies of the martyrs! Scarcely had their spirits fled, when fire was kindled among the fagots under them; and the bodies being consumed, the ashes were thrown into the river Arno. The pope's brief, read aloud at the place of execution, designated Savonarola as "the son of blasphemy, the nursling of perdition, and the seducer of the people."

Thus perished by the hand of bigotry, one of Italy's most gifted and most upright men, and one of the greatest among the forerunners of the reformation of the sixteenth century. Undoubtedly his true place is among the early reformers; for although he did not testify against the doctrinal errors of the Romish church, yet his life and teaching were a testimony against its corruption, and greatly tended to draw men from an implicit confidence in its authority, and to lead them to think for themselves respecting the all-important subject of religion, under the guidance of something better than lifeless dogmas and pompous ceremonies.

The author whom we have so often quoted in reference to this eminent man, says of his death: " The 23d of May, 1498, Alexander VI. sent Savonarola to the judgment-seat of God to answer for his efforts to renovate religion. The 7th of August, 1518, Leo X. cited Luther to appear at Rome to answer for a revolution commenced against the church. Twenty years only had elapsed since the attempted renovation was quenched in blood, before the revolution broke out that was to shake the pillars of Catholicity, and even Christianity itself."

A divine retribution seems to have visited several of the most violent persecutors of Savonarola. Ceccone, the bribed notary, it is said, only obtained one-tenth part of the four hundred scudi that had been promised him; and afterward, struck with remorse, or with vexation at not having obtained the wages of his iniquity, he disclosed the particulars of the falsification of the report of the examination to several persons, among whom was Lucretia de Medici, a sister of Leo X. This wretched man, Burlamacchi relates, falling sick at his villa in Mugello, a very lonely and desert place, two Dominican monks called at the house for assistance, and were implored to visit him. Approaching his bed, they began to speak of the divine mercy to the dying man. But the word mercy seemed dreadful to him. "There was no mercy," he said, "for his guilt. Judas had betrayed only one just one, but he had betrayed three!" No words of comfort or exhortation had any effect; he died in their presence, despairing of salvation.

The chief executioner, who had almost tumbled from the scaffold in making his mockery and antics while Savonarola by his hands was dying, perished himself on the scaffold some time afterward, being stoned to death by the mob for the bungling manner in which he had decapitated a young brigand.

Corsini, one of the examiners, who had upbraided Savonarola with the falsity of his predictions, lived just long enough to see those predictions fulfilled, and died in a state of frenzy.

Another of the examiners, Maretti, who was present at the torture of Savonarola, and "had the indecency as well as the cruelty to aggravate the sufferings of the prisoners by a scandalous indignity, perished miserably, without hope, crying out in terrible mental anguish, 'Oh, this hand! this hand! The friar is torturing me!'"

One of the pope's commissaries, Romolino, receiving a large sum of money the night before the execution, soon returned to Rome with it, and bought a cardinal's hat; but is said to have died a miserable death in Naples.

Madden says of Savonarola's ministry: "In the abundance of the divine mercy, a mission was given to him from on high, to labor for the renovation of the church, as he most firmly and piously believed. And in the discharge of the duties of that mission, the conviction was never absent from his mind, that he was to encounter great trials, grievous sufferings, and eventually death. He had three weapons for the fearful struggle. 1. Ardent love for the honor and glory of God. 2. A spirit of prayer, that exalted his mind above all worldly influences, fears, and affections. 3. A power of preaching, in which the highest order of eloquence was united with a spiritualized piety, and a pervading stream of gospel light, that gave an unction to his sermons, such as at once touched the hearts of all classes of his hearers, and was alike appreciated by the learned and the illiterate, the young and the old, by men and women—and alike also by laity and clergy. All his cotemporaries are agreed on this point. And many of those in subsequent times, who have taken unfavorable views of his character in general, seem to leave the question of the power of his preaching undisputed. . . . . . He died in the struggle, and the enemies of truth and justice thought they had a signal triumph. But his death only served to send his opinions throughout the civilized world."

CHAPTER XIV.

JUAN VALDÉS.

THIS enlightened man, who, though a layman, may be said to have been a preacher of righteousness; who, though cotemporary with Luther, and in reality, though unconsciously, a colaborer with him, was nevertheless entirely independent of him, apparently without any communication with him, and in some respects in advance of him in the experimental work of religion; was one of those reformers who did much to overturn the corruptions of sentiment and practice in the Romish church, without directly opposing its claims to be the church of Christ. Like Molinos and Guion in the subsequent century, he remained within its pale, but was a thorn in the sides of the formal professors, whose corrupt practices were constantly testified against by the Christian integrity of his own life, no less than through the flat contradiction which he gave to their tenets by the clear manner in which, both in his writings and in his oral teachings, he upheld many of the truths of the gospel. McCrie* calls him the first who was active in spreading the reformed opinions in Spain.

By many authors Juan de Valdés appears to have been confounded with his twin-brother, Alfonso, who was Latin Secretary to the Emperor Charles V. They were the sons of Hernando de Valdés, a *hidalgo* of liberal estate and circumstances, and were born about the end of the fifteenth century, probably in the mountain city of Cuença, in the old Kingdom of Leon, in Spain, of which city their father was

* History of the Reformation in Spain, p. 140.

hereditary *Regidor*, or Mayor.* It was then a flourishing town, though now much declined; but its picturesque position still remains, at the confluence of two beautiful streams, and rising like a terraced pyramid from luxuriant gardens, and rocks covered with creeping vines, which form its suburbs; while the town itself climbs by steep and tortuous streets and lanes, tier above tier, and roof above roof, "up to the square and cathedral which occupy almost the only level space," and afford a lovely view of the valleys below.

Of his early life, little is known, except that, together with his brother Alfonso, after leaving the paternal roof, he was educated in the court of Ferdinand and Isabella. Juan had received a good knowledge of school learning, and of the original languages of the Holy Scriptures, the Hebrew and the Greek; which he failed not to make use of in his more mature life, in translating into Spanish the Book of Psalms from the one, and the gospel narrative of Matthew and some of Paul's epistles from the other. In the royal court, amid doubtless a great deal that was calculated to dazzle the minds of these youths and lead them into a love of the lustre and pleasures of this world, they had the advantage of the instruction of Pedro Martir de Angleria, a man of great attainments, and of sentiments decidedly favorable to a reformation of the corruptions of the Romish hierarchy. It was through his influence that Alfonso Valdés was made Latin Secretary to the Emperor Charles V. in the beginning of 1520, an office which he retained for more than ten years.

When Adrian of Utrecht, a friend of Erasmus, and an advocate of reform, was elected pope, in the year 1521, Juan de Valdés accompanied him to Rome in the capacity of chamberlain; an office, however, which, from the short reign of that pontiff, he held but for a few months. After

* Wiffen's Life of Juan de Valdés. Lond. 1865.

the death of Adrian, he rejoined his brother in Spain, in the court of the emperor. Respecting this portion of his life, it is believed* that he has described his own condition in a Dialogue written a few years afterward. The expressions are as follows, attributed to a soul relating in the dialogue what passed during its life on earth: "When a youth, although I naturally loathed the vices, yet through bad companions I was held enslaved by them for many years. When I attained twenty years of age, I began to know myself, and to learn what it is to be a Christian. . . . But I did not lay aside vices that had become habitual. At twenty-five years of age I began seriously to reflect on my manner of life, and on my abuse of the knowledge God had given me. And I reasoned thus: either the doctrines of the New Testament are true, or they are not. If they are true, is it not gross folly for me to live as I am doing, in opposition to them? . . . . . . Then God enlightened my mind; and knowing the doctrines of the New Testament to be true, I determined to lay aside superstitions and vices in all their forms, and to occupy myself in following out the former to the best of my poor ability, although friends and relations placed immense obstacles in the way of my doing so. Some said I was going mad, and others that I was about to turn monk. . . . . . . But from love to Jesus Christ, I bore it all patiently." . . . . . . "I was told that the monks had seldom opportunity to sin, compared with men living in the world. To which I replied, that sinful desire developed itself as fully inside a monastery as outside; and, moreover, that sinful man never wanted, let him be where he may, time and opportunities for being so, and that those persons who hold themselves far above all temptation, frequently fall more heinously and more disgracefully. True it is that I was once inclined to turn

* Wiffen's Life of Valdés, p. 56.

monk, to escape the indulgence of ambition; but on going to confess myself to a monk, my personal friend, he told me that ambition was as prevalent among them as among men outside. Whereupon I determined not to change my garb." And in another work, the "Dialogo de la Lengua," somewhat celebrated as a lively treatise on certain elegancies of the Spanish language, he says of this period of his life: "Ten years, the best of my life, which I spent in palaces and courts, I did not employ myself in more virtuous exercises than in reading these lying romances, in which I took so much relish, that I ate my food with the books in my hand. And notice what a thing it is to have a depraved taste. For if I took in hand a work translated from the Latin that was true history, or at least what was held as such, I had not patience to read it."

The Dialogue first quoted, shows also the estimation in which he held the superstitious practice of pilgrimage, so much relied on in the dark ages:—" Did you ever go on a pilgrimage?—No; because it seems to me that Jesus Christ manifests himself everywhere, to those who truly seek him; and because I saw many who returned from pilgrimage worse than when they set out. And it likewise appeared to me to be an act of folly, to *seek at Jerusalem what I had within me.*"

This dialogue was mainly a conversational development of the history of those troubled times which followed the battle of Pavia, and in which Charles V. and Francis I. bore so prominent a part. Another treatise in the same conversational form (the "Dialogo di Lactancio") was composed by himself and his brother* about the year 1528; in which they attributed the recent dreadful sacking of Rome

* M. Young (Life of Paleario) states that both these Dialogues were written by Alfonso; but from Wiffen's account it seems probable that the twin-brothers were jointly concerned in each.

to the divine displeasure for the vices of that city and of the hierarchy, and brought into view many subjects relating to the corruption of religion. On the subject of war, they express the following sentiments:—"All (brute) animals are naturally provided with defensive and offensive arms; but to man, as a creature come down from heaven, impersonating perfect concord, as an object that should here represent the image of God, He left him disarmed. It was His will there should prevail amongst men a harmony, rivalling that amongst the angels in heaven. Alas! that we should now have become so excessively blind, that, more brutish than the brutes themselves, we should kill each other! .... Where do you find that Jesus Christ commanded his people to go to war? Peruse all the gospels, peruse all the apostolic epistles, you will find nothing but peace, concord, unity, love, and charity. When Jesus Christ was born, the angels did not sound an alarm, but they sang, 'Glory to God in the highest, and on earth peace and good will unto men.' He gave us peace when he was born, and peace when he suffered on the cross. How frequently did he enjoin peace and love upon his people! And not even satisfied with this, he besought his Father that his people should be at one amongst themselves, as he with his Father." .... "We call ourselves Christians, and we live worse than Turks and brute beasts. If the Christian doctrine appear to us to be a farce, why do we not wholly give it up, that so, at least, we might not so frequently and deeply insult Him, from whom we have received so many benefits? But since we know it to be true, and pride ourselves on being called Christians, and treat with contempt those who are not so, why do we not seek to be such in reality? Why do we live as if there were neither faith nor law amongst us?"

In this work Valdés inveighed boldly against the pope

for undertaking to provoke a war against the emperor. He says, "What Jew, Turk, Moor, or Infidel will now ever wish to come to the faith of Jesus Christ, since our experience of His Vicar's works is such? Which of them will ever serve or honor him? . . . . Does it appear to you that this is the mode of teaching Christian people? . . . . Does it appear to you that these are the works of Jesus Christ? Does it appear to you that this dignity was instituted to the end that the Christian body should be destroyed by it?"

He also exposed in this treatise many of the gross corruptions of religion then prevalent. A few extracts from his remarks on the popular superstitions of the day, may serve to show in some degree the heathenism that had become mixed with the Christianity (so called) of that period. After mentioning many great absurdities in the way of pretended relics, which, he says, even if true, "are stumbling-blocks to cause men to fall into idolatry," he exclaims, "How far are we from being Christians! How opposed are our works to the doctrine of Jesus Christ! How laden are we with superstitions! And according to my views, the whole proceeds from the pestilential avarice and pestiferous ambition which now reign among Christians more absolutely than they ever previously did." . . . . "He that would honor a saint, let him labor to follow his saint-like virtues. We now-a-days, instead of doing so, hold bull-fights on his feast-day, and practise other levities. We say that we hold it devout, to kill four bulls upon St. Bartholomew's day, and that were we not to kill them, we should have cause to fear that he would lay our vines waste with hail! What greater heathenism than this could you adduce? . . . . Would you see another similar heathenism no less glaring than this? Look how we have distributed among our saints the offices held by the gods of the heathen.

The god Mars has been superseded by St. James and St. George, Neptune by St. Elmo, Bacchus by St. Martin, Æolus by St. Barbara, Venus by the Magdalen, etc. . . . . I know not to what these inventions tend, unless it be to give us a wholly Pagan character, to divert us from that love to Jesus Christ, which we ought to cherish for Him alone, by giving us the habit of asking that of others, which, in truth, He alone can give us Hence it comes to pass, that some think because they rehearse a mass of psalms, or handfuls of rosaries; some because they don the habit of a Franciscan or of a Merced; some because they do not eat meat on Wednesdays; some because they dress in blue or orange, that they indeed come short in nothing of being very good Christians; retaining, on the other hand, their envy, rancor, avarice, ambition, and other similar vices, as fully as though they had never heard tell what it is to be a Christian."

The pope's nuncio at the court of Spain was highly indignant at the contents of this treatise, and sought to bring the authors of it into trouble with the Spanish Inquisition. Juan, being a private individual, was most open to the danger of being called to account; and Alfonso, knowing this, assumed the whole responsibility of the authorship, thus screening his brother under the shadow of his own official position. The process was commenced against them both, but the nuncio, receiving Alfonso's assumption of authorship, thundered forth a threatening reply, and soon after died, early in the year 1529.

But the danger to the brothers did not cease with the death of Castiglione. The anger of the friars and Romish party was aroused, and might have proceeded to extremities had not circumstances about this time taken both the brothers out of Spain. The emperor, soon after midsummer, took his departure to meet the pope at Bologna, Alfonso being a part of his suite;* and Juan, feeling increasingly unsafe in his isolated condition, and desiring to be placed in a position of more freedom for the expression of his convictions, left his native country, and proceeded to Naples. It does not appear, however, that he waited for his brother's actual departure with the emperor, but probably left for Italy early in the spring. In Naples he soon became acquainted with various intelligent and virtuously disposed persons, and spent much time with some of them afterward in facilitating a thorough acquaintance with the Spanish language. After a few months he visited Rome, where he spent about two years, and then returned to Naples. It has been said that he here occupied the position of secretary to the Spanish viceroy, Don Pedro de Toledo.

He was in the practice of assembling his intimate friends, at times, for social conversation on instructive topics, often mingling with it the perusal of Holy Scripture. A series of conversations of this kind at his country residence, near the promontory of Pausilippo, overlooking a beautiful part of the bay of Naples, when the main subject of conversation turned on the elegancies of the Spanish language and literature, and was, without his knowledge, taken down secretly in short-hand, was afterward, at the urgent entreaty of his friends, written out at large by Juan, and circulated among his acquaintances, under the title of "Dialogo de la Lengua." It was first printed about two hundred years after his death. Of this treatise his biographer, Wiffen, speaks as "a production of great beauty, which will be read with pleasure by every

* McCrie says (Hist. of Reformation in Spain, p. 131, etc.) that Alfonso was in company with the emperor at the Diet of Augsburg in 1530, became acquainted there with Melancthon, translated the Augsburg Confession into Spanish, and exerted his influence with Charles V. in favor of the Lutherans, but that on his return to Spain he was (p. 134) condemned by the Inquisition. This is the last we hear of him.

student of the Spanish language, for its intelligence and discriminating good sense."

In 1536, Charles V. passing through Naples from Tunis to Rome, Juan Valdés accompanied him to that city, and on that prince's departure, returned to Naples, making his residence there for the rest of his life. He is described at this time as a man " of a fair countenance, very sweet manners, and soft and attractive speech, professing a knowledge of languages, and of the Holy Scriptures." It appears that from the time of his permanently settling in Naples, his mind deepened in a knowledge of divine things. His most important and instructive works were written during the few short years of his life that elapsed from that event to the time of his death. Wiffen says that "he devoted himself to study, and the improvement of his own moral and intellectual nature. His society was sought by such of the nobility as were most distinguished for piety and learning. . . . His religious teaching was of a private and individual character. It was attained by personal moral influence of a remarkable kind, by conversations, and letters on special subjects and occasions." Among his most intimate friends, and, as we may say, disciples, were Peter Martyr Vermeglio, many years afterward the hospitable host, at Zurich, of the exiled Bishop Jewel, of England; Bernardino Ochino, a well-known preacher in Naples, of whom Charles V. said that "his eloquence might make the very stones shed tears," and who was afterward invited by Cranmer into England; Fabio Mario Galeota, a Neapolitan, who was some years afterward confined in the Inquisition, but escaped on the occasion of the populace attacking that dreaded and hated institution on the death of Paul IV.; Caserta, a learned and wealthy man, an ardent disciple of Peter Martyr, who many years afterward testified his constancy by suffering death in the market-place of Naples; Flaminio, a Latin poet, and a "man after Valdés's own spirit;" Carnesecchi, who though at one time secretary to Pope Clement VII., was afterward engaged in procuring the publication of some of the writings of Valdés, and being accused at Rome of holding erroneous sentiments, was burned at the stake in 1567. There were also among those who enjoyed his society and instruction some pious and noble women, particularly Vittoria Colonna, Marchioness of Pescara, whose residence on the island of Ischia was only about three miles from Pausilippo; and Giulia Gonzaga, Duchess of Trajetto, "the one who drank deepest of his instructions, and toward whom his mind was most forcibly brought into exercise. Her noble faculties, her pursuit of the highest virtue, and the loveliness of her mind and person, alike engaged his regard. He longed to lead her into the way of Christian perfection by the royal road of the Gospel, and strove to guide her in the path by the most assiduous endeavors."*

To her he presented a volume, detailing a conversation which had passed between them on religious subjects, and which he modestly entitled "Alfabeto Christiano," telling her that she might therein, as a first book, "learn the rudiments of Christian perfection," and afterward "leave the alphabet, and apply her soul to things more important, more excellent, more divine." In his epistle addressing the work to her, after warning her against a reliance on the mere writings of men, in her pursuit after Christian perfection, he gives her the following advice: "Now, desiring that your ladyship may never judge yourself perfect, but that you may be so in reality, both in the view of God and of the world, I wish you not so to read this composition, nor to hold it in greater estimation than ought to be given to the writings of one who, desirous to gratify you in this

* Wiffen's Life of Valdés, p. 109.

Christian object, only points out to you the way by which you may arrive at Christ himself, and become united to Him. And I desire that your Christian intention may be to make Christ the peaceful possessor of your heart, in such a manner that He may absolutely and without contradiction rule and regulate all your affairs."

The dialogue was a protracted one, embracing many subjects connected with the Christian life; but we may venture on a few striking extracts, showing Juan's deeply spiritual views, and his characteristic method of instilling them. Giulia Gonzaga had developed to him her state of inquietude and perplexity respecting the condition of her soul. "Valdes :—Then, in order to understand whence proceed the travail and confusion which you say you have felt for so many years, I wish you would turn over in your memory how man is made *in the image and likeness of God.*

" Giulia :—Let me understand what this image and likeness of God is.

"Valdes :—I wish rather that St. Paul may explain it to you; and thus you will understand it by what he says to the Colossians, where, admonishing them to speak the truth one to another, he counsels them to 'put off the old man with his deeds, and to put on the *new man,* who is renewed in knowledge conformable to the *image and likeness* of Him who created him.' And you will also understand it by what St. Paul again says to the Ephesians, reminding them that by becoming Christians, they have learned to put off the old man, and to be renewed in the spirit, and clothed with the *new man,* who is created in the *image and likeness of God.* From this, it appears that in whatever degree a man possesses and retains in himself the image and likeness of God, in the same measure he sees and knows, understands and relishes spiritual things in a spiritual life and conversation. This truly known, and what objects you set before your mind well scrutinized, you will understand clearly how all the inquietude, all the travail, all the confusion you feel, arise; because your soul desires you to procure its restitution to the image of God." . . . "This state of mind that happens to you ever befalls worldly persons, who, having attained to a reflective intellect and clear judgment, knowing truly that their souls find not, nor ever can find, entire satisfaction in outward things, turn themselves to seek for it in things relating to the mind. Yet, as *the supernatural light*, by which *alone* truth is discovered, seen, and known, is wanting to them, they go wandering in a labyrinth of appearances and opinions. And thus some seek happiness in one thing, some in another. . . . All these persons deceive themselves, and can never shadow out, nor reach to the symbols of the things in which true happiness consists; who, if they had had a little of the light of faith, would most easily, and with the grace of God, have acquired it; and thus they would have quieted and pacified their souls. Do you now understand the cause whence your inquietude, confusion, and labor proceed?

"Giulia:—Yes, very well."

"Valdés [after some intervening conversation]:—We are all born and created to know God, to believe God, to love God, and after our present existence to enjoy God. And yet there are some who feed on the pleasures of this world, not only delighting and giving themselves up to rest in them, but who are wholly forgetful of that other life for which they were created. . . . . Like him who knows how to taste of the things of this world, yet does not enjoy them as things suitable to his better nature, or that will be lasting, but looks at them as the curious beholder views them, turning away from the recreations and banquets offered to him by the way; so I wish you, Signora, to act. *Turn within yourself, open the ears of your soul, so that you may hear the voice of God;* and think as a true Christian, that in this life you can have no other real contentment and ease, than what will come to you by means of the knowledge of God, through the faith and love of God. Settle your mind in this consideration; most earnestly putting aside all those things that are transitory and cannot endure. Doing this, I promise that you will occupy a much shorter time in quieting, soothing, and giving peace to your mind, than you have spent in disturbing it."

After some conversation on the necessity of banishing self-love entirely from the heart, so that the Holy Spirit may come and dwell there, Valdés instructs his friend, that there are three ways of acquiring some knowledge of God —the first, by the light of nature, and reading in the volume of created things—the second, by reading the Holy Scriptures, as the Hebrews through the Old Testament—but "the third way of knowing God is by Christ. This way is the certain, clear, and safe way; this is the straight, royal, and noble way. And be assured, Signora, that in knowing God through Christ, consists the whole being of a Christian; for to know God through Christ, it is necessary first to know Christ himself. And because we cannot know Christ by the light of nature, nor by other human industry, if God does not internally illumine and open the vision of our souls, I say, that this knowledge of God through Christ is a supernatural knowledge, for which the special grace of God is necessary. And that it is the truth, that we cannot have the true knowledge of God except through Christ, Christ himself demonstrates, saying, 'No man can come to me, except the eternal Father draw him.' And he shows it again by his answer to Peter, when Peter acknowledged him to be the true Son of God, saying to him, 'Blessed art thou, Simon, son of Jonas, for this thou hast not gained by human reason, nor by the light of nature, but my Father who is in heaven has revealed it unto thee.' .... In order that this exercise may be profitable, it is proper that you should learn to know Christ, not by knowledge gained by custom, nor acquired by the intellect and human industry, but *by the light of faith inspired by the Holy Spirit.* It is needful for you in this manner to learn rightly to know Christ, if you wish to come perfectly to know God through Christ. .... Now this secret cognizance is what I said persons must come to *by inspiration;* and therefore we should not think the public acknowledgment of Christ sufficient. An assassin or a traitor has such. St. John undeceives us, saying, 'He that saith, I know Him, and keepeth not his commandments, is a liar.'" And respecting regeneration, Valdés tells his friend, "The spiritual resurrection is when through dying to the 'old man,' we come to be revived in the 'new man.' This is the passing from death unto life; and thus as Christ, through dying, came to the resurrection, so we by denial of self come to the 'newness of life.' And this is what Christ said to Nicodemus, 'Except a man be born of water and of the Holy Spirit, he cannot enter the Kingdom of God.'"

And further on, he tells her,—" Finally, when you shall feel and enjoy so much of the sweetness and love of Christ here in this world, as is to be felt and enjoyed, taking this sense and enjoyment for an earnest of what you will yet have to feel and enjoy in the other life, to which you will expect certainly to go, to rejoice perpetually with Christ, you will not hesitate to confess the Life Eternal. And now, when you possess such inward experience, yours will be living and true faith, because you will have *the experience of it within you.*"

After conversing upon various other topics, Valdés concludes the whole by the following advice: "Be careful that you always entreat God that he would guide and conduct you by his grace, without ever consenting to withdraw yourself from Him. Because this is the way to arrive at Christian perfection, and to enjoy Christian liberty, to which, when you shall become united, you will be able with truth to say with the prophet David, 'The Lord is my shepherd, I shall not want. He maketh me to lie down in green pastures, he leadeth me beside the still waters.'"

We have already seen that Juan de Valdés translated the Book of Psalms from the Hebrew into the Castilian or Spanish language. He also wrote translations of Paul's Epistle to the Romans, and the First Epistle to the Corinthians, from the Greek, adding simple and practical commentaries on the text, which he had already read to his friends at their usual gatherings at his house. After commenting on a passage of Romans, he modestly says, "This is all the knowledge that I can attain of this divine epistle at present, having availed myself of *my two books*, prayer, and consideration. These books have helped me as far as prayer has been aided by the Holy Spirit, and as far as consideration has been helped by personal experience and daily reading. And I hold it for certain, that in proportion as the spirit has been more fervent and the hope greater, the apprehension of St. Paul's words will have been more perfect, prayer and consideration having been more aided."

In his commentary on I. Cor. i. 17—"Not with wisdom of words," etc.—he says: "And this desire of knowledge is to such a degree pernicious and dangerous, that even in the reading of the Holy Scriptures it injures the mind, when the reader is not very guarded, lest he should be guided by curiosity and self-esteem. And I understand that a man reads the Holy Scriptures with curiosity, when he does so solely with the view of acquiring knowledge.

And I understand that a man reads the Holy Scriptures with self-esteem, when he avails himself of his knowledge to talk about them and criticise them. And should some one ask me, 'With what purpose may I then come to read the Holy Scriptures?' I shall answer him, for the purpose of personal edification, reading them at times for your consolation under tribulation and affliction, and at other times to awaken in your mind fresh desires after God, and to conceive fresh views of spiritual and divine things; and, again, in order that the same reading may be to you as a testimony of what God shall give you inwardly to feel and know of your own soul. And one of the greatest advantages in reading the Holy Scriptures is, that the man doing so ascertains the extent to which his feelings and experience concur with those of [other] persons who possess the Holy Spirit. . . . . And, returning to St. Paul, I understand that by the expression, 'Not with wisdom of words,' he means to say, God sent me to preach the gospel; and this with no ornate discourse blended with science and human wisdom; and this, lest the cross of Christ should be made of no effect; which would be made of no effect, were I to preach the gospel after such fashion; for men would attribute the effect of my preaching, not to the efficacy which there is in the cross of Christ, but to the efficacy of my words."

On the passage, Rom. x. 15, he remarks: "So that all the force of St. Paul's words consists in this, '*except they be sent.*' And hence it is easy to understand why our preachers do not move the hearts of men, withdrawing them from the world to God, and separating them from themselves for Christ, and making them more readily accept the grace of the gospel. The reason is, because they are not sent; because they are not apostles; and that may be affirmed of them, which God says by Jeremiah

(xxiii. 21), 'I have not sent these prophets, yet they ran; I have not spoken to them, yet they prophesied.' Here likewise it is to be understood, that they who preach Christian things, not being apostles of Christ, do not preach Christ, however much they may use his name in the pulpit. But they preach themselves, their own fancies and imaginations, that which they imagine and invent, taking Christ as their subject. ...... To preach Christ, it is necessary that the preacher be an apostle, sent of God to preach Christ, he having accepted the righteousness of Christ. Those who have not accepted it do not understand it; and not understanding it, they are ill able to preach it, nor can they make their hearers understand it. Besides, all they may say will be opposed to it, because the human mind [of itself] is incapable of receiving it."

Commenting on the next two verses of the same chapter, he remarks thus respecting Christian ministry: "I understand that St. Paul, employing this expression, 'our report,' infers that man cannot believe unless it be told what it is he has to believe, and that the mere telling is inadequate unless the individual telling him be *inspired, moved, and sent by God* to tell him it; so that the whole transaction depends upon the mere will of God who inspires the speaker, instructing him what to say, and disposing the listener to hearken. ..... Hence, the apostles, the ministers of Christ, are called in the Holy Scriptures, the mouth of God, because God speaks by them and in them. By this one may understand well what God speaks by Esaias (lv. 11), 'That the word which goeth forth from his mouth shall not return unto him void, but that it shall accomplish that which he pleases.' And hence we may understand how necessary it always is, that, following the advice which Christ gave to his disciples, and which he gives to all of us, we should ask God that he would send among us persons who shall speak the words of God; that they speak, *being inspired*, and *not taught of men;* speaking *by divine experience*, and not by human science."

Valdés addressed the translation of the Psalms and Epistles to his friend Giulia Gonzaga, prefixing to the Commentary on the Epistle to the Romans a letter of Christian counsel to the duchess, concluding with the following excellent advice: "The object for which you set yourself to read St. Paul, is not to comprehend all that St. Paul says; but to form your mind by that which God gives you to understand, and feel, and relish, in St. Paul. . . . . But all these advices [of mine] are as nothing. There is yet another of more value than all of them. This is, that whenever you take St. Paul in hand, you commend yourself to God, praying Him to send his Holy Spirit, who may guide you in this reading; and seek to receive it by means of the only-begotten Son of God, Jesus Christ our Lord, to whom be glory forever, amen!"

We now come to that which appears to have been his latest, as it was his largest and most important work, "The Hundred and Ten Considerations;" which has recently been translated anew from the Italian by John T. Betts, and published with Wiffen's account of his life and writings. This work also Juan addressed to Giulia Gonzaga, for whose religious welfare he was so deeply interested. These "Considerations," embracing some of the most important doctrines of the Christian religion, though not free from error, and perhaps too speculative on some subjects, are extremely interesting to the serious reader, showing as they do the workings of a very original mind, accustomed to deep thoughtfulness on the things that accompany salvation, and cherishing a dependence on the teaching of that Spirit which was promised by the Saviour to lead us into all truth. It is very clear that Juan de Valdés derived great advantage from never having pursued his early inclination to become a monk, nor entangled his intellect in the sophistry and false philosophy taught in the theological schools of that day. He was thus left at liberty to think and feel for himself on subjects of the highest importance, as he knew them to be, to his immortal soul. During the latter portion of his life especially, he was deeply in earnest in his search after divine truth, as the greatest good. And though encompassed with the thick darkness of the Romanism of Spain and Italy in that day of superstition, and in some points of doctrine biassed by the prevailing views, yet looking to the Holy Spirit for instruction, he became wonderfully enlightened in regard to the spiritual nature and inward efficacy of true religion, and looked *over* the formalities of the papal system, as something that did not concern him, while his soul was ardently pursuing the substance. We must here be satisfied with a few scattered extracts from this very original treatise. Written by Valdés in Spanish, it was printed in Italian at Basle ten years after his death, and has since been translated and published in various languages.

From Consideration x.—"I am clearly of opinion, that he who believes, without having been taught by the Spirit of God, relies more upon opinion than upon faith, and is ever involved in error and false conceits. Whence it should be understood, that when a man believes alike all the statements made to him, he is without the Spirit of God; he believes upon report, by human suasion, and by received opinion, and not by revelation, nor by inspiration. And it being true that the Christian's happiness does not consist in believing merely, but in believing through revelation, and not by report,—we are to conclude that the Christian's faith is not what is based upon report, but that the Christian's faith is by revelation alone: and this is what makes us happy; it is what brings with it love and hope; and is what purifies the heart, and is in every respect pleasing to God. May we be enriched with it by God himself, through Jesus Christ our Lord!"

From Consideration xii.—"The first man, proud of his reason, wished to know God without God; as if one wished to see the sun without the sun; and he deprived himself of the knowledge of God, and was left to the government of his own reason. And he, and all men who have imitated him, seeking to know God simply with their reason, by means of the Scriptures and of the creature, are still more rash than those who, not wishing to see the sun by the sun, attempt to see it by the light of a candle. Now, this being true, we understand that God has placed reason in man, in order that he, by it, may know God; but it *must be by God*, and *not by his own speculations*. It is well that God requires man to mortify his reason, so far as it presumes to know God, and the things of God, by itself alone, without the Spirit of God,—if he desire to know God and to abide in His kingdom in the way it behoves him to do. Of this mortification we have already spoken many times, and said it is that which is revealed to us by our Lord Jesus Christ."

From Consideration xxiii.—"Finding my mind wholly sterile and dried up, and as it were alienated from God, and understanding that this proceeded from God's having hidden his presence from me, I thought to remedy this my necessity by imposing on my memory that it should occupy its meditations with God solely. Scarcely had I conceived this purpose—scarcely had I begun to put it in execution, than I understood that, although it be in my power to occupy my memory in meditation upon God, as upon anything else, still, however, it is not in my power to cause my mind to feel the presence of God, and thus free it from barrenness, aridity, and alienation from God. Moreover, I understood what an utter difference there is between the state of the soul when it *labors* to realize the presence of God, from that in which it is when *God makes it conscious of His presence*. And being desirous of knowing in what this difference consisted, I perceived it consisted in this, that in one instance there is the operation of the human mind, and in the other that of the Holy Spirit; and thus I concluded that the same difference exists between these two states of mind, that there is between flesh and spirit."

From Consideration xxxvi.—"Among the Jewish people there were some who applied themselves to the law from inspiration, and others from opinion. They who applied themselves to the law from opinion—knew the Jewish bondage, but did not practise it as was right; because, being ruled by their own spirit, they were in some things superstitious, and in other things licentious. They who applied themselves to the law from inspiration, and exercised themselves in it as was right, desiring its promises and fearing its threats, these knew the Jewish bondage, seeing that they must ever remain bound to the law; and they exercised themselves in it as was fit, holding themselves to be bondsmen and dependent upon the will of God, because, being ruled by the Holy Spirit, who inspired them to fulfil the law, they became pious, holy, and just. Thus Jewish bondage was brought about by the law, and was known when men applied themselves to the observance of the law, and was exercised when the application proceeded from the Holy Spirit. On the other hand, Christian liberty consists in the abrogation of the law; which was wholly abrogated at the coming of the Holy Spirit, who succeeded to the government of the people of God, superseding the law."

From Consideration xxxvii.—"They who, by accepting

the gospel, and who, by the covenant of justification established by Jesus Christ our Lord, are made sons of God, and sustaining intimate relations with God, know God and acquire a fresh opinion of God, and form new conceptions of God, not indeed by report, but by knowledge and experience,—when these persons have recourse to the Holy Scriptures with their fresh opinion and their new conceptions, they find that written in them which they know and experience."

From Consideration xlvi.—"All they who, guided only by the light of nature, and by human wisdom, presume to understand things that belong to the Spirit of God, and to tread the Christian path, that is to say, to live in a Christian-like manner, I compare to a man who walks at night by a way that is full of perils and obstacles, simply with the light of his eyes. And it appears to me, that just as to this man a tree will at one time appear to be a foot-pad, and he will fly from it; a rock, to be an armed man, and he will be dismayed; and at other moments, water will appear to him to be stone, and he will be plunged in it; and a shadow will appear to be a tree, and trying to lean against it he will fall flat on the ground; exactly in a similar manner, the man who, guided by the light of nature, treads the road to God, at times is frightened by things that ought never to have terrified him at all, and at other times he feels secure, and reposes trust in things in which he ought never to have felt secure, nor reposed trust at all, and thus groping his way, he walks like one bewildered, and knows not whither he is going. He who walks by the light of Holy Writ, and after the example of the saints, but without the Spirit, I compare to a man who walks at night, carrying a candle in his hand, so that he does not go wholly in the dark; but neither does he go without fear, nor does he in his mind feel safe, nor is he sure that he shall not fall into many difficulties.

"Whence I understand, that just as to the traveller of whom I have spoken as walking by night simply by the light of his eyes, the best and safest counsel is, that he suspend his journey as long as the night lasts, till the sun be risen to show him the way and the objects upon it, and he be enabled to travel, aided by the light of his eyes; so to him that travels on the road to God, simply by the light of nature, by the testimony of Scripture, and by the example of the lives of the saints, the best, the soundest advice that can be given to him is, that he stop on the way, during the night of his own blindness, until God send him His Spirit,—that he may know his way, and see all that is in it."

From Consideration xlviii. — "From Romans, viii. 26, we collect that St. Paul considered prayer to be one amongst the things with which, in our weakness and infirmities, we are favored and helped by the Spirit of God; and thus he says, that forasmuch as we know not how to pray as we ought, the Spirit of God prays for us. Hence I understand that the Holy Spirit then prays for us, when he impels us and moves us to pray, because at such a time he prays in us himself. And I understand, that he who prays with the Spirit of God, asks that which is the will of God, and thus obtains what he desires; and he who prays with his own spirit, asks that which is his own will; and hence the reason why man knows neither for what, nor how, he ought to pray." ...... "When he who prays with the human spirit, utters these words of the Lord's prayer,—'Thy will be done,'—although the words were dictated by the Spirit of God, he does not pray with the Spirit of God, because he does not pray being inspired, but instructed [taught naturally]. And St. Paul does not say that the Holy Spirit should teach us to pray, but that He prays for us and in us." ......

"They who work with human wisdom find satisfaction in their works, but mixed with arrogance and presumption; and they who work with the Holy Spirit, find also satisfaction in their works, but of a very different kind, and mixed with humility and mortification. So that a person, by examining his mind after the work is completed, shall be able by this consideration to understand whether human wisdom, or the Spirit of God, has wrought in him."

From Consideration 1.—"I come to the conclusion, that the proper duty of the Christian in the present life is, to be intent upon the reinstatement of his soul, and the recovery of the image and likeness of God. . . . . . . And I understand that Christian perfection consists in this exercise. I mean to say, that a Christian is more or less perfect in this life, just as, being more or less engaged in this exercise [the progressive restoration of his soul], he gains more or less of that part of the image and likeness of God in which [man] was created, and which is attainable in this life. And this I understand to be the reason why Jesus Christ our Lord concludes his exhortation upon Christian perfection, by saying, 'Be ye perfect, as your Father in heaven is perfect' (Matt. v.)."

From Consideration liv.—"I hold it to be a thing most true and most certain for the understanding of Holy Scripture, that the best, the surest, the highest interpreters that man can find are these two—Prayer and Consideration. I understand that Prayer discovers the way, opens it, and makes it plain; and that Consideration puts the man into it, and makes him walk by it. Furthermore, I understand it to be indispensable that these two interpreters, or books, be assisted by God, himself inspiring the man who prays, to pray. Because I understand, that he who prays without being inspired to pray, does so at the suggestion of his own fancy, of his own affection, and of his own will; and that, not knowing how to pray as he ought, he is not heard in his prayer; and he who prays, being inspired to pray, prays to the glory of God, and prays by the will of God; and knowing how to pray as he ought, his prayer is heard, and what he seeks is granted. As to Consideration, I hold it to be indispensable on the part of the man who would consider of spiritual things, that it be assisted with his own experience of them. I mean, that he who considers, should have inwardly experienced those things of which Holy Scripture speaks, in such a manner, that by what he finds and knows in himself, he comes to understand what is written in the Holy Scriptures. And they who consider without this experience, walk in the dark and grope their way. . . . . . While those persons who are aided in Prayer by the Holy Spirit, and in Consideration by their individual experience, frequently attain certainty, nay, ordinarily do so; they know what they ascertain, and also relish it."

From Consideration lvii.—"Day by day I acquire a stronger conviction, that the Christian should be concerned about experience, and not about theoretical knowledge. I mean to say, that his business is not learned by speculation, but by experience. In the first place, I understand that it is peculiarly the Christian's duty to exercise himself in mortification. By persevering in it, he feels that its usefulness consists in this: that by mortifying his affections and appetites, man gradually attains to the apprehension of that divine Christian perfection, of which he is himself apprehended by union with Christ, a union brought about by faith." . . . .

"The Christian has not to busy himself in speculative knowledge, but in experience. If it were a *science*, it would have the effect that other sorts of science [tend to] produce, which is to inflate and to puff up those who acquire them. But because it is experience, it produces the effect . . . .

to humble and cast down to the earth everything that is associated with human wisdom, and to elevate and exalt to heaven all that is associated with the Spirit."

From Consideration lxxv.—"Just as all men who have the clear vision of their outward eyes, know the external forms of things through the aid of the sun, in which God has placed his outward light, so all men who have the clear vision of their inward eyes, know all inward things through the aid of Christ, in whom, as says St. Paul (Col. ii.), 'God has placed all the treasures of his divinity' [in the English version, 'of wisdom and knowledge']. . . . . I likewise understand the manner in which Christ is the Head of the church. I mean to say, that I understand that just as vital energy descends from my head to all my members, they being each sustained and governed by it, so vital energy descends from Christ to all those who belong to the church, they being each sustained and governed by the divine gifts which are communicated to them by Christ. And I understand that those persons belong to the church, who, being called of God and brought to the knowledge of Christ, are capable of effectively receiving the divine treasures which are showered down most abundantly upon all men by the only begotten Son of God, Jesus Christ our Lord."

From Consideration lxxxv.—"I understand that the Christian knows God by the communication of the Holy Spirit; because I understand that the Holy Spirit is given to them who believe in Christ; and I understand by St. Paul (I. Cor. ii. 10), 'that the Spirit searcheth all the deep things of God.' I understand likewise that we know God himself, through Christ, inasmuch as through Christ the Holy Spirit is given to us, it being Christ himself who gives us Him by the will and command of God, just as, by the same will and ordinance, light is given unto us through the sun. And certain it is that the Holy Spirit is efficacious in me who am a Christian, to make me know the omnipotence that is in God, by the mighty power which he manifests in me, in mortifying me, and in quickening me; to make me know the wisdom that is in God, by the wisdom which I acquire by the Holy Spirit; to make me know the justice that is in God, for that he justifies me in Christ; to make me know the truth that is in God, inasmuch as he fulfils to me what he has promised; and to make me know the goodness and mercy of God, forasmuch as he bears with my infirmities and sins. And thus I am brought to recognize all these things in God, not indeed by relation of Scripture, but by that which the Holy Spirit works within me, who communicates himself unto me through Christ.

"I understand that a Christian knows God by regeneration and Christian renovation; because I understand that he who has been regenerated, and renewed by the Holy Spirit, who is communicated to him by Christ, gradually rids himself of and renounces the image of Adam, which is peculiar to us by human generation, through which we 'are by nature children of wrath,' enemies of God, wicked, rebellious, and infidel; and gradually assumes and recovers the image of God, which is peculiar to us by Christian regeneration; through which we as it were naturally become children of grace, the adopted sons of God—friends of God, pious, obedient, and faithful."

We have thus spread before the reader, from this remarkable book of Valdés, sufficient to show the admirable spirit which he brought to the contemplation of divine truth, and the deep views which he had of the operative nature of true religion—altogether at variance with the outward and ceremonious system which prevailed around him. He was accustomed to say that a Christian's proper study should be in *his own book*, and that this book was *his own mind;* and he found in his own experience that no occupation need interrupt this reading. In a letter written at a late period of his life, he alludes to this self-examination in an instructive and beautiful manner, saying among other things that bespeak his earnestness in the search, and his conviction of its importance in the Christian life, that sometimes—"I consider whether the Christian's faith has its efficacy within me, causing me to change my natural disposition; and whether the Christian life has made me change my former state and manners; because such alteration is Christian renovation and regeneration. I enter at other times into a very strict account with myself, examining how far I love God and Christ; whether I love Him more than myself; and how far I love my neighbors, and whether I love them as well as I love myself. If, then, I perceive that I am going forward, purely directed to the glory of God and of Christ, and to the spiritual and eternal good of my neighbors, I know that I go forward in love. This is the way I study in *my own book*. The fruit I gain from such perusal is, that I arrive at a much better knowledge of what I am, and of what I am worth in myself, and what through God and through Christ; and so I arrive at a more intimate knowledge of *the benefit to be received from Christ*. And this is the consequence, that the more constantly I read in this my book, so much the more the life I have by the grace of God and of Christ grows within me, and that which I have as a son of Adam becomes less."

In this manner, with constant self-scrutiny, and a cherished and humble reliance on the mercy of God through Jesus Christ—on the inward experience of it, and not on any pompous ceremonial profession of it—he drew toward the close of life, serene and peaceful, and in the midst of friends who loved him and whom he loved. Though enmity existed in the minds of the priesthood and hierarchy, yet that enmity had not ripened into open persecution, partly from his early death, and partly from the fact that his writings, though spread extensively among his friends by manuscript copies, were not printed or openly published until some years after his decease.

He died at Naples in the year 1540, about middle age. He was never married, and maintained throughout his life a character of unblemished integrity. Wiffen says of him, —"To Valdés the internal word of inspiration was not *mystical*. He knew that the Word of God within, earnestly sought for, patiently believed in, and obediently complied with, was also the highest reason; and that its commands were practicable just in proportion to the degree of the reliance of faith reposed in them. ..... Neither did Valdés inculcate an *ascetic* life. He mixed with men and with their affairs, striving alike by his practice and instruction to direct them to a foretaste of that true felicity in this life which they might hope to enjoy perpetually hereafter; and in this also he was practical. ..... Valdés, as a reformer, entered less than almost any thoughtful man of his time into the battle of hierarchies. He was less a destroyer of error and evil, than a builder-up of truth and goodness. He left not, himself, the profession of the church of Rome, nor incited others so to do. ..... He looked *beyond* her ceremonies and pompous ritual—aware, to use his own words, how outward ceremonies breed inward vices, and how the mind which is inclined to superstition is naturally inclined to persecution. ..... He made not theology, that is, a doctrinal science of religion, his study; and therefore had not, in his more enlightened years, to unlearn the sophistical formulas of the schools. ..... In person, Valdés was spare in body, of fair and pleasing countenance, of sweet and courteous manners, of soft and winning speech, clear and logical in discourse, active, and diligently studious. ..... He died greatly beloved and honored by his numerous friends."

His views were of the very essence of the Reformation. How then was it that he never fraternized with Luther?* The fact that he did not, seems to prove that he was indeed not brought into his knowledge of divine truth "by man, neither was he taught it but by the revelation of the Spirit of God."

CHAPTER XV.

ANNE ASKEW.

ANNE ASKEW was the second daughter of Sir William Askew, of Kelsey, in Lincolnshire, England, one of the knights who attended Henry VIII. on his pageantry of the "Field of the Cloth of Gold." She was born about the year 1522.† While still quite youthful, she was married, against her own wishes, and at the urgent instigation of her father, to a young man of great wealth, but of no congeniality of character or disposition. The result, as might have been anticipated, was great unhappiness. In her distress her mind was mercifully visited by the love of God, and enabled to turn to Him for support. She had, while younger, been encouraged by her tutor in reading the Holy Scriptures (probably Wycliffe's version into

* McCrie (Reformation in Spain, p. 142) appears to think it probable that Juan Valdés had read the works of Luther and Tauler; but the remarkable originality both of the modes and trains of thought in the writings of Valdés seems to indicate that his religious views were the product of his own meditations, rather than borrowed from those of other men. The volume he most particularly delighted in, was evidently the Holy Scriptures.

† See M. Webb's "Fells of Swarthmoor Hall," whence we also learn that she was great-grandmother to Margaret Askew, wife of Judge Fell of Swarthmoor, afterward Margaret Fox.

English), and now she derived great comfort from a frequent recourse to them. But this practice, together with the still more offensive one to the priests, of absenting herself from auricular confession, aroused the displeasure of her husband and his family; and as she remained firm to what she believed to be her duty, and felt the consolation of faithfulness therein, her husband, after the birth of their second child, threatened to dismiss her from his house. She endeavored to show him that she could not change her course with a clear conscience. She had been enabled to see that priestly confession was contrary to the Scriptures, as well as other superstitions of the Romish system, and she could not give up her convictions, or go so directly contrary to them as he, at the suggestion of the priests, required of her. Whereupon, says Bishop Bale, "he drove her from his house." We may imagine the lacerated feelings with which the young repudiated wife returned to the home of her childhood, with her two little children. Yet she had the support of inward consolation from her Lord and Master, and that, to her, was of more value than all else.

On being turned out by her husband, she considered that he had broken his marriage covenant, and accordingly renounced his name, which was Kyme, and resumed for herself and her children the name of Askew. Her husband's family continuing to persecute her, after a time she removed to London, where she had relations and friends, hoping thus to escape their animosity, and to live in peace with her children. But the distance did not prevent them from sending information against her to the bishop and the chief magistrate of that city, to the effect that she was a dangerous heretic. Hearing that her enemies had reported that she had left Lincolnshire for fear of her heresies being made public, she returned for a short time; and, with a view to confront the priests who had raised the report, and expecting that they would then specify what they had against her to justify a charge of heresy, she entered the cathedral of Lincoln, and for several days placed herself conspicuously in front of a large Bible, fixed there by the king's order, near which great numbers of the priests continually passed. But they looked upon her, and passed by without saying anything of importance to her. "She had not the slightest fear," it is said, "of what they could say or do; for she felt her cause was good, and that the Lord was on her side."

After this she returned to London, and during the next spring was summoned before a body of Inquisitors (the "quest," as she calls them), who endeavored to ensnare her by their questions. She says, "Christopher Dare asked me if I did not believe that the Sacrament hanging over the altar was the very body of Christ really. Then I demanded of him, wherefore was St. Stephen stoned to death? And he said, he could not tell. Then I answered, that no more would I assoil his vain question.

"Secondly, he said, that there was a woman who did testify that I read how God was not in temples made with hands. Then I showed him chapters vii. and xviii. of the Acts of the Apostles, what Stephen and Paul had said therein.

"Thirdly, he asked, wherefore I said I had rather read five lines in the Bible, than to hear five masses in the temple. I confessed that I had said no less, because the one did greatly edify me, and the other nothing at all. He asked me what I said concerning confession. I answered him my meaning, which was, as St. James saith, that every man ought to acknowledge his faults to another, and one to pray for the other.

"He asked me what I said to the king's book [a book published by King Henry VIII., for which he obtained from the pope the title of "Defender of the Faith"]; and I answered that I could say nothing to it, because I never saw it. He asked me, if I had the Spirit of God in me? I answered, if I had not, I was but a reprobate or castaway.

"Then he said, he had sent for a priest to examine me, who was then at hand. The priest asked me what I said to the Sacrament of the altar, and required much to know my meaning thereof. But I desired him to hold me excused concerning that matter. None other answer would I make him, because I perceived him to be a papist.

"Lastly, he asked me, if I did not think private masses did help the souls departed? I said, it was great idolatry to rely more in them than in the death Christ died for us.

"Then they had me to my Lord Mayor, and he examined me as they had before, and I answered him directly in all things as I answered the quest. Besides this, my Lord Mayor laid one thing to my charge which was never spoken of [by] me, but by them; and that was, whether a mouse, eating the host, received God, or no? This question did I never ask, but indeed they asked it of me; whereunto I made them no answer, but smiled."

The Chancellor of the Bishop of London then found fault with her for "uttering the Scriptures," saying that the apostle Paul had forbidden women "to talk of the word of God." But she showed him that the prohibition of the apostle did not apply to anything that she had done.

The Lord Mayor then committed her to the prison called the Compter, refusing her request to be permitted to put in surety for her appearance, and not admitting any of her friends to speak to her during the eleven days that she remained there. Two priests however came to the prison, and endeavored to entangle her by questions respecting transubstantiation and confession; but she firmly maintained her ground from Holy Scripture. Bishop Bonner himself came afterward, to try what he could accomplish toward the ensnaring of this innocent woman; but she was on her guard, and to all his doctrinal questions she merely replied that she believed "as the Scripture doth teach," or "as Christ and his apostles did leave them." Disappointed in his repeated attempts to induce her to answer him in a way that he could take hold of to her disadvantage, he asked her, why she had so few words? To which she replied, that God had given her the gift of knowledge, but not of utterance, and that Solomon had said that a woman of few words is the gift of God. Some other conversation took place, near the conclusion of which she appealed to the bishop for proof of any blame that might be attached to her. He then went away, and writing a statement of her avowal of her belief in transubstantiation, and in the holiness and regenerating efficacy of "all the Sacraments of the Catholic church," he brought it to her for her consent to it. She was willing to say that "she believed so much thereof as the Holy Scripture doth agree unto," and requested him to add that to the writing. But desiring her not to teach him what to write, he took the paper to the assembly in his great chamber, who demanded her signature to it. Bonner handing the paper to her for that purpose, she wrote thus: "I, Anne Askew, do believe all manner of things contained in the faith of the Catholic church."

The bishop, seeing that she did not mean by that expression, the Roman church, "flung into his chamber," she says, "in a great fury." But one of her cousins afterward interceding for her release on bail, in a few days she was allowed to go home.

With regard to the contrivances set on foot for her subsequent persecution, we may take the following brief statement from the work before referred to.

"After this, a year passed, during which Gardiner, Bishop of Winchester, Bonner, Bishop of London, and others of their stamp, were watching with much apprehension the decided interest taken by Queen Catherine Parr in the Reformation. The grandeur of the hierarchy, the personal consequence and the revenues of the clergy, seemed in greater danger than ever. They determined that a stop should be put to the spirit of religious inquiry, manifesting itself among the people, and to the discussions about church-government and principles. They sorely repented that they had sanctioned the introduction of the English Bible into the cathedrals; and they thought that if they could only get the Queen out of the way, they might induce the King to have the Bibles withdrawn, and succeed in turning the tide of royal favor in the direction they would point out. They dreaded so much her clear head, her prudence, and her influence over her capricious husband, that nothing short of her destruction would satisfy them. But they must needs begin cautiously, and cunningly hide the end in view. The bishops again turned their attention to Anne Askew. They knew she was much favored by the queen and her friends. Might they not get something out of her that would implicate some about the court, perhaps even Queen Catherine herself? They determined to try; and Lord Chancellor Wriothesley, who was as anxious to get rid of the queen as the bishops were, went into the plot with his characteristic artful cruelty.

"Anne Askew, who, Fuller says, was distinguished for wit, beauty, learning, and religion, was again seized and imprisoned. Nevertheless her heart did not sink, for it was anchored on the Rock of ages. Bishop Bale has preserved a hymn which she composed during her imprisonment in

Newgate. She seems to have well understood the characters of the two bishops and of the lord chancellor, who were banded together against her; and evidently expected neither truth nor justice from them."

At her examination before the King's Council, she was interrogated respecting her domestic difficulties with her husband, which she very properly declined to expose. Then they asked her concerning the Sacrament; to which she replied briefly according to her belief. The Bishop of Winchester not being satisfied with her answer, and desiring a more direct one, she said: "If I show the open truth, ye will not accept it." On this he told her she was a parrot; to which she said to him, that "she was ready to suffer all things at his hands—not only his rebukes, but all that should follow besides."

The Council rebuked her several times during the five hours that she was detained by them, because she did not express herself as they wished.

"The next day," she relates, "I was brought again before the Council. Then would they needs know of me what I said of the Sacrament. I answered, that I had already said what I could say. Then came my Lord Lisle, Lord Essex, and the Bishop of Winchester, requiring me earnestly to confess the Sacrament to be flesh, blood, and bone. I said to Lord Parre and Lord Lisle, that it was a great shame for them to counsel contrary to their knowledge. The bishop (Gardiner) said he would speak with me familiarly. I said, so did Judas when he betrayed Christ. Then desired the bishop to speak with me alone. But I refused. He asked me, why? I said, that in the mouth of two or three witnesses every matter should stand, after Christ's and Paul's doctrine. Then the Lord Chancellor began again to examine me of the Sacrament. I asked him, how long he would halt on both sides?

He needs would know where I found that. I said, in the Scriptures. Then the bishop said, I should be burned. I answered, that I had searched all the Scriptures, yet could I never find that either Christ or his apostles put any creature to death.

"Then came Master Paget to me, with many glorious words, and desired me to speak my mind to him. I might, he said, deny it again, if need were. I said, I would not deny the truth. He asked me, how I could avoid the very words of Christ—'Take, eat, this is my body which shall be broken for you?' I answered, that Christ's meaning was there, as in these other places of Scripture, viz., 'I am the door'—'behold the Lamb of God'—the rock—the stone—only figured by these things. Ye may not here, said I, take Christ for the material thing that he is signified by; for these would make him in that way a very door, a vine, a lamb, a stone, clean contrary to the Holy Ghost's meaning. All these do but signify Christ—like as the bread doth signify his body in that place. And though he did say there, 'Take, eat this in remembrance of me,' yet he did not bid them hang up the bread in a box, and make it a god, to bow to it.

"Then they made me a bill of the Sacrament, willing me to set my hand thereunto; but I would not. On Sunday I was sore sick, thinking no less than to die—therefore I desired to speak with Master Latimer, but it would not be. I was sent to Newgate in my extremity of sickness; for in all my life afore, I was never in such pain."

After this she was examined at the Guildhall. She says: "They said to me there that I was a heretic, and condemned by the law, if I would stand in my opinion. I answered, that I was no heretic, neither yet deserved I death by the law of God. But as concerning the faith which I uttered and wrote to the Council, I would not, I said, deny it, because I knew it true. Then would they needs know if I would deny the Sacrament to be Christ's body and blood. I said, yea; for the same Son of God that was born of the Virgin Mary is now glorious in heaven, and will come again from thence at the latter day as he went up. And as for that ye call your god, it is a piece of bread. For proof thereof, mark it when you list, let it but lie in the box three months, and it will be mouldy, and so turn to nothing that is good. Whereupon I am persuaded that it cannot be God.

"After that, they willed me to have a priest; and then I smiled. Then they asked me if it were not good. I said, I would confess my faults unto God; for I was sure that he would hear me with favor. And so we were condemned without a quest."

Three men, similarly accused, were condemned along with her; one of whom was her former tutor, John Lacels, another had been a Romish priest, and the third was a poor artisan. There was no jury to try the case, nor had she any counsel to plead her cause; but was summarily condemned to be burned at the stake. Yet how calmly does she relate the circumstances!

After her condemnation, she wrote to the king, as follows:

"My faith, briefly written to the King's Grace.—I, Anne Askew, of good memory, although God hath given me the bread of adversity and the water of trouble, yet not so much as my sins have deserved, desire this to be known to your Grace, that forasmuch as I am by the law condemned for an evil-doer, here I take heaven and earth to record, that I shall die in my innocency; and according to that I have said first, and will say last, I utterly abhor and detest all heresies. As concerning the Supper of the Lord, I believe so much as Christ hath said therein, which he confirmed with his most blessed blood. I believe also so much as He willed me to follow, and believe so much as the Catholic church of Him doth teach; for I will not forsake the commandment of his holy lips. But look, what God hath charged me with his mouth, that have I shut up in my heart. And thus briefly I end, for lack of learning.

"ANNE ASKEW."

The account before referred to relates, that when Gardiner and the Lord Chancellor failed to frighten their victim into recantation by the threat of the stake, or, by cross-questioning, to lead her unconsciously to implicate others, they determined on trying the rack. They thought that prolonged agony might extort revelations which might bear on the queen's household, or on the queen herself. Her own account of the proceedings shows that her previous means of maintenance had been cut off after her first imprisonment. It is as follows:

"The effect of my examination and handling since my departure from Newgate:—

"On Tuesday I was sent from Newgate to the sign of the Crown, where Master Rich and the Bishop of London, with all their power and flattering words, went about to persuade me from God. But I did not esteem their glosing pretences. Then came there to me Nicholas Shaxton, and counselled me to recant, as *he had done.* I told him that it had been good for him never to have been born, with many other like words. Then Master Rich sent me to the Tower, where I remained till three o'clock. Rich and one of the Council charged me, upon my obedience, to show them if I knew any man or woman of my sect. My answer was that I knew none. Then they asked me of my Lady Suffolk, my Lady of Hertford, my Lady Denny, and my Lady Fitzwilliam; to which I answered, if I should pronounce anything against them, that I were not able to prove it. Then said they to me, that the king was informed that I could name, if I would, a great number of my sect. I answered, that the king was as well deceived in that behalf, as dissembled with in other matters.

"They commanded me to show how I was maintained in the Compter, and who willed me to stick to my opinions. I said, there was no creature that therein did strengthen me; and as for the help I had in the Compter, it was by means of my maid. For as she went abroad in the streets, she made moan to the 'prentices, and they, by her, did send me money; but who they were I never knew.

"Then they said that there were divers gentlewomen that gave me money; but I knew not their names. And they said there were divers ladies that sent me money. I answered, that there was a man in a blue coat, who delivered me ten shillings, and said that my Lady Hertford sent it to me; and another in a violet coat gave me eight shillings, and said my Lady Denny sent it me; whether it were true or no, I cannot tell, for I am not sure who sent it me but as the maid did say. They said there were of the Council, that did maintain me; and I said, No.

"Then they put me on the rack, because I confessed no ladies or gentlewomen to be of my opinion; and thereupon they kept me a long while; and because I lay still, and did not cry, my Lord Chancellor and Master Rich took pains to rack me with their own hands, till I was nigh dead. The lieutenant caused me to be loosed from the rack. Incontinently I swooned, but they recovered me again.

"After that, I sat two long hours, reasoning with my Lord Chancellor, upon the bare floor; where he, with many flattering words, persuaded me to leave my opinions. But the Lord my God (I thank his everlasting goodness) gave me grace to persevere, and will do, I hope, to the very end.

Then was I brought to a house, and laid in a bed, with as weary and painful bones as ever had patient Job; I thank my Lord God therefor. Then my Lord Chancellor sent me word, if I would leave my opinions, I should want nothing; but if I would not, I should forthwith again to Newgate, and so be burned. I sent him word, that I would rather die than break my faith.

"Thus, Lord, open the eyes of their blind hearts, that the truth may take place.

" Farewell, dear friend; and pray, pray, pray."

Foxe's account* adds a few more particulars respecting this cruel transaction. "First," he says, "she was let down into a dungeon, where Sir Anthony Knevet, the lieutenant, commanded the jailer to pinch her with the rack. Which being done as much as he thought sufficient, he went about to take her down. But the chancellor, not contented that she was loosed so soon, confessing nothing, commanded the lieutenant to strain her again; which because he denied to do, tendering the weakness of the woman, he was threatened therefore grievously of the said Wriothesley, saying that he would signify his disobedience to the king. And so consequently upon the same, he and Master Rich, throwing off their gowns, would need play the tormentors themselves. Quietly and patiently, praying unto the Lord, she abode their tyranny, till her bones and joints were almost plucked asunder, in such sort as she was carried away in a chair."

Sir A. Knevet, the lieutenant, expecting to be promptly complained of for his compassionate leniency to his poor prisoner, sped with all haste in a boat to the court, and explained the circumstances to the king, before the others had time to get there by horse; whereupon the king "seemed

* Acts and Monuments of the Martyrs, as quoted in Webb's "Fells of Swarthmoor."

not very well to like their so extreme handling of the woman," and granted the lieutenant his pardon, though he did nothing toward the liberation of the innocent sufferer.

Her enemies, now fearing the effects of the public sympathy and indignation, printed and spread the paper which they had previously prepared for her to sign, falsely saying that she had signed it, and that their now placing her on the rack was only with a view to induce her to a similar recantation, in order to save her life. Her old tutor and fellow-prisoner, John Lacels, hearing of it, wrote to her, expressing solicitude for her faithfulness, to which she made the following noble reply:

"Oh, friend most dearly beloved in God, I marvel not a little what should move you to judge in me so slender a faith as to fear death, which is the end of all misery. In the Lord I desire you not to believe of me such wickedness; for I doubt it not, God will perform his work in me like as he hath begun. I understand the Council is not a little displeased that it should be reported abroad that I was racked in the tower. They say now, that what they did there was but to fear me; whereby I perceive they are ashamed of their uncomely doings, and fear much least the king's majesty should have information thereof. Wherefore they would no man to noise it. Well, their cruelty, God forgive them!

"Your heart in Christ Jesus. Farewell, and pray."

She also wrote a paper for the public, to contradict the injurious falsehoods spread abroad, of her recantation; in which she explains the facts in regard to her refusal to sign the declaration presented to her, and states what she did eventually write upon the paper; and she declares solemnly that she "never meant a thing less, than to recant."

Before her execution she wrote a confession of her faith, and likewise a prayer; which latter is as follows: "O

Lord! I have more enemies now than there be hairs in my head! Yet, Lord, let them never overcome me with vain words, but fight them, Lord, in my stead, for on thee cast I my care. With all the spite they can imagine, they fall upon me, who am thy poor creature. Yet, sweet Lord, let me not set by them that are against me; for in thee is my delight. And, Lord, I heartily desire of thee that thou wilt, of thy most merciful goodness, forgive them that violence which they do, and have done, unto me. Open also thou their blind hearts, that they may hereafter do that thing in thy sight which is only acceptable before thee, and to set forth thy verity aright, without all vain fantasies of sinful men. So be it, O Lord, so be it!"

One who saw her about this time declared: "I must needs confess of Mrs. Askew, now departed to the Lord, that on the day afore her execution, and the same day also, she had on an angel's countenance, and a smiling face; though, when the hour of darkness came, she was so racked that she could not stand, but was holden up between two serjeants."

Her execution, along with that of three men who were under the same condemnation, was appointed to take place in the evening, that the scene might be all the more terrific from approaching darkness. She was now in the twenty-fifth year of her age. We may imagine the yearnings with which her heart turned toward her helpless children; but she was sustained by that faith that "overcometh the world." The last scene is thus described by Foxe: "The day of her execution she was brought into Smithfield in a chair, because she could not go on her feet. When she was brought to the stake, she was tied by the middle with a chain that held up her body. When all things were thus prepared, Dr. Shaxton, who was appointed to preach, began his sermon. Anne, hearing, answered unto him where he said well, confirming the same. Where he said amiss, 'There!' said she, 'he speaketh contrary to the Book.'

"The sermon being finished, the martyrs standing there, tied at three several stakes, ready for their martyrdom, began their prayers. The multitude of the people was exceeding—the place where they stood being railed about, to keep out the press. Upon the bench, under St. Bartholomew's church, sat Wriothesley, Chancellor of England, the old Duke of Norfolk, the old Earl of Bedford, the Lord Mayor, with divers others. Before the fire should be set unto them, one of the bench, hearing that they had gunpowder about them, and being alarmed lest the faggots, by strength of the powder, would come flying about their ears, began to be afraid. But the Earl of Bedford declared unto him how the gunpowder was not laid under the faggots, but only about their bodies, to rid them quickly of their pain; so diminished that fear. Then Wriothesley, the Lord Chancellor, sent to Anne Askew letters, offering her the king's pardon if she would recant. Refusing to look upon them, she made this answer: 'I came not hither to deny my Lord and Master!' Then were the letters likewise offered unto the others, who in like manner, following the constancy of the woman, denied not only to receive them, but also to look upon them. Whereupon the Lord Mayor, commanding fire to be put unto them, cried with a loud voice: 'Fiat justitia!'

"And thus died the good Anne Askew, with these blessed martyrs; being compassed in with flames of fire, she slept in the Lord, leaving behind a singular example of Christian constancy for all men to follow."

CHAPTER XVI.

MICHAEL DE MOLINOS.

MIGUEL DE MOLINOS was descended from a wealthy and honorable family in Spain, and was born in the diocese of Saragossa in the year 1627. After studying at Pampeluna and Coimbra, he early entered into priest's orders, and received the degree of Doctor in Theology, though he would not accept of any ecclesiastical preferment or benefice, from which to derive worldly advantage. His talents were superior, and his conduct is said to have been uniformly consistent with his profession of piety; though he did not accustom himself to the austerities so prevalent among the Romish priesthood. His mind appears to have been enlightened from early life to perceive the great inferiority of ceremonial and outward religion, when compared with the possession of that which is interior and spiritual, and effectual to the purification of man's nature, and his exaltation into a capacity for communion with his Maker and Redeemer. His reputation for piety extended considerably in his native country; but in 1663, or as some have it, in 1669, he left Spain, to fix his habitation in Rome.

Here, we are told in Foxe's "Acts and Monuments of the Martyrs," that he soon made acquaintance with distinguished men of learning, who approved of his religious views, and assisted him in propagating them. His disciples rapidly increased in number, and from the peculiar contemplative character of their doctrine and practices, were soon distinguished by the name of Quietists. This appellation was afterward given to the adherents of the views of Jeanne M. Guion in France; and the famous Archbishop Fenelon has been generally considered as among that comparatively enlightened portion of the Romish church. In the papal city Molinos was regarded as a man of extraordinary piety, and was highly esteemed by the pope.

In the year 1675 he published in Spanish his principal and celebrated work, entitled "Spiritual Guide," which, it is probable, was afterward published by him in Italian, as some writers date the publication of the work at Rome in 1681.* This book was afterward translated into several different languages, and in less than six years passed through twenty editions. Mosheim says of the principles advocated in it, that according to the author, "the whole of religion consists in the perfect calm and tranquillity of a mind removed from all external and finite things, and centred in God, and in such a pure love of the Supreme Being as is independent on all prospect of interest or reward." This book was at first received with almost universal favor. Many even of the high dignitaries of the papal court were found among its admirers. Five celebrated doctors had given their sanction in the first instance to its publication, among whom one was a Jesuit, and the other four were members of the Inquisition. Many of the priests, both in Rome and Naples, openly declared in favor of the views advocated in the book. Three of these were afterward raised to the cardinalate. One of them was Cardinal Petrucci; and one of Molinos's most zealous partisans, for a time, was the Cardinal D'Etrees, ambassador to Rome from the king of France. This man professed a great approval of his principles, and entered into intimate friendship with him. Soon after the publication of the

* See Rose's Biog. Dict. compared with Am. Encyclop. and Foxe's Book of Martyrs,—also Life of Molinos, translated by Brooke.

work, the Cardinal Odescalchi, one of Molinos's friends, was elected to the papal chair (Innocent XI.), and gave him signal marks of his regard, lodging him in the palace of the Vatican, and openly favoring his sentiments. Many of those who thus favored him were doubtless convinced, for the time, of the truth and excellency of his sentiments, and of the spiritual efficacy of his religion; though they may not have had depth enough in a living experience for themselves, to adhere to such convictions when the tide of public feeling turned, and persecution commenced. The great Christian doctrine of the possibility, through divine grace and perseverance, of attaining to freedom from sin even in this life, seems to have been appreciated and advocated by Molinos; and he earnestly pressed upon all, the great benefit of silent waiting on the Most High, under the name of inward recollection, wherein the soul is withdrawn from all outward things, and fixed upon God in watchfulness unto prayer. But a few detached extracts from the "Spiritual Guide" itself, will give a more vivid insight into his main and distinguishing tenets, than any mere description of the work. We find him expressing his sentiments, in different places, in the following beautiful and impressive manner:—

"Oh, how many souls are called to the inward way! And spiritual directors, for want of understanding their case, instead of guiding and helping them forward, stop them in their course, and ruin them."

"How much are many souls to be pitied, who, from the beginning of their life to the end, employ themselves in mere meditation; constraining themselves to reason, although God Almighty deprives them of reasoning, that he may promote them to another state, and carry them on to a more perfect kind of prayer. And for many years they continue imperfect, and are always beginning, without any progress, or having as yet made one step in the way of the Spirit; cumbering themselves about times and places, the choice of particular subjects, imaginations, and strained reasonings; seeking God without, when in the mean time they have him within themselves."

"It is certain that our Lord Jesus Christ taught perfection to all, and is willing that all should be perfect, particularly the ignorant and simple. He clearly manifested this truth, when for his apostles he chose illiterate men, saying to his eternal Father, 'I thank thee, O Father, Lord of heaven and earth, because thou hast hid these things from the wise and prudent, and hast revealed them unto babes.' And it is certain that these cannot acquire perfection by acute meditations and subtile reasonings, though they are as capable as the most learned to attain to perfection by the purification of the affections and the will, wherein principally it consists."

"It is not to be said that the soul is idle, when, as to acts, it is silent; because, though it work not actively, yet the Holy Ghost operates in it. Besides that, it is not without all activity; for it operates spiritually, simply, and intimately. For, to be attentive to God, to draw near to Him, to follow his internal inspirations, receive his divine influences, adore him in his own intimate centre, reverence him with the pious affections of the will, to cast away multitudes of fantastical imaginations, and with composure to overcome so many temptations; all these, I say, are true acts, though simple, wholly spiritual, and in a manner imperceptible, through the great tranquillity wherewith the soul exerts them."

"The prayer of internal recollection may be well typified by that wrestling which the Holy Scriptures say the patriarch Jacob had all night with God, until day broke, and He blessed him. Wherefore the soul is to persevere, and wrestle with the difficulties that it will find in internal recollection, without desisting, until the sun of internal light begins to appear, and the Lord gives it his blessing."

"'The Lord intimated to Francesca Lopaz of Valenza, three things of great weight and consequence, in order to internal recollection: 'In the first place, that a quarter of an hour of prayer, with introversion of the senses and faculties, and with resignation and humility, does more good to the soul than five days of penitential exercises, hairclothes, disciplines, fastings, and sleeping on bare boards; because these are only mortifications of the body, but with recollection the *soul* is purified.

"'Secondly, that it is more pleasing to the Divine Majesty, to have the soul in quiet and devout prayer for the space of an hour, than to make long pilgrimages; because that in prayer it receives good for itself, and for those for whom it prays, gives delight to God, and procures a high degree of glory; but in pilgrimage, commonly the soul is distracted, and the senses are diverted, to which succeeds a decay of virtue, besides many other dangers.

"'Thirdly, that constant prayer consists in keeping the heart always upright toward God; and that a soul, to be internal, ought rather to act with the affection of the will, than the toil of the intellect.'"

"There are three kinds of silence. The first is of words, the second of desires, and the third of thoughts. The first is good; the second better; and the third best and most perfect. In the first, that is, of words, virtue is acquired; in the second, of desires, quietness is attained to; in the third, of thoughts, internal recollection is gained. By not speaking, nor desiring, nor thinking [our own selfish thoughts], we arrive at the true, perfect, and mystical silence, wherein God speaks with the soul, communicates himself to it, and in the abyss of its own depth teaches it the most perfect and exalted wisdom. Thou art to keep thyself in this mystical silence, if thou wouldst hear the sweet and divine voice. Rest in this mystical silence, and open the door, that so God may communicate himself unto thee, unite with thee, and then form thee into himself."

"There are two sorts of spiritual persons, internal and external. These last seek God without, by discourse, by imagination, and consideration. They chiefly endeavor to get virtues by many abstinences, by macerations of the body, and mortification of the senses. They give themselves to rigorous penance; they put on sackcloth, chastise the flesh by discipline, keeping outwardly silent in the presence of God, forming him present in their imagination, sometimes as a pastor, sometimes as a physician, and sometimes as a father and Lord. They delight to be continually seeking God, very often making fervent acts of love; and all this is art and meditation. By this way they desire to be great, and by the power of voluntary and exterior mortification they go in quest of sensible affections and warm sentiments, thinking that God resides in them only when they have these things. This is the external way, and the way of beginners. But there is no arriving at perfection by it. Nay, there is not so much as one step toward it; as experience shows in many, who, after fifty years of this external exercise, are void of God, and full of themselves, having nothing of a spiritual man, but the name only.

"There are others truly spiritual, who have got beyond the beginnings of the interior way, which leads to perfection and union with God; and to which the Lord called them by his infinite mercy, from that outward way, in which before they had exercised themselves. These men, retired, in the inward part of their souls, with true resignation into the hands of God, with a total putting off and even forgetting of themselves, do always go with a raised spirit to the presence of the Lord, by the means of pure faith; without image, form, or figure, but with great assurance founded in tranquillity and internal rest; in which infused recollection, the Spirit attracts with so much force, that it makes the soul turn inward with all its powers. These souls, as they are already passed through the interior mortification, and have been cleansed by God with the fire of tribulation, ordained by his hand and after his way, are masters of themselves, because they are entirely subdued and denied, which makes them live with great repose and internal peace. And although on many occasions they feel resistance and temptations, yet they become presently victorious, because being already proved, and endued with divine strength, the motions of passions cannot last long upon them; and although vehement temptations and troublesome suggestions of the enemy may continue a long time about them, they are all conquered with infinite gain; God being he that fights within them.

"These souls have already attained a great light, and a true knowledge of Christ our Lord, both of his divinity and his humanity. They exercise this infused knowledge with a quiet silence in the inward recollection of the superior part of their souls, with a spirit free from images and external ideas, with a love that is pure and divested of all creaturely affection. . . . . . . There is no news that terrifies them; no success that elevates them; tribulations never disturb them; nor do the interior, continual, and divine communications which they receive, make them vain and conceited. They remain always full of holy and filial fear, in a wonderful peace, constancy, and serenity."

"Oh, how much is there to be purified in a soul, before it arrives at the holy mountain of perfection, and transformation with God! Oh, how self-divested, naked, and brought to nothing, ought the soul to be, which would not hinder the entrance of the Divine Lord into it, nor his continual communication with it!"

"There are two sorts of humility; one false and counterfeit, the other true. The false humility is like fountains or falling waters, which must mount upward before they fall. Those who possess this feigned humility, avoid esteem and honor that so they may be taken to be humble. They say of themselves, that they are evil, that they may be thought good; and though they know their own misery, yet they are loth that others should know it. This dissembled humility is nothing but secret pride. . . . . . . As much, nay more, does false humility displease God, than pride does; because false humility is hypocrisy besides."

"That thou mayst be acquainted with interior or true humility, know, that it doth not consist in external acts, in taking the lowest place, in wearing mean clothes, in speaking submissively, in shutting the eyes, in affectionate sighings, nor in condemning thy ways, calling thyself miserable, to give others to understand that thou art humble. It consists only in the contempt of thyself, and a willingness to be despised, with a low and profound knowledge of thyself, without concerning thyself whether thou art esteemed humble or not. . . . . . . The light, wherewith the Lord with his grace enlightens the soul, discovers the greatness of God, and at the same time shows the soul its own misery; insomuch that no tongue is able to express the depth in which it is overwhelmed; being willing that every one should know its baseness; and it is so far from vain-glory and complacency, that it sees this grace of God to be the effect of his mere goodness, and nothing but his mercy, which is pleased to take pity on it."

"Although outward solitude doth much assist for the obtaining of internal peace, yet the Lord did not mean this, when he spake by his prophet (Hos. ii. 14), 'I will bring her into the wilderness, and speak comfortably to her.' But he meant the interior solitude, which jointly conduces to obtaining the precious jewel of internal peace. Internal solitude consists in the forgetting of the creatures, in disengaging one's self from them, in a perfect strippedness of all the affections, desires, and thoughts, of one's own will. This is the true solitude, where the soul reposes with a sweet and inward serenity in the arms of its Chief Good. ...... There the Lord converses, and communicates himself inwardly with the soul; there he fills it with himself, because it is empty; clothes it with light and with his love, because it is naked; lifts it up, because it is low; and unites it with himself and transforms it, because it is alone. Oh, delightful solitude, and earnest of eternal blessings! Oh, mirror, in which the Eternal Father is always beheld! ...... Oh, Divine Lord! how is it that souls do not seek this glory on earth? How come they to lose so great a good, through the love and desire of created things? ...... Blessed soul, how happy wilt thou be, if thou dost but leave all for God—seek him only—breathe after none but him—let him only have thy sighs!" ......

"By these six steps the abstracted soul rises higher, and gains experience in the spiritual and internal way:—In the first step, which is fire, the soul is illuminated by the means of a divine and ardent ray, enkindling the divine affections, and drying up those which are but human.

"The second is, the anointing, a sweet and spiritual unction, which diffusing itself over the soul, teaches it, strengthens it, and disposes it to receive and contemplate the divine truth. And sometimes it extends even to nature itself, corroborating and strengthening it with a sensible pleasure that seems celestial.

"The third is, the elevation of the inner man above itself, by which it is introduced into the clear fountain of pure love.

"The fourth step, which is illumination, is an infused knowledge, whereby the soul sweetly contemplates the divine truths, rising still from one clearness to another, from one light to another, from knowledge to knowledge; being guided by the Divine Spirit.

"The fifth is, a savory pleasure of the divine sweetness, issuing forth from the plentiful and precious fountain of the Holy Spirit.

"The sixth is, a sweet and admirable tranquillity, arising from the victory obtained after inward fightings and continual prayer. And this, very few have experience of. Here, the abundance of joy and peace is so great, that the soul seems to be in a sweet sleep, solacing and reposing itself in divine love."

"The sermons of men of learning, who want the Spirit, though they are made up of divers stories, elegant descriptions, acute discourses, and exquisite proofs, yet are by no means the word of God, but the word of men, plated over with false gold. These preachers spoil Christians, feeding them with wind and vanity; and so both speakers and hearers become void of God. These teachers feed their hearers with the wind of hurtful subtleties, giving them stones instead of bread, leaves instead of fruit, and unsavory earth mixed with poisoned honey, instead of true food. These are they that hunt after honor, raising up an idol of reputation and applause, instead of seeking God's glory, and the spiritual edification of men. Those that preach with zeal and sincerity, preach for God. Those that preach without these, preach for themselves. Those who preach the word of God with the Spirit, make it take hold on the heart; but those who preach without the Spirit, carry it no farther than the ear."

"O Divine Majesty! in whose presence the pillars of heaven do quake and tremble! O thou Goodness Infinite, in whose love the seraphim burn! Permit me, O Lord! to lament our blindness and ingratitude! We live in a delusion, seeking the foolish world, and forsaking thee, who art our God. We forsake thee, the fountain of living waters, for the stinking dirt of the world!

"O, we children of men! how long shall we follow after lying and vanity? Who is it that hath thus deceived us, that we should forsake God, our greatest good? Who is it that speaks the most truth to us? Who is it that loves us most? Who defends us most? Who is it that doth more to show himself a friend? Who more tender to show himself a husband, and more good to be a father? How great must our blindness be, that we should forsake this greatest and infinite goodness!

"O Divine Lord, how few souls are there in the world, who serve thee in perfection! How small is the number of those who are willing to suffer, that they may follow Christ crucified, that they may embrace the cross, that they may deny and contemn themselves! . . . What a scarcity of souls is there, who are disposed to let the Divine Creator work in them a willingness to suffer, that they may reign; to die, that they may live! . . . . Great reason hath heaven to lament, that there are so few souls to follow its precious path-way! 'The ways of Zion mourn, because none come to the solemn feasts;' but 'Him that cometh unto me, I will in no wise cast out.'"

Such sentiments as these, so contrary to the outward and formal profession of the church of Rome, nevertheless circulated freely in and from the papal metropolis itself, for several years. The pope was a personal friend of the author, and several of his high officers had already committed themselves to the work on its first appearance, and before its inconsistency with the prevalent system was suspected, or at least much talked of. So that it had time to be so widely distributed that all attempts afterward to suppress it were in vain. But at length the Jesuits and Dominican monks took the alarm. In the words of an anonymous writer of a few years afterward (supposed to be the Chevalier Ramsay), whose biography of Molinos has been translated into English by T. Digby Brooke, and furnishes perhaps the most complete account of any now to be found of the life of this excellent man—and which we shall occasionally quote in regard to the succeeding portion of his life—these priests "saw their trade decay, and branded Molinos with the infamous name of a heretic. They got the Inquisition to take cognizance of his book. And as the Jesuit Esparsa had given it an authentic approbation, it is said, they privately shut him up within four walls. Whatever way they dispatched him, he was seen no more. So dangerous it is to do any good or honest thing which incurs the wrath of the Jesuits."

Molinos and his friend, the Cardinal Petrucci, were arraigned before the Inquisition; but they defended themselves so well, and so fully refuted the attacks of their accusers, that these were condemned as scandalous and defamatory libels, to the great joy and encouragement of Molinos's numerous disciples. Petrucci was made by the pope, Bishop of Jessi, and we are told that his "life and manners were in every respect so exemplary, that his enemies could find no occasion against him, except that he omitted those exteriors of religion, which in the Romish church make a person pass for a saint."

The Jesuits and their partisans were excessively chagrined at their defeat, and began even to find fault with what they thought the blindness of the pope, in not seeing through the pernicious designs which they attributed to

Molinos and his friends. "On the other hand, it was observed, concerning the exemplary life of Molinos, with his disinterestedness, which induced him not to accept of any worldly dignity or ecclesiastical benefice, though for a long time in very high favor both with the pope and cardinals— with the unspotted conduct of his disciples, to which all Italy bore witness,—that there could be no stronger proof of his and their piety and sincerity."

But the Jesuits determined to leave no stone unturned to accomplish their object. "They sent privately to Spain, to examine the registers of his native place, in order to find out whether he might not be descended from the ancient stock of the Jews or Moors; and in that case they would have raised a clamor of his having sucked in their impieties with his milk." They also applied to the King of France, through the Père la Chaise, who represented to Louis XIV. that it would be a great glory to him, not only to destroy heresy in France, which he was then attempting by the destruction of the Huguenots, but in Italy also, where "one Molinos had infected it with pernicious errors," which were spreading not only there but in France also, and that by inducing the pope (who was thought to be favorable to Austria) to busy himself with a persecution against Molinos, the king would, first, ruin heresy,—second, weaken the party of Spain,—and third, by making work for the pope, prevent his disturbing the interests of France.

These reasons, unworthy as they were, prevailed with the great monarch. He ordered his ambassador, Cardinal d'Etrees, to pursue the matter with the utmost rigor; and the cardinal, not willing to lose the favor of his prince and his lucrative and important position, preferred to belie his own convictions, betray his friend, and become the ready tool of despotism and persecution. Through his intrigues and influence, Molinos was suddenly cited to appear before the Inquisition, and detained in custody. The cardinal, who had some years before translated into Italian a book of Francis Malaval's of much the same tenor as the writings of Molinos, had now turned traitor to his best feelings, and had presented to the pope a remonstrance from the King of France, wherein that monarch boldly set forth, "that it was a strange thing, that while he himself, as eldest son of the church, was employing all his power in the extirpation of heresies, his holiness was entertaining even in the Vatican an impious seducer of souls, and protecting a public despiser of the sacred ceremonies." The cardinal seconded this expostulation of Louis, by adding that he was ready to prove Molinos to be a heretic. To this the pope, who doubtless felt that he was in the power of the machinations of the French king, only replied, that the cardinal might address himself to the Inquisition; thus also giving up his friend to the power of his enemies, from a slavish fear of the result of standing to his convictions.

To the Inquisition accordingly d'Etrees presented himself, with extracts from the books of Molinos, and from papers of his which had been seized. "He would not allow Molinos to give the sense and meaning of his own writings, 'because,' said he, 'his obscure terms enclose mysteries, which he has discovered to me.' The Inquisitors, astonished, and at that time apparently loth to proceed against Molinos, asked the cardinal, 'how he could for so long a time be the particular friend of a man whom he now represented to be so wicked?' To this the cardinal, without shame, readily replied, 'All that he had done was in disguise, in order to discover the more easily the pernicious designs of the Quietists; that from the very first he had seen into the impious consequences of their doctrine; but that he had prudently dissembled, to see how far they would carry their impiety; that he had often approved *with the mouth*, what he detested *in his heart!* But that the necessity of penetrating to the bottom of those abominable mysteries had obliged him to have recourse to such dissimulation;—that in all this, he had done nothing but what was conformable to the holy Inquisition, which allows of those pious frauds, when one can by no other way come at clear and convincing proofs against a heretic,'" etc.

This was in the year 1685, and Molinos was thereupon cast into prison. During several months, however, his treatment was not characterized by the usual cruelty of the Inquisition, as the pope could not readily forget all at once their mutual affection, and said that "Molinos might have fallen into some errors, yet he believed him to be a good man." Thus he remained for nearly two years, public sentiment being greatly divided in regard to his guilt or innocence. Meantime, however, a storm broke out against some of his disciples. "The Count and Countess Vespiniani, with others to the number of seventy, and among them some eminent for learning and piety, were put into prison, accused of omitting the exterior practices of religion, and giving themselves entirely to solitude and inward prayer. The answers of the countess on this occasion astonished her judges. She said, 'she had never discovered her manner of devotion to any but her confessor—that it was impossible for them to have learned it but from him—consequently he was a wicked man, who had betrayed her, and revealed her confession—and who but idiots would go to confess, when priests let it be seen that they make use of confessions only to discover secrets,—but that she was resolved in future to confess to God only.' The noble firmness of the countess quite confounded them. Not daring to act with rigor against a person of her quality, and not willing to give room to any more such bold answers, by keeping her any longer in prison, they set her and her husband at liberty, on their promise to appear before them as often as they should be required."

"It is impossible to describe the consternation of the people, both at Rome and almost over all Italy, when they saw, in less than a month, nearly two hundred persons put into the Inquisition." The Inquisitors even went so far as to send deputies to examine the pope in regard to his favoring the new heresy, partly, it is most probable, with a view to intimidate him into a compliance with the contemplated measures. It was said that "they held strange discourses about it at Rome," but what passed at that extraordinary conference was not allowed to transpire.

Meantime measures were set on foot by the Inquisitors to crush out the novel views, which were spreading among the people through the influence of those writings of Molinos, the circulation of which had been at first sanctioned by some of their own number. The bishops in various dioceses through Italy were enjoined to forbid and disperse the assemblies of those who favored these novelties, their books were ordered to be seized, and they were to be compelled to resume those ceremonious exercises which for conscience' sake they had discontinued. Many of the bishops, however, had become so favorable to the sentiments of Molinos, that they were in no haste to obey the inquisitorial order; and by some means the letter of the Inquisitors being translated from the Latin to the Italian, and spread among the common people, contrary to their usual custom to maintain the secrecy of their transactions, it produced great dissatisfaction through the city. "This letter was followed up with nineteen articles imputed to the Quietists, to every one of which a short pretended refutation was subjoined. The sentiments of Molinos and his disciples were portrayed therein in the blackest colors with much malignity. But they never mentioned whence they drew those sentiments, for fear lest such as had made those extracts might be convicted of infidelity and malice."

"The prisons of the Inquisition filled fast every day. The fright all over the city was so general and so great, that only they whose public debauch and riot, or whose ignorance and stupidity screened them, thought themselves out of danger. It was said that the Inquisitors, in their examination of the prisoners, found some who answered nobly, and showed more knowledge than their examiners.

"The pope still showed regard for Cardinal Petrucci, and permitted him to visit Molinos in prison, with whom he had a long conversation. The pope's mildness had given some hopes to the friends of Molinos; but their fears redoubled when they thought of the number and credit of his adversaries. Very formidable enemies, especially in Italy, are all the different orders of monks joined together; of whom they reckon 500,000; among them 40,000 Jesuits; and in the single city of Naples 25,000 ecclesiastics, both regular and secular. This reflection made them look upon the condemnation of Molinos as inevitable. They foresaw that the Inquisitors (like Caiaphas) would conclude that it was *better that one man perish*, though innocent, than that the whole nation of monks should be starved, and superstition, to which they owe their subsistence, authority, and riches, destroyed.

"The condemnation of Molinos was then resolved on, and the noise of it spread in the city. Of a million of persons who were thought to be engaged (through Italy) in the sentiments of the Quietists, not one was found who dared to open his mouth in favor of their chief. So completely had the Inquisition, like some hurricane or earthquake, struck an universal panic, that innocence turned pale, fortitude trembled and was dumb, while cowardice and baseness joined the general cry, and easily carried all before them."

"The Inquisitors gave out that they had not condemned Molinos till they had heard the depositions of fourteen witnesses; eight of whom presented themselves; and the truth was *drawn from* the other six (*by tortures*). But these fourteen witnesses, it is more than probable, were not worth one good one. Such as come to present themselves to accuse an unhappy man, are generally people hardened in wickedness; and for the others, how common is it for tortures to force men to utter falsehoods."

The Jesuits appear to have aroused the feelings of the lowest classes of the people, not only against the reformer, whom they had in confinement, but also against the pope, whose assent to his restraint and condemnation had been obtained with difficulty. But having granted his assent, that functionary dared no longer to interfere in behalf of his former friend, unless we may attribute to his influence the fact that Molinos was never publicly condemned to the flames.

On the day appointed for the mock ceremony of his condemnation, a great crowd was assembled in the hall set apart for the purpose, the old Temple of Minerva, and a *plenary indulgence* was offered to all who should assist at it. Molinos was conveyed from his prison in an open carriage, with a monk at his side, and arriving at the Minerva, was left for some time in a gallery. When at length conducted to the place assigned to him, he showed not the least mark of fear or confusion. He had his hands bound together, and a lighted wax-taper placed within them. "His countenance and carriage manifested a steady firmness, such as showed no consciousness of any guilt, however charged with it by his enemies. Meantime, two monks, clad in long robes, read his process with a loud voice. Some people were suborned to cry out, at the reading of certain articles, 'To the fire—to the fire!' All the people joining, echoed the cry, and became so animated to madness, that if the guards, in leading him back to prison, had not opposed the insolence of the mob, he must have fallen the speedy victim of their fury. When he was near the little cell, in which he was to be shut up for the rest of his life, he entered it with great tranquillity, naming it his closet. Then taking leave of the friar who had attended him, he said, 'Farewell; at the day of judgment we shall see each other again; and then it will appear on which side the truth is, whether on yours or on mine.'

"After this we hear no more of him; his life and death being kept private among the Inquisitors and their officers." It was said that, in seizing his papers, they had collected above 20,000 letters, which had been received by him, asking spiritual counsel; which, if correct, shows the extent of his influence among the people abroad. He is said, in Foxe's "Acts and Monuments," to have suffered many cruelties from his keepers in the Inquisition, and that at length his physical strength gave way under his accumulated sufferings and privations. It is asserted in the American Encyclopedia that he died in the year 1696. But there has always been a mystery in regard to the mode and time of the death of this spiritually-minded man; and the silence maintained by the authorities at Rome has led to many doubts, whether his days were not shortened by that hand of violence so often resorted to in that institution.

Some authors have undertaken to say that he was compelled to a public recantation of his sentiments; but of this we have no information of an authentic and clear character, and it may be deemed at least extremely doubtful, and probably a mere calumny of his enemies. No hint of such a thing appears in the account from which we have so freely quoted; which seems to have been written either by a cotemporary, or by one entirely conversant with all the circumstances.

In the year 1819, Stephen Grellet, a citizen of the United States, though born in France, travelling in Italy, visited Rome, and was allowed to see the interior of the Inquisition. His account of his visit (published in his Journal after his decease) is as follows: "The entrance is into a spacious yard, in which nothing is in view but extensive and sumptuous buildings, containing their very large library, paintings, etc. On the left hand is a door, hardly to be noticed, which opens through a very thick wall into an open space, round which are buildings of three stories, with many cells. The doors of all these open into passages fronting the yard. These cells, or small prisons, are very strongly built. The walls are of great thickness, all arched over. Some were appropriated to men, others to women. There was no possibility for any of the inmates to see or communicate with each other. The prison where Molinos was confined, was particularly pointed out. I visited also the prisons or cells underground, and was in the place where the Inquisitors sat, and where tortures were inflicted on the poor sufferers. But everything bore marks that for many years these abodes of misery had not been at all frequented."

He went likewise into the public library, and was afterward introduced into the secret library. "It is," he says, "a spacious place, shelved round up to the ceiling, and contains books, manuscripts, and papers condemned by the Inquisition after they had read them. In the fore part of each book, the objections to it are stated in general terms, or a particular page, and even a line, is referred to, dated and signed by the Inquisitor. . . . Some of them contain very interesting matter, and evince that the writers were, in many particulars, learned in the school of Christ. I could have spent days in that place. . . . There are many Bibles in the several languages; whole editions of some thousand volumes, of the writings of Molinos."

He afterward went into the "Secretairerie," where the records of the Inquisition for many centuries are kept. He says, "They are kept as the books of a merchant's journal and ledger, so that looking into the ledger for any name, and turning thence to the various entries in the journal, a full statement is found, from the entrance of the poor sufferer into the Inquisition, to the time of his release or death, and in what way it took place, by fire or other torture, or by natural death. The kind of torture he underwent at each examination is described, and also what confessions were extorted from him. All these books are alphabetically arranged. . . . . I could have spent days in this place also; but the examination of some of the books, of several centuries, gave a pretty full view of the whole subject. This is an examination that probably very few have made, or are allowed to make."

With such an opportunity, it is matter of regret that he did not examine the record of the incarceration of Michael de Molinos, and thereby obtain the requisite information once for all to settle the very doubtful question of the duration of his sufferings, and by what means his spirit was at length released to its eternal rest.

CHAPTER XVII.

JANE MARY GUION.

OF the life and voluminous writings of this eminently gifted woman and true reformer, our limits will only permit a comparatively brief outline. She and Fenelon, though not professing any fellowship or connection either with the Protestants or with the Jansenists, have become identified with the history of the religious awakenings in France during the reign of Louis XIV.

Neither of them, it is true, saw through the whole of the great mass of errors in the doctrines of the Romish church; though they seem to have looked *over* them to something far better, and to have seen much *further* than the ceremonial limits of popery. This was especially the case with the subject of this notice. Fenelon himself, as a man, may almost be said to have been an unconscious Protestant; but, as a priest, he was nevertheless a Papist. Both of them, though still cherishing their connection with the papal system, in which they had been educated, were in reality permanently efficient in the work of reformation, and in spirit were unquestionably more evangelical than many of the acknowledged reformers themselves.

Jeanne Marie Bouviéres de la Mothe was born in the year 1648, at Montargis, a town about fifty miles south of Paris, and was the daughter of Claude Bouviéres, Seigneur de la Mothe Vergonville. When she was about four years of age, at the solicitation of the Duchess of Montbason, a friend of her father's, who requested the favor of his little daughter's company in her temporary retirement, she was placed with her in the convent of the Benedictine Nuns in Montargis. During this early period of her life, through the merciful visitations of divine love, she had many religious impressions, and made resolutions to lead a life of devotion to her Heavenly Father.

How long she remained in this convent does not appear. But her health failing, she returned home, and in the seventh year of her age was again sent away, to be under the charge of a half-sister in a convent of Ursuline Nuns. Some of her early religious impressions seem to have given way under the various temptations to which this period of her youth was exposed. She became less watchful over her conduct and temper, and less careful in regard to strict truthfulness in her words; yet her general deportment was such as to attract the esteem of those by whom she was surrounded, and she made rapid progress in her studies. When ten years of age she returned home; but was soon again sent away from the parental roof, and placed for further instruction in a Dominican convent, where she remained eight months. While here, though the pupils had not generally any opportunity of reading the Bible, a copy of it had, by some means which has not been explained, been left in her room. She gladly seized the opportunity thus, as it were, providentially afforded her, of an acquaintance with its contents. In her own account of her life she says: "I spent whole days in reading it, giving no attention to other books or other subjects from morning to night. And having great powers of recollection, I committed the historical parts to memory." After returning home, however, she once more gave way to youthful temptations and the influence of surrounding persons, and began to think she was none the better for what she had as yet attained, or for the restraints to which she had submitted. Her religion at this time, as she afterward acknowledged, was too much outward, and self-love was at the bottom of it, rather than the pure love of her Heavenly Father. Of course it was liable to great fluctuations, and by no means proof against the temptations of the cunning enemy. As she grew up, the comeliness of her person attracted many admirers; the world began to beguile her with its charms; and her mother indulging her in elegance of attire, she incurred great danger of entire forgetfulness of God, or of the necessity of walking in the narrow way of self-denial. From this state her mind, after a time, was somewhat aroused, by being disappointed of an interview with an esteemed relative, who called at her father's house on his way to Cochin China as a missionary. She was led to reproach herself with her want of obedience to the heavenly calls with which she had from time to time been favored; and in too much of her own strength she formed resolutions of amendment. "She resisted her passions," says her American biographer, Upham, "which were liable to be too strongly moved—asked forgiveness of those whom she had displeased—visited the poor, gave them food and clothing, and taught them the catechism. She spent much time in private reading and prayer. She inscribed the name of the Saviour in large characters upon a piece of paper, and so attached it to her person as to be continually reminded of Him. With an erroneous notion of expiating her sin by her own suffering, she voluntarily subjected herself to various bodily austerities." And she even entertained thoughts of "endeavoring to secure her spiritual interests and her salvation by becoming a nun;" a plan which was frustrated by the affectionate care of her father.

Thus she endeavored, for about a year, to satisfy the uneasiness of her conscience by contrivances made in her own will and wisdom, and the exercise of what the apostle calls "voluntary humility;" but her religious feelings gradually grew cooler, and from this time until after her marriage, she appears to have given way to the fascinations of the world. Her parents removed in 1663 to Paris, and she was introduced into the vortex of gaiety and amusement which characterized the court of Louis XIV. Here she was married, before completing her sixteenth year, to James Guion,* a man of great wealth but of little congeniality of disposition, and of considerably more than double her age. This marriage, accomplished at the instigation of her father, after an actual acquaintance of only three days, and consented to by her merely out of filial obedience, was fraught with many bitter sorrows to her during the twelve years of her husband's subsequent life.

Her husband, though he appears to have had a degree of affection for her, especially when out of the way of the influence of others, was a man of strong impulses and fluctuating temper, but little governed or brought under control by religious principle. His mother lived with them, and continued to claim the management of domestic affairs in his house. She was a woman of very little if any cultivation of mind, of no refinement of feeling, sordidly penurious, and of a violent temper. And James Guion, being often severely afflicted with disease, had moreover a female nurse constantly in attendance, who by her long assiduities had acquired an undue influence over his mind. The animosity of this woman, combined with the ill-nature of his mother, made the position of his young wife one of constant humiliation and unhappiness. She was sneered at for her refined sensibilities, listened to only to be rudely contradicted or rebuked, allowed no control in the family,

* It does not appear that either her husband or herself, as sometimes supposed, had any title of nobility.

insolently told to hold her tongue, and "scolded from morning to night." The contrast was indeed painful between her late condition in her father's indulgent mansion, and what she was now subjected to. When we reflect on her intellectual character as it afterward developed, and look upon the great susceptibility of her feelings, the liveliness of her imagination, and the extraordinary ability of her mind, and when we call to mind the fact that she became the author in after-life of more than thirty small volumes of religious writings, and was a chief instrument in clearing the views of the Abbé Fenelon to perceive the spirituality of true religion, we cannot but feel for her under the heartless treatment to which she was now subjected, and from which it was her husband's obvious duty to have protected her. To add to her annoyances, she had no room in the house which she could call strictly her own, or in which she could escape from the constant presence of those who combined to act as spies on all her actions. In describing her situation she says: "My condition was every way deplorable—my proud spirit broke down—married to a person of rank and wealth, I found myself a slave in my own dwelling—terror took possession of my mind—I found no one to share my grief, or help me to bear it—I was alone and helpless." But in a review of these trials in after-life, she could acknowledge that the Almighty permitted these things because he would not have her perish, and that such was the strength of her natural pride, that nothing short of some dispensation of sorrow could have broken down her high spirit and turned her unto God. "Thou* hast ordered these things, O my

* Her addresses to the Almighty, in accordance with the practice of the French, are all in the plural number; but this is so repulsive to our ears, that the author has, in rendering them into English, taken the liberty of changing them into the singular.

God! for my salvation. In goodness thou hast afflicted me."

In less than two years, she was visited with the additional affliction of severe illness, and the loss of her mother. In her distress, she was led once more to look for support to her Heavenly Father, entered into serious self-examination, and changed her reading from works of a worldly tendency to those of a religious character. The "Imitation of Christ," by Thomas à Kempis, was one of the books which now engaged her attention, and was probably one means whereby her heart was attracted to the inward work that was needed. Many of her efforts, however, she acknowledges, were made in her own strength.

A remarkable circumstance occurred to her soon after completing her twentieth year. After much striving to attain a knowledge of religious truth, in the best manner that she was then acquainted with (which was chiefly in the practice of outward acts of charity, piety, or ceremony), without arriving at any satisfaction to her tossed mind, she was induced by her father to visit a certain monk of the Franciscan order, who had spent much time in retirement, and whose spiritual views had proved very acceptable to her father during a late severe sickness, leading him to more inwardness in the work of religion. She told him her condition, and her want of success in all her endeavors. He remained a long time entirely silent, and not able to speak to her. At length he said, "Madame, it is because you seek *without* that which you have *within*. Accustom yourself to seek God in your own heart, and you will there find him." Saying this, he quitted her presence. These few words were as a watchword for all her subsequent life; and they were not lost upon her. They went, she says, through her heart like an arrow. They met there the Witness for truth, which told her that this was the way of life. And though the instrument of this good to her soul was a Franciscan monk, we cannot doubt that he spoke at that time by a wisdom better than that of man.

In narrating this occurrence, she exclaims from the fulness of her feelings: "O my Lord, thou wast in my heart, and requiredst of me only a simple return inward, to enable me to feel thy presence! O infinite goodness, thou wast so near, and I was going about running hither and thither to seek thee, and found thee not. O beauty, ancient and new, wherefore have I been so tardy in knowing thee?—It was for want of understanding thy gospel declaration: 'The kingdom of God is not here and there; but the kingdom of God is within you.' Thenceforward thou wast my King, and my heart became thy kingdom!"

From this time, though with fluctuations, her daily walk became more strict, and less conformed to the manners of the world. She gradually renounced all companies of pleasure, plays, diversions, dancing, and ostentatious promenades; and employed herself in domestic duties, and especially in attending to the necessities of her poor and sick neighbors, to whom she was a bountiful giver, and a kind and tender adviser. But her main solicitude was to attain to a pure knowledge and love of God, and entire resignation and conformity to his holy will. Her domestic griefs still continued to be sources of much affliction; but she bore them with great patience and meekness, believing that they would thus be made a means of crucifixion of the flesh with the affections and lusts of fallen nature. To this work, the subjugation of her own will, the reduction of her natural inclination to the cross of Christ, and the sanctification of body, soul, and spirit, through obedience to the power of divine grace, she devoted her most earnest endeavors; and though her course was marked by fluctuations in faithfulness, and she had at times to acknowledge with grief, that she had failed in entire fidelity to her convictions, yet on the whole she appears to have sustained for some years a gradual progress in religious life and experience. She increasingly found that the way of life is "a strait and narrow way," and that her own powers, unassisted by the power of divine grace, could not enable her to walk therein. To this divine assistance, then, she endeavored continually to have recourse.

About this period of her life she formed an acquaintance with a spiritually-minded individual, Genevieve Granger, the Prioress of a community of Benedictine nuns near Paris, and appears to have been greatly helped by the pious intercourse which resulted.* About this time also, a remarkable and unexpected interview with an entire stranger in the streets of Paris, was a means of reanimating her in the pursuit of holiness. She was walking to a place of public worship in the city, when, in crossing a bridge, she met with a man in very mean attire, whom at first she took for a pauper, and offered him alms. He thanked her, but told her he was not requesting any gratuity. He entered into conversation with her on the infinite greatness of God, and so sublimely did he speak of the "Three that bear record in heaven," that she thought she had never before heard the subject so clearly opened. He appears to have been of the Romish church; for he recommended the ceremony of the mass. He proceeded to depict to her, in an astonishing manner, her character and disposition, her virtues and her faults, though a total stranger to her. She listened to him in respectful silence, and while those who witnessed the interview thought she was conversing with a crazy man, she felt convinced that he was enlightened by the true Wisdom. He concluded by exhort-

* Some of the Benedictines had adopted several of the spiritual views of Jansenius.

ing her to endeavor after perfect salvation and freedom from sin in this life, without waiting for the work to be accomplished hereafter. His discourse made the way, though long, appear quite short; so that she was not sensible of her fatigue from having walked much further than was usual for her, until her arrival at "Notre Dame," when she sank down exhausted. In reply to her inquiry who he was, he only told her that he had been a porter, but was not so now; and suddenly disappearing, she never saw him again.

Although, during a large portion of her life, she was in the midst of society, surrounded by social, and by (so called) religious influences, yet in one sense she may be said to have been as it were alone—left to work out her soul's salvation without the usual aids of the religious fellowship of such as were truly of a kindred spirit. For though many sought her religious help, and many others officiously sought to influence her, yet having learned her experience in a good measure from the Lord himself, the great and sure teacher of his children, she outran her teachers, and had no one, or scarcely any, with whom walking at an equal pace, she might have been helped with the instrumental help of spiritual communion in her various and successive trials and difficulties. Perhaps this may in part account for her never having seen clearly the emptiness of many rites and ceremonies practised by the Romish church. She had been educated in strict conformity with its routine of outward observances, and her feelings had through habit interwoven them in some degree with her sentiments of duty. For she cherished at all times, and even under circumstances of outrageous persecution by the ecclesiastical authorities, a conscientious sentiment of obedience to the functionaries of the Romish church, whenever this obedience did not come in direct collision with what she had already been instructed was the divine will in her own particular. It is, however, surprising that, with views so clear as she was favored to attain to, respecting many portions of Christian doctrine, yet on various other matters, relating chiefly to the outward ceremonies of their worship, she retained, at least to a late period of her life, the prejudices of her early education and associations. Among these prejudices was an abhorrence of all that appeared to her to be novelty or innovations on the doctrines of the church, so that she could never bring herself to depart so far from its fidelity (as she supposed) as to make herself really acquainted with the principles of the Reformers; yet the tendency of her life and doctrines, and the deep inward tenor of her loving spirit, waiting constantly on God for its supplies, was (though unknown to herself) in harmony with the purest spirits of the Reformation.

In the summer of 1672, she was called upon to sustain a double privation very afflicting to her sensitive nature. She had already lost her mother. She was now to give up her father and her only daughter. While on a visit of religious retirement at an abbey, the residence of one of her friends, at four o'clock in the morning she suddenly awoke, with a lively impression on her mind that her father was dead; and the strong conviction of it remaining with her, so overcame her bodily strength, that when she arose and went into the chapel, she fainted, and for some time did not regain the power of speech. Yet her grief was accompanied with a feeling of divine support and inward peace. She heard nothing in regard to it until after dinner, when a messenger arrived, bringing a letter from her husband, announcing that her father, who was at that time staying at their house, had been taken extremely ill. She said at once, "He is dead, I cannot doubt it;" and immediately sent to Paris for a coach to take her to him. Her account of the journey states that she departed at nine o'clock at night, with none but strangers to accompany her, and against the remonstrances of her friend the abbess, who knew the danger of travelling on so bad a road, especially at that time of the night. She replied to her that she felt it her indispensable duty to go to her father.

"So I set out," she says, "alone, resigned to Providence, with people unknown to me. My bodily weakness was such that I could not retain my seat in the coach; and nevertheless I was often compelled to get out of it, from the perilous condition of the roads. I had to pass in this way by midnight through a forest which is styled 'cut-throat,' renowned for the murders and thefts which have been committed there; on account of which it is feared by the boldest people. As for me, I could fear nothing, my entire resignation of myself to the Lord's care, having enabled me to forget myself so much, that I could not dwell upon the danger. Oh, how many terrors and sorrows does a resigned soul avoid! I had gone to within five leagues of our own house, thus accompanied by my grief and by divine Love alone, when I met my confessor, who had opposed me, with one of my relatives, waiting for me. I cannot express the pain I suffered when I saw my confessor; for, while alone, I was tasting of an inexplicable contentment; but he knew nothing of my condition, but contended with me and gave me no liberty. My grief was of such a nature that I could not shed a tear, though I was ashamed of not being able to show any external signs of grief, when informed of a circumstance which I knew too well already; for my inward peace was so profound that it spread itself over my countenance; and, moreover, the state I was in permitted me not to talk, nor to behave as is commonly expected even of pious persons:

I could only dwell in love and silence. When I arrived at home, at ten o'clock in the evening, I found they had already buried my father, on account of the great heat of the weather; and all were in the habits of mourning. I had travelled thirty leagues in a day and night; and as I was very weak from exhaustion and want of nourishment, they put me at once to bed."

About two o'clock in the morning her husband, for some purpose, arose and left her chamber; but immediately returned, exclaiming with a loud voice, that her little daughter was dead! This was, then, her only daughter, a beautiful and lovely child about three years of age, a great comfort to her, being warmly attached to her mother, and evincing "an extraordinary love" for her Heavenly Father for one of such tender years. She had died, it appears, of a sudden hemorrhage, without her mother's knowledge that she was sick. Thus she was deprived of two earthly comforts at once, her father and her daughter, and left among connections whose delight it was continually to thwart her, and persecute her, and show in every possible way their contempt for her, and their disgust at her religious life. She bore her sorrows with extraordinary submission, believing that Divine Love was at the bottom of the bitter draught.

Some time after this event, a governess well known in the neighborhood sought her acquaintance from admiration of her character and deportment. This person, though somewhat serious in her sentiments, had no scruple against attending public entertainments, and one day invited Jane M. Guion to accompany her to the play. This, as she dared not comply, brought her (after finding that a subterfuge would not answer as an excuse for declining) to the necessity of giving her true conscientious ground of objection to such diversions; and her friend, though much further advanced in age than herself, was so much impressed in her spirit by what she said, as to abandon the practice from that time, of going to the theatre.

This friend once afterward, being at her house with an acquaintance who talked much, and who had studied the writings of "the fathers," they entered into a great deal of conversation concerning the Almighty. Jane M. Guion says, in relating the occurrence, "the lady spoke scientifically. I scarcely said anything; for I was drawn to keep silence, feeling even trouble at this manner of speaking concerning God. My friend came to see me in the morning, and told me, that God had so touched her that she could no longer resist. I thought she meant that she was touched by the conversation of the other lady: but she said to me, '*Your silence* had something in it which spoke to the bottom of my soul, and I had no taste for what the other was saying to me.' . . . It was thus, O my God, that thou madest such an entrance into the depths of her heart, that thou didst not withdraw therefrom, to the day of her death! . . . After the death of her husband and the loss of nearly all her property, she came to live on a remnant of her estate about four leagues from us. I obtained from my husband permission to pass some days with her for her consolation, and the Lord gave her, through my instrumentality, all that was necessary for her. My natural mind was not capable of such things; it was thou, O my God, who didst give them to me for her sake, causing the waters of thy grace to flow into her soul, without considering the unworthiness of the channel which it was thy pleasure to make use of. From this time the soul of my friend has been the temple of the Holy Spirit, and our hearts have been united by an indissoluble tie."

Soon came another privation, in the death of her intimate friend and confidant, Genevieve Granger; and this was followed by a long period of deep poverty of spirit, and apparent desertion, so that she seemed to herself incapable of doing anything acceptable to the Almighty, or even of feeling the comforting evidences of his presence in her soul. This barren and desolate state of mind lasted for seven years. It may have been intended by Him who knew what she needed, to draw her away from a dependence on outward observances and austerities, and reliance on them as means of spiritual strength, and to fix her faith more firmly on His immediate and inspeaking Word in her soul; and it seems to have had to some extent such an effect. She had been accustomed, in her great zeal to mortify the flesh, and doubtless in a compliance with what had been instilled into her mind as duties by her priestly directors, to subject herself to a surprising variety of austerities by way of penance for her sins, and in order to overcome the self-love and vanity which she felt so strong in her nature. She describes how she used not only to long for crosses (as if her many domestic tribulations were not enough of their kind), but plentifully to multiply them by compelling herself to do things exceedingly disagreeable to her feelings. She willingly undertook the most repulsive offices of the nurse toward the sick poor, when others might have relieved her; she sent away from her own portion at table to the poor, the things which were particularly agreeable to her palate; she tormented her flesh with rough bandages with iron points in them, and also with brambles, nettles, and such things, which often prevented her from sleeping; she would hold wormwood in her mouth, and put bitter apple into her food; she would place pebbles in her shoes when she went to go out; she would have teeth drawn when they did not ache, and would not have them extracted when they did; she once poured melted lead on her bare flesh, but finding that it flowed off immediately, she let melted sealing-wax fall on her skin, which stuck and made a sore; and when she held a lighted match or taper, she would allow it to burn down to the end, so that it might burn her fingers. But in recounting some such things in after-life, she says, "These are not in reality crosses nor pains; our own choice can only make trifling crosses; it is for thee, O my crucified Lord, to fashion them to thy will, and make them weighty." And in another place she remarks, as the result of further experience, that "austerities, how great soever, if not accompanied by what I have been speaking of [the living inward prayer of faith], always leave the natural senses in vigor, and never really mortify them: but *this*, with mental introversion, destroys their very life." And toward the close of her life, in allusion to a certain period of trial, when the words of David (Ps. lxix. 10) were impressed upon her mind, she made this acknowledgment—"Thus, as long as my health permitted it, I made very rigorous fasts and austere penances; but that appeared to me [afterward] to be but as burnt straw: one moment of the leadings of God is a thousand times greater help."

Probably it was in the latter part of her life that she wrote as follows, on the subject of austerities, in a letter to one of her friends: "I have great hopes of your soul, if you continue faithful to the beginnings of the inward work." . . . "Do not think of undergoing austerities; but die to the taste and liking you have for them. Your health will not admit of it. The enemy is very busy when he sees a soul willing to betake itself to silent prayer, and whose body is weak and unhealthy, to give it a taste and liking for austerities. He does this upon a twofold account—first. that the mind may be turned outward, and so hindered from bending its strength inward; secondly, that he may destroy its health, and frustrate by that means the good purpose of God. If you had a strong and sound body, and suffered yourself to be ruled by your appetite, I should not talk to you in this manner.

"But I will teach you another kind of mortification, which, without hurting your health, will have a greater effect than the austerities chosen by you. Mortify your peculiar tastes, your propensities, and your inclinations; and as for your own will, never adhere to it. Bear with patience and resignation your excessive and frequent sufferings of body. Suffer, out of love to God, all that may happen of contradiction, ill manners, or negligence in those who serve you; bear with what thwarts, displeases, and incommodes you, in fellowship with the sufferings of Christ. By this practice you will take bitter remedies, to honor the gall and vinegar which Jesus partook of." . . . . "Die to all sorts of height and magnificence; and you will make a greater sacrifice to God than if you fasted every day of your life with only bread and water. All depends on the mortifying of our own will and corrupt affections. This is what St. Paul calls the circumcision of the heart."

During the above mentioned period of deep trial from the feeling of desertion and poverty of spirit, her husband, who had long been subject to severe attacks of gout and other diseases, died. She believed that his last illness was blest to him; and she had the satisfaction of knowing that during it he had conducted himself affectionately toward her, and had even begged her to forgive him, and acknowledged his unworthiness of her. For more than three weeks of his illness she scarcely left his bedside. He died in the summer of 1676, leaving her a widow in the twenty-ninth year of her age, with two sons and one infant daughter. This daughter afterward married Louis Nicolas Fouquet, Count de Vaux, son of a celebrated financier under Louis XIV.

Her husband's death placed in her charge the arrangement of his large estate, and of many affairs belonging to other parties in his hands, which she was enabled to accomplish to their great satisfaction. She believed that she was divinely assisted in these matters, for she was of herself very ignorant in regard to business affairs. But her feeling of desolation was extreme. One day, she says, when she was more than ordinarily oppressed with it, she opened the New Testament, without thinking what she was doing, and found these words: "My grace is sufficient for thee; my strength is made perfect in weakness." For some moments she derived consolation from these expressions, but it was only for a brief period; the feeling of desolation and desertion again overwhelmed her. In these distresses she was brought to see more clearly than ever before, the exceeding sinfulness of sin, so that she was induced to prefer death rather than to live to grieve her Lord, and even cried out, in her grief, for "hell, rather than sin!" All that she had done appeared full of faults—her charities, her prayers, her penitences, all rose up against her and appeared to call for condemnation. She found no remedy in her usual resort, confession. She turned everywhere to find where she could receive help, "but," she says, "my help could come only from Him who made heaven and earth." "When I saw that there was nothing of my own to rely upon for safety, it seemed to me that I had in Jesus Christ all that I wanted in myself. I was, O Lord Jesus, that wandering sheep from the house of Israel, whom thou camest to save! Thou becamest indeed the Saviour to her who could find no salvation out of thee. Oh, ye strong and righteous men! find such safety as you can in what you have done at all good and glorious for God; as for me, I will glory only in my infirmities."

Some months after her husband's decease, at the instigation of her mother-in-law, who still remained implacable in her disposition toward her, she removed with her children to another house, and had at length the comfort and satisfaction of a quiet home. It was in the neighborhood of Paris. Here, particularly after the period of desolation and apparent desertion had given way to a peaceful consciousness of her Saviour's love to her soul—in short, of her having the unspeakable mercy and favor of being accepted as a spouse of Christ (to use her own expression)— which filled her heart with gratitude and love, she employed herself in deeds of kindness and benevolence, in frequent retirement and prayer, and in the diligent practice of those rites of the Romish religion which she still considered incumbent upon her, as having the sanction of the church in which she had been educated, and which, organized and carried on as it had been with great pomp and the highest assumptions of sacredness and authority for a thousand years, appeared to her to be the true church of Christ, although she saw and felt the wickedness of many of its officials. Her views of religious truth were indeed in many respects truly surprising, when we consider her education and constant associations, and can only be accounted for on the ground of an inward experimental acquaintance with the "inspeaking Word of Divine Grace," to which it was her earnest concern to take heed. Yet, in reading her own account of her life, we are continually met by remarks and facts which might stumble us in our belief of the depth of her inward experience after all, did we not know that the divine will and wisdom are not developed to mankind all at once, but gradually, *as we are able to bear it.* Even the immediate apostles of our Lord were told: "I have many things to say unto you, but ye cannot bear them now; when He, the Spirit of Truth, is come, He shall lead and guide you into all truth." Yet this likewise was experienced by the primitive church, after our Lord's ascension, to be somewhat gradual in its development. Many things were seen by the apostles at an early day very clearly. Other things were opened to them more gradually. The way of life shined more and more clearly to their view, unto the perfect day. We need not then, considering the strong hold of early impressions upon us all, and the powerful influence of priestly domination in France, and the pervading desire in J. M. Guion's mind, so far as the dictates of her conscience would allow her, to comply with all the requisitions of the church of which she found herself a member—we need not greatly wonder that, notwithstanding an extraordinary growth in religious experience, she continued to cling to certain superstitions, such as the Mass, priestly confession, praying to the Virgin Mary, a high esteem of certain days called saints' days, and an undue estimation, to say the least, of images of our Saviour, and such things. She must also be acknowledged, perhaps from a natural tendency, to have been over-credulous in regard to certain circumstances or appearances of a marvellous character, to which her own account at times alludes. Her regard for dreams was a discriminating one. She made a clear distinction between ordinary dreams and those which she deemed to be divine communications for our instruction, warning, or encouragement. The latter, which are often mentioned in Holy Scripture, she said, are characterized by a certain sense attending them that they have a mysterious application, by not being so easily effaced from the memory as common dreams, by even an increasing sense on the mind in recurring to them that there was a certain truth in them, and particularly, that they are mostly followed, on awaking, by a measure of solemnizing unction to the spirit. Her belief was, that the Almighty still speaks to mankind in various ways, partly in condescension to their various degrees of attainment; but that the highest and most pure and certain mode of his communication is by his "inspeaking Word" in the introverted, humbled, and obedient soul.

While residing apart from her mother-in-law, she had the satisfaction of witnessing a softening of her animosity toward her, and eventually, to her great comfort, an appearance of reconciliation, and even of affectionate regard.

But here she was not to dwell. She was given to understand that this was not to be the place of her rest. During the remainder of her life she could scarcely be said indeed to have had a home. In the various places where, during her middle life, she made her temporary abode, and to which she believed herself led successively by Divine Providence, she was diligent in laboring for the spiritual and temporal good of her fellow-creatures, generously expending her ample means, and giving up her own personal ease indefatigably for that object. And she did this without taking credit to herself, or seeking praise of men— indeed often concealing the hand that held forth the donation—and acknowledged that all praise was due to Him alone whom she felt to be the true owner of all she had, while she herself was only the unworthy agent. In like manner, when she was made the means of spiritual good to others, of which there were many instances, she was careful to seek no honor to herself, but earnestly to avow that all the good was from the Almighty, and though it came through her as his handmaid, yet it was not of her, nor at her own command.

Our limits will not permit more than a cursory view of this middle period of her pilgrimage, interesting though it would be to follow her in the detail she has given of her everyday life. Many remarkable occurrences of this period have been detailed in the beautiful portraiture given by her American biographer, Upham, and still more by herself in her own account of her life.* We must confine ourselves to what is necessary, to understand clearly the general course of her life, and to develope the gradual progress of those shameful and relentless persecutions which afflicted her latter years, and by which she was not only vilified with an extreme degree of baseness and malignity, but subjected to three solitary imprisonments; once under bars and bolts in a convent, once in the Castle of Vincennes and then at Vaugirard, and once in that most terrible of all French prisons, the Bastile—those imprisonments occupying many years—and finally condemned to banishment to a distant part of France, where she ended her days.

It was about the year 1680 that she felt a secret and often recurring impression that the Almighty had a work for her to do, away from her present home, in the neighborhood of Geneva. What this work was, she did not know; but thither was the attraction. After long deliberation and many doubts, and hesitation on account of her young family, encouraged at length by several friends whom she privately consulted—(among whom was one who in after-years became very dear to her in the bonds of the gospel, and in the fellowship of deep suffering for his testimony to inward religion, viz., Francis de la Combe, a priest then residing at Thonon, about sixteen miles from Geneva)—she placed her two sons in charge of preceptors, and taking her little daughter with her, left Paris in the summer of 1681, for a period of several years. She seems simply to have gone forth in faith, in obedience to what she fully believed the Lord required of her, "not knowing whither she went," or what was to befall her in the way of His leadings.

After her arrival in the neighborhood of the Jura

* "Vie de Madame Guion, écrite par ellemême:" en trois volumes; à Cologne, 1720.

Mountains, she resided sometimes at Gex, in a small community called New Catholics, under the patronage of D'Aranthon, Bishop of Geneva; sometimes at Geneva itself for a short time; and sometimes at Thonon, where she placed her daughter at a seminary under the immediate eye of her friend La Combe.

At first she seems to have imagined that her duty in coming into that country might be in some way to draw back the Protestant population of Geneva to the Romish faith; but this came to nothing. She then supposed it might be to help the poor and the sick; and accordingly she employed herself in preparing medicines and plasters, dressing sores, nursing, etc. But she soon had reason to believe that she had been sent thither for a higher purpose; and she found many opportunities of affording religious instruction and comfort to those needing instrumental help. In pursuing this course, she failed not to endeavor, as she felt called upon, to instil those deep views of the inward work of true religion and the necessity of an inward impulse in true prayer, with which her own spirit had been so sweetly imbued. And it looks probable after all, that one of the objects of her being called into that part of the vineyard may have been for the instruction and advancement of Francis La Combe in the way of life and salvation. It is at least evident that their frequent interviews during her tarriance were a means of leading him to a far clearer appreciation of the inward operations of the Holy Spirit, than he had before attained to. He had, in after-life, to suffer grievous calumnies and persecutions for his adherence to his conscientious convictions in this respect, and eventually was subjected to an imprisonment of many years' duration, terminating only with his life, after wearing out the powers of his mind.

In a letter written by her to La Combe in 1683, referring

to the storms which appeared to be gathering over them both, she uses the following remarkable and somewhat prophetic language:—" There will be many crosses common to us both; but you will observe that they will unite us more in God by an inviolable firmness to sustain all sorts of evils. It seems to me that God will give me many spiritual children—many children of grace...... You will have crosses and prisons which will separate us personally, but the union in God will be firm and inviolable.

"I had last night a dream denoting strange overturnings, so that when I awoke, all my senses were moved by it. There will happen only what the Master wills. But the tempest growls long, and I know not what the thunder will be; but it seems to me that all Hell will league itself to hinder the progress of the inward work, and the formation of Jesus Christ in souls. This tempest will be so strong, that but for great protection and faithfulness, scarcely could any withstand it. . . . It seems to me, it will cause agitation and doubt—and will be such as to leave not one stone upon another. All your friends will be scattered, and renounce you, and be ashamed of you; so that scarcely shall one be left to you; and such a succession of crosses and afflictions, and such strange confusions, as will utterly surprise you. . . . And as the children of God, who are inseparably with Him, will be spread over all the earth, it must be that the prince of this world will shake all the earth with divisions, signs and miseries, which, the stronger they are, the nearer will peace approach. . . . I warn you to listen as little as possible to your reasonings and reflections. And I have a strong inward impression to tell you to keep this letter, and even to seal it with your hand, in order that when these things occur, you may see they have been foretold to you. . . . .

"I know not what I am writing. Come, it is no time now for either you or me to be sick. Let us arise; for the prince of this world cometh. In the same manner as, before the coming of Christ, there were many killings of the prophets, many wars, and the Jewish people had been as it were brought to nothing; so true piety, which is the inward worship, will be almost destroyed, and will be persecuted in the person of the prophets—that is to say—of those who have inculcated it. The desolation on the earth will be great. During this time, the Woman [the true church] will be full of this inward spirit; and the Dragon will stand up before her, though without hurting her; because she is encircled by the Sun of righteousness, and has the moon, which is changeableness and inconstancy, under her feet; and the divine virtues will serve for her crown. . . . But though she may suffer many terrible pains, so as to cry out for their vehemence, yet God will protect her offspring, which will be hidden with Him until the day of its manifestation, until peace may be upon the earth. The woman will be in the wilderness without human aid, hidden, and unknown; there will be vomited against her rivers of calumny and persecution; but she shall be helped with the wings of the dove, and not touching the earth, the river will be swallowed up in it, while she will remain inwardly free, so that she will fly as the dove, and will rest truly without fear, without care, and without sorrow. It is said that she will *be nourished*, not that she will nourish herself there. . . . God will take care for her. I pray God, if it be for his glory, to give you an understanding of these things."

The spiritual views inculcated by Jane Mary Guion produced a marked salutary effect in the neighborhood; but startled some as a novelty compared with the common teachings of the priests. Her faithful counsels to one of the female inmates of the institution at Gex, by which she was made instrumental in rescuing the young woman from the evil designs of a priest who was confessor there, raised a spirit of resentment in this man, who thenceforward determined to endeavor to drive her from the place, and her friend La Combe also He spared no pains to prejudice the inmates against her, and insinuated likewise ill feelings into the mind of the bishop, to that degree that a real persecution soon arose, which never afterward ceased during her life. The bishop, finding that her pious counsels and example had gained many over as converts more or less to her spiritual views, and pressed by this corrupt ecclesiastic, endeavored at first to limit her influence, by urging her to accept the office of Prioress of the institution at Gex, with the condition annexed, that she should make over to it all her available funds, and confine herself to its care altogether. This, though strongly urged by him, she could not by any means consent to, for she felt convinced that it was not the way in which her Divine Master designed her to walk. The bishop insisted on La Combe's using his influence to bring this about, and threatened to have him silenced and removed, unless he consented to induce her compliance; but La Combe would have nothing to do with it, feeling convinced that her own judgment was adequate, and should be left to decide the question. The storm accordingly gathered more and more strength against them both—the bishop became exasperated—and she found she could not remain in that diocese. Not knowing whither to direct her steps, she concluded to pass into Italy, where she had a friend residing near Turin, the Marchioness de Prunai, who had invited her to spend some time with her.

It was in the summer of 1684, after remaining near Geneva about three years, that she left Thonon, and passed through Chamberri and over Mount Cenis to the city of Turin; an arduous and trying journey in those days, when the mountain passes had to be threaded by mules for the men, and the female travellers were carried on litters. She was hospitably received by her friend, and remained in Italy until the autumn; when she believed it best to return into France, by way of the ancient city of Grenoble, about one hundred miles northwest of Turin. She had a personal friend in that city, but she took up her abode with a pious widow previously unknown to her, placing her daughter under the care of a religious institution of the place, probably connected with a seminary for youth. She purposed a retired life; but very soon after her arrival, to her surprise, she was visited by many religious individuals, and found herself called upon in an unusual manner to minister to their spiritual condition. She was brought into deep feeling for many of them in their respective besetments, trials, and weaknesses. She describes the qualification she now received as a divine gift, communicated to her in an incomprehensible manner for the discernment of spirits, and to enable her to express to each, that which was suitable for them. She compared it to being clothed with an apostolic condition, and says, "I discerned the state of the souls of those who spoke to me, with such facility that they were astonished, and said one to another, that I had given to each one that of which they respectively had need. It was thou, O my God, who performed all these things!" Such was the succession of individuals of all classes who thus flocked to her for counsel, that she was often closely engaged in speaking of the things of God, from six o'clock in the morning until eight in the evening, and many marvellous changes were the result, through the Divine Grace which accompanied her labors. Some likewise came, she says, for the evil purpose of taking some advantage of her, or spying her out; but without her knowing this, she found, to her subsequent surprise, that she had not a word to say to such, and when she would try to compel herself to speak to them, she found herself divinely restrained. Some of these, on returning to their own people, declared, "People are mad, to go to see that lady—she cannot speak." "Others treated me," she says, "like a brute. I knew not that they came as spies, but when they had gone away, some one came to me saying, 'I could not come soon enough to tell you not to say anything to those persons; they came on the part of such and such an one, to spy you out and lay snares for you.' I replied, 'Our Lord has anticipated your kindness, for I could not say a word to them.' . . . . I felt that what I had to say was from the true source, and that I was but the instrument of Him who caused me to speak. During this general applause, our Lord made me sensible that this apostolic qualification with which he had honored me, and the resignation to help souls in purity of spirit, was likely to expose me to the most cruel persecutions." Here she was forcibly reminded that the multitude round our Saviour had sang, "Blessed is he that cometh in the name of the Lord," and yet this was very soon changed into, "Take him away, crucify him!" She says, "One of my friends speaking of the general esteem which people had for me, I replied, Take notice of what I tell you to-day—that you will hear maledictions expressed by the same lips that now pronounce benedictions!" And she adds these instructive remarks: "Souls who are really employed by God as apostles, really sent with an apostolic qualification, have to suffer extremely. I speak not of those who put *themselves* forth as apostles, and who not being called of God in a singular manner, and having none of the graces of the apostleship, have likewise nothing of the cross of the apostleship; but of those who resign themselves to God without reserve, and who desire with all their heart to be led or even tossed about without restriction by His providence; ah, these will assuredly be 'a spectacle to God, and to angels, and to men'—to God, of glory, by conformity to Jesus Christ—to angels, of joy—and to men, of cruelty and ignominy."

In speaking of the priests of a certain order, some of whom came to Grenoble, she mentions an interesting occurrence, which is said to have taken place at Dijon, a small town where she spent a day or two on her return to Paris. She says: "I have never in my life had such comfort, as in seeing in this little town so many good souls who gave themselves to God with all their heart. There were young girls of twelve or thirteen years old, who labored almost all day, in silence, in order to converse with God..... Being poor, they united together in pairs, and those who could read would read something to those who could not. It seemed as if the innocence of the first Christians was revived. There was a poor laundress, who had five children, and a paralytic husband, whose little remaining strength was only exerted in beating his wife. Yet this poor woman bore it all with the sweetness of an angel, and procured a maintenance for this man and her five children. This woman had a wonderful gift of prayer, and preserved her equanimity and a sense of God's presence, through the greatest miseries and in the most extreme poverty. There was also a pious tradeswoman, and a locksmith's wife—these three were friends together, and the two latter would read sometimes to this laundress, and were surprised to find that she was instructed by our Lord in all that they read to her, and could speak of those things in a divine manner. The priests (above mentioned) sought out this woman, and threatened her greatly if she did not cease praying, telling her that it was only for priests, and that it was very bold in her to attempt to pray. She replied to them (or rather He who instructed her, for she was of herself quite ignorant), that our Lord had commanded all to pray, declaring, 'I say it unto you all,' not specifying priests nor ecclesiastics; and she added, that without prayer, she could not support the crosses and poverty which were her lot; that she had once been without prayer, and that she was exceedingly wicked (*un Démon*); but since she had known what it was to pray to God, she had loved Him with all her heart; that thus to cease to pray, would be to renounce her salvation, and she could not do it.'" The priests threatened that she should have no absolution till she promised to cease from praying; but she told them "that it depended not on herself; and that our Lord was the master, and it was his right to communicate with his creatures, and make of them whatsoever might please him." These priests collected together all the books that they could find in the place, which inculcated prayer, to the number of about three hundred, and burned them in the public square, being "much elated" with their achievement.

At Thonon also, she says, there were young women— poor village girls—who, with one accord, wishing to serve their Maker while they were gaining their living, assembled together at their needlework, and one would read from time to time, while the others worked. None would go out without asking permission of the oldest, and the strong contributed to the support of the weak. These poor girls were separated, as well as others in several villages, and were cast out from the church.

A monk of the same order as those who burned her books at Dijon, was here greatly reached by what she said to him, and by the savor of her spirit as they communed silently before the Lord. She says, in reference to it, "Christ has declared, 'where two or three are gathered together in my name, there am I in the midst of them.' With the greatest certainty, through his blessed operation, is this experienced. . . . . In proportion as this person's soul advanced sufficiently for continuing in silence before God, and as the Word operated on him in silence, being vivid and fruitful, and not in a state of indolence as some ignorantly imagine, he thereby grew in grace. Oh, immediate ineffable Word, who tellest us everything without articulating anything!" .... "How well I comprehended in this silence, that in souls wholly the Lord's, his grace flows like a river! This is that 'well of water springing up into everlasting life;' the great mystery which Christ spoke of and revealed to the Samaritan woman." .... " The water of life will flow from the sacred source into the souls of all those who have lived by grace, more or less as they are fitted or enlarged to receive of its abundance." She adds, that the Superior and the Master of the monks "were grievously chagrined that a woman, as they said, should be so much flocked to and sought after. For, looking at things as they were in themselves, and not as they were in God, who does whatever pleases Him, they had nothing but contempt for the gift which was lodged in so mean an instrument; and instead of rightly estimating God and his grace, they attended to the meanness of the subject in which he was pleased to shed it." Yet she informs us that this Superior was himself eventually reached in his conscience, and acknowledged the benefits they had received; and he became so fully convinced of her rectitude, that some time afterward he distributed many of the same books which his brethren had destroyed.

In describing the manner in which she was often led, in her ministrations to various individuals at Grenoble, she says that some would ask her over again at different times the same questions, merely from a talkative disposition. To such she could not reply, and then it was made clear to her that no response was given to her because it would have been useless. There were others who, while undergoing those mortifications by which the Lord was conducting them to a death of self, came to her to seek human consolation. She says, "For these I had only what was barely needful, after which I could say no more. I would rather have talked about indifferent things, being willing to be all things unto all, and to be disagreeable to none; but as to the word of the Lord, He is himself the dispenser of it. Oh, if preachers would speak in the Spirit, what fruits would they not bring forth! There were others, to whom, as I have said, I could communicate only in silence, but a silence as ineffable as it was efficacious—this is the communion of blessed spirits!"

Soon after mentioning these things, in speaking of the relation between John the Baptist and our Lord Jesus Christ, she says, "He [John] only baptized with water, to show what was his function—the water, in flowing off, leaves nothing behind it—it is only the Word, which impresses itself. John was to introduce the Word, but he was not the Word; and He who was the Word baptized with the Holy Spirit, because he had the power of impression into souls, and communicating himself to them by the Holy Spirit."

No wonder, if such doctrines were inculcated in her daily ministrations, so savoring of primitive Christianity revived, so calculated to shake from all false dependence on outward rites, that the adherents of formal religion took alarm, and a party was raised in Grenoble, as it had been around Geneva, to prevent, by calumniating the promulgator, the spread of such innovations upon the craft of the priests. But was the woman who could express herself thus, who, like King David (Ps. cxix. 99), saw so far beyond all her teachers, who received her instructions evidently from the heavenly Source of all true Wisdom, through the "In-speaking Word," was this woman indeed a Papist? Was she not a Protestant, unknown and unsuspected by herself? Was not the Romish system, in her case, like the mere dead shell which binds and clogs the limbs of the chrysalis, until its wings are sufficiently matured to be ready to expand, and enable it to soar aloft in its kindred element, the sunshine of perfect day?

Whether it was about this time or not, does not appear; but once, on the subject of simplicity of dress, she thus addressed one of her female friends : "Why do you make a difficulty of speaking to me about your dress? Should you not be free, and tell me all? You have done well in laying aside that superfluity. I entreat you never to wear it again. I am also sure that if you would hearken to that which speaks in the bottom of your heart, you would find more things to put off. For though we are not to make the putting off of such things the capital, yet it is necessary; and I am persuaded that in the disposition your husband is in at present, you will please him as well without those ornaments as with them. But nature will find some pretext to keep those things it likes. However, a little sacrifice of this kind which you shall make to God, will often draw down His grace upon you; and He who has promised to recompense even a cup of cold water given for his sake, will much more recompense the denial of yourself in a matter of dress. And I must tell you likewise, that it would draw down the blessings of Heaven upon your husband.

"A Christian woman must be distinguished from others, not by an affected outside, nor by an untidy dress, but by a neat and modest exterior. You may wear clothes and linen suitable to your quality; but I would put off all those superfluous ribbons; and I am sure you would be never the less pleasing in the eyes of your spouse, and much more so in the eyes of Him whom you desire to please above all.

"Never make any scruple or difficulty of writing plainly and nakedly as things are. Do not be afraid, in so doing, of lessening my esteem for you; for it has a quite different effect, because I gather from that, that you have truly a mind to be given up to God, and that God is leading you; since He makes you attentive and careful about things so small; and it is a good sign that He is at work at the bottom of your heart. Be faithful to him, I earnestly beseech you, and you will find a thousand times more satisfaction in listening to Him within, and in following His inspirations, than in all the foolish toys of the world, which can never give true satisfaction."

It was about this time that she completed the manuscript of her celebrated little book, entitled "A Short Method of Prayer;" a book which in after-years was made a plea for her most grievous persecutions. She had previously, while at Thonon, written another small work, entitled "Spiritual Torrents," comparing the religious life to a stream, in allusion to Amos, v. 24—" Let judgment run down as waters, and righteousness as a mighty stream"— which, in the French and Latin translations to which she had access, is rendered "A mighty torrent." She now commenced writing her largest work, which was eventually published in twenty volumes 12mo., being Commentaries on the Bible—the Old Testament in twelve volumes, and the New in eight—a work which has probably never been translated into the English language, and is now very scarce in the French. In writing this book she had no doubt that she was divinely led and qualified. She says she used no other book in preparing it than the Bible itself, that the references made from the Old to the New, or from the New to the Old Testament, were not the result of study

on her part, but were such as were immediately given to
her at the time; and that though, when she commenced at
any time to write, she did not know at all what she was
going to say, yet as soon as she had written any passage,
the commentary was given her, without the least premeditation or study of her own; and she was enabled to write
down, with a quickness inconceivable to herself, things
which before she was quite ignorant of. "All the faults in
my writings," she says, "arise from this, that not being
accustomed to the work of the Lord, I was often unfaithful
in it, thinking it was well to continue to write when I had
time for it, without having the inward motion for it—anxious to finish the work—so that it is easy to see places
which are good and sustainable, and others which have
neither taste nor unction. I have left them as they are
(until directed otherwise by the light given me), that the
difference may be seen between the Spirit of God and the
natural human spirit." . . . . . . "I continued to write with
wonderful rapidity. My hand could scarcely keep pace
with the dictation of the spirit. The copyist, however diligent, could not copy in five days what I had written in a
night. Whatever is good therein came from thee, O my
God, and whatever is bad is from myself, and of my own
unfaithfulness, and of the mixture which I unconsciously
made of my own impurity with thy pure and chaste doctrine."

Her "Short Method of Prayer" was not originally published by herself, but by one of her friends, a Counsellor of
the Parliament, who saw it lying in manuscript on her
table at Grenoble, borrowed it, lent it, and was so much
pleased with it that he concluded to print it. Many thousands have since that time been spread abroad in the
world, particularly in France, and have doubtless acted as
a wholesome leaven, in promoting more spiritual views of

this subject and of the nature of religion at large, among a people otherwise much held under the blighting influence of formality. It is not to be denied that there are portions of this work more or less tarnished by the imperfections of the prevalent form of religion; but as a whole its tendency is eminently spiritual, as may be seen by the following extracts taken from various parts of the treatise:

"For the attainment of salvation, it is absolutely necessary that we should forsake outward sin, and turn unto righteousness; but this alone is not perfect conversion, which consists in a total change of the whole man from an outward to an inward life."

"We must urge it as a matter of the highest import, to cease from self-action and self-exertion, that God himself may act alone. He saith by the mouth of his prophet David, 'Be still, and know that I am God.'"

"'The Lord is in his holy temple, let all the earth keep silence before Him.' Inward silence is absolutely indispensable, for The Word is essential and eternal, and necessarily requires dispositions in the soul in some degree correspondent to his nature, as a capacity for the reception of himself. Hearing is a sense formed to receive sounds, and is rather passive than active, admitting, but not communicating sensation; and if we would hear, we must lend the ear for that purpose. So Christ the Eternal Word, without whose divine inspeaking the soul is dead, dark, and barren, when he would speak within us, requires the most silent attention to his all-quickening and efficacious voice."

"When, through imbecility or unfaithfulness, we become dissipated, or as it were uncentred, it is of immediate importance to turn again gently and sweetly inward; and thus we may learn to preserve the spirit and unction of prayer throughout the day; for if prayer and recollection were wholly confined to any appointed half-hour or hour, we should reap but little fruit."

"A direct contest and struggle with distractions and temptations, rather serves to augment them, and withdraws the soul from that adherence to God, which should ever be its principal occupation. The surest and safest method of conquest is simply to turn away from the evil, and draw yet nearer and closer to our God. A little child, on perceiving a monster, does not wait to fight with it, and will scarcely turn its eyes toward it, but quickly shrinks into the bosom of its mother, in confidence of safety. So likewise should the soul turn from the dangers of temptation to her God. 'God is in the midst of her,' saith the psalmist, 'she shall not be moved; God shall help her, and that right early.'"

"St. Paul saith, 'If any man hath not the Spirit of Christ, he is none of His:' therefore, to be Christ's, we must be filled with his Spirit; and to be filled with his Spirit, we must be emptied of our own. The apostle, in the same passage, proves the necessity of this divine influence or motion. 'As many,' saith he, 'as are led by the Spirit of God, they are the sons of God.' The spirit of divine filiation is then the spirit of divine action or motion. He therefore adds, 'Ye have not received the spirit of bondage again to fear, but ye have received the spirit of adoption, whereby ye cry, Abba, Father.' This spirit is no other than the Spirit of Christ, through which we participate of his filiation; 'And this Spirit beareth witness with our spirit, that we are the children of God.' When the soul yields itself to the influence and motions of this blessed Spirit, it feels the testimony of its divine filiation; and it feels also, with superadded joy, that it hath received, not the spirit of bondage, but of liberty, even 'the liberty of the children of God.' It then finds that it acteth freely and sweetly, though with vigor and infallibility. The spirit of divine action is so necessary in all things, that St. Paul, in the same passage, foundeth that necessity on our ignorance with respect to what we pray for. 'The Spirit,' saith he, 'also helpeth our infirmities; for we know not what we should pray for as we ought; but the Spirit itself maketh intercession for us with groanings which cannot be uttered.' This is positive. If we know not what we stand in need of, nor pray as we ought to do for those things which are necessary; and if the Spirit which is in us, and to which we resign ourselves, asks and intercedes for us; should we not give unlimited freedom to its action, to its ineffable groanings on our behalf? This Spirit is the Spirit of The Word, which is always heard, as He saith himself, 'I know that thou hearest me always.' And if we freely admit this Spirit to pray and intercede for us, we also shall always be heard."

"When the vessel is in port, the mariners are obliged to exert all their strength, that they may clear her thence and put to sea; but at length they turn her with facility as they please. In like manner, while the soul remains in sin and creaturely entanglements, very frequent and strenuous endeavors are requisite to effect her freedom; the cords which withhold her must be loosed; and then by strong and vigorous efforts she gathers herself inward, pushing off gradually from her old port; and in leaving that at a distance, she proceeds to the interior, the haven to which she wishes to steer. .... The further she departs from the old harbor, the less difficulty and labor is requisite in moving her forward. At length she begins to get sweetly under sail, and now proceeds so swiftly on her course that the oar, which has become useless, is laid aside. How is the mariner now engaged? He is content with spreading the sails and holding the rudder. To spread the sails, is to lay one's self before God in the prayer of simple exposition, that we may be acted upon by His Spirit. To hold the rudder, is to restrain our heart from wandering from the true course, recalling it gently, and guiding it steadily to the dictates of the Blessed Spirit, which gradually gain possession and dominion of the heart, just as the wind by degrees fills the sails and impels the vessel. While the winds are fair, the mariners rest from their labors, and the vessel glides rapidly along without their toil. And when they thus repose, and leave the vessel to the wind, they make more way in one hour than they had done in a length of time by all their former efforts. Were they even now to attempt using the oar, they would not only fatigue themselves, but retard the vessel by their ill-timed labors. This is the manner of acting we should pursue interiorly. It will indeed advance us in a very short time, by the divine impulsion, infinitely further than a whole life spent in reiterated acts of self-exertion. .... If the wind be contrary and blow a storm, we must cast anchor to withhold the vessel. Our anchor is a firm confidence and hope in God, waiting patiently the calming of the tempest and the return of a more favorable gale; as David 'waited patiently for the Lord, and He inclined unto him and heard his cry.' We must, therefore, be resigned to the Spirit of God, giving up ourselves wholly to His divine guidance."

"Few and transient fruits must attend that [ministerial] labor which is confined to outward matters; such as burdening the disciple with a thousand precepts for external exercises; instead of leaving the soul to Christ by the occupation of the heart in him. If ministers were solicitous thus to instruct their parishioners, shepherds while watching their flocks might have the spirit of the primitive Christians, and the husbandman at the plough might maintain a blessed intercourse with his God; the manufacturer, while he exhausts his outward man with labor, would.be renewed in internal strength; every species of vice would shortly disappear, and every parishioner might become a true follower of the Good Shepherd."

"The Spirit of God needs none of our arrangements and methods. When it pleaseth Him, he turns shepherds into prophets; and, so far from excluding any from the temple of prayer, he throws wide the gates, that all may enter; while Wisdom cries aloud in the highways, 'Whoso is simple let him turn in hither,' and to the fools she saith, 'Come, eat of my bread, and drink of the wine which I have mingled.' And doth not Jesus Christ himself thank his Father for having 'hid' the secrets of his kingdom 'from the wise and prudent, and revealed them unto babes'?"

"Divine justice and wisdom, as an unremitting fire, must devour and destroy all that is earthly, sensual, and carnal, and all self-activity, before the soul can be fitted for, and capable of union with God. Now, this purification can never be accomplished by the industry of fallen man. On the contrary, he submits to it always with reluctance; he is so enamored of self, and so averse to its destruction, that did not God act on him powerfully and with authority, he would forever resist."

"Would you not say that he had lost his senses, who having undertaken an important journey, should fix his abode at the first inn, because he had been told that many travellers who had come that way had lodged in the house and made it their place of residence? All that we should wish then is, that souls should 'press toward the mark,' should pursue their journey, and take the shortest and easiest road; not stopping at the first stage, but, following the counsel and example of St. Paul, suffer themselves to be guided and governed by the Spirit of Grace; which would infallibly conduct them to the end of their creation, the enjoyment of God. But while we confess, that the enjoyment of God is the end for which we were created; that 'without holiness' none can attain it; and that to attain it we must necessarily pass through a severe and purifying process; how strange it is, that we should dread and avoid this process, as if that could be the cause of evil and imperfection in the present life, which is to be productive of glory and blessedness in the life to come!"

"Some say that we should not attempt, by our own ability, to place ourselves in this state [of union with God]. I grant it. But what a poor subterfuge is this!—since I have all along asserted and proved, that the utmost exertion of the highest created being could never accomplish this of itself; it is God alone must do it. The creature may indeed open the window; but it is the Sun himself, that must give the light."

"Oh, ye blind and foolish men, who pride yourselves on science, wisdom, wit, and power, how well do you verify what God hath said, that his secrets are hidden from the wise and prudent, and revealed unto the little ones—the babes!"

Fifteen hundred copies of this little book were taken at Grenoble very soon after it was printed, and five or six editions were subsequently published during her life, notwithstanding the calumnies and opposition of the priests.

During her residence at Grenoble, Jane Mary Guion made a visit to the celebrated Carthusian monastery of La Grande Chartreuse, situated among the mountains about eight miles from that city. She makes no mention of it in her own very minute account of her life; which seems singular; as, from the objection which she says she had to visiting such places unless required to do so, it may be supposed that she did not go thither from any other motive than an impression of religious duty. Though the distance from Grenoble was not great, yet the journey must have been attended with considerable fatigue and risk, from the recluseness of the spot among precipitous and snow-clad mountains. Upham gives the following description of the ascent to it, taken principally from an account given by Claude Lancelot, of a Tour to this place and Alet:

"As the traveller approaches the Grande Chartreuse, he emerges from a long and gloomy forest, which is abruptly terminated by immense mountains that rise before him. The pass, through which the ascent of the mountains is commenced, winds through stupendous granite rocks, which overhang from above. At the end of this terrific defile, the road is crossed by a romantic mountain torrent, over which is a rude stone bridge. The road no sooner leaves the bridge than it turns suddenly in another direction, and thus presents at once before the traveller a lofty mountain, on the flattened summit of which the Carthusian monastery is situated, enclosed on either side by other mountain peaks still more elevated, whose tops are whitened with perpetual snows. 'No sooner is the defile passed,' says Lancelot, 'than nothing which possesses either animal or vegetable life is seen. No huntsman winds his horn in these dreary solitudes; no shepherd's pipe is allowed to disturb the deep repose. It is not permitted to the mountaineers ever to lead their flocks beyond the entrance of the defile; and even beasts of prey seem to shrink back from that dreaded pass, and instinctively to keep away from a desert which furnishes neither subsistence nor covert. Nothing, as we passed upward, met the eye, but tremendous precipices and huge fragments of rock, diversified with glaciers in every possible fantastic form. Sometimes the rocks overhung us till they formed a complete arch over our heads, and rendered the path so dark that we could scarcely see to pick our way. Once we had to pass over a narrow pine plank which shook at every step. This was placed by way of bridge over a yawning chasm, which every moment threatened to engulf the traveller. We often passed close by the side of abysses so profound as to be totally lost in darkness; while the awful roaring of the waters, struggling in their cavities, shook the very rocks on which we trod.' From the bridge at the termination of the defile, to the level opening on the top of the mountain where the monastery is situated, the ascent is a little more than two miles. The monastery itself is a very striking object, from its massive strength and high antiquity. Although correctly described as situated on the summit, it is nevertheless enclosed on two sides by stupendous rocks and peaks of still greater height, which reach far above the clouds, and almost shut out the light of the sun."

All that is known of the visit of J. M. Guion to this wild retreat of some forty monks, is from the account given of it by the Prior of the institution in his Life of D'Aranthon, Bishop of Geneva. He says, as quoted by Upham: "Some six or seven years ago, Madame Guion left the city of Grenoble, and found her way upward to our solitary home in the rocks. Although contrary to our usual custom [to admit females into the monastery], I thought it an occasion on which I might be excused for conversing with this lady. I took with me, however, a number of the brethren, who might be witnesses of what passed between us. And they will now bear me testimony that, after the conversation, and when Madame Guion had left us, I immediately expressed my suspicions in very strong terms, of the soundness of her views."

We have no information what the views were which she felt it her duty to spread before these monks; but if they were such as we have just seen to characterize the pages of her work on prayer, we cannot wonder that they were unpalatable to the Prior of this celebrated monastery, however conformable they were to primitive Christianity. He soon became fixedly hostile to her, and joined his efforts to those of Bishop D'Aranthon, to lay obstacles in her path, and raise a party at Grenoble to oppose and persecute her.

While she was in Grenoble, she was as usual constantly concerned for the help of the poor and sick, and was instrumental in the founding of a hospital near the city. But the storm which had been for some time gathering against her, at length attained such a height, that she concluded, with the advice of some of her friends, to leave the place, at least for a time. She went first to Marseilles, where she met with some remarkable circumstances, which seemed to her like seals of the rectitude of her apostolic labors; and having some time previously been pressingly invited to revisit her friend, the Marchioness de Prunai, she passed on for Italy. In her voyage from Nice to Genoa, which was with a wicked crew in a very small and inadequate vessel for the open sea, a storm arising, she had a narrow escape from death; but was preserved in great calmness of mind, and even more than a willingness to end her days in the waves of the ocean, if such were the will of God, feeling all the world against her, and no refuge nor comfort but in the Saviour whose love she experienced in her soul.

In proceeding afterward by land, she had to pass through a forest infested by robbers, four of whom, armed, stopped the litter in which she travelled, and looked in upon her. She says: "I nodded and smiled, for I had no fear, and was resigned to Providence to that degree that it was indifferent to me whether to die in this manner or some other, whether by the sea, or by the hands of robbers. But, O my God, how great has been thy protecting care over me! And what was my state of resignation in thy hand! How many perils have I encountered on the mountains and on the brinks of precipices! How many times have I thought I was being plunged from those frightful mountains into dreadful torrents of a depth beyond sight, but which made themselves heard by their fearful noise! When the danger was the most imminent, my faith was the strongest—all was equal to me, in thy will! .... The robbers came to the litter, but I had no sooner saluted them, than the Almighty changed their design, and they gave each other hints not to hurt me. They saluted me very civilly, and retired with an air of compassion little common among such people."

After this, the muleteer who conducted them, considering that he had in his charge only three lonely women, herself and two girls who attended on her, thought to put an affront on her, with the purpose, as she believed, of extracting money from her. Toward night he stopped at a mill in a lonely place, nearly a mile from the inn to which they should have been carried—a place where there was only one room for all to sleep in, millers, muleteers, travellers, and every one else—and declared he would go no further. In vain did she protest to him that she was not such a person as to submit to such lodgings. Finding he was not to be turned from his purpose, she and the two girls took up such portion of their baggage as they could carry, and proceeded on foot, in the midst of the darkness of night, unacquainted with the road, and through one end of the infested forest, and even followed by the sneers and insults of this evil-designing man; but they were favored to arrive safely at the inn.

Contrary to her own desire, she was compelled to go to Vercelli, instead of proceeding directly to Turin, which caused her some trial of mind, and occasioned also some uneasiness to Fras. La Combe, who was then stationed at Vercelli; for they were not ignorant of the slanderous and groundless reports which had been spread in France, that she was encouraging an unbecoming intimacy with him, though the fellowship mutually felt between them was in fact easily seen by unbiassed eyes to be of a purely religious nature, from a close similarity of experience and oneness of inward feeling and views. She was, however, very kindly received by the Bishop of Vercelli, who was anxious to retain her there, and even offered to found a religious house in the place, if she would consent to remain to superintend it. But she says she was inwardly sensible that this was not what the Almighty's will was for her to be engaged in. She was confined here for some time by fatigue and sickness, after which she pursued her plan of visiting her friend near Turin.

After a short visit to the Marchioness de Prunai, she believed it best to return into France, through Chamberri and Grenoble. Throughout her journey she says she was deeply impressed with the words of the apostle Paul when going up to Jerusalem, that the Holy Ghost testified to him "that bonds and afflictions awaited him;" and she was favored with calm resignation, under the full belief that this would be her own portion in returning to her native land. It happened that Fras. La Combe had at this time been directed to repair to Paris, to take a position of some importance to the Order to which he belonged; and as the Order was poor, and it seemed likely that his travelling as her escort would save some of the expenses of his journey, he was requested to accompany her. This he did as far as Chamberri, where he obtained permission to leave her, in order to visit his relations at Thonon before proceeding to Paris. This journey proved to be, both to him and J. M. Guion, a progress into increased trials and persecutions. These were in part instigated by her own half-brother, the Abbé La Mothe, a priest of the same Order as Fras. La Combe, who happened to meet them at Chamberri, and whose secret hostility (of which they were both of them convinced by their inward feelings) was then studiously concealed under professions of kindness and esteem.

She proceeded to Grenoble, where she rejoined her daughter, whom she had left in charge of a religious institution in that city. The excitement against her here seemed to have been allayed during her absence, and she was very cordially received by Bishop Camus, and by many of her former friends. But after a short tarriance she thought it best to proceed to Paris. She arrived in that city in the summer of 1686, just five years after her departure from it.

Scarcely had she returned to Paris, when she clearly discovered the evil designs of her half-brother La Mothe, who secretly combined with others to injure both herself and La Combe. Indeed her brother from this time seemed to her to take the lead in all the insidious attacks that were made upon her. This was instigated partly by a desire to extract from her that portion of her estate which she had not hitherto either appropriated to her children or distributed for charitable uses. His hostility against La Combe arose partly from jealousy of his success as a preacher, and partly from disappointment in finding that the latter would not suffer himself to be made a tool, to persuade Jane Mary Guion to transfer to him a small sum of money, which she had appropriated to the assistance of a poor but talented and religious young woman, who stood greatly in need of protection and help. La Mothe and his colleagues descended so far as to employ a wicked woman and her husband, who were ready for any malicious business which they could accomplish with impunity. The man was a skilful counterfeiter of writing, and the woman was no less skilful in counterfeiting the character of a devout person, to win the confidence of the unsuspecting. Among these was F. La

Combe, to whom she went to confess, and whom she persuaded to believe that she was a true saint. While J. M. Guion was on a visit to the Duchess of Chevreuse in the country, along with certain other religious persons of kindred feelings, La Combe wrote to her respecting this insinuating woman, in terms that led her to fear that he was being imposed upon. She felt an inward conviction that she was a dangerous person. "Nevertheless," she says, "as our Lord gave me nothing in particular in regard to it, and as I then apprehended that if I said anything of my thoughts it might not be well taken, and as the Lord did not impress it upon me to say anything (for if he had exacted it of me I would have done it, whatever it might have cost me)— but as he left me at rest, I merely replied that I left him to God in that matter, as in everything else." While La Combe was being thus deceived by her, this woman and her husband were employed in forging and circulating papers calculated to convey the belief that La Combe was not sound in the faith, and that he and J. M. Guion were unduly intimate. They invented some vile calumnies of this sort against them in a forged letter which they got up, pretending to come from a person of Marseilles, containing scandalous stories of what, they said, occurred while they were in that city together. These gross falsehoods, however, they were easily able to disprove, especially as La Combe had never been near Marseilles. We cannot here enter into a detail of all the plots which were formed to entrap and to destroy the reputation of these two worthy and pious persons. These plots were participated in by many ecclesiastics, and ended only when the object was attained, of indefinite imprisonment.

Being fully convinced herself that this woman was a wicked and dangerous character, she avoided as much as possible her repeated importunities for access to her, and endeavored to warn her friend of his danger in putting confidence in her; but he would not, for a long time, believe but that she was indeed a saint. Meantime these calumnies were spread abroad with great success. At length, however, La Combe's eyes were opened to perceive her deception and wickedness. Their enemies now, foiled in their attempts to substantiate their falsehood, endeavored to persuade them to leave Paris, with a view to circulating the report that, now they had fled, there could no longer be any doubt of their guilt. J. M. Guion relates that her half-brother La Mothe summoned her to him, along with La Combe, and said to her in the presence of the latter, "My sister, it is necessary for you to think of flying, for there are execrable statements against you. They say you have committed crimes which would make one shudder." She was not moved at all by what he said, but replied with her ordinary tranquillity, "If I have committed the crimes of which you speak, I could not be too severely punished. I am therefore far from being willing to fly; for if, after having made profession all my life of a particular devotion to my Maker, I should make use of [an appearance of] piety to commit offenses against Him whom I would love and cause to be loved at the expense of my life, I ought to be made an example, and to be punished with the most extreme rigor. If I am innocent, flight is not the way to make my innocence believed." La Mothe knew this as well as she, but it was for that very reason that he desired to induce her to fly. He then endeavored to induce the tutor of her children to use his influence to bring it about. But not being able at once to see him, he applied to his sister, charging J. M. Guion with fearful crimes. In astonishment she replied, "If Madame Guion has committed such crimes as you say, I should believe that I had committed them myself! What! One who has lived as she has lived! I would answer for her, body for body. As to making her fly, flight is by no means a matter of indifference to her; for if she is innocent, it would be declaring herself guilty." La Mothe still urged, "that she must absolutely be made to fly—that this was the wish of the archbishop." At the naming of the archbishop, she said she would see her brother the tutor on the subject, and have the archbishop spoken to about it; which alarmed La Mothe and put him into great confusion. The tutor, who was a Parliamentary Counsellor, went to the archbishop, although earnestly dissuaded from it by La Mothe, and told him of the terrible crimes alleged against J. M. Guion, and that it was said that he (the prelate) had counselled that she should fly; adding that he had long known her as a virtuous woman, and that he would answer for her, body for body—that he would plead her cause if anything was brought against her. The archbishop declared that he knew nothing at all of it, and that the thing was false; and causing La Mothe to be called in, he repeated before him that he had never heard of the matter, and confounded him still further by demanding the source of his information.

The enemies of La Combe now applied to the king (Louis XIV.), and managing to persuade him that the former was a friend of Michael de Molinos, and of dangerous views, obtained a royal order that he should confine himself to his monastery, until he had been officially examined concerning his doctrines. But they insidiously concealed this order from him, in order that by finding him abroad, they might accuse him of rebelling against the king's command. Meanwhile, La Combe, not knowing anything of the order, preached two remarkable sermons in different places of worship, which aroused all who heard them. He was also induced to go abroad to administer comfort to a young woman dying from an accident, who was one of his penitents. Scarcely had he gone out, when one of them went and reported to the authorities, that he had not found him at the monastery, and that he was rebelling against the royal order. This treatment was several times repeated, under various pleas, and report made accordingly of his disobedience.

He had, some time before this, when persecuted by the Bishop of Geneva, betaken himself to Rome, and there appealed in person so effectually on his own behalf, as to obtain very satisfactory testimonials of his orthodoxy from the Inquisition, and from the cardinals and "Congregation of Rites" in that city. These papers were now very important to him; but La Mothe, finding them to stand in his way, determined to procure possession of them. Still insidiously professing friendship for him, he said to him, that having such testimonials as these from such a source, ought to secure him against being found fault with by subordinate officers of the church. La Combe, still thinking that La Mothe was his friend, was easily persuaded to put the papers into his hands; and, as might have been anticipated, he never saw them again. One subterfuge or another was made, to explain their not being returned to him. J. M. Guion happened to have copies. Finding that to be so, La Mothe, by false pretenses, obtained them from her, and would never return them, making dreadfully false assertions that she had never given them to him.

A few days after the loss of his papers, La Combe was arrested while at dinner, and under the most grossly false pretenses, was, without any trial, committed to the Bastile. This was in 1687. J. M. Guion adds that, "As his enemies learned that in the first fortress the captains esteemed him, and treated him rather mildly, not content with having shut up so eminent a servant of God, they caused him to be put into a place where they believed he would have more to suffer. The Lord, who sees everything, will render to every one according to his works. I am satisfied from my inward feelings, that he is very content and resigned to God."

Having got him out of the way, the persecution was now concentrated against J. M. Guion herself; who says, nevertheless, "I bore all with great tranquillity, without anxiety to justify or defend myself, leaving it to my God to order all concerning me as it might please him. He increased my peace according as Father La Mothe continued to decry me. I cannot express how great was my inward content, leaving myself to the Lord without reserve, entirely ready to endure extreme sufferings, or punishment, if that should be His will."

Soon after this, she was put in possession of ample and clear evidence of the abandoned wickedness of the woman who had been employed against La Combe, and offered to her half-brother La Mothe the means of readily proving her crimes and La Combe's innocence; but he would not listen to anything of the kind. They now accused her to the king, as a heretic, and a correspondent of Molinos (though she says she had no knowledge whatever of him, except through the Gazette); that she had written a dangerous book, and needed to be closely confined; and they forged a letter in her name, in order to show to the king that she was still holding meetings with great and secret designs. On this a royal order was issued for her imprisonment in a convent. She was taken very ill about this time, which delayed the execution of the order for about five weeks; but before she quite recovered, about the beginning of the year 1688, she was arrested by a *lettre de cachet*, which consigned her to the "Convent of the Visitation" at the "Faubourg S. Antoine.". She had hoped that they would at least allow her the consolation of having with her

her daughter, now nearly twelve years old; but this was denied. She was to be entirely alone, except a woman who at times waited on her; and not only so, but they interdicted all manner of communication between the mother and daughter. No one else, but this woman, was to come into her little room, which was kept closely locked. And this woman made all the mischief in her power, by false representations of her conversation and conduct. She says, "I had need for the exercise of patience, and the Lord suffered it not to escape from me." She was treated with great injustice while in this confinement. Several times she was subjected to ensnaring interrogations, and another forged letter, purporting to be from her, was produced, by which they endeavored to alarm her into a confession of guilt. When she denied the authorship of the letter, and showed that it was in a handwriting altogether different from her own, they alleged that it was a copy, and that they had the original at home; but they would never produce the original. She continued to deny the authorship of the letter, or even any knowledge of the person to whom it was addressed; and offered the clearest proof of its being fictitious, but to no purpose. Her continued imprisonment was a thing determined on, and she was kept still more strictly locked up. A cousin of hers at length ventured to request the Marchioness de Maintenon, who was in fact wife to Louis XIV., to intercede with the monarch on her behalf; but she found him very much prejudiced against her by what La Mothe had said. Eventually, however, he granted an order for her discharge, and she was set at liberty, after a confinement, for no crime, of nearly eight months.

A few days after her liberation, she first became acquainted with the Abbé de Fenelon, soon afterward appointed to the Ducal Archbishopric of Cambray. She felt a remarkable attraction to this amiable and eminent man; and having several interviews with him, found his mind open to appreciate, to a great extent, her spiritual views. From this time she reckoned him among those with whom she had the comfort of religious fellowship and union. How far this fellowship was indeed reciprocal, how far it may have extended on his part beyond a mere conviction of his understanding, of the truth of her doctrine, and an admiration of her innocent and pious life, in consonance with his own views of a truly Christian character, may be a matter of some question. There is no doubt that he did, for a time at least, seek and enjoy her company and conversation, and was deeply impressed with a piety which carried its own evidence to his finest feelings; and he has generally been regarded as, through life, pre-eminently one with her in the advocacy of the "interior spiritual life." Yet it is evident, from his own words, which are to be found in Bishop Bausset's Memoir of his Life, that Fenelon was by no means prepared to suffer persecution on her account, or for the cause which she maintained so firmly; or to lose his position in ecclesiastical and courtly society, by coming out openly in defense of a woman, of whose innocence he was nevertheless clearly convinced. T. C. Upham, in his biography of Jane Mary Guion, says respecting Fenelon, that "the principles of the inward life, which he had learned from the conversations and correspondence of Madame Guion, commended themselves entirely to the mind of Fenelon." . . . . . "These important views, which strike so deeply at the life of nature—were new to him in a considerable degree, until he learned them in his acquaintance and correspondence" with her. She herself remarks, as Upham informs us, that she was enabled so fully to explain everything to Fenelon, that he gradually entered into the views which the Lord had led her to entertain, and gave them his unqualified assent; and that the persecutions which he afterward suffered were an evidence of the sincerity of his belief. Upham also says that Fenelon was known to be "too conscientious, either to abandon his position, or to be unfaithful in defending it, without a change in his convictions. Naturally mild and forbearing in his dispositions, he was inflexible in his principles," and that "he felt himself morally bound to defend the ground he had taken, although he had no disposition to do it otherwise than in the spirit of humility and candor." This was eminently evinced in his controversy with Bossuet, respecting the doctrines of spiritual religion advanced by him. That he was also averse to all persecution for religious belief, is well known. He said on one occasion, " No human power can force the impenetrable bulwarks of the liberty of the heart. Force never can persuade men ; it only makes hypocrites of them."* And when the religious house of Port Royal was destroyed in 1709, " Fenelon could not (says Bausset, vol. ii. p. 90) avoid raising his voice against the proceeding, in a letter to the Duke de Chevreuse, and regretting that other measures, of a more conciliatory and gentle nature, had not been adopted." That Fenelon participated in the spiritual views of religion advocated by J. M. Guion, may be clearly seen in many of his writings, especially in his controversy with Bossuet, and in the following scattered extracts.†

"By Scripture it is certain that the Spirit of God dwells in us, that it acts there, that it prays there; that it groans there, that it desires there, that it asketh for us what we know not to ask for ourselves; that it excites us, animates us, speaks to us in silence, suggests all truth to us, and so unites us to itself that we become one spirit with God.

* Bausset's Life of Fenelon, vol. ii. p. 53.
† See "Œuvres Spirituelles," tome i.

This is what Scripture teaches us. This is what the doctors or teachers, who are furthest off from the inward life, cannot but acknowledge. And yet, notwithstanding these positive principles, we always see by their practice that they suppose the outward written law, or at most a light drawn from Scripture and reasoning, to be what enlightens us inwardly, and that it is our reason afterward which acts of itself by that instruction. These men set not enough by the Inward Teacher, the Holy Spirit, who does all in us. He is the soul of our soul. We cannot frame a [holy] thought or desire but through Him." ..... "Perhaps you will say to me, 'What! then, are we inspired?' Yes, without doubt. But not as the prophets and apostles [probably meaning, not according to their measure]. Without the actual inspiration of the Spirit of Grace, we can neither do, will, nor believe, any good." ..... "We must silence every creature, and ourselves too, to hear in a profound stillness of soul the inexpressible voice of Christ, the bridegroom of our souls. We must listen diligently; for it is a very still and soft voice, which is not to be heard but by such as hearken to nothing else. Oh, how seldom it is that the soul is silent enough to let God speak! The least whisper of our vain desires, or of self-love, attentive to itself, confounds all the words of the Spirit of God—we do not perceive what it is." ..... "To what purpose would the outward expressions of teachers be, and even of the Scriptures themselves, were it not for the Inward Voice of the Holy Spirit, which gives the other all its efficacy? The outward words, without this living efficacious Word within, would be but an empty sound. 'It is the letter that killeth, but the Spirit giveth life' (II. Cor. iii. 16). Oh, eternal and all-powerful Word of the Father, it is thou who speakest in the very bottom of souls!" .... "It is not the exterior law or rule of the gospel, which God lets us see by the

light of reason and Scripture; it is His Spirit, that speaks, that touches us, that operates in us, and that animates us; so that it is the Spirit that 'worketh in us, both to will and to do' what is good; as it is our soul that animates our body, and regulates its motions. It is certain, therefore, that we are inspired continually, and that we live not the life of grace, but in proportion as we partake of this inward inspiration." ..... "I have often remarked that persons of small natural parts and understanding, when they begin to be made sensible of their sins, and livingly touched with the love of God, are more disposed to hear this inward language of the Spirit than some enlightened and learned persons grown old in their own wisdom" ..... "God sees these simple ones, and it is in them he loves to dwell. 'My Father and I,' says Jesus Christ, 'we will come unto them, and make our abode with them.' Oh, how does a soul, given up entirely to the Spirit of God, esteeming itself as nothing, and directed wholly by pure love; I say, how does that soul taste of the love and goodness of God, which the wise of this world can neither experience nor comprehend. I have myself been wise, I may venture to say, as well as others. But then, imagining that I saw everything, I saw nothing. I went groping by a chain of reasons, but the Light shined not in my darkness. I satisfied myself with reasoning. But when once we come to silence everything in us in order to hear God, we know all things without knowing anything, and we plainly see that we were before ignorant of those things which we thought we understood. .... Not that we have the presumption to believe that we possess in ourselves all truth and knowledge. No, no, quite the contrary—we then feel that we of *ourselves* see nothing, that we can do nothing, and are nothing." .....
"But in this entire resignation of all without reserve, we find from time to time, in the immensity of God, all that

18

we stand in need of, in the course of his providence. It is there that we find the daily bread of Truth, as well as everything else, without making provision. It is there 'the Anointing teacheth us all truth,' by taking from us all our own wisdom, our own glory, our own interest, our own wills" .... "in this state the Spirit teaches us all truth; for all truth is eminently comprised in this sacrifice of love, in which the soul strips itself of all, to give all to God."

In another place (Meditation of God's operation in the Soul), he says of his own experience, "I tried, by collecting together in my mind all the wonderful works of nature, to form an idea of Thy grandeur. I sought thee among thy creatures, and did not think to find thee in my own heart, where thou art never absent. No, there is no need, O my God, 'to descend into the deep, nor to go over the sea,' as say the Scriptures, 'nor to ascend into heaven' to find thee, for thou art nearer to us than we are to ourselves."

And in his "Directions for a Holy Life," he thus expresses himself: "Let us seek God within us, and we shall infallibly find him, and with him joy and peace. In our outward occupations let us be occupied more with God than all the rest. To do them well, we must do them as in his presence, and for his sake." ...... "We must often lift up our heart to God; he will purify, enlighten, and direct it. It was the daily practice of the holy prophet David. 'I have set,' says he, 'the Lord always before me.'" .... "We must endeavor to have a continual correspondence and fellowship with God. Let us be persuaded that the most profitable and desirable state in this life is Christian Perfection; which consists in the union of the soul with God, an union that includes in it all spiritual good. This is the happy state to which we are called; we, whom God hath separated from the corruptions of this world. If we do not partake of these heavenly blessings, it is our own fault; since the Spirit of God disposes and excites us continually to aspire after them. . . . . . As saith the apostle, let us 'walk circumspectly, not as fools, but as wise, redeeming the time, because the days are evil.'"

Yet it is painful to be obliged to believe, that so amiable and in many respects so enlightened a man should not have stood uprightly faithful to the responsibilities entailed by his religious position, when the persecution which assailed the friend who placed so much confidence in him, threatened to involve himself likewise; and the truthfulness of history demands that our admiration of his character should not be suffered to blind us to the fact that he was nevertheless a Romish dignitary, and not prepared to imperil his high ecclesiastical position, for the sake of defending a defenseless woman. Even the estimable Tronson, in writing to Fenelon immediately after his appointment, in 1689, as Preceptor of the Duke of Burgundy, heir-presumptive to the throne of France, held language tending to encourage him in what, in these days, we should consider as a compromise with "the spirit that now rules in the children of disobedience," unworthy of a Christian pastor. He says,* "A thousand occasions will present themselves, in which you will consider yourself bound, by prudence and even by benevolence, to concede something to the world; and yet [as if recoiling with shame from his own doctrine] what a strange state it is for a Christian to be in, and still more for a priest, to behold himself obliged to enter into a compact with the enemy of his salvation!"

While the acrimony of the persecution of his friend was at its height, in 1695, and alarmed that the tempest was lowering upon himself in the clouds of that controversy in which he became involved with Bossuet, Fenelon wrote to the latter, respecting the articles against J. M. Guion,

* Bausset, vol. i. p. 49.

"that he would sign them from deference, *against his conviction;* but if they would add certain things to them, he would cheerfully sign them with his blood." (Bausset, p. 117) "He had," says Bausset, "concurred with sincerity in the intentions of Madame de Maintenon, of checking, at St. Cyr, that inclination to religious novelty, which had alarmed her ; he was *the first* to advise her to withdraw, from the hands of the nuns, not only the printed works of Madame Guion, but her written notions also."

These, it is true, are the words of the Bishop of Alais, who might easily be supposed anxious to show that J. M. Guion's course was not altogether sanctioned by the Archbishop of Cambray. But we have Fenelon's own words, evidencing how he flinched from the danger of being involved with her in suffering for the cause of Christ. In writing to Tronson (Bausset, p. 136), he speaks of being urged to condemn her and her writings, and excuses himself thus: "But this is what even the Inquisition would not demand; nor will I ever do it, *unless in obedience to the church,* when it shall be thought fit to devise a formula such as was employed against the Jansenists.* What does it signify, that I believe Madame Guion to be neither wicked nor mad, if at the same time I *abandon her by my silence,* and *suffer her to perish in prison,* without interfering either directly or indirectly with anything that concerns her?"

How sorrowful is it to be obliged to acknowledge that these are the words of the great and amiable Fenelon! And not only this; but that in writing to the Marchioness de Maintenon,† he could, while professing some degree of regret at the unfairness with which Bossuet was misrepresenting her, yet hold such language as the following, to ex-

* Doubtless meaning, one so ambiguously worded as to admit of a double construction.

† Bausset, vol. i. pp. 139–145.

cuse his leaving her to the malice of those who had not, as he had, tasted of the sweetness and loveliness of her spirit and of her sentiments! He says, in the first place: "It is quite unpardonable in the Bishop of Meaux to represent to you, as the doctrine of Madame Guion, what is nothing but idle fancy, or some figurative expression, or something tantamount to it, which she herself disclosed to him only in the secrecy of confession." And again: "Nothing has been said of her morals, but what was calumny! Nothing can be imputed to her but an indiscreet zeal, and a mode of speaking of herself, which are too advantageous to her doctrine. Admitting that she had erred, without duplicity, was it a crime?" And yet with all this, and knowing that her enemies were urging the persecution against her to the utmost, he could acknowledge that he might be in error in esteeming her as "a person whom I believe to be holy," and add, "As I will never either speak or write, so as to patronize or vindicate this woman, my error is as harmless toward the church, as it is innoxious toward myself." . . . "I never had any predilection either for her or her writings. I have never experienced anything extraordinary in her, which could at all prepossess me in her favor." And after proposing to obtain from her some explanations or concessions under certain circumstances, to appease her enemies and his own, he adds: "After that, let her die in prison. I am content that she should die there; that we never see her again, that we never hear speak of her again!"

It can scarcely be doubted that Fenelon, occupying as he did a post of great importance in the French church, having much influence among the enlightened portion of the French people, and holding the position of preceptor to the grandsons of the monarch, might, by a bold and fearless advocacy of the innocence of his friend, have been of essential service to that deeply calumniated and afflicted woman. How wretched must be that system of church policy, which could promote views and conduct so averse to Christian charity, honor, and faithfulness, even in one of the most estimable and amiable of men!

For a few years after the termination of this imprisonment, Jane M. Guion lived more or less a retired life; partly with her daughter, who had married the Count de Vaux, and who, being quite youthful, needed her maternal advice and assistance, and partly in religious houses where she had hoped to be exempt from further persecution. But her half-brother, La Mothe, and others, were still bent on continuing their efforts to destroy her character, and they gradually enlisted men of greater eminence and influence than themselves in the work. The Marchioness de Maintenon, however, at this time, continued to befriend her, and for about four years promoted her frequent visits to her favorite seminary for orphan girls, which she had established at the village of "St. Cyr," and where J. M. Guion's influence had a marked effect in the increase of true piety among the pupils. At length the jealousy of her enemies invaded even this limited field of her labors for the good of souls, and she was compelled to desist from visiting that seminary. About this time her persecutors procured an attempt to poison her, by one of her domestics, who immediately fled. The result was not fatal, but she was taken alarmingly ill, and had to retire for a time to Bourbon, for the recovery of her health.

It was near this time also, that she was strongly solicited by some of her friends to become acquainted with the celebrated J. B. Bossuet, Bishop of Meaux; who, they told her, was not averse to inward religion "I knew," she says, "that he had read, about eight or ten years before, the 'Short Method of Prayer,' and the 'Commentaries on the Canticles,' and had approved of them; so that I consented to see him with pleasure. But, oh, how greatly have I found, during my life, that everything done from motives of mere human contrivance turns into shame, confusion, and grief! I flattered myself at that time (and I acknowledge my fault therein) that he would sustain me against those who were oppressing me: but how far was I from knowing him! And how greatly is that liable to fail, which we do not see in the light of the Lord, and which He does not discover to us!"

Bossuet was introduced to her by her friend the Duke de Chevreuse from motives of kindness; but it proved to be the means of throwing her still more completely into the hands of her enemies. This learned and accomplished prelate professed at first a great esteem for her writings, and for the inward work of religion advocated in them, and thereby gained her confidence for a time. He held long conversations with her on religious subjects, and she put copies of her works, and even the manuscript history of her life, into his hands for examination. This latter was accompanied with a strict condition, acceded to by him, that it was under the same secrecy as if communicated at the confessional. He requested four or five months, to enable him to read them at his leisure.

About the beginning of the year 1694, he desired to see her again. He had two interviews with her, and in the last of them he developed himself quite differently, seemed like another man, made many objections to her writings, and produced a memorandum of these objections, containing twenty articles. She thought she was sensible of being divinely aided in her replies to his objections, yet she could not entirely satisfy him. He had a quick, arrogant, and imperious manner when speaking to females, or to persons of humble demeanor, and he scarcely gave her an opportunity to explain her sentiments; so that she found herself afterward so overcome and exhausted with the mental effort to explain herself to him, that she was sick for several days.

"He ordered me," she says, "to justify my books; but this I declined as much as I could; because, having submitted them with all my heart, I did not wish to undertake to justify them. But he would have it. I protested then that I did it only out of obedience, and was sincerely willing to condemn all that was to be condemned. I have always held this language, which was in fact that of my heart even more than of my mouth. He desired me to give him a reason for an infinity of things which I knew nothing about [not professing to be a theologian]. I had often written things which I had not studied or thought much of, and I had not premeditated any replies before seeing him. I would have desired him to judge of me, not by his mere reason, but by his heart. Truth alone was my strength, and I was willing that my mistakes should be known. I hoped that the same God, who formerly caused the ass to speak, could cause a woman to speak, who often knew no more of the subjects of which she spoke, than did Balaam's ass. This was the disposition of my heart, in my conferences with the Bishop of Meaux."

"He made many objections to what I had said in the account of my life, respecting the apostolic state. What I wished to express was, that persons whose condition renders them far from fit to help souls (such as laymen and women) should not meddle with it *of themselves;* but that when God wills to make use of them by his own authority, they must be put into that state of which I spoke. Many good souls who experience the first effects of the unction of grace, of that anointing spoken of by St. John (I. John ii. 20 and 27), which teaches all truth, when they begin to feel this unction, are so charmed with it that they desire all the world as it were to partake with them. But not yet being actually brought to the fountain, and this unction being given them for themselves and not for others, if they scatter it abroad they lose little by little the sacred oil, and become like the foolish virgins: the wise ones on the other hand keep their oil for themselves until they are introduced into the marriage chamber of Christ; then can they give of their oil, because the Lamb is the lamp which enlightens them. That this state is possible, it is only needful to open the history of all times, to show that God has made use of laymen, and women without learning, to instruct, edify, direct, and lead souls to true perfection. I believe that one of the reasons why God has seen meet to do this, has been in order that he should not be robbed of his glory. 'He has chosen the weak things of the world to confound the things that are mighty.' . . . . I pray the Lord with all my heart, that he would crush me (*m'écraseroit*) by all the most terrible means, rather than let me rob him of the least measure of his glory. I am a mere nothing; but my God is all-powerful, who is pleased to exert his power on that which is nothing."

Bossuet thought her cautions against self-activity were dangerous and liable to abuse, and that there were but four or five persons in the world who held her views of prayer and her objections against activity: but she maintained that the abuse of her precautions might be guarded against; that there were, on the contrary, more than a hundred thousand souls in the world to whom they would be acceptable, and that it was for such that she had written.

At length Bossuet professed to be satisfied that she was at least no heretic, and offered to testify to that effect; though he still objected to some of her sentiments, as not satisfactory to himself. She soon found rumors again afloat against her character; and being informed that the Marchioness de Maintenon had given an ear to those rumors to such a degree as to become entirely alienated in her feelings, she wrote to this influential personage, earnestly requesting that a commission might be appointed, of persons of known probity and without prejudice, half laymen and half ecclesiastics, for a thorough examination of her conduct. This she claimed as due to the church, to her family, and to herself. The letter was delivered by the hand of one of her friends, the Duke de Beauvilliers; to whom the marchioness declared that she gave no credence to the rumors against J. M. Guion's moral character; but that it was her doctrines that she was afraid of; and that if her moral character was cleared, it was to be feared that her sentiments would thereby more easily find currency; and she declined to have anything to do with the appointment so earnestly requested.

Jane M. Guion was deeply affected at this refusal; but she was made willing to leave it all to her Maker, to order as it might please Him; and she now saw no way left for her but to go into close retirement from the notice of the world. She thus expresses a portion of her feelings: "People will say, 'But what! pass for a heretic?'—What can I do? I have written candidly my thoughts. I submit them, with all my heart, to be judged. It is said they can have a good or a bad sense. I know that I wrote them in a good sense, that I know nothing of the bad sense, and that I willingly submit them as to both. What can I do more? When I wrote, I was always ready to burn what I wrote, at the least signal. Let it be burnt or censured, I wish to take no part. It is sufficient for me that my heart bears me testimony of my faith, since they will not have any public testimony, which I have freely offered. They want to corrupt my character, in order to corrupt my faith. I wish to justify my character, in order to justify my faith; but they will not have it done. What can I do more? I cannot acknowledge thoughts which I never entertained, nor crimes which I have never known, much less committed; for this would be to lie against the Holy Spirit; and while I am ready to die for my faith and the decisions of the church, I am also ready to die to maintain that I have not thought that which they have wished me to appear to think, in my writings, and that I have not committed the crimes which they impute to me."

After some time, the Duke de Chevreuse informed her that the Marchioness de Maintenon, and some others about the court, had concluded to have a commission appointed, to examine, not the assaults on her moral character, as requested, which would have been an act of simple justice, but the supposed errors of her writings. Even this, she thought, composed of men of knowledge and integrity, would have tended to correct the current opinions and remove prejudices, if they had proceeded with such intentions; "but," she says, "it was condemnation that they desired to secure, and to confirm it in the minds of those favorable to me, by their authority."

In attacking her writings, she believed they had another object now in view, which was to bring the Abbé Fenelon into disrepute, and eventually into persecution. The commissioners now appointed, and who appear indeed to have been suggested by herself, under the belief that they were candid and upright men, were Bossuet, Bishop of Meaux, the Cardinal De Noailles, then Bishop of Châlons, and Tronson, Superior of the Sulpitian Seminary. In order to facilitate their examination, and at their request, she undertook to prepare a work of considerable labor, which she entitled "Justifications" of her writings. This took her nearly two months to accomplish;* but when finished, she

---

* There is a copy of this rare work in the Philadelphia Library. It is in three volumes 8vo., containing over 1000 pages; yet she says she wrote it in about fifty days. It comprises quotations from sixty-three authors of repute in the Romish church.

soon found that Bossuet had again turned against her, for he would neither read it himself nor let the others see it. He had in fact evidently determined to bring about her condemnation, and it afterward appeared that he had actually promised this to the Marchioness de Maintenon. J. M. Guion requested, as a favor, that her friend, the Duke de Chevreuse, might be permitted to be present at the examinations, and that the successive conclusions should be put in writing. But Bossuet would consent to neither of these reasonable requests. The amiable Tronson was prevented by sickness from leaving his home, and Bossuet not being willing to go thither, he and the Bishop of Châlons went on without him. Bossuet endeavored by all means to intimidate and confound her. "He reproached me," says she, "with my ignorance—told me that I knew nothing—and repeated unceasingly, after having made ridiculous nonsense (*des galimatias*) of all that I said, that he was astonished at my ignorance. I replied nothing to these reproaches, and the ignorance of which he accused me ought to have shown him, at least, that I said truly, that what I had written had been by an actual light vouchsafed, as nothing dwelt on my spirit when that was withdrawn."

.... "It is impossible to reply to a man who throws you down (*qui vous terrasse*), who *will not* understand you, and who crushes you incessantly. For my part, I lose the thread of what I want to say, and can remember nothing more."

After this conference, Bossuet told the Marchioness de Maintenon, that having convicted J. M. Guion of her errors, he hoped after a while to induce her to go into a convent in his diocesan city, where he should be able quietly to accomplish what he designed. The Bishop of Châlons, on the contrary, seemed satisfied with her; and told her that he saw nothing for her to change in her present practice of prayer, or otherwise; and that he prayed God to increase more and more his mercies and grace to her.* She sought an interview with Tronson at Issi, who, though still sick, entered closely and candidly into an investigation of the affair; after which the Duke de Chevreuse said to him, "You see that she is right?" To which he replied, "I perceive it well;" and appeared to be content.

In hopes of at length appeasing the Bishop of Meaux, and satisfying him of her innocence by further intercourse, she offered to place herself for a time under his supervision, in a convent in Meaux. To this, as being exactly what he thought would answer his present purpose, he gladly acceded, named the convent, and fixed the time for her going thither. She remarks: "This pleased Bossuet extremely, in the idea that he would thence derive great temporal advantages, as I learned afterward. He said to the Mother Picard, the Superior of the Convent, that it was worth to him the Archbishopric of Paris and a cardinal's hat. I replied to this Mother, when she told me of it, that God would permit him to have neither the one nor the other."

She accordingly went to Meaux at the time appointed, the beginning of the year 1695, though at the risk of her life; as the weather was unusually severe, and the coach in which she travelled was almost overwhelmed in a deep

---

* The poor Cardinal De Noailles seems to have been subject to many conflicts and fluctuations, indicating a mind of good intentions, but easily turned aside from its convictions by designing men. He had hitherto been known as a defender of the spiritual writings of Quesnel; but being made Archbishop of Paris the next year, he soon weakly complied with the wishes of the Jesuits and the king, and became an opponent of the views of the Jansenists. In 1709 he was induced to issue the order for the suppression of the Monastery of Port Royal; a deed, of which he afterward bitterly repented, visiting the spot in deep remorse, and pouring out many tears and prayers for forgiveness over its ruins. See Tregelles's "Jansenists," pp. 37 and 39.

snowdrift, in which she had to remain for several hours. The result of this was an illness of six weeks. Bossuet, though at first expressing pleasure at her obedience to him, in coming so punctually through such a storm, afterward charged her with doing it through artifice and hypocrisy. She keenly felt his unkindness, but says that the Lord's invisible hand sustained her, without which she must have sunk under so many trials. "All thy waves and thy billows," she sometimes exclaimed, "have come over me!" Yet when she remembered that Christ himself was "reckoned among transgressors," she was content that the handmaid should be as her Master. While she remained here, her enemies again set afloat the most wicked tales respecting her, employing abandoned individuals to invent and spread abroad accounts of her being guilty of various things which she knew nothing about, but which led people to believe that her conduct was very reprehensible. Some of these things were in forged letters, which were afterward found to be falsifications; yet her persecutors did not stop for that. They cared not whether they were true or false, so that they accomplished their end.

Bossuet gave himself but little opportunity of any better acquaintance with her; for he almost immediately left Meaux for Paris, where he remained for many weeks. When he at length returned, he found her quite sick; but entering her chamber, the first thing he said to her was, that she had many enemies, and that every one was exasperated against her. He brought her some articles, prepared for her to sign, in order to ensnare her.

A few days after this, he again came into her room, and when the nuns who had been with her had retired, he approached her bed, and told her that he wished her to sign an acknowledgment that she "did not believe in the Incarnate Word!" Many of the nuns, being still in the antechamber, heard him distinctly. Astonished at such a proposal, she told him she could not sign what was false. He repeated, that "he would make her do it." She answered him: "I know how to suffer, by the grace of God —I can die—but I cannot sign falsehoods." He then begged her to do it, saying that if she would comply, he would re-establish her reputation, and say all manner of good things of her. She replied, that "it was for God to take care of her reputation, if it pleased him; and for her to maintain her faith at the peril of her life." Seeing that he gained nothing, he retired. The inmates of the convent were greatly shocked, and wrote to the bishop their convictions of her piety, but all to no purpose. He acknowledged to them that he himself found no evil in her, but good; but that *her enemies tormented him*, and desired to find something wrong in her—that in her writings he had only found certain terms not strictly theological; but that a woman might be excused for not being a theologist.

It will be necessary to go somewhat into details with regard to what passed between Bossuet and J. M. Guion shortly afterward, as related by herself, in order to develope the shameful artifices and oppressions by which her enemies endeavored to get her into their power, and how ready that renowned prelate, who ought to have protected this innocent and helpless woman, was to become a tool for the accomplishment of their ends against her. It is the more needful to do this, inasmuch as the anonymous English translator of her "Life," for some reason, probably with a view to screen this celebrated ecclesiastic from the reprobation so palpably due to his conduct when clearly known, has thought fit to omit the particulars of his outrageous treatment of her on this occasion, condensing the whole matter into three sentences.

"Some days afterward," she says,* "the Bishop of Meaux returned. He brought me a paper written by his own hand, which was only a profession of faith, that I had always been an apostolic Roman Catholic, and including a submission of my books to the church; such as I would have made of myself whenever it might have been required. He then read to me another, which he said he would give me, which was a Certificate such as he gave me some time afterward, yet even more advantageous. As I was then too sick to be able to transcribe the paper of Submission, which was in his handwriting, he told me to have it copied by one of the nuns, and then sign it. He took back his Certificate, to finish it off completely, as he said; and he assured me that on my giving him the one, he would give me the other; that he wished to treat me as his sister, and that he should indeed be a knave to act otherwise. This proceeding, apparently so honorable, charmed me. I said to him, that I had put myself entirely into his hands, not only as into the hands of a bishop, but as into those of a man of honor.

"I found myself so ill after his departure, being extremely weak, and fatigued with my exertions in speaking to him, that it was necessary to revive me with cordials. The Superior, fearing that if he returned in the morning I might not be able to bear it, wrote to request him to leave me that one day for repose; but he would not. On the contrary, he came that very day, and demanded of me whether I had signed the writing which he had left with me; and opening a blue portfolio, which was locked, he said to me: 'Here is my Certificate—where is your Submission?' He held a paper while he said that. I pointed out to him my Submission, which was on my bed, and which I had not strength to reach to him. He took it, and I had no doubt he was going to give me his writing. But

---

* "La Vie de Madame Guion, écrite par ellemême," vol. iii. p. 220.

not at all; he shut up the whole in his portfolio, and told me that he would give me nothing—that I was not yet at the end—that he was going to torment me still more, and that he wanted other signatures—among them, this: that I *did not believe in the Incarnate Word.* Judge of my surprise! I was speechless from weakness and astonishment. He then departed. The nuns were astounded at such behavior. He was under no obligation to have promised me a Certificate—I had not requested it of him. But I then thought it needful to make a protestation, in presence of a notary of Meaux.

"Some time after this, the bishop came to see me again. He demanded of me that I should sign his Pastoral Letter, avowing that I had held the errors which were therein condemned. I endeavored to convince him that the paper I had given him comprised a complete submission; and although in this Pastoral Letter he had numbered me with transgressors, I was endeavoring to honor this state of suffering with Christ without complaint. He said to me: 'But you promised to submit to my condemnation.'— 'That I do with all my heart,' replied I; 'and I now take no more interest in those little books than if I had not written them myself. If it please God, I will never depart from the submission and respect due to you, whatever way things may turn; but, my lord, you promised me a discharge.'—'I will give it you when you will do what I wish,' said he. I replied: 'You did me the honor to say that when I gave you, signed, this act of submission, dictated by yourself, you would give me my discharge.'— 'Those were words,' said he, 'which escaped me before I had maturely considered what could and ought to be done.' ..... 'It is not for the sake of complaining to you, that I say this,' replied I; 'but to call to your recollection that you promised it to me; and to convince you of my submission, I will write at the foot of your Pastoral Letter all that I can put there.' After having done this, and he having read it, he told me that he found it good enough; then, after putting it in his pocket, he said: 'That is not to the point; you did not say that you were strictly a heretic, which I want you to declare; and also that the Pastoral Letter is very just, and that you acknowledge having been in all the errors which it condemns.' I replied: 'I believe it is to try me, that you say that; for I will never persuade myself that a prelate of such piety and honor would make use of the good faith with which I have come to put myself in his diocese, for the purpose of compelling me to do things against my conscience. I believed I found in you a father—I entreat that I may not be deceived in my expectation.'—'I am a father of the church,' said he to me; 'but, in short, this is not a question of words. Unless you sign this according to my wishes, I will come with witnesses, and after having admonished you in their presence, I will deliver you over to the church, and we will excommunicate you (*retrancherons*—literally, suppress, or put you down) according to the gospel.' . . . . I said to him: 'I have no one but my God for *my* witness; I am prepared to suffer everything; and I hope that God will give me of his grace to do nothing contrary to my conscience, without ever departing from the respect which I owe to you.' He desired, in the same conversation, to induce me to make an acknowledgment, that there were errors in the Latin book of Father La Combe, and yet at the same time to declare that I had not read it.

"The young women who witnessed a portion of the violence and angriness of the bishop, could not recover from their astonishment; and the Mother Picard (the superior) told me that my too great mildness had emboldened him to treat me ill; for his turn of mind was such, that he usually acted in this manner toward mild people, but was more pliant with those who stood high. Yet I never changed my behavior toward him, and preferred to take the portion of suffering, rather than to be wanting in any of the respect due to his character.

"Sometimes, when he came, he told me that, as for himself, he was satisfied with me, but that my enemies told him to torment me. At other times he would come full of fury, to demand of me that signature which he well knew I would not give. He threatened me with all that has since been done to me, saying, he was not going to lose his fortune for me, and many other such things. After these fiery outbreaks, he returned to Paris, and did not come back for some time.

"At length, after I had been six months at Meaux, he gave me a Certificate of his own accord, without asking me any more for a signature. What is astonishing, he expressed a willingness that I should continue in his diocese, acknowledging that God had given me a very certain light on the subject of the inward life ; and a little before my departure, he remarked to the Archbishops of Paris and of Sens, how much he was satisfied and edified with me; and at the mass he wished me to take the communion from his own hand. On that occasion he preached an astonishing sermon on the inward life, advancing things much stronger than what I had myself advanced, and saying that he was not master of himself in the midst of these awful mysteries; that he was obliged to speak the truth, and not at all to dissimulate ; that this avowal of the truth was absolutely necessary, since God had required it of him, as if in spite of himself. The Superior went to salute him after his sermon, and asked him, how he could so torment me, with such sentiments as he had avowed ? He answered her, that it was not he, it was my enemies." We may well say, Is Saul also among the prophets ?

Soon after this she departed from Meaux, with the esteem and love of the inmates of the convent. The Certificate given to her by Bossuet demands a passing notice. It recited that in consequence of her having submitted to his prohibitions against her "writing, teaching, dogmatizing in the church, or spreading her printed books or manuscripts, or conducting souls in the ways of prayer, or otherwise, together with her good character while in the Convent of St. Mary, he rested satisfied with her conduct, and had continued to grant her the sacraments; and declared that he found her by no means implicated in the abominations of Molinos, or other condemned writers, and did not intend to include her in the mention made of them in his Ordinance of 6th April, 1695."

. Whether J. M. Guion really did submit to be governed in the matters referred to, by the bishop's prohibition, as implied in his Certificate, does not appear. If she did, she seems to have carried her apprehension of the duty of obedience to ecclesiastical authority rather too far; as she had merely been exercising, according to her conscientious convictions, and as she verily believed under the constraining influence of divine grace and gospel love, a liberty allowed to all under the gospel dispensation, and entirely consistent with gospel order. But we have no evidence that the statement is anything more than Bossuet's own construction of her submission, in order to get rid of the difficulty in which he felt himself placed, in his attempts to inculpate this innocent woman. And if that "Ordinance of 6th April" refers to his Pastoral Letter above alluded to, we can at once perceive, from the foregoing relation, how much reliance is to be placed on his assertion, when he says he had *not intended to include her* in the statement made therein!

But scarcely had she left the city of Meaux, when the

bishop, calling on the Marchioness de Maintenon in Paris, found that the Certificate which he had given was by no means palatable to that personage, as it did not at all accomplish the desired end. He therefore set about to procure possession again of that document. He wrote another, and desired the Superior of the convent to deliver it to J. M. Guion, and require her to give up the first. She sent it by letter to her persecuted friend, at the same time advising her not to trust herself again into Bossuet's hands; for that she was convinced he was endeavoring once more to entrap her. Accordingly, seeing that the second paper was an artful attempt to do away the justifying effect of the first, by carefully contrived expressions really intended to promote the idea of her continued unsoundness and contumacy, she declined any further interview, and replied that the first paper having been placed in the hands of her family for her own safety and justification, was not now within her own power, and would scarcely be likely to be returned by them. She soon found that Bossuet was exasperated at this refusal and apparent escape from him; and her enemies now showed such a determination to pursue her, that she concluded it would be needful to retire into complete privacy. Not wishing to involve any of her friends in difficulty on her account, she took a small house in an obscure part of Paris; where she spent her time, for some months, unknown to the world, in prayer, reading, needlework, etc., accompanied only by a few confidential domestics. Her place of retreat was however at length discovered by the police; and about the end of the year 1695, she was arrested, and, by a despotic process which was a disgrace to the reign of Louis XIV., was consigned to the Castle of Vincennes, without a trial, and without specification of the charges against her.

In her own account of her life, she has drawn a veil over

the sufferings which she endured in her imprisonments; partly, as she says, out of charity for those who were the instigators of those sufferings; but chiefly, as we may suppose, owing to the circumstance that all prisoners in the Bastile were bound under oath not to divulge what passed in that doleful place. Her American biographer Upham has collected a few particulars of this portion of her life, from which we may in some measure supply the deficiency.

She remained in the Castle of Vincennes about nine months, and was then transferred to a place of confinement connected with a monastery in the village of Vaugirard, near Paris; where she had a little more liberty to see her friends. But the Archbishop of Paris becoming alarmed at this, compelled her to sign a paper agreeing "to receive no visits, hold no conversations, and write no letters, without the express permission of the Curate of St. Sulpitius." Being now entirely in the power of her enemies, she could not easily do otherwise than submit to them. Yet we may query, how far the servant of the Lord is at liberty to submit, by a voluntary signature, to power clearly exercised against His own divine commands. About this time likewise, Godet Marais, the Bishop of Chartres, within whose diocese was the "Seminary of St. Cyr," where her labors had been attended with remarkably awakening results in the minds of many of the pupils, issued an ecclesiastical ordinance, condemning her writings as "false, rash, impious, heretical, and tending to renew the errors of Luther and Calvin;" and caused all her books to be removed from the seminary, to the great grief of the pious female who had charge of the institution.

A nefarious attempt to ruin both her and Francis La Combe, transpired when she had been about two years at Vaugirard. The Archbishop of Paris came into her prison, accompanied by the above-mentioned "Curate of St. Sulpitius;" and read to her, without letting her see the writing, a letter purporting to come from La Combe, addressed to herself, referring to irregularities of conduct on the part of both of them, and exhorting her to repent. These priests, after reading the letter to her, urged her earnestly to merit forgiveness by confessing her guilt. Astonished at the transaction, but conscious of her innocence, she meekly replied, that either that letter was a forgery, or that La Combe, worn out mentally and bodily by his long incarceration, had lost his intellectual powers, and had written it, or signed it, at the instigation of some one, without knowing what it was. Upham adds, that "her perfect self-possession, her serious and unaffected air of innocence, the conviction which suddenly flashed upon their own minds, that an attempt had been made to destroy the most devoted and virtuous of women by the foulest of means, compelled them to leave her prison with a shame to themselves hardly less than the sorrow which they brought to her. The secret history of this atrocious movement is not well known." La Combe's mental and physical system had indeed given way at length under the sufferings which he had so long endured; so that it had been deemed needful to transfer him from his prison to a public hospital for sick and insane persons, in the village of Charenton. "On his way he was lodged for a short time in the Castle of Vincennes, where the above paper was prepared, and his signature obtained to it. Shortly after his arrival at Charenton he died; but it was satisfactorily ascertained, that at the time of his death, and for some time before, he had not sufficient power of perception and reasoning, to know what he did, and to render him accountable for his acts."

The failure of this wicked attempt to ruin her character, exasperated her enemies, who thereupon obtained an order from the king to transfer her to one of the towers in the Bastile. Upham has given an interesting description of this dismal place. It was mainly composed of eight large and immensely strong towers, four storied, and eighty feet high, united by very thick walls enclosing two large courts and several other apartments, and the whole surrounded by a deep and wide ditch. At the base of the towers were dungeons below the level of the ground, with no fireplace in any of them. The walls of the towers were twelve feet thick at the highest part, and thicker still near the base. The doors of the four rooms in each tower were double; and the single window allotted to each room, twelve feet from the broad light of day, was, as well as the chimney, secured by prodigiously strong iron grates. The floors were of stone or tile. The furniture usually consisted of a bed, a table, a chair, a basin, and a large earthen water-pitcher, a brass candlestick, a broom, and a tinder-box. Everything was taken from the prisoners, on their entrance, except such clothing as was absolutely necessary. These stony rooms were exceedingly cold in winter, and badly ventilated in summer, and rendered more offensive by the putrid exhalations from the ditch below.

We can now picture to ourselves this virtuous and highly gifted woman, shut up in one of these gloomy abodes, in the fifty-first year of her age, and with no prospect of release from it during her life. She went thither in the autumn of 1698, and continued there four years, as far as appears in entire seclusion. She was not even allowed to write to her friends. The "Man of the Iron Mask," who has been supposed to have been a twin-brother of Louis XIV., and confined during his whole life by his brother, from motives of jealousy, was a prisoner there at the same time. "For the purpose of entire concealment, he wore a mask, of which the lower part had steel springs, contrived so that he could eat without taking it off." Even the physician of the prison had never seen his face, though he had several times examined his tongue or his pulse. At this time he had been a prisoner thirty seven years; "shut out from nature, from knowledge, and from man;" without any fault but that of his twin-birth of royalty!

A pious woman also, who had long been a faithful domestic assistant to J. M. Guion, was imprisoned about the same time in the Bastile, though in a separate apartment. "She was a person of a strong understanding, as well as of a pious heart. Her letters show this. She took a strong hold of the truth, and her purpose was fixed to maintain it. Nothing could turn her from what she believed to be the will of God.". . . . . "If she had consented to say a word unfavorable to Madame Guion, she would undoubtedly have been set at liberty, and perhaps rewarded. But although she was poor and in prison, the world had not riches enough to seduce her principles, or pervert her integrity." She died in that prison.

While J. M. Guion was thus confined in the Bastile, she was several times strictly interrogated by order of the king; but she is said to have defended herself with great ability and firmness.

Her feelings and experience during her imprisonments and subsequent banishment, may be gathered from the following extracts from her own account. While it appears that both her intellectual and physical energy had been much worn down by her long and accumulated afflictions, yet there is a beautiful evidence in her writings of this period, brief as they were, that her soul had attained to a still nearer access to the Source of all wisdom and purity, and that her spirit had increased in weightiness, and in clearness of vision in divine things.

She says that she looked upon these greatest persecutions, which overtook her in the latter part of her life, as favors rather than as evils, and her most violent persecutors as instruments whereby her beloved Lord saw fit to accomplish the purification of her soul. Thus she says, "I was, in the prison, as in a place of delicacies and refreshment; this seclusion from all fellow-creatures giving me more opportunity of being alone with God; and the privation of things which appeared the most necessary, enabling me to taste of an exterior poverty which I could not otherwise have experienced. Thus I regarded all these great apparent evils, and this universal outcry against me, as the greatest of all benefits. It seemed to me to be the work of the hand of the Almighty, who saw meet to cover his tabernacle with the skins of beasts, and thus to hide it from the sight of those to whom he would not that it should be manifested."

But, she says, "Besides suffering many heavy and grievous maladies, the Lord permitted an inward experience of great desolation for some months, so that I could only exclaim, 'My God, my God! why hast thou forsaken me?' It seemed as if the Almighty, and also all his creatures, were against me, and I was at length ready to take part with them even against myself, and to crave that everything of self might be entirely sacrificed and given up. And so I have preferred to consecrate all these sufferings by silence. If the Lord should permit that in a future day anything of them should be known, for his glory, I should adore his judgments; but as for myself personally, my part is taken." . . . . . "I have believed that I owed it to religion, to piety, to my friends, to my family, and to myself, to develope those things, from time to time, in which others were sought to be implicated with me, or might be weakened or endangered by any faults of mine; but as far as regarded my personal ill-treatment, I have believed it my duty to sacrifice and sanctify them by profound silence."

"During the time that I was at Vincennes, I rested in great peace, entirely content to pass my life there, if such was the will of God. I wrote hymns, and the young woman who attended on me learned them by heart as I wrote them, and we sang together thy praises, O my God! I looked upon myself as a little bird held in a cage at thy will, and felt that I must sing, to fulfil my allotment. The stones of my tower seemed like rubies—that is to say—I esteemed them more than all the magnificence of the age. My joy was founded on thy love, O my God! and on the pleasure of being thy captive. The bottom of my heart was filled with that joy which thou givest to them who love thee in the midst of the greatest afflictions.

"This peace was broken for a little time by my unfaithfulness. This was in one day premeditating what I should answer to an interrogation, to which I was expecting to be subjected the next day. I had before been greatly helped to reply to difficult questions with much facility and presence of mind; but now, the Lord knew well how to punish me for my forethought. He permitted me to be unable to answer very simple questions, or to know scarcely what to say at all. This unfaithfulness, I say, interrupted my peace for some days, but it soon returned, and I believe this fault was permitted, in order to show the inutility of our own contrivances, and the safety of trusting in God. They whose foundation is on human reason will say that we must take forethought, and endeavor to pre-arrange, and that to act otherwise is to tempt God and expect miracles. I leave others to think what they will; but for myself, I find no safety but in resignation to the Lord. All Scripture is full of testimonies to the need of this resignation. 'Commit thy way unto the Lord; trust also in him, and he shall bring it to pass. And he shall bring forth thy righteousness as the light, and thy judgment as the noon-day.' God has not, in saying this, undertaken to lay snares for us; nor yet in enjoining us 'not to take thought beforehand what ye shall answer.'"

"While I was in the Bastile, and things were carried to the greatest extremity, having been apprised of the outcry and dreadful excitement that existed against me, I said, 'O my God! if it is thy will to make me a new spectacle to angels and to men, thy holy will be done! All that I ask of thee, is that thou wouldst save those who are thine, and not permit them to be scattered—that neither principalities, nor powers, nor the sword, may ever separate us from the love of God which is in Christ Jesus! For my own particular, what matters it what men think of me? What matters it if they cause me to suffer, since they cannot separate me from Jesus Christ, who is graven in the bottom of my heart! ..... Their blows will polish what is defective in me, in order that I may be presented to Him for whom I die daily, until he come to finish this death; and I pray thee, O Lord, to make of me an offering pure and clean in thy blood, that I may soon be offered unto thee!'"

In the year 1702, she was tardily liberated from her cruel imprisonment, one year after Bossuet had at length declared before the assembled ecclesiastics of Paris, his belief that she was an innocent woman. She was allowed for a short time to visit her daughter, and then banished to Blois,* about one hundred miles southwest from Paris; where her eldest son, who had given her much trouble during his youth, and had since been bitterly at variance

---

* In 1709 or 1710, the last Prioress of the Monastery of Port Royal des Champs, was, after the demolition of that convent, sent likewise to Blois, where she died after a captivity of about six years. (Tregelles's History of "The Jansenists," p. 39.)

with her, now resided. It was probably thought that his proximity to her would be a check upon her during the rest of her days. Here she lived in comparative quietness and retirement, and, though closely watched, was able occasionally to see her friends. To an eminent person who visited her from England, whose name has not come down to us, she entrusted, near the close of her pilgrimage, the account of her Life, which she had originally undertaken at the earnest request of Francis La Combe.

After her liberation from the Bastile, she says: " No sooner had my spirit begun as it were again to breathe freely, than my body found itself overwhelmed with all sorts of infirmities, and I had almost continual and dangerous sicknesses. In these last days I can speak but little of my feelings. My condition has been simple and without variety, founded on a deep sense of nothingness. I know that God is infinitely holy, just, good, and happy, including in himself all that is good;—but I see nothing baser than myself, nothing more unworthy than myself. . . . . . If any one thinks there is any good in me, he deceives himself and wrongs the Almighty. All good is in Him and for Him. . . . . . If he save me, it will be of his free grace, for I have neither merit nor worthiness. . . . . I desire neither to go nor to stay—the will and the natural instincts appear to be gone—poverty and nakedness are my portion. . . . . . There are times when I could wish, at the peril of a thousand lives, that God was duly known and loved."

"I seek for nothing, but words of strength are immediately afforded me. If I wish to retain them, they escape —if I would repeat them, they are gone. . . . . The Lord keeps me in extreme simplicity, rectitude of heart, and enlargement, and I perceive things only as it is needful—without the occasion for it, I see nothing. . . . . He gives me a liberty in conversation with people, not according to my own disposition, but according to their state. . . . . Sometimes people tell me, 'You have said such and such things; these persons can put a bad interpretation on them; you are too simple.' I believe it; but I cannot do otherwise. Oh, carnal prudence! how opposed do I find thee to the simplicity of Christ! . . . . . For me, Christ is my prudence and my wisdom."

"Nothing is greater than God; nothing smaller than myself. He is rich; I am poor; yet I want nothing—I feel the lack of nothing. Death or life, eternity or time, all is equal to me. . . . . . God is love, and love is God, and all in God and for God."

She thus pours forth the travail of her soul on behalf of those whom she accounted her children in Christ; apparently conscious that she should see their faces no more, and that this was her last appeal for their preservation: "Oh, my children, open your eyes to the light of truth! . . . . . Holy Father, sanctify them in thy truth! I have told them thy truth, since I have not spoken of myself. Thy Divine Word hath spoken to them by my mouth. He only is the Truth; and He hath said, 'For their sakes I sanctify myself.' Say thou the same to my children. Sanctify thyself in them and for them. But how well do thy words agree together, O, Divine Word! Thou hast said, 'Sanctify them through thy truth; thy word is truth' —and again—'For their sakes I sanctify myself.' . . . . . This is to be sanctified with all holiness in the truth, when we have no other holiness than that of Jesus Christ. Let him alone be holy in us and for us. He will be the holy one in us, when we are sanctified in the truth by this experimental knowledge, that to him alone belongs all holiness, all justice, all strength, all greatness, all power, all glory; and to us all poverty, and all weakness. Let us dwell in our nothingness, in honor to the holiness of God, and we shall be sanctified and instructed by the Truth. Jesus Christ will be holiness for us, and will be everything to us; we shall find in him all that we need. If we seek anything for ourselves out of him, if we seek anything in ourselves as belonging to ourselves; however holy it may appear to us, we are liars, and the truth is not in us; we deceive ourselves, and shall never be the saints of the Lord; who, having no other holiness than His, have renounced all arrogance of self.

"Holy Father! I have given back into thy hands those whom thou hast given me. Keep them in thy truth, that that which is false should not at all come nigh them. To attribute the least thing to self, or to think ourselves able to do anything of ourselves, or that we possess anything of ourselves, is to be in that which is false—in a lie. Cause them to know, O my God! that this is that truth of which thou art very jealous. All language that departs from this principle is falsehood; he that approaches it, approaches the truth; but he that says 'all of God, and nothing of the creature,' is in the truth, and the truth dwells in him; for self and arrogancy being banished from that soul, the truth must needs abide there.

"My children, receive this instruction from your mother, and it will procure you life. Receive it through her, but not as from her, or as belonging to her, but as from God and belonging to God.

"In Jesus, amen. I will sing of the righteousness of the Lord forever."

With these fervent aspirations she concludes the account of her own life. Are these the sentiments of a criminal— of one worthy of incarceration in one of the most dreadful of all prisons? Are they not rather the outpourings of a soul which had come out of great tribulation, whose garments had been made white in the blood of the Lamb, and which was soon to be called before the throne of God, to sing, Great and marvellous are thy works, Lord, God, Almighty, just and true are all thy ways, thou King of saints! Who shall not fear before thee, and glorify thy name; for thou only art holy!

She had a long and painful illness. It was probably during this sickness that she wrote, as follows, to one of her friends, as given by Upham.—"I can only say at present, my dear friend, that my physical sufferings are very severe, and almost without intermission. It is impossible for me, without a miraculous interposition, to continue long in this world under them. I solicit your prayers to God, that I may be kept faithful to Him in these last hours of my trials.

"Last night, in particular, my pains were so great, as to call into exercise all the resources and aids of faith. God heard the prayer of his poor sufferer; Grace was triumphant. It is trying to nature; but I can say in this last struggle, that I love the hand that smites me."

She died in peace, early in the summer of 1717, aged about sixty-nine years.

CHAPTER XVIII.

WILLIAM DELL.

WILLIAM DELL was an Episcopal minister, and rector of Yelden, in Bedfordshire, England. Of his early life we have no account. While at Yelden, in the year 1645, and during the religious agitations which followed the expulsion of Charles I. and the establishment of the Commonwealth, he published a treatise, entitled "Christ's Spirit a Christian's Strength." His object in this discourse was to show that the Spirit of Christ is absolutely necessary in the church, to furnish with power to overcome the world, and that a dependence on human strength and learning, without the unction of this Spirit, can only lead into "the form of godliness," as distinguished from "the power" thereof. This doctrine pervades all his subsequent writings. The tenor of his views in this work, very contrary to the prevalent dogmas of that time, may be gathered from the following brief extracts:

"'The receiving of the Spirit," says he, "is the receiving of power. ['Ye shall receive power, when the Holy Ghost is come upon you.'] Till we receive the Spirit, we are altogether without power; and when we receive the Spirit, then first of all, do we receive power—power from on high. By nature we are all without strength, weak, impotent creatures, utterly unable to do anything that is truly and spiritually righteous and good."

"The Spirit is power operatively in us, by being in us a spirit of knowledge. For the Holy Spirit teaches us to know 'the things that are freely given to us of God;' yea, he teaches us to know what sin is, and what righteousness; what death is, and what life; what heaven is, and what hell; what ourselves are, and what God is. And these things he teaches us to know otherwise than other men know them."

He maintains that this gift of the Spirit is common to all true Christians, and that all must needs have it, if they are really in the life and power of Christianity; but that for ministers of the gospel it is especially necessary.

" The ministers of the gospel must needs have this power of the Holy Spirit, because otherwise they are not sufficient for the ministry. For no man is sufficient for the work of the ministry, by any natural parts and abilities of his own, nor yet by any acquired parts of human learning and knowledge; but only by this power of the Holy Spirit; and till he be endued with this, notwithstanding all his other accomplishments, he is altogether insufficient. And therefore, the very apostles were to keep silence, till they were endued with this power. They were to wait at Jerusalem till they had received the promise of the Spirit. . . . . Without this power of the Spirit, ministers are utterly unable to preach the word; that is, the true, spiritual and living word of God. For to preach this word of God, requires the power of God. One may speak the word of man, by the power of man; but he cannot speak the word of God, but by the power of God."

"Human reason, and human wisdom, and righteousness, and power, and knowledge, cannot receive the Holy Spirit. But we must be emptied of these, if ever we would receive Him. . . . . . And when a man is thus empty of himself, and of other things, then he becomes 'poor in spirit;' and such the Spirit fills, and descends into with a wonderful and irresistible power, and fills the outer and inner man, and all the faculties of the soul, with himself and all the things of God."

And he winds up the whole by the following remark:—
"We must ascribe to the Spirit the whole glory of his own works, and acknowledge that we ourselves are nothing, and can do nothing; and that it is He only that is all in all, and works all in all. And we ourselves, among all the excellent works of the Spirit in us, must so remain as if we were and wrought nothing at all; that so, all that is of flesh and blood may be laid low in us, and the Spirit alone may be exalted; first, to do all in us, and then, to have all the glory of all that is done." . . . .

"And by the daily use and improvement of these means,

we may attain to a great degree of spiritual strength, that we may walk and not be weary, and may run and not faint, and may mount up as eagles, yea, and may walk as angels among men, and as the powers of heaven upon earth; to His praise and honor, who first communicates to us his own strength, and then, by that strength of his own, works all our works in us. And thus is He glorified in his saints, and admired in all that believe."

In a treatise put forth probably soon afterward, he argues that the true spiritual church of Christ is composed of living stones—precious stones—"and therefore," says he, "the Lord calls them [the faithful] his jewels—'In the day wherein I make up my jewels'—and elsewhere they are called 'the precious sons of Zion.' The people of God are a most precious people, men and women of a precious anointing; though some wicked and scurrilous libellers against the spiritual church will not allow them this name, but reproach it. And yet still it is a truth, that the gates of hell shall not prevail against, that the truly faithful are precious stones in the building of the church, partaking of the nature and Spirit of God."

But though these true members of Christ have all received of the same anointing, yet "let us not expect all gifts in all men, and that every man should excel in every gift; for then one would be saying to another, 'I have no need of thee.'" ..... "If thou hast the gift of utterance in the ministration of the Spirit, it is to build me up. If I have the spirit of prayer, it commends thee as carefully to God as myself. One watches over another, as over his own soul. And if any be weak, the strong support them; if any be doubtful, they that have the gift of knowledge direct them; if one be troubled, the rest mourn with him; if one be comforted, the rest rejoice with him; and they are all so linked together in the body of Christ, that the good and evil of one extends to all. Where thou canst find such another communion, there join thyself. But if this be the only excellent communion in the world, who would not willingly join himself to that spiritual people, where no man calls his grace his own, but all gifts are in common among all, every one having a share in the faith, hope, love, prayer, peace, joy, wisdom, strength of all; and all having a share in these gifts and graces, that are in any one? And thus much for the diversity of the stones, as well as for the preciousness of them."

And further on, in the same work, he says: "Now we perceive how few true children of the church there be among those commonly called Christians. For among all these, how few are there who have the teaching of God! But most have their teaching only from men, and no higher. Consider therefore, I pray, whether the knowledge you have be from the teaching of God, or the teaching of man. You all pretend to know that Christ is the Son of the living God, and that redemption and salvation is by him alone. But how came ye by this knowledge? Did you read it in the letter, or did somebody tell you so, or hath God himself taught you this? For 'no man knoweth the Son but the Father, and he to whom the Father will reveal him.'" . . . "Oh, consider whether you have the teaching of God in these things or no. And if you have not the teaching of God, you are none of the children of the church; whatever truth thou knowest from the letter, if thou hast not the teaching of the Spirit, it will do thee no good; thou knowest not anything spiritually and savingly, wherein thou hast not the teaching of God. 'All thy children shall be taught of the Lord.'"

In the year 1646, Wm. Dell preached a sermon before the House of Commons, on the Right Reformation of the Church; wherein, after contrasting inward and spiritual with outward, civil, and ecclesiastical reformation, he earnestly appealed to the Parliament, to stop all persecution and attempts to force men's consciences by the power of the magistrate; showing that this can never produce true reformation, but only outward conformity, with inward and dangerous dissatisfaction.

Among many other excellent sentiments, he boldly held forth to them the following language:

"It is an inward reformation [that is needed]. For as the kingdom of God is an inward kingdom ('the kingdom of God is within you'), so the reformation that belongs to it is an inward reformation. This true gospel reformation lays hold upon the heart, and soul, and inner man; and changes, and alters, and renews, and reforms that; and when the heart is reformed, all is reformed. . . . . . And, therefore, saith Christ, touching the worship of the New Testament, 'God is a Spirit; and they that worship him must worship him in spirit and in truth;' but speaks not one word of any outward form. So that God, in this gospel reformation, aims at nothing but the heart, according to the tenor of the new covenant: 'This shall be the covevant that I will make with them after those days, saith the Lord, I will put my law in their inward parts, and write it in their hearts' (Jer. xxxi. 33); so that they shall not only have the word of the letter in their books, but the living Word of God in their hearts; and God, intending to reform the church, begins with their hearts; and, intending to reform their hearts, puts his Word there; and that living Word put into the heart reforms it indeed."

"The word whereby Christ reforms, is not the word without us, as the word of the law is; but the word within us, as it is written, 'The Word is nigh thee, even in thy mouth, and in thy heart;' and this is the 'word of faith.' If thou live under the word many years, and if it come not into thy heart, it will never change thee, nor reform thee. And, therefore, the reforming Word is the Word within us, and the word within us is 'the word of faith.'"

"Forcible reformation is unbeseeming the gospel; for the gospel is the gospel of peace, and not of force and fury. Civil ecclesiastical reformation reforms by breathing out threatenings, punishments, prisons, fire, and death; but the gospel, by preaching peace. And therefore it is most unbeseeming the gospel to do anything rashly and violently for the advancement thereof, for the gospel of peace is not to be advanced by violence; and therefore violent reformers live in contradiction to the gospel of peace, and cannot be truly reckoned Christians, but enemies to Christianity; since Christianity doth all by the power of the anointing, but anti-christianity doth all by the power of the world. Forcible reformation is unsuitable to Christ's kingdom, for Christ's kingdom stands in the Spirit; and the force of flesh and blood can contribute nothing to this."

Toward the close of his discourse, he thus pleads with the Parliament: "I have a few more things to say, touching God's kingdom:—1. That as Christ's kingdom and the kingdoms of the world are distinct, so you would be pleased to keep them so; and not mingle them together yourselves, nor suffer others to do it, to the great prejudice and disturbance of both.

"2. That you would be pleased to think that Christ's kingdom (which is not of this world) hath sufficient power in itself to manage all the affairs of it, without standing in need of any aid or help from the world; seeing the power of man is of no place or use in the kingdom of God, which is not a temporal, or an ecclesiastical dominion, but a spiritual.

"3. That you would suffer the little stone of Christ's kingdom to be hewn out of the mountain of the Roman monarchy (whereof this kingdom is a part) without hands, even by the power and efficacy of the Word and Spirit; seeing the hands of man cannot help, but hinder this work, which is to be done without hands. . . . . .

"4. That you would be pleased to suffer the assemblings of the saints, both publicly and privately, as occasion serves, seeing this can be no prejudice to the State, but a great advantage; inasmuch as they meet peaceably, and make no tumults, and in their assembling pray for the peace and welfare of this divided and distracted kingdom. And also that you take heed of scattering those churches that meet in the name and Spirit of Jesus Christ (which are Christ's own gatherings together), lest Christ so scatter you abroad that you never be gathered together again."

. . . . . "When I see the generality of the people of all sorts rise up against the ministration of the Spirit, which God hath now in these days of ours set up, ... I am then exceedingly distressed, and pained at the very heart, for thee, O England! and for all thy cities and towns and inhabitants; for thou that dashest against the Spirit in the gospel, how shalt thou be dashed in pieces thyself, and there shall be no healing for thee!"

And in another address to the Parliament, he tells them: "It shall be your wisdom to be built up, together with the church, on Christ; but it would be your confusion to go about to build the church on yourselves and your power; seeing this building is too weighty for any foundation but Christ himself. . . . It will be no less dangerous an evil, for the magistrate to make himself lord and lawgiver in the church, than for the pope, or general council, in all the kingdoms called Christian; as for the archbishop or national assembly in particular kingdoms. . . . Wherefore do you look to the care of the State, and trust Christ with the care of his church, seeing he is both faithful and able to save it perfectly.... Why should the church any longer be ignorant of the things that belong unto its peace? And why should the members of it any longer lie as scattered bones, dry and dead, and not gathered up into the unity of a living body?"

About this time, or soon after, appears to have been published one of his largest as well as most clear and deeply spiritual works, entitled "The Way of True Peace and Unity in the True Church of Christ;" which also was addressed to the Parliament, and likewise to General Fairfax and Oliver Cromwell. It was a time of great agitation among all classes of professors of religion—the country was full of commotions and changes, so that he said "there was no silence in heaven for so much as half an hour"— none of the high-soaring rulers of the various professing churches knew what it was to come into that silence of all fleshly tumults and impulses, wherein they might have experienced Jerusalem to be a quiet habitation, a place of safety from the powers and storms of the world.

In this work on the Peace and Unity of the Church, he entirely disavows any aim to reconcile the true church of Christ with the world; for, says he, the Lord never intended such reconciliation between the seed of the woman and the seed of the serpent; neither does he endeavor to bring about an agreement between the children of Ishmael and those of Isaac, in the professing church; for "they that are born after the flesh," says Dell, "are always persecuting them that are born after the Spirit, but never agreeing with them." But he says, "the way of peace I shall speak of, is between the children of peace, touching whom God hath promised that He will give them one heart and one way; and for whom Christ hath prayed, 'That they all may be one, as thou, Father, art in me, and I in thee, that they also may be one in us.'"

. . "The peace then I seek by this discourse, is the peace of the true church." And this true church he describes as "a spiritual and invisible fellowship, gathered together in the unity of faith, hope, and love, and so into the unity of the Son, and of the Father by the Spirit." . . . . . "The true church is knit into their society among themselves by being first knit unto Christ their head; and as soon as ever they are one with him, they are also one with another in him; and not first one among themselves, and then one with Christ." . . . . . And again he says, "The churches of men have human officers who act in the strength of natural or acquired parts, who do all by the help of study, learning, and the like. But in the true church, Christ and the Spirit are the only officers, and men only so far as Christ and the Spirit dwell and manifest themselves in them. And so, when they do anything in the church, it is not they that do it, but Christ and his Spirit in them and by them. And therefore saith Paul, 'Seek ye a proof of Christ speaking in me? which to youwards is not weak, but mighty.' Whoever is the instrument, Christ is the only preacher of the New Testament; and that which is the true gospel, is the ministration of the Spirit; for 'holy men spake as they were moved by the Holy Spirit;' and were first anointed with the Spirit, before they preached." . . . . . "Against the churches of men, the gates of hell (which are sin and death) shall certainly prevail: but the true church of Christ, though the gates of hell do always fight against it, yet they shall never prevail against it; as Christ hath promised, 'Upon this rock I will build my church, and the gates of hell shall not prevail against it.'"

"Christ was known [to John Baptist] by the Spirit's resting on him. . . . . . After the same manner the church of Christ is known, to wit, by the Spirit's coming and remaining on it. So that whatever people have received the

Spirit of Christ, of what sort or condition soever they be, they are the church of Christ; and they that are destitute of this Spirit, are not of the church."

"They that do content themselves in joining to some outward and visible society and corporation of men, though called a church, and think that by being knit to them in ways of outward worship and ordinances, they live in the unity of the church, when as yet, all this while, they live out of that one body that is born of the Spirit, which is the only true church, and body of Christ—he that lives out of this spiritual body, though he live in the most excellent society in the world, yet he breaks the unity of the church, not living in one body with it."

"Hence it is evident, that it is nothing to have the outward form of a church, even as our souls could wish, except there be inwardly, in that church, the Spirit of Christ. For it is not unity of form, will ever make the church one, but unity of Spirit. That church then that is destitute of the Spirit, in its laws, orders, constitutions, forms, members, and officers; what unity can that have, in all its uniformity?"

"They that, being of the church, do anything in it by their own spirits, and not by Christ's, prejudice the peace of the church; for the true church is such a body, which is to have all its communion in the Spirit. And therefore, when any pray or prophesy, or the like, in the strength of natural parts, or human studies and invention only, and do not pray and prophesy in the Spirit, they break the unity of the church; for the faithful have communion with one another, only so far as the Spirit is manifested in each."

"One Lord, one faith, one baptism." . . . . . "The true church, which is the body of Christ, hath but one and the self-same baptism, by which it is purified; which is the baptism of the Spirit. For the apostle speaks here of that baptism, wherein the whole church is one; which is not the baptism of the sign, which hath often been altered and changed, but the baptism of the substance, which comprehends all believers, and all ages, and under several and various dispensations; and was the same before Christ's coming in the flesh, as since; believers, both of the Jews and Gentiles, of the Old and New Testaments, drinking all alike into one spirit, though these more plentifully than those. So that, though many have wanted the baptism of water, yet not one member of the true church hath wanted the baptism of the Spirit, from whence our true Christianity begins." . . . . . "So that it is not the washing of water, but the washing of the Spirit, that is the true ground of the true church's unity; and they that want this baptism of the Spirit, though they have been baptized with water never so much, live quite out of the unity of the church."

"The right church is the city of God, and hath God in the midst of it, being built and framed, and that according to every part of it, by the Spirit, to be the habitation of God. This is 'the temple of the living God,' as God hath said, and God is in it of a truth. And if any would know what this church is called, the name of it is, THE LORD IS THERE. And so the whole guiding and ordering of this church depends wholly on God, who dwells within it. For God will not dwell in his own church and sit still, while others that are without it shall govern it; but the government of the right church lies on His shoulders, who is Immanuel, God with us, and in us."

"Peter had said to Christ, 'Thou art Christ, the Son of the living God:' and Christ replied to Peter, 'Blessed art thou; for flesh and blood hath not revealed it unto thee, but my Father which is in heaven;' and then adds, 'unto thee will I give the keys of the kingdom of heaven,' etc.— that is, not to Peter, as an apostle, or minister, but as a believer, who had the revelation of the Father, touching the Son. And so also, they are given equally to each faithful Christian, who hath the same revelation with Peter, as also to the whole communion of saints."

"What officers are to be chosen? Paul teaches us this; saying, They must be faithful men, apt and able to teach others. For as, among natural men of the world, they that have most natural power and abilities, are fittest to be the officers; so among spiritual men in the church, they are fittest to be the officers, that have most spiritual power, that is, such in whom Christ and the Spirit are most manifest; and of this, the faithful of all sorts are judges. Wherefore, no natural parts and abilities, nor human learning and degrees in the schools or universities, nor ecclesiastical ordination or orders, are to be reckoned sufficient to make a man a minister; but only the teaching of God, and gifts received of Christ, by the Spirit, for the work of the ministry, which the faithful are able to discern and judge of."

He adds that these officers "are to be chosen out of the flock of Christ, and nowhere else. Indeed antichrist, bringing in human learning instead of the Spirit, chose his ministers only out of the universities; but the right church chooses them out of the faithful; seeing it reckons no man learned, and so fit to speak in the church, but he that hath 'heard and learned from the Father.'"

"The true church is to preserve itself distinct from the world; and is neither to mingle itself with the world, nor to suffer the world to mingle itself with it. For if the church and the world be mingled together in one society, the same common laws will no more agree to them who are of such different natures, principles, and ends, than the same common laws will agree to light and darkness, life and death, sin and righteousness, flesh and spirit. For the true church are a spiritual people, being born of God; and so they worship God in the spirit, according to the law of the Spirit of life that was in Christ, and is in them. But the carnal church is of the world, and only savors of the world, and so will have a worldly religion, forms, orders, government, and all worldly as itself is. Now, while these two are mingled together, what peace can there be?"

"By what means may the church be able to keep out error?—1. Let the church suffer none to teach among them that are not themselves taught of God; though they have never so great natural parts, and never so much human learning. For, when they are the teachers that are taught of God, they will only teach the truth, which they have heard and learned from God; and the line of every man's teaching must extend no further. But when they teach that are not so taught, they will, in many things, vary from the truth as it is in Jesus." . . . . .

"2. Let the church examine everything—and not receive doctrines on trust—and compare the present doctrine, preached and printed, and generally received, with the doctrines of the prophets and apostles, which without doubt is sure and certain, seeing those 'holy men of God spake as they were moved by the Holy Spirit.' And whatever doctrine shall be found contrary to, or different from that doctrine, let them reject it as reprobate silver." . . . . .

"3. The church, that it may be able to keep out errors, must desire of God the Spirit which he hath promised; that this Spirit of truth may lead them into the true and spiritual knowledge of the word, and understanding of the mind of Christ. For no man can make any right judgment of the word he hears or reads, without the teaching of the Spirit. And by this anointing, as we shall be certainly taught which is truth, so also shall we discern which is error, and that by so clear and true a light, that we shall not mistake."

"4. Another notable means to keep error out of the church, is to restore in it that most ancient gospel ordinance of prophesying; which, how much soever it hath been out of use during the reign of antichrist, yet is no other than the very commandment of the Lord; as Paul witnesseth, I. Cor. xiv. 31, where he saith, 'When the whole church is met together, ye may all prophesy one by one, that all may learn, and all may be comforted,' etc."

"Through the exercise of prophesying, the church knows and discerns which of its members are most spiritual and most clearly taught of God in divine things; and who have received the most excellent gifts from Christ, and so are most fit and able to hold forth the word of life, in most evidence and power of the Spirit, that so the church may be supplied with pastors of her own sons, and not seek after unknown persons; nor be constrained to use mercenary men, who have been brought up to preaching, as their trade to live by; whereupon but few of them can be expected to be other than hirelings, who will make their ministry serve their own advantage, and frame the Scripture to found such doctrine as may best serve their own turns.". . .

"Yea, further, in this society, God will have him who is most unlearned, according to human literature, to speak; that the virtues of Christ may the more evidently appear in the saints; and the knowledge of heavenly and divine truths may not be attributable to gifts, parts, learning or studies, but only to His Spirit; which can even in a moment teach the ignorant, and make the simple wise, and open the mouths of babes and sucklings, yea, and the very dumb, to perfect his praise by."

"It will be objected—Yea, but if every one have liberty to speak in the church, will not this breed great confusion and disturbance? I answer, no; not in the true church, which are a people met in the name of Christ, and who have

Christ himself present in the midst of them; and so every one demeans himself answerably to the presence of Christ; that is, in the wisdom, meekness, and modesty of the Spirit. And there also every one speaks, not after the rashness of his own brain, but according to the revelation of God; as it is written, 'If anything be revealed to another, let the first hold his peace;' so that no man is to speak here but by revelation, or an inward teaching and discovery of God. And where men speak thus, as the true church is to speak, there can be no confusion, but most excellent order and decency. Yea, God himself, who is not the author of confusion, but of peace, in all the churches of the saints, hath appointed and commanded prophesying as the way of peace; and, therefore, do not thou dare to say it is the way of confusion, seeing God knows better how to order the affairs of his own church than thou dost."

The above extracts will afford a little glimpse at the truly Christian doctrine advocated in this treatise, a treatise which must have sorely grated on the ears of those who were interested in the maintenance of a religion of mere outside form, so framed as to gain the favor of the world, without subjection to the cross of Christ.

The next treatise in the order in which the successive pieces appear in his printed works, and probably the next in the order of their original publication, is one which appears to have been put forth after his appointment as Master of Gonville and Caius College in the University of Cambridge. It is the first in which he so designates himself in the title. This is a discourse on "The crucified and quickened Christian," the substance of which, founded on Gal. ii. 19, 20, was spoken at the residence of Oliver Cromwell, and was afterward more amply delivered to a congregation in Cambridge. He herein argues, in accordance with the apostle's teaching, that the true Christian must be indeed crucified as to the affections and lusts of fallen nature, that he may know what it is to arise with Christ, to have Christ living in him, and to live by the faith of the Son of God. He says, among other things:

"Let us know, that it is not enough to salvation, to believe that Jesus Christ, according to his human nature, was outwardly crucified on a cross at Jerusalem for us, except we also be crucified with him, through his living word and Spirit dwelling in us; through which we must be powerfully planted into a true likeness of his death, in such sort that we must be dead unto all sin whatever, even to all our own corruptions and lusts, and to all the corruptions that are in the world through lust; and we must be dead to ourselves, to our own fleshly reason, understanding, will, desires, ends, and to our own human life; and we must be dead to the world, and to all that is in it and of it; to all the pleasures, profits, and honors of it; we must thus truly be dead with Christ, ere we can live with him."

"Seeing Christ himself lives in all true believers, let us all, who profess ourselves to be such, so live, that Christ may be seen to live in us, more than ourselves; that they that have known us, may know *us* no more, but may know Christ in us; and that they that have communion with us, may acknowledge Christ himself speaking, working, and living his own life in us, in all self-denial, humility, holiness, love, resignation of ourselves to the will of God, and in all diligence to do the work of God, and readiness to suffer the will of God."

This publication, advocating too thorough a work in the soul, to be pleasing to the lovers of easy religion, drew forth a certain Humphrey Chambers, "Doctor in Divinity and Pastor of Pewsy," who published "Animadversions" on the doctrine promulgated by Dell. The latter therefore came forth with a treatise entitled "The Stumbling-Stone," showing how it was that carnal professors, and hangers on to the authority of universities in matters of religion, should be offended with sound Christian doctrine. In this work he spares not to speak boldly for the spiritual qualification of ministers of the gospel, and against a ministry of university appointment, quoting Huss and Luther in support of his positions.

"By this," says he, speaking of the very weak and unsound "Animadversions" published by Chambers, "the true church may judge also, what a sad ministry these poor nations have received from antichrist's ordination, when the chief doctors, the very Scribes and Pharisees among the clergy, do not know the very first principles of the gospel in any spiritual light, or by any teaching from God; but all their cold, faint, and uncertain doctrine they scrape from fathers and schoolmen, and from other ordinary systems of divinity; without any presence of faith, or anointing of the Spirit: whereby all their doctrine becomes carnal and corrupt, and contrary to Christ's mind, and agreeable to antichrist's. So that I cannot choose but conclude with John Huss, 'that all the clergy must be quite taken away, ere the church of Christ can have any true reformation.'"*

In this work he reasserts his position that Christ alone, by his Spirit, can qualify any to preach the gospel; saying " He chose fishermen, and tent-makers, and publicans, plain men, and of ordinary employment in the world ; and only put his Spirit on them, and this was their sufficient unction to the ministry. And thus it was foretold by Joel (chap. ii. 28), 'And it shall come to pass in the last days, saith the Lord, that I will pour out of my Spirit on all flesh, and your sons and your daughters shall prophesy.' There needs

* Joan. Hus. De Vitâ et regn. antichrist., cap. 37.

nothing to the ministry of the New Testament, but only God's pouring out his Spirit. Wherefore Christ bids his disciples stay at Jerusalem till they should receive the promise of the Spirit, and then they should go forth and teach." And again,—after quoting I. Cor. ii. 8–10,—"We learn that the things of the gospel, and of the Kingdom of God, are not known at all, nor discerned in the least measure, but by God's Spirit; which Spirit is given to all that believe; and this Spirit alone is sufficient, both to enable us to know clearly and certainly the things of God, and also to publish them to others; and nothing of man, or the creature, can add to it. Wherefore, when Christ chose his ministers, he chose not the wise and learned, but plain simple men; that it might appear to all the world, throughout all ages, how infinitely able the unction of his Spirit alone is, without any addition of anything else, for the ministry of the New Testament. And Christ breaks forth (Matt. xi. 25) into this thanksgiving: 'I thank thee, O Father, Lord of heaven and earth, that thou hast hid these things from the wise and prudent, and hast revealed them unto babes; even so, Father, for so it seemed good in thy sight.'" . . . .

"Now at these things how grievously are the worldly wise, and deep learned ones (as they esteem themselves) offended; that God's Spirit alone should be a sufficient unction for the ministry of the New Testament, and that God should, on set purpose, lay aside the wise and prudent men, and choose babes, and out of their mouths ordain his great strength, to set up Christ's kingdom in the world, and to destroy antichrist's! Yea, this doctrine will chiefly offend the university."

"Let us consider, that it is no new thing that Christ and his gospel should be stumbled at, and contradicted by the world and worldly church. For thus it was foretold by the prophets, and thus it hath been done ever since Christ was manifested in the flesh. In the days of his ministry, his doctrine was so contrary to carnal reason, and the human apprehensions of men in matters of religion, that many of his disciples said, 'This is a hard saying, who can bear it?' Yea, many of his disciples murmured at his doctrine, and went back, and walked no more with him. And all along, during Christ's ministry, many were snared, and stumbled, and fell, and were broken thereby; and he that is troubled and offended at this, must get him another Christ, and another gospel; for the true Christ is set for a sign to be spoken against; and the true gospel is set for a word of contention and contradiction to the carnal Christians and to the whole world."

But of all the writings of this intrepid reformer, excepting his direct attacks upon the universities, perhaps no one was more calculated to provoke the animosity of the advocates of formality, and especially of those who were conscious that "by this craft they had their wealth," than his short but cogent and unanswerable treatise, "The Doctrine of Baptisms, reduced from its ancient and modern corruptions, and restored to its primitive soundness and integrity;" in which he rescues that great and grossly abused doctrine from the hands of the priests, and shows conclusively from the Scriptures that baptism belongs to the One great High Priest of our profession, Christ Jesus, through the operation of the Holy Spirit; and that the baptism of water, which was John's, was merely preparatory and to pass away, to make room for that of Christ, with the Holy Ghost and fire. We cannot here undertake to follow up his reasoning; but a few extracts may suffice to show the scope and tendency of his argument.

He adduces John's own clear acknowledgment of the superior character of the baptism of Christ; "saying, 'I indeed baptize you with water,' that is, my baptism is but water baptism, that washes the body only with a corporeal element; but 'one mightier than I cometh;' for I am but a creature, He the power of God; I but a servant, He the Lord of all; and one so infinitely excellent above all that I am, that 'the latchet of his shoes I am not worthy to unloose;' that is, I am unworthy to perform the meanest and lowest office for him. . . . . He shall baptize you with the Holy Ghost and with fire; that is, I that am a servant do baptize with water; but He that is the Son, baptizes with the Spirit; my baptism washes but the body from the filth of the flesh; but his, the soul from the filth of sin; so that, by how much the Spirit excels water, and God the creature, so much his baptism transcends mine."

He goes on to show the great and essential distinction between John's baptism and that of Christ, and that though the former was honorable in itself and excellent in its place, being especially honored by Christ himself, as a man, submitting to it, as he did also to circumcision, for the fulfilment of all righteousness; yet that it could not give repentance nor remission of sins, nor any entrance into the kingdom of God; but that Christ's baptism, which is of the Spirit, gives a new nature, translates into the church and kingdom of God, teaches us by the divine anointing, enables those who partake of it "to put on Christ," truly washes and cleanses from sin, dips us into the death of Christ, makes us one with Christ, the Head, and saves us "by the washing of regeneration and renewing of the Holy Ghost."

"The baptism of John," says Dell, "was but a sign and ceremony, though it had more life and light in it than any of the signs of the law, as being nearer to Christ, and more newly revived by God; and so, though useful in its season, yet the efficacy of it (after the manner of signs) was but weak. For first, it did not give the Spirit, not one drop of the Spirit; yea, some who were baptized with John's baptism did not know the way of the Lord perfectly; that is, had no certain knowledge of Christ, the only way to God, as Apollos (Acts, xviii.); yea, some of them did not so much as know whether there were any Holy Ghost or not, as those twelve disciples (Acts, xix.),—much less had received the Spirit."

"And thus you see that the baptism of John, as it is distinct from Christ's, so it is far inferior to his. And therefore great hath been the mistake of many, for several ages, who have made John's baptism equal to Christ's; for what is this but to make the servant equal to the Lord, and to set down the creature in the throne of the only begotten of the Father? Yea, and it is quite perverting of John's office; for John was to be 'a burning and a shining light,' to usher in Christ, the true light. He was to be as the morning star, to usher in Christ, the Sun of Righteousness; and was not to be so much clouds and darkness to obscure him. He was but to point out Christ, and depart again, and not to sit in equal glory with him, on his throne in the New Testament. John said he was not worthy to bear his shoes; and therefore they do not well, who have prepared an equal crown for him with Christ, who is King of kings, and Lord of lords."

"*Objection.* Why, this would rob us of our Christianity! I answer, No; for it is not water, but Spirit-baptism that makes us Christians; and water-baptism hath been an unlawful blending or mixing of the church and world together; so that hitherto they could not be well distinguished from each other, to the great prejudice of the congregation of Christ."

" That which seems the strongest objection is, that the apostles practised water-baptism, not only before Christ's baptism came in, but after. . . . . .

" True, indeed, the apostles did practise water-baptism,

but not from Christ, but from John, whose baptism they took up; and an outward ceremony of honor and account is not easily and suddenly laid down; and hence some of the apostles used circumcision, and that after the ascension of Christ; for circumcision was an honorable ceremony, used from Abraham's time, and so they could not suddenly and abruptly leave it off, but did use it for a time, for their sakes who were weak, well knowing that the circumcision without hands would by degrees put an end to the circumcision made with hands. . . . And so, in like manner, the apostles used the baptism of John, or water-baptism, it having been of high account in the dawning of the day of the gospel, ... but they knew that Spirit or fire-baptism would by degrees consume water-baptism, and lick up all the drops of it; for so John himself intimates, saying: 'He must increase, but I must decrease!'"

"Christ's Spirit or fire-baptism is the one and only baptism of the New Testament, as we find Paul affirming, Ephes. iv. 6, where he saith, that in Christ's kingdom, where is but one body, and one Spirit, and one hope of our calling, one Lord, and one faith, there is also but 'εν βαπτισμα, one baptism; and this is the baptism of the Spirit, as the apostle elsewhere shows, saying (I. Cor. xii. 13): 'For by one Spirit we are all baptized into one body, and have been all made to drink into one Spirit.'"

"Now this baptism that makes us one with Christ, makes us to partake both of his death and resurrection. Through baptism of the Spirit we are dipt into the death of Christ (Rom. vi. 3, 4): 'Know ye not that so many of us as are baptized into Jesus Christ are baptized into his death?' And this is, as the apostle unfolds it (ver. 6), the crucifying of the old man with him, 'that the body of sin may be destroyed, that henceforth we should not serve sin.' And all this is done, not through any water-washing, but through the gift of the Spirit; for it is through the Spirit only, that we are able to mortify the deeds of the flesh; and nothing but the presence of this Spirit in us is the destruction of sin ; so that the Spirit of Christ baptizes us into the death of Christ."

"'By one Spirit are we all baptized into one body, whether we be Jews or Gentiles, whether we be bond or free, and have been all made to drink into one Spirit' (I. Cor. xii. 13). So that, by drinking into one Spirit with the church, we become one body with it, and no other ways: I say, not by being dipt into the same water, but by receiving the same Spirit, do we become one body with the church; and it is not the being of one judgment or opinion, or form, or the like, that makes men one true church or body of Christ; but the being of one Spirit; and none are of that church, which is the body of Christ, but those who are baptized with that one Spirit of Christ."

Toward the conclusion, comparing I. Peter, iii. 20, with Rom. ii. 28, he remarks that as Paul here puts an end to circumcision in the flesh, so Peter there also puts an end to baptism in the flesh; and that the reasoning of the two apostles may be thus stated—that he is not a Christian who is one outwardly, neither is that baptism which is outward in the flesh; but he is a Christian who is one inwardly, and baptism is that of the heart, in the Spirit, and not in the letter, whose praise also is not of men, but of God. . . . Christ hath put an end to all outward, carnal, and earthly things of the first Testament, by the inward, spiritual, and heavenly things of a second and better Testament. And by his own death and resurrection only, not without us [only] but within us, through the power and efficacy of his Spirit, all the baptism of the New Testament is fully and perfectly performed.

"And thus, in all these particulars, you see the infinite

excellency and glory of the Spirit-baptism, above water-baptism. And this only is sufficient in the days of the gospel, as being the true and proper baptism of the New Testament. For as Christ himself only, is sufficient to the faithful without John, though John were of use in his season, to point out Christ; so the baptism of Christ only, is sufficient to the faithful, without the baptism of John, though the baptism of John were of use in its season, to point out the baptism of Christ. And the baptist himself was of this judgment, who said to Christ, 'I have need to be baptized of thee;' which he means, not of water baptism (for so Christ himself did not baptize), but of the baptism of the Spirit." . . . .

"Now this, it may be, may seem strange and dangerous to some of low, and fleshly, and customary religion; but let all such (if it be possible) consider, that where the substance comes, the shadow is at an end. . . . . And if they understand not this for the present, I hope they may understand it afterward; for we speak not at uncertainties in this point; but 'what we have in some measure seen, and felt, and handled of the word of life, that we deliver unto you, that ye may have fellowship with us; and truly our fellowship is with the Father, and with his Son Jesus Christ,' through the Spirit." And he winds up the whole matter, by the following remarkable prophetic appeal, in the conclusion of the preface to the reader:—

"But because I see this present generation so rooted and built up in the doctrines of men, I have the less hope that this truth will prevail with them. And therefore I appeal to the next generation; which will be further removed from those evils, and will be brought nearer to the word; but *especially to that people, whom God hath and shall form by his Spirit for himself;* for these only will be able to make just and righteous judgment in this matter, seeing *they have the Anointing* to be *their teacher,* and *the Lamb* to be *their light."*

A certain Sydrach Simpson, Master of Pembroke Hall, in the University of Cambridge, undertook to controvert what he considered dangerous errors in Wm. Dell's doctrines, particularly his denial of the authority of universities to qualify for the ministry of the gospel. In the year 1653 this man delivered a discourse with this view before the University Congregation, at the public Commencement in Cambridge. He endeavored to show that the universities now were answerable to the schools of the prophets in the times of the Old Testament, and were therefore of right capable of sending forth gospel teachers—that they who endeavored to pull down schools, were always enemies to religion,—that "divinity is swaddled in human learning"— that Paul was brought up at the feet of Gamaliel—that men now are not to receive the Spirit in that immediate way, to understand the Scriptures, in which it was given to them who wrote the Scriptures—that men now are to get knowledge by studies and human learning, and not by inspiration—that it is wrong for believers to speak of being one with Christ, and partaking of his divine nature, whereas they are at an infinite distance from him—that arts and tongues are the cups in which God drinks to us! —and that when learning goes down, religion goes down too, so that "religious foundations" [*i.e.* colleges of divinity] must be kept up, if we do not wish to go to destruction.

Whereupon Wm. Dell addressed to the Congregation of the University a counter Discourse on "The Trial of Spirits, both in Teachers and Hearers;" which he published, with a Confutation of Simpson's gross and foolish errors, and a Brief Testimony against divinity degrees in the universities. This altogether was a pretty large work, containing much excellent Christian doctrine, but of a nature very similar to his former works noticed above; so that we must be satisfied with bringing forward a few detached extracts.

He says: "Had not Christian people thus unchristianly delivered up their judgments to the clergy, and that in the very highest points of religion, Christianity had not been so miserably blinded and corrupted as it is, and the mystery of iniquity had not so much prevailed in the world as now it hath. For when Christians would not try the spirits, whether they were of God, and the doctrines, whether they were the word of God or no, but thought this a matter too high for them, and would refer and submit all to the judgment of their ministers; then antichrist (the apostle of the devil) came forth boldly, and proudly exalted himself above all that is called God, and his kingdom above all the kingdoms of the world."

"The trial of spirits doth unquestionably belong to all men who have received the Spirit of God. For to this Spirit of God, which dwells in the faithful, the gift of discerning spirits is inseparably annexed; and the Spirit of Christ, which truly dwells in all true Christians, cannot deceive, nor be deceived in the trial of spirits. So that this now is a common grace, that in some measure belongs to all true Christians, who have received the unction that teacheth them all things, and is truth, and is no lie."

"Now the true prophets, speaking the word of God by and in his Spirit, do also speak it in the right sense, and after the true mind of Christ; as Paul saith of himself and of other believers who had received the Spirit, 'We have the mind of Christ.' But the false prophets, though they speak the word of the letter exactly, and that according to the very original, and curiosity of criticisms, yet speaking it without the Spirit, they are false prophets before God, and his true church; seeing all right prophecy hath proceeded from the Spirit in all ages of the world, but especially it must so proceed in the days of the New Testament, wherein God hath promised the largest effusion of his Spirit."

In the latter part of the treatise, after making some remarks on the text, "They are of the world, therefore speak they of the world, and the world heareth them," he says: "Hence we may learn, that it is not study, parts, breeding, learning, nor any natural endowments or acquired accomplishments, that will deliver any man out of this world (or corrupt state of mankind), or that can change his nature, or give him the least place or interest in the kingdom of God; but only a new birth, and true faith in Jesus Christ, whereby we are made the children of God; without which, men are still of the world, notwithstanding all their other improvements."

In his preface to the Confutation of Simpson, after quoting Wycliffe, Huss, Luther, and Melancthon, he says: "Now, as it was necessary that this work [of exposing the carnal clergy, and the false pretenses and heathenish instruction of the universities of that day] should be done, so, through the grace of Christ, was I made willing to do it, seeing nobody else more fit and able did appear. And well knowing that he that provokes the universities and clergy against him, provokes 'principalities and powers, and the rulers of the darkness of this world' against him; as is evident in the example of Wycliffe, Huss, Luther, Tindal, and others; I have, therefore, according to Christ's counsel, sat down and counted the cost of this undertaking, and after all, do say, 'the Lord is on my side, I will not fear what man can do unto me.'"

"If any say, I myself relate [belong] to the university, why then do I speak against it thus? I answer, that I neither do, nor will relate to the university, as it is polluted with any of the abominations herein mentioned. But as, by the providence of God alone, I have been brought to that relation in which I now stand, and continue in it, against the wills and workings of many; so, through his good pleasure, I will remain, till he shall otherwise dispose of me; and during my sojourning with them, I will not fail to testify against their evil, and to endeavor to win all those whom God shall persuade to receive his truth, from heathenism to the gospel, and from antichrist to Christ. Wherefore, let none be offended that I am made willing to hazard and part with my worldly accommodations for Christ's name's sake. But let them rather praise the grace of God, which hath enabled me to witness a good confession, whatever worldly disadvantage I might run into thereby. Wherefore, welcome the righteousness, power, wisdom, truth, word, and whole kingdom of Christ, though they swallow up all my earthly accommodations. For such fear and love of his name hath the Lord graciously put into my heart, that I would not willingly conceal anything of his most precious truth, either to gain or to preserve to myself the whole world. And so, righteous Father, not my will be done, nor theirs, but 'thy will be done in earth as it is in heaven.'"

He then rehearses Simpson's errors, and shows their utter inconsistency with sound doctrine, and with the state of the facts as regarded the universities; where, though professing to teach religion, a vast amount of the *falsities* and *impurities* of the *heathen mythology* was daily taught, to the great contamination of the morals of the youth subjected to the influence of such poison.

In regard to schools, it is well to understand clearly his position, as expressed in the following paragraph:

"True it is, that they who have sought the subversion of Christian schools, wherein the doctrine of the gospel is purely taught, without the mixture of philosophy and heathenism, they all have been and are very enemies to true religion. But they that seek to put down heathenish schools, and to erect Christian, or to reform the schools of heathen into Christian, or to remove heathenism out of Christian schools, they are not, before God and good men, enemies to true religion, but the great friends of it."

In accordance with these views, in a small treatise on "the Right Reformation of Learning," he states his sentiments respecting a Christian education more fully; a part of which is as follows:

"There neither is, nor can be any greater evil, than to bring up children in ease and idleness, and to suffer them to live freely and without control, according to [their] natural lusts and corruptions," etc.

"I conceive it meet that the civil power should take great care of the education of youth, as one of the greatest works that concern them, and as one of the worthiest things they can do in the world; inasmuch as what the youth now is, the whole commonwealth will shortly be.

"To this end, it is meet that schools, if wanting, be erected throughout the whole nation, and that not only in cities and great towns, but also, as much as may be, in smaller villages; and that the authority of the nation take great care that godly men especially have the charge of greater schools; and also that no women be permitted to teach little children in villages, but such as are the most sober and grave; and that the magistrate afford all suitable encouragement and assistance.

"That in such schools they first teach them to read their native tongue, which they speak without teaching; and then presently, as they understand, bring them to read the Holy Scriptures; which, though for the present they understand not, yet may they, through the blessing of God, come to understand them afterward.

"That in cities and greater towns, where are the greater schools, and the greater opportunities to send children to them, they teach them also the Latin and Greek tongues, and the Hebrew also, which is the easiest of them all, and ought to be in great account with us, for the Old Testament's sake. And it is most heedfully to be regarded, that in teaching youth the tongues, to wit, the Greek and Latin, such heathenish authors be most carefully avoided, be their language never so good, whose writings are full of the fables, vanities, filthiness, lasciviousness, idolatries, and wickedness of the heathen. Seeing usually, while youth do learn the language of the heathen, they also learn their wickedness in that language; whereas it were far better for them to want their language, than to be possessed with their wickedness. And what should Christian youth have to do with the heathenish poets, who were, for the most part, the devil's prophets, and delivered forth their writings in his spirit?" . . . .

"It may be convenient also, that there may be some universities or colleges, for the instructing youth in the knowledge of the liberal arts, beyond grammar and rhetoric . . . . . but the mathematics especially are to be had in good esteem in universities . . . . . which, as they carry no wickedness in them, so are they besides, very useful to human society, and the affairs of this present life."

He then advocates the scattering of colleges through various parts of the nation, and recommends, with Luther, that a portion of the education should be devoted to the useful arts or some lawful calling; and adds:—"If this course were taken in the disposing and ordering colleges and studies, it would come to pass that twenty would learn then, where one learns now; and also by degrees, many men, on whom God shall please to pour forth his Spirit, may grow up to teach the people, while yet they live in an honest calling and employment, as the apostles did. And this would give them great efficacy and power in teaching, while they lived by faith, through their honest labor, and were delivered from the mischief of idleness." ...

"And by this means may the chargeable and burdensome maintenance of the carnal clergy, by degrees be taken away, and the church of Christ, and the very nations themselves, be supplied with a more faithful, Christian, and spiritual ministry than now it hath, at a far less rate. For God hath promised, in the last days 'to pour out his Spirit on all flesh, and the sons, and daughters, and servants, and handmaids, shall prophesy,' and then 'shall knowledge cover the earth, as waters do the seas.'"

But now briefly to return to his Confutation of Simpson's Errors—in animadverting on his absurd assumption, that all divinity is swaddled in human learning, he conceives that all Christians must, at first reading of this, acknowledge that such doctrine is not divine, but philosophical; and affirms, that "if all divinity be swaddled in human learning, all such divinity hath no great depth, seeing the bottom of human learning is easily fathomed;" adding, "I conceive he might speak thus, that all divinity is wrapped up in human learning, to deter the common people from the study and inquiry after it, and to cause them still to expect all divinity from the clergy, who, by their education, have attained to that human learning which the plain people are destitute of. For it is the old and new design of antichrist, to make the people depend on the clergy for all divinity, though the people have the Scriptures as near them, and the grace of God usually nearer to them, than they; seeing 'God resisteth the proud, and giveth grace to the humble.'"

"And now," he reverentially concludes, "O blessed Lord Jesus, who wast crucified, dead, and buried, but yet art risen from the dead by the eternal Spirit, and art ascended on high to fill all things, have mercy on thy poor church, which is so grievously rent and torn this day by wolves in sheeps' clothing; and is thus hurt and consumed by poisonous doctrines of men, who seek themselves, and their own things, to the harm and ruin of thy poor people! O, thou Son of the living God, who art the way, the truth, and the life, how shall the kingdom of antichrist be brought down, when the hands of such men, who seem pillars in the church, are stretched forth so strongly to hold it up? And how shall the days of antichrist be shortened, when his kingdom is coming forth again, in the greatest deceivableness of unrighteousness that hath ever yet appeared in the world to delude the nations? O Lord, remember all thy promises, and make haste to destroy Babylon the great, with all its mysteries of righteousness and unrighteousness, and let it sink as a millstone in the sea, without any hope or possibility of a resurrection. And seeing there is no hand of man stretched out for this work, but all hands are against it; do thou destroy it, O Lord, without hand, even with the Spirit of thy mouth, and the brightness of thy coming, according to the truth of thy promises, and the unutterable sighs and groans of thy Spirit, occasioned thereby, in the hearts of all thy faithful and elect. Even so, Lord, and let thy kingdom come, and make no long tarrying. Amen."

We have no further account of this spiritually-minded and enlightened man, until the year 1662, about two years after the restoration of Charles II. to the throne of England, when he was ejected from his position in the college, as a non-conformist.

CONCLUSION.

It was well said by a Dutch historian about one hundred and fifty years ago,* in reference to the gradual progress of reform during the dark ages:—" That the wonderful work of reformation was small, and of very little account [apparently] in its beginning, and yet hath been advanced with remarkable progress, will, I believe, be denied by none that have with attention and due consideration read the history of its first rise ; since God, the beginner and author of this glorious work, proceeding *by steps and degrees*, used therein such singular wisdom and prudence, that (every circumstance duly considered) instead of censuring any part thereof, we shall be obliged to cry out, ' Thou, O Lord, alone knowest the right times and seasons to open the eyes of the people, and to make them capable of thy truth' " . . . And in allusion to the fact that John Huss saw not through all the errors of the Romish doctrine, the same author adds : —" He had been faithful according to his knowledge, and had not hid his talent in the earth, but improved it ; having shown himself a zealous promoter of that small illumination which God was pleased to grant him—it being without question great enough in that grievous night of darkness, when idolatry had so universally blinded mankind, that morally speaking, it would have been impossible for them to have understood the declaration of an entirely reformed religion ; whereas it is evident that the most sober and discreet people of that age were capable to understand the doctrine and sermons of that honest man."

The "steps and degrees" by which it pleased the Most

* William Sewell, of Amsterdam.

High to lead his poor benighted professing church into more and more light, as they were able to bear it, are observable not only in doctrinal development, but also in the gradual amelioration and civilization of professing Christendom, by which the human mind, at large and as a whole, became more capable of performing its most important functions. And though the successive reforms were often partial, and apparently ephemeral and local, and were in their scope by no means perfect, nor free from many of the errors of the prevalent system, nevertheless it is plainly observable that their local and ephemeral character was more in appearance than in reality; for though the active instruments therein from time to time perished, often without being permitted to "see of the travail of their souls," and the strong hand of authority covered their names with reproach, and seemed for a time to succeed in stifling the voice of their testimony; yet the virtue of it continued to flow in an under current, and was like the "bread cast upon the waters," which was "found after many days," to the strength and animation of those who came afterward to "fight the good fight" of the faith once delivered to the saints. So that the right promulgation of the truth may be said never to fall entirely to the ground, without the word of the Lord accomplishing, in his own time, that whereunto it was sent. Its secret but irrepressible influence has formed a sort of platform for succeeding reformers to stand upon, who found the hearts of increasing numbers prepared more or less to examine into the nature of divine truth. Thus the standard that had been raised was by no means lost, from century to century, although for a season trodden under foot by the powers of the world. This was conspicuously the case with John Huss, whose views were to an eminent degree cleared and strengthened and enlarged by the previous course and testimony of Wycliffe; and in like manner, though at first unconsciously, did Martin Luther derive advantage and enlarge the field of his success, from the results of the labors of Wycliffe and of Huss; although many years had elapsed between him and them, and great efforts had been made to vilify their memory as heretics, and bury the results of their teachings under a load of obloquy, overwhelming to anything short of that which has a measure of divine approval to sustain it.

Nevertheless the principles of a perfect reformation were reserved (as to their development in the world) to a later day. Even the great reformation under the instrumentality of Luther and his associates (which falls not within our present scope), is acknowledged to have been short of arriving at a clear revival of pure primitive Christianity in life and doctrine; and conspicuously was this the case with the English reformation under Henry VIII. Previous reforms fell certainly still more short of bringing mankind back to the primeval state of the Christian religion, as it had emanated from the very "lip of truth," and from which the world had so widely departed into the "traditions" and "commandments of men." Yet how animating is it to look upon the successive efforts made by faithful men and women, through all the darkness which surrounded them, to walk worthy of the vocation wherewith they felt themselves called; and to behold them sustained by faith in the succor of the Son of God, through all the sufferings which overtook them! And although seeing in some things "as through a glass, darkly," yet, on the whole, how eminently were they made instrumental (by Him who called them and in degree enlightened and qualified them), in clearing away idolatry and priestcraft, and encouraging men to love and serve the living and true God, from a principle operative in the heart and soul.

After the Lutheran reformation, the reader will have perceived the advocacy of still purer views of the sweetness of the love of God, and the efficacy of true and living faith, exemplified in the accounts of Molinos, Guion, and Dell; although the two former never left the profession of the church of Rome, sorely persecuted as they were by its authorities; and the latter, for aught that has appeared in history, continued in connection with the Episcopal church of England. As regards William Dell, he saw so clearly that the professing church of his day was very far from the purity of the primitive times, and felt so fully convinced that more of a putting on of the beautiful garments of righteousness was called for at its hands, that he might almost be said to have adopted the language of the apostle Paul: "And yet show I unto you a more excellent way"—when his pen prophetically declared, in reference to the unbelief of that age in the spiritual doctrines which he advocated: "But because I see this present generation so rooted and built up in the doctrines of men, I have the less hope that this truth will prevail with them. And therefore I appeal to the next generation, which will be further removed from those evils, and will be brought nearer to the Word; but *especially to that people whom God hath and shall form by His Spirit for himself;* for these only will be able to make righteous judgment in this matter, seeing *they have the Anointing* to be *their teacher*, and *the Lamb* to be *their light.*"*

It is probable that but few of our readers will at first sight be able to appreciate this notable testimony, given about the middle of the seventeenth century, to the approaching rise of a people who should practically carry out the spiritual views, some of which Dell had a glimpse of, and to which he testified as characteristic of the true

* See Works of William Dell, Master of Gonville and Caius College, Cambridge, in the treatise on Baptism.

church of Christ. And probably Dell himself never realized fully, or followed out, the application of his own words. Yet the reader who will take the pains candidly to pursue the subject of vital religion, as historically sketched or depicted in another work by the author of the present volume (and put forth by the same publishers), may not find it so difficult, as prejudiced minds might suppose, to ascertain whether the foresight of William Dell was not fully realized, during that same and the following century, in the raising up by the Lord of the harvest, of a people who showed not only by profession, but by practice also, and that through severe persecutions, that they had the clear light of the gospel itself to walk by, experimentally knowing "the Anointing to be their teacher, and the Lamb to be their light."

THE END.

www.ingramcontent.com/pod-product-compliance
Lightning Source LLC
Chambersburg PA
CBHW031956300426
44117CB00008B/779